AN ABRIDGEMENT OF
THE
SECRET
DOCTRINE

from a painting by Hermann Schmiechen

AN ABRIDGEMENT OF
THE
SECRET
DOCTRINE

H. P. BLAVATSKY

EDITED BY
ELIZABETH PRESTON &
CHRISTMAS HUMPHREYS

A publication supported by
THE KERN FOUNDATION

Quest Books
Theosophical Publishing House

Wheaton, Illinois ◆ Madras, India

© The Theosophical Publishing House, London, Ltd., 1966.
All rights reserved
First Quest Book edition, 1967, published by
The Theosophical Publishing House, Wheaton, Illinois,
a department of The Theosophical Society in America,
by arrangement with The Theosophical Publishing House,
London, Ltd.
Seventh Printing, 1996
ISBN: 0-8356-0009-2

Printed in the United States of America

TABLE OF CONTENTS

VOLUME FIRST

COSMOGENESIS

PART I

COSMIC EVOLUTION

PART II

THE EVOLUTION OF SYMBOLISM

PART III

SCIENCE AND THE SECRET DOCTRINE CONTRASTED

VOLUME SECOND

ANTHROPOGENESIS

PART I

EDITORIAL FOREWORD TO THIS ABRIDGEMENT

THERE has long been a need for some abridgement or condensed version of *The Secret Doctrine* by H. P. Blavatsky, partly for the general reader unwilling to embark on the thirteen hundred pages of the original two volumes, and partly for the serious student, to serve as an introduction and guide to the larger work.

The Secret Doctrine has sold steadily since its first appearance in 1888, but succeeding editions have increased in price, and the present Adyar Edition contains no fewer than six volumes. In any edition, the work is large and heavy to handle and contains a good deal of material that is now of secondary importance, and even a hindrance in a first attempt to grasp the main tremendous theme.

The author herself left no work that can be used as an introduction to the great sweep of Cosmogenesis and Anthropogenesis outlined in *The Secret Doctrine*, for *The Key to Theosophy*, published a year later, does not cover this ground at all.

The first attempt to produce a shortened version was the Abridgement by Katharine Hillard, published in 1907, and the present Editors considered reproducing this by some modern process. But it was found to be itself too long. Moreover, Miss Hillard had changed the order of whole paragraphs with a view to easier reading, had translated Sanskrit terms with equivalents no longer acceptable, and made actual changes in the text.

For these reasons it was decided to prepare an entirely new abridgement, to be taken from the First Edition, to be entirely in the words of the author, and entirely in her own order of writing. The present work is based on such an abridgement made by Miss Elizabeth Preston for her own studies. Mr. Christmas Humphreys who, with Mrs. Elsie Benjamin, edited the new edition of *The Mahatma Letters to A. P. Sinnett*, worked over Miss Preston's MSS. at her request, making minor restorations and equivalent cuts. The revised MS. was then examined by Miss Grace Blanch with reference to the comparable cuts made in Miss Hillard's original abridgement, and further suggestions from Mr. Wallace Slater, then General Secretary of The Theosophical Society in England, Mr. Leslie Leslie-Smith, now General Secretary and Chairman in charge of the

Theosophical Publishing House in London, Mrs. Elsie Benjamin, Hon. Secretary of the Corresponding Fellows Lodge of Theosophists, and Mr. Boris de Zirkoff, now editing the *Collected Writings of H. P. Blavatsky*, were carefully considered. The present work is therefore the result of long and careful study by a team of experienced students of *The Secret Doctrine*. It is appreciated, however, that no other student of the same experience will be entirely satisfied with the result, and it is therefore important that the principles devised and followed by the Editors in making their decisions should be clearly set out.

Only the two volumes of the original First Edition of 1888 have been used, and in the form therein printed. The alterations made for the Third Edition of 1893 have been carefully examined line by line. In many places, particularly in the more consistent use of capitals, these revisions have been adopted, but in no instance has a change been made unless made visible to the reader by the use of square brackets. The so-called Third Volume, which appeared for the first time in 1897, has not been used. It may be that those who collected from the author's unpublished MSS. and other writings the material which appeared as a separate "Third Volume" in 1897 were in error only in giving such a collation such a name. The result, however, has been unfortunate, for a large section of the Theosophical Movement has refused to recognize this altered and additional material as part of *The Secret Doctrine*, and these Theosophists have produced and thereafter used their own exact reproductions of the original edition. All Theosophists, of any Theosophical Society or none, may accept the present work as a genuine attempt to produce a shortened version, and no more, of *The Secret Doctrine* of H. P. Blavatsky.

To reduce some thirteen hundred pages to some three hundred pages meant that the Editors had to decide what to leave in, rather than what to cut out. Clearly, the Introduction, the Proem, the actual Stanzas of Dzyan and the Commentaries thereon take precedence. Clearly the long quotations from contemporary writers which the author refutes in equal detail are the first to be cut out. It is in the large remaining field that difficulties of choice arise. Much that is off the main axis of the book's development, on symbolism, comparative religion and scientific theories of the 1880's must also go, for this material does not actively enlarge our knowledge of Cosmogenesis and Anthropogenesis, the coming into being of the Universe and the origin of Man. Within this field the Editors have made such cuts as were inevitable, realizing that much material of value would be thereby omitted. At times the continuity from surviving portion to portion was difficult to keep smooth, and a line of dots (...) has been inserted to warn the reader of a big break.

At all times the Editors had in mind the reader who would be using the Abridgement as an introduction to the larger work, and have therefore published the original Contents in full. It will be thus obvious which whole sections have been removed and which remain in part only.

It has been thought right to include a brief Biography of H. P. Blavatsky and a note on the Genesis of *The Secret Doctrine*. At the end, the reader will find a selected Bibliography of works on H. P. Blavatsky and *The Secret Doctrine*, and an Index suitable to this Abridgement.

For the rest, this work is offered in the spirit in which it was conceived, to encourage an ever-increasing number of those in search of the meaning of life to study, with the intellect and the intuition, this new-old presentation of *The Secret Doctrine*.

ELIZABETH PRESTON
CHRISTMAS HUMPHREYS

H. P. BLAVATSKY

A BRIEF BIOGRAPHY

THE author of the two volumes of *The Secret Doctrine*, of which this is an abridgement, was born on July 31 (August 12 new style) 1831, at Ekaterinoslav in South Russia. Her father was Colonel Peter von Hahn, son of General Alexis Hahn von Rottenstern Hahn. Her mother, Helena de Fadeyev, was the daughter of the gifted Princess Helena Pavlovna Dolgoroukov, but she died when her daughter was only eleven, and the young Helena was brought up in her grandmother's house at Saratov, where her grandfather was Civil Governor.

She was clearly an exceptional child, and at an early age was aware of being different from those around her. Her precocious psychic powers puzzled her relations and friends. At once impatient of all authority, yet deeply sensitive, she was gifted in many ways that are seldom found in the same girl. A clever linguist, an exceptionally fine pianist and a clever artist, she was yet a fearless and skilled rider of half-broken horses, and always in a remarkable degree at one with nature about her. Quite early she sensed that she was in some way dedicated to a life of service, in which her developing spiritual powers would be harnessed in the service of mankind. When just eighteen she married, not from affection or desire, but because, it is said, her governess taunted her that, with her rebellious disposition, she would never marry anyone, not even the middle-aged Nikifor V. Blavatsky, a friend of the family who was then Vice-Governor of the Province of Erivan. She accepted the challenge, and in three days made him propose. The marriage meant nothing to her and was never consummated. In a few months she escaped, and travelled widely in Egypt, Greece and lesser known parts of Eastern Europe on money supplied by her father. In 1851 she was in London and there, on her twentieth birthday met the Master Morya, or M. as he became known in the Theosophical Movement. He told her something of the work that was in store for her, and from that moment she accepted his guidance both in her inner development and her outward work for mankind.

In 1852, after adventurous travels in America, she made her first attempt to enter Tibet, where her Master lived, but the time was apparently not ripe, and she got no farther than Nepal. She returned to London and thence sailed to the United States where she spent some two years. She then went to India via Japan, and this time succeeded in entering Tibet, from Kashmir and Ladakh. Here, her real training began, but after three years with her Master she returned to India, leaving it for Europe during the troubled times of the Mutiny. She returned home unannounced, but was soon off on her travels again, through the Caucasus, Georgia, and we do not quite know where.

During the period from 1867 to 1870 she was again in Tibet, and there completed her control of her occult powers, cleansing herself of what she called her "psycho-physical weakness," by which she meant the last trace of negative mediumship. There followed a period of further wandering during which she visited Egypt, Syria and Constantinople. While at Odessa she was instructed by her Master to go to Paris, where she received direct instruction to proceed to New York. She landed on July 7, 1873.

In 1873 Mme. Blavatsky was forty-two and at the height of her exceptional spiritual, mental and psychic powers. In the opinion of those who had trained her she was the best available instrument for the work they had in mind, to offer to the world a new presentation, though only in brief outline, of Theosophy, meaning "Divine Wisdom," "the accumulated Wisdom of the ages, tested and verified by generations of Seers . . . ," that body of Truth of which religions, great and small, are but as branches of the parent Tree. The task laid on her was tremendous, to challenge on the one hand the entrenched beliefs and dogmas of established Christianity, and on the other the equally dogmatic views of the science of her day. But a crack had recently appeared in this twofold set of mental fortifications. It was caused by Spiritualism, then sweeping America, and the work entrusted to this brilliant yet excitable Russian woman was, as she understood it, clear. "I was sent to prove the phenomena and their reality, and show the fallacy of the spiritualistic theory of spirits."

The double nature of this objective was soon to embarrass her. In proving, by her own astonishing phenomena, the presence of a psychic plane beyond the physical, she identified herself with the Spiritualists, yet by teaching in considerable detail the immemorial Wisdom, and in particular the principles it taught as to the sevenfold nature of man, she made enemies of the Spiritualists.

In New York she was put in touch by those instructing her with Col. H. S. Olcott, an American lawyer who had fought in the Civil War, and with W. Q. Judge, an Irish lawyer, who were both interested in the new phenomena. In 1875, these three, with a number of others interested, founded a new society "to collect and diffuse a knowledge of the laws which govern the Universe."

She chose for it the name Theosophy, "Divine Wisdom, or the aggregate of the knowledge and wisdom that underlie the Universe," a word originally coined in the third century A.D. by the Neo-Platonists. The Theosophical Society was founded in New York on November 17, 1875 with Objects which were later formulated as follows:

1. To form a nucleus of the Universal Brotherhood of Humanity, without distinction of race, creed, sex, caste or colour.

2. To encourage the study of Comparative Religion, Philosophy and Science.

3. To investigate unexplained laws of Nature, and the powers latent in man.

Col. Olcott was elected President and Mme. Blavatsky Recording Secretary.

To prepare the way for the new movement she began to write *Isis Unveiled*, "a Master-Key to the Mysteries of Ancient and Modern Science and Theology," and while Col. Olcott was organizing the new Society, worked on it for the next two years.

Isis Unveiled was published in 1877 in New York and proved an immediate success. The Theosophical Society, which had by its very Objects roused considerable interest, support and opposition, expanded rapidly. In 1878, again on the instructions of her Master, Mme. Blavatsky sailed with Col. Olcott for India. Soon after landing in Bombay they received a letter from A. P. Sinnett, then Editor of *The Pioneer*, of Allahabad. In due course Mme. Blavatsky put Sinnett in touch with the two Masters who were sponsoring the Theosophical Movement, and from this introduction came the long correspondence, from 1880 to 1884, which was later published as *The Mahatma Letters to A. P. Sinnett*.

Sinnett compiled from the Letters his understanding of the Masters and their Teaching, first in *The Occult World* (1881) and later in *Esoteric Buddhism* (1883), and these two volumes, together with the Mahatma Letters, flowing in a sense from the same source as Mme. Blavatsky's own knowledge of the occult Teaching, may well be studied in conjunction with *The Secret Doctrine*.

After an extensive tour of India, the Founders returned to Bombay and published, in October, 1879, the first issue of *The Theosophist*, with H. P. Blavatsky as Editor, the Masters themselves being early contributors.

In May, 1880, they visited Ceylon, and publicly took "Pancha Sila." According to Col. Olcott, "We had previously declared ourselves Buddhists, in America, both privately and publicly, so this was but a formal confirmation of our previous professions." In May, 1882, the Founders bought a large estate at Adyar, near Madras, and this has remained the Headquarters of The Theosophical Society to this day. Here they settled down, with very little help, to found new Lodges, receive visitors, conduct an enormous range of correspondence and produce *The Theosophist*. Col. Olcott began his remarkable career as a lecturer and healer. In Ceylon he stimulated the revival of Buddhism, and in 1884 left for London to petition the British Government on behalf of the Sinhalese Buddhists. Mme. Blavatsky, then in very poor health, went with him.

In Europe she recovered and was widely received with great enthusiasm, her brilliance of conversation, profound knowledge, and reputation for psychic powers everywhere drawing attention to her work. Meanwhile, a vicious and dangerous attack on her by two of her servants at Adyar, a Mr. and Mrs. Coulomb, was rapidly building up. She returned to Adyar in November, 1884, and learnt the details of the attack. She wished to sue the couple, already dismissed by the committee left in charge before the attack began, for their gross libel on her concerning the supposed fraudulent production of phenomena at Adyar. She was, however, overruled by the committee, and in disgust resigned all her appointments. In March, 1885, she left for Europe, never to return.

The attack, as was later proved, had no foundation. In the absence of the Founders in Europe, the two servants, already dismissed by the committee for incompetence and worse, sent to a Christian missionary newspaper in Madras two letters, purporting to be written to them by Mme. Blavatsky, containing instructions to arrange fraudulent phenomena. The Society for Psychic Research in London, ignoring Mme. Blavatsky's flat repudiation of the letters, which she was at no time allowed to see, sent a young man, Richard Hodgson, to India to report on the Coulombs' allegations. This Report, published in December, 1885, has been the basis for all subsequent attacks on Mme. Blavatsky, as to her morals, the worthlessness of "Theosophy" and even the non-existence of the Masters, and has been repeated with variations and additions by ill-wishers ever since. At last, in 1963, with the aid of hitherto unpublished documents, Mr. Adlai Waterman, in his *Obituary: The "Hodgson Report" on Madame Blavatsky*, published by the Theosophical Publishing House at Adyar, has analysed the whole sad story, and to any impartial mind destroyed it utterly.

But the effect on Mme. Blavatsky of this violent attack by a couple whom she had long befriended was serious. She was already grossly overworked and in poor health, and on her arrival in Europe she fell seriously ill. In August, however, she began work at Würzburg in Germany on her magnum opus, *The Secret Doctrine*, a brief history of which follows this Biography. In 1886, she moved to Ostende, and in the following year, at the invitation of English Theosophists, to a small house taken for her at Norwood, London. Soon, however, the Norwood premises proved too small, and she moved to 17 Lansdowne Road, Notting Hill, where, with the aid of Archibald and Bertram Keightley, she completed *The Secret Doctrine*, which was published in 1888. In 1887, as she had lost control of *The Theosophist*, which was published in Adyar, she founded *Lucifer*, a monthly magazine designed, as she said on the title-page, "to bring to light the hidden things of darkness."

In 1889, she moved to 19 Avenue Road, St. John's Wood, and from there published *The Key to Theosophy*, "a clear Exposition, in the form of Question and Answer, of the Ethics, Science and Philosophy for the study of which the Theosophical Society has been founded." In the same year she translated selected passages from a Tibetan scripture which she had learnt by heart during her training in Tibet, and published it as *The Voice of the Silence*, "Dedicated to the Few."

She died peacefully at 19 Avenue Road on May 8, 1891, and her body was cremated at Woking.

This is no place for the history of the Theosophical Movement, nor for an account of its considerable influence on the religious thought of the day, but Mme. Blavatsky gave to her own students a description of the ideal theosophical student and this, allowing for all the faults of her outer personality, is surely a true and sufficient epitaph.

Behold the truth before you: A clean life, an open mind, a pure heart, an eager intellect, an unveiled spiritual perception, a brotherliness for all, a readiness to give and receive advice and instruction, a loyal sense of duty to the Teacher, a willing obedience to the behests of TRUTH once we have placed our confidence in and believe that Teacher to be in possession of it; a courageous endurance of personal injustice, a brave declaration of principles, a valiant defence of those who are unjustly attacked, and a constant eye to the ideal of human progression and perfection which the sacred science depicts—these are the Golden Stairs up the steps of which the learner may climb to the Temple of Divine Wisdom.

THE GENESIS OF THE SECRET DOCTRINE

Isis Unveiled was published, as already described, in 1877. It was an immediate success, and the first edition was exhausted in ten days. Two years later Mme. Blavatsky had in mind a successor, and even drafted a Preface for it, but pressure of work for the expanding Theosophical Society, and the promotion of *The Theosophist* put other work aside, and it was not until January, 1884, that an announcement appeared in *The Theosophist* concerning "The Secret Doctrine, a New Version of *Isis Unveiled*," to appear in monthly parts. The scheme of monthly parts never materialized, but later in the year the author returned from India to Europe, and began work in earnest. She had assistance, in Würzburg and in Ostende, but as the Master K. H. wrote in 1885 to a German doctor, a member of the Society, "The Secret Doctrine, when ready, will be the triple production of M. [the Master M.], Upasika [Mme. Blavatsky] and the Doctor's most humble servant, K. H."

All who watched her at work on the manuscript, in different parts of Europe and at different times, speak with amazement of the smallness of her reference library. As one of her helpers wrote, "Quotations, with full references, from books which were never in the house—quotations verified after hours of search, sometimes at the British Museum for a rare book—of such I saw and verified not a few." Only rarely did her helpers find a reference for her; in most cases they merely verified what was already written down.

Early in 1886 she told Col. Olcott that the forthcoming work would be utterly new, and not merely an improved version of *Isis Unveiled*. That summer she was working with the help of the Countess Wachtmeister at Ostende. Dr. Archibald Keightley and Mr. E. C. Fawcett helped in the arrangement of the sections and in general research, while Mme. Blavatsky was busy "re-writing it, pasting and repasting, scratching out and replacing with notes from my AUTHORITIES." In Ostende she was seriously ill, but with her Master's help she recovered, and in September sent the material for Volume I., as copied out by Countess Wachtmeister, to Col. Olcott in Adyar. This version is extant in the Society's archives, and differs to some extent from the version finally published.

In May, 1888, she moved to London, and it was at 17 Lansdowne Road that, with the help of Dr. Archibald Keightley and his uncle, Bertram Keightley, the final version was prepared. A fund was raised to pay for the publication, and the printing was begun for the Theosophical Publishing Co. Ltd. of Duke Street, Adelphi. Many assisted in the proof-reading, during which Mme. Blavatsky sorely tried the printer's patience and pocket with voluminous corrections. The Preface was written last, and dated October, 1888. In it she apologized for the delay "occasioned by ill-health and the magnitude of the undertaking." She made it clear what the book contained. "These truths are in no sense put forward as a revelation ... for what is contained in this work is to be found scattered throughout thousands of volumes embodying the great Asiatic and early European religions, hidden under glyph and symbol, and hitherto left unnoticed because of this veil. What is now attempted is to gather the oldest of the tenets together and to make of them one harmonious and unbroken whole." Later she adds, "The teachings, however fragmentary and incomplete, contained in these volumes, belong neither to the Hindu, the Zoroastrian, the Chaldean nor the Egyptian religion, neither to Buddhism, Islam, Judaism nor Christianity exclusively. *The Secret Doctrine* is the essence of all these. Sprung from it in their origins, the various religious schemes are now made to merge back into their original element, out of which every mystery and dogma has grown, developed and become materialized." The aim of the work, in brief, was "To show that Nature is not 'a fortuitous concurrence of atoms', and to assign to man his rightful place in the scheme of the Universe ... "

In October, 1888, *The Secret Doctrine* was published simultaneously in London and New York. The first English edition of five hundred copies was exhausted before the day of publication. It was immediately reprinted, with the words "Second Edition" added to the title-page, although in modern usage this would be called a second impression or reprint.

While in London "H. P. B.", as she was affectionately known, founded the Blavatsky Lodge, and in 1889 attended a series of its meetings at 19 Avenue Road. At these discussions she answered questions on the Stanzas in Volume I. of *The Secret Doctrine*, and these Questions and her Answers, later published as *Transactions of the Blavatsky Lodge of the Theosophical Society*, may be usefully studied in conjunction with the major work.

In 1893, two years after the author's death in 1891, a "Third and Revised Edition" appeared, edited by Annie Besant and G. R. S. Mead. It contained a great many changes in the text, correcting references, improving faulty English and making a more consistent transliteration of foreign terms. But some of the corrections substantially altered the sense, and many later students do not accept them as justified.

In 1897, the Theosophical Publishing House published a new work described as Volume III. This, however, was never planned as such by Mme. Blavatsky, and is clearly not either of the "volumes three and four" to which she more than once referred.

Since then, many editions of *The Secret Doctrine* have appeared, in London, India and America. Some are careful reprints of the First Edition, in two volumes or in one; others are further revisions of the Third Edition. The current Adyar Edition has been carefully collated with this Abridgement in order that every change in the text, trivial or substantial, might be carefully considered. But, as explained in the Editorial Preface, on the rare occasions when a change, other than a purely editorial improvement has been made, that change is clear to the eye.

The work itself is difficult reading, for its teaching is, to modern Western minds, entirely new. It needs considerable mental effort to digest, but as H. P. Blavatsky wrote in the preface to *The Key to Theosophy*, "To the mentally lazy or obtuse, Theosophy must remain a riddle; for in the world mental as in the world spiritual each man must progress by his own efforts." It is hoped that this Abridgement will make the effort of digestion easier.

PREFACE

THE author does not feel it necessary to ask the indulgence of her readers and critics for the many defects of literary style, and the imperfect English which may be found in these pages. She is a foreigner, and her knowledge of the language was acquired late in life. The English tongue is employed because it offers the most widely-diffused medium for conveying the truths which it had become her duty to place before the world.

These truths are in no sense put forward as a *revelation*; nor does the author claim the position of a revealer of mystic lore, now made public for the first time in the world's history. For what is contained in this work is to be found scattered throughout thousands of volumes embodying the scriptures of the great Asiatic and early European religions, hidden under glyph and symbol, and hitherto left unnoticed because of this veil. What is now attempted is to gather the oldest tenets together and to make of them one harmonious and unbroken whole. The sole advantage which the writer has over her predecessors, is that she need not resort to personal speculations and theories. For this work is a partial statement of what she herself has been taught by more advanced students, supplemented, in a few details only, by the results of her own study and observation.

This book is not the Secret Doctrine in its entirety, but a select number of fragments of its fundamental tenets. It is perhaps desirable to state unequivocally that the teachings, however fragmentary and incomplete, contained in these volumes, belong neither to the Hindu, the Zoroastrian, the Chaldean, nor the Egyptian religion, neither to Buddhism, Islam, Judaism nor Christianity exclusively. The Secret Doctrine is the essence of all these. Sprung from it in their origins, the various religious schemes are now made to merge back into their original element, out of which every mystery and dogma has grown, developed, and become materialised.

The writer is fully prepared to take all the responsibility for what is contained in this work, and even to face the charge of having invented the whole of it. That it has many shortcomings she is fully aware; all that she claims is that its logical coherence and consistency entitle this new Genesis to rank, at any rate, on a level with the "working hypotheses" so freely accepted by modern science. Further, it claims consideration, not by reason of any appeal to dogmatic authority, but because it closely adheres to Nature, and follows the laws of uniformity and analogy.

The aim of this work may be thus stated: to show that Nature is not "a fortuitous concurrence of atoms," and to assign to man his rightful place in the scheme of the Universe; to rescue from degradation the archaic truths which are the basis of all religions; and to uncover, to some extent, the fundamental unity from which they all spring; finally, to show that the occult side of Nature has never been approached by the Science of modern civilization.

If this is in any degree accomplished, the writer is content. It is written in the service of humanity, and by humanity and the future generations it must be judged.

H. P. B.

London, October, 1888.

INTRODUCTORY

SINCE the appearance of Theosophical literature in England, it has become customary to call its teachings "Esoteric Buddhism." *Esoteric Buddhism*[1] was an excellent work with a very unfortunate title, though it meant no more than does the title of this work, *The Secret Doctrine*. It proved unfortunate, because people are always in the habit of judging things by their appearance, rather than their meaning. From the first, protests were raised by Brahmins and others against the title; and, in justice to myself, I must add that *Esoteric Buddhism* was presented to me as a completed volume, and that I was entirely unaware of the manner in which the author intended to spell the word "Budh-ism." This has to be laid directly at the door of those who neglected to point out the difference between "Buddhism"—the religious system of ethics preached by the Lord Gautama, and named after his title of Buddha, "the Enlightened"—and *Budha*, "Wisdom," or knowledge (*Vidya*), the faculty of cognizing, from the Sanskrit root "Budh," *to know*.

In etymology *Adi*, the *one* (or the First) and "Supreme Wisdom" is a term used by Aryasanga in his secret treatises, and now by all the mystic Northern Buddhists. It is a Sanskrit term, and an appellation given by the earliest Aryans to the Unknown deity; the word "Brahma" not being found in the Vedas and the early works. It means the absolute Wisdom, and "Adi-bhuta" is translated "the primeval uncreated cause of all" by Fitzedward Hall. Aeons of untold duration must have elapsed before the epithet of Buddha was so humanized, so to speak, as to allow of the term being applied to mortals and finally appropriated to one whose unparalleled virtues and knowledge caused him to receive the title of the "Buddha of Wisdom unmoved." *Bodha* means the innate possession of divine intellect or "understanding"; *Buddha*, the acquirement of it by personal efforts and merit; while *Buddhi* is the faculty of cognizing, the channel through which divine knowledge reaches the "Ego," the discernment of good and evil, "divine conscience" also; and "Spiritual Soul," which is the vehicle of *Atma*. "When *Buddhi* absorbs our Egotism (destroys it) with all its *Vikaras*, Avalokiteshvara

---

[1] [By A. P. Sinnett, 1883.]

becomes manifested to us, and Nirvana, or *Mukti*, is reached,'' Mukti being the same as Nirvana, *i.e.*, freedom from the trammels of "Maya" or *illusion*.

Unwise are those who, in their hatred of Buddhism, and, by reaction, of "Budhism," deny its esoteric teachings (which are those also of the Brahmins). For the Esoteric philosophy is alone calculated to withstand, in this age of crass and illogical materialism, the repeated attacks on all and everything man holds most dear and sacred, in his inner spiritual life. The true philosopher, the student of the Esoteric Wisdom, entirely loses sight of personalities, dogmatic beliefs and special religions. Moreover, Esoteric philosophy reconciles all religions, strips every one of its outward, human garments, and shows the root of each to be identical with that of every other great religion. It proves the necessity of an absolute Divine Principle in nature. It denies Deity no more than it does the Sun. Esoteric philosophy has never rejected God in Nature, nor Deity as the absolute and abstract *Ens*. It only refuses to accept any of the gods of the so-called monotheistic religions, gods created by man in his own image and likeness, a blasphemous and sorry caricature of the Ever-Unknowable. Furthermore, the records we mean to place before the reader embrace the esoteric tenets of the whole world since the beginning of our humanity, and Buddhistic occultism occupies therein only its legitimate place, and no more. Indeed, the secret portions of the "*Dan*" or "*Jan-na*"[2] ("Dhyan") of Gautama's metaphysics—grand as they appear to one unacquainted with the tenets of the Wisdom Religion of antiquity—are but a very small portion of the whole. The Hindu Reformer limited his public teachings to the purely moral and physiological aspect of the Wisdom-Religion, to Ethics and MAN alone. Things "unseen and incorporeal," the mystery of Being outside our terrestrial sphere, the great Teacher left entirely untouched in his public lectures, reserving the hidden Truths for a select circle of his Arhats.

Time and human imagination made short work of the purity and philosophy of these teachings, once that they were transplanted from the secret and sacred circle of the Arhats, during the course of their work of proselytism, into a soil less prepared for metaphysical conceptions than India; *i.e.*, once they were transferred into China, Japan, Siam, and Burma. How the pristine purity of these grand revelations was dealt with may be seen in studying some of the so-

---

[2] *Dan*, now become in modern Chinese and Tibetan phonetics *ch'an*, is the general term for the esoteric schools, and their literature. In the old books, the word *Janna* is defined as "to reform one's self by meditation and knowledge," a second *inner* birth. Hence Dzan, *Djan* phonetically, the "Book of *Dzyan*."

called "esoteric" Buddhist schools of antiquity in their modern garb, not only in China and other Buddhist countries in general, but even in not a few schools in Tibet, left to the care of uninitiated Lamas and Mongolian innovators.

Thus the reader is asked to bear in mind the very important difference between *orthodox* Buddhism—*i.e.*, the public teachings of Gautama the Buddha, and his esoteric *Budhism*. His Secret Doctrine, however, differed in no wise from that of the initiated Brahmins of his day. The Buddha was a child of the Aryan soil, a born Hindu, a Kshatrya and a disciple of the "twice born" (the initiated Brahmins). His teachings, therefore, could not be different from their doctrines, for the whole Buddhist reform merely consisted in giving out a portion of that which had been kept secret from every man outside of the "enchanted" circle of Temple-Initiates and ascetics. Unable to teach *all* that had been imparted to him—owing to his pledges—though he taught a philosophy built upon the ground-work of the true esoteric knowledge, the Buddha gave to the world only its *outward* material body and kept its *soul* for his Elect.

Towards the end of the first quarter of this century, a distinct class of literature appeared in the world. Being based, *soi-disant*, on the scholarly researches of Sanskritists and Orientalists in general, it was held scientific. Hindu, Egyptian, and other ancient religions, myths, and emblems were made to yield anything the symbologist wanted them to yield, thus often giving out the rude *outward* form in place of the *inner* meaning. This is the true reason, perhaps, why the outline of a few fundamental truths from the Secret Doctrine of the Archaic Ages is now permitted to see the light, after long millenniums of the most profound silence and secrecy. I say "a *few* truths," advisedly, because that which must remain unsaid could not be contained in a hundred such volumes, nor could it be imparted to the present generation of Sadducees. But, even the little that is now given is better than complete silence upon those vital truths. The world of today, in its mad career towards the unknown—which it is too ready to confound with the unknowable, whenever the problem eludes the grasp of the physicist—is rapidly progressing on the reverse, material plane of spirituality. It has now become a vast arena—a true valley of discord and of eternal strife—a necropolis, wherein lie buried the highest and the most holy aspirations of our Spirit-Soul.

The most serious objection to the correctness and reliability of the whole work will be the preliminary STANZAS: How can the statements contained in them be verified? True, if a great portion of the Sanskrit, Chinese, and Mongolian works quoted in the present volumes are known to some Orientalists, the chief work—that one from which the Stanzas are given—is not in the possession of European libraries. The Book of Dzyan (or "Dzan") is utterly unknown to our philologists, or at any rate was never heard of by them under its present name. The main body of the Doctrines given is found scattered throughout hundreds and thousands of Sanskrit MSS., some already translated, others still awaiting their turn. Every scholar, therefore, has an opportunity of verifying the statements herein made, and of checking most of the quotations. A few new facts (*new* to the profane Orientalist, only) and passages quoted from the Commentaries will be found difficult to trace. Several of the teachings, also, have hitherto been transmitted orally: yet even those are in every instance hinted at in the almost countless volumes of Brahminical, Chinese and Tibetan temple-literature.

The members of several esoteric schools—the seat of which is beyond the Himalayas, and whose ramifications may be found in China, Japan, India, Tibet, and even in Syria, besides South America—claim to have in their possession the *sum total* of sacred and philosophical works in MSS. and type: all the works, in fact, that have ever been written, in whatever language or characters, since the art of writing began; from the ideographic hieroglyphs down to the alphabet of Cadmus and the Devanagari.

It has been claimed in all ages that ever since the destruction of the Alexandrian Library (see *Isis Unveiled*, Vol. II., p. 27), every work of a character that might have led the profane to the ultimate discovery and comprehension of some of the mysteries of the Secret Science, was, owing to the combined efforts of the members of the Brotherhoods, diligently searched for. It is added, moreover, by those who know, that once found, save three copies left and stored safely away, such works were all destroyed. In India, the last of the precious manuscripts were secured and hidden during the reign of the Emperor Akbar.

Moreover in all the large and wealthy lamasaries, there are subterranean crypts and *cave-libraries*, cut in the rock, whenever the *gonpa*[3] and the *lhakhang*[4] are situated in the mountains. Beyond the Western Tsaydam, in the solitary passes of *Kuen-lun*[5] there are several such hiding-places. Along the ridge of Altyn-Taga, whose soil no European foot has ever trodden so far, there exists a certain hamlet, lost in a deep gorge. It is a small cluster of houses, a hamlet rather than a monastery, with a poor-looking temple in it, with one old lama, a hermit, living near by to watch it. Pilgrims say that the

---

[3] [Monastery.]
[4] [Temple.]
[5] Karakorum mountains, Western Tibet.

subterranean galleries and halls under it contain a collection of books, the number of which, according to the accounts given, is too large to find room even in the British Museum.⁶. . .

Traces of an immense civilization, even in Central Asia, are still to be found. This civilization is undeniably *prehistoric*. And how can there be civilization without a literature, in some form, without annals or chronicles? Common sense alone ought to supplement the broken links in the history of departed nations. The gigantic, unbroken wall of the mountains that hem in the whole tableland of Tibet, from the upper course of the river Khuan-Khé down to the Karakorum hills, witnessed a civilization during milleniums of years, and would have strange secrets to tell mankind. The Eastern and Central portions of those regions—the Nan-Shan and the Altyn-taga—were once upon a time covered with cities that could well vie with Babylon. A whole geological period has swept over the land, since those cities breathed their last, as the mounds of shifting sand, and the sterile and now dead soil of the immense central plains of the basin of Tarim testify. The borderlands alone are superficially known to the traveller. Within those tablelands of sand there is water, and fresh oases are found blooming there, wherein no European foot has ever yet ventured, or trodden the now treacherous soil.

The traces of such civilization, and these and like traditions, give us the right to credit other legendary lore warranted by well educated and learned natives of India and Mongolia, when they speak of immense libraries reclaimed from the sand, together with various reliques of ancient MAGIC lore, which have all been safely stowed away.

To recapitulate. The Secret Doctrine was the universally diffused religion of the ancient and prehistoric world. Proofs of its diffusion, authentic records of its history, a complete chain of documents, showing its character and presence in every land, together with the teaching of all its great adepts, exist to this day in the secret crypts of libraries belonging to the Occult Fraternity.

In the twentieth century of our era scholars will begin to recognize that the *Secret Doctrine* has neither been invented nor exaggerated,

⁶ According to the same tradition the now desolate regions of the waterless land of Tarim—a true wilderness in the heart of Turkestan—were in the days of old covered with flourishing and wealthy cities. At present, hardly a few verdant oases relieve its dead solitude. One such, sprung on the sepulchre of a vast city swallowed by and buried under the sandy soil of the desert, belongs to no one, but is often visited by Mongolians and Buddhists. The same tradition speaks of immense subterranean abodes, of large corridors filled with tiles and cylinders. It may be an idle rumour, and it may be an actual fact.

but, on the contrary, simply outlined; and finally, that its teachings antedate the Vedas.[7] Such a work as this has to be introduced with no simple *Preface*, but with a volume rather; one that would give *facts*, not mere disquisitions, since THE SECRET DOCTRINE is not a treatise, or a series of vague theories, but contains all that can be given out to the world in this century.

The Secret Doctrine is not a version of *Isis Unveiled*—as originally intended. It is a volume explanatory of it rather, and, though entirely independent of the earlier work, an indispensable corollary to it. Much of what was in *Isis* could hardly be understood by theosophists in those days. *The Secret Doctrine* will now throw light on many a problem left unsolved in the first work, especially on the opening pages, which have never been understood.

Concerned simply with the philosophies within our historical times and the respective symbolism of the fallen nations, only a hurried glance could be thrown at the panorama of Occultism in the two volumes of *Isis*. In the present work, detailed Cosmogony and the evolution of the four races that preceded our Fifth-race Humanity are given, and now two large volumes explain that which was stated on the first page of *Isis Unveiled* alone, and in a few allusions scattered hither and thither throughout that work.

Volume I. of *Isis* begins with a reference to "an old book." The "very old Book" is the original work from which the many volumes of *Kiu-ti* were compiled. Not only this latter and the *Siphrah Dzeniouta* but even the *Sepher Jezirah*, the work attributed by the Hebrew Kabalists to their Patriarch Abraham (!), the book of *Shu-king*, China's primitive Bible, the sacred volumes of the Egyptian Thoth-Hermes, the Puranas in India, and the Chaldean *Book of Numbers* and the *Pentateuch* itself, are all derived from that one small parent volume. Tradition says that it was taken down in *Senzar*, the secret sacerdotal tongue, from the words of the Divine Beings, who dictated it to the sons of Light, in Central Asia, at the very beginning of the 5th (our) race; for there was a time when its language (the *Sen-zar*) was known to the Initiates of every nation, when the forefathers of the Toltec understood it as easily as the inhabitants of the lost Atlantis, who inherited it, in their turn, from the sages of the 3rd Race, the *Manushis*, who learnt it direct from the *Devas* of the 2nd and 1st Races. The "illustration" spoken of in *Isis* relates to the evolution of these Races and of our 4th and 5th Race Humanity

[7] This is no pretension to *prophecy*, but simply a statement based on the knowledge of facts. Every century an attempt is being made to show the world that Occultism is no vain superstition. Once the door is permitted to be kept a little ajar, it will be opened wider with every new century.

in the Vaivasvata Manvantara or "Round"; each Round being composed of the Yugas of the seven periods of Humanity; four of which
are now passed in *our* life cycle, the middle point of the 5th being
nearly reached. The old book, having described Cosmic Evolution
and explained the origin of everything on earth, including physical
man, after giving the true history of the races from the First down to
the Fifth (our) race, goes no further. It stops short at the beginning
of the *Kali Yuga* just 4989 years ago at the death of Krishna, the
bright "Sun-god," the once living hero and reformer.

But there exists another book. None of its possessors regard it as
very ancient, as it was born with, and is only as old as the Black Age,
namely, about 5,000 years. In about nine years hence, the first
cycle of the first five millenniums, that began with the great cycle
of the Kali-Yuga, will end. And then the last prophecy contained in
that book (the first volume of the prophetic record for the Black
Age) will be accomplished. We have not long to wait, and many of
us will witness the Dawn of the New Cycle, at the end of which not
a few accounts will be settled and squared between the races.

One more important point must be noticed, one that stands fore-
most in the series of proofs given of the existence of one primeval,
universal Wisdom—at any rate for the Christian Kabalists and
students. The teachings were, at least, partially known to several of
the Fathers of the Church. It is maintained, on purely historical
grounds, that Origen, Synesius, and even Clemens Alexandrinus,
had been themselves initiated into the Mysteries before adding to the
Neo-Platonism of the Alexandrian school that of the Gnostics, under
the Christian veil. More than this, some of the doctrines of the Secret
schools—though by no means all—were preserved in the Vatican,
and have since become part and parcel of the Mysteries, in the shape
of disfigured additions made to the original Christian programme
by the Latin Church. Such is the now materialized dogma of the
Immaculate Conception. This accounts for the great persecutions
set on foot by the Roman Catholic Church against Occultism,
Masonry, and *heterodox* mysticism generally.

The days of Constantine were the last turning-point in history, the
period of the supreme struggle that ended in the Western world
throttling the old religions in favour of the new one, built on their
bodies. Thence the vista into the far distant Past, beyond the
"Deluge" and the Garden of Eden, began to be forcibly and relent-
lessly closed by every fair and unfair means against the indiscreet
gaze of posterity. Every issue was blocked up, every record that
hands could be laid upon destroyed. Yet there remains enough, even
among such mutilated records, to warrant us in saying that there is

in them every possible evidence of the actual existence of a Parent Doctrine. Fragments have survived geological and political cataclysms to tell the story; and every survival shows evidence that the now *Secret* Wisdom was once the one fountain head, the everflowing perennial source, at which were fed all its streamlets—the later religions of all nations—from the first down to the last. This period, beginning with Buddha and Pythagoras at the one end and the Neo-Platonists and Gnostics at the other, is the only focus left in history wherein converge for the last time the bright rays of light streaming from the aeons of time gone by, unobscured by the hand of bigotry and fanaticism.

To my judges, past and future—whether they are serious literary critics, or those howling dervishes in literature who judge a book according to the popularity or unpopularity of the author's name, I have nothing to say. To the public in general and the readers of *The Secret Doctrine* I may repeat what I have stated all along, and which I now clothe in the words of Montaigne: Gentlemen, "I HAVE HERE MADE ONLY A NOSEGAY OF CULLED FLOWERS, AND HAVE BROUGHT NOTHING OF MY OWN BUT THE STRING THAT TIES THEM."

VOLUME FIRST
COSMOGENESIS

PROEM

PAGES FROM A PREHISTORIC PERIOD

An Archaic Manuscript—a collection of palm leaves made impermeable to water, fire, and air, by some specific unknown process —is before the writer's eye. On the first page is an immaculate white disk within a dull black ground. On the following page, the same disk, but with a central point. The first, the student knows to represent Kosmos in Eternity, before the re-awakening of still slumbering Energy, the emanation of the Word in later sys‘ems. The point in the hitherto immaculate Disk, Space and Eternity in Pralaya, denotes the dawn of differentiation. It is the Point in the Mundane Egg (see Part II., "The Mundane Egg"), the germ within the latter which will become the Universe, the ALL, the boundless, periodical Kosmos, this germ being latent and active, periodically and by turns. The one circle is divine Unity, from which all proceeds, whither all returns. Its circumference—a forcibly limited symbol, in view of the limitation of the human mind—indicates the abstract, ever incognizable PRESENCE, and its plane, the Universal Soul, although the two are one. Only the face of the Disk being white and the ground all around black, shows clearly that its plane is the only knowledge, dim and hazy though it still is, that is attainable by man. It is on this plane that the Manvantaric manifestations begin; for it is in this SOUL that slumbers, during the Pralaya, the Divine Thought, wherein lies concealed the plan of every future Cosmogony and Theogony.

It is the ONE LIFE, eternal, invisible, yet Omnipresent, without beginning or end, yet periodical in its regular manifestations, between which periods reigns the dark mystery of non-Being; unconscious, yet absolute Consciousness; unrealizable, yet the one self-existing reality; truly, "a chaos to the sense, a Kosmos to the reason." Its one absolute attribute, which is ITSELF, eternal, ceaseless Motion, is called in esoteric parlance the "Great Breath," which is the perpetual motion of the universe, in the sense of limitless, ever-present SPACE. That which is motionless cannot be Divine. But then there is nothing in fact and reality absolutely motionless within the Universal Soul.

From the beginning of man's inheritance, from the first appearance of the architects of the globe he lives in, the unrevealed Deity was recognized and considered under its only philosophical aspect—universal motion, the thrill of the creative Breath in Nature. Occultism sums up the "One Existence" thus: "Deity is an arcane, living (or moving) FIRE, and the eternal witnesses to this unseen Presence are Light, Heat, Moisture,"—this trinity including, and being the cause of, every phenomenon in Nature. Intra-Cosmic motion is eternal and ceaseless; cosmic motion (the visible, or that which is subject to perception) is finite and periodical. As an eternal abstraction it is the EVER-PRESENT; as a manifestation, it is finite both in the coming direction and the opposite, the two being the alpha and omega of successive reconstructions. Kosmos—the NOUMENON—has nought to do with the causal relations of the phenomenal World. It is only with reference to the intra-cosmic soul, the ideal Kosmos in the immutable Divine Thought, that we may say: "It never had a beginning nor will it have an end." With regard to its body or cosmic organization, though it cannot be said that it had a first, or will ever have a last construction, yet at each new Manvantara its organization may be regarded as the first and the last of its kind, as it evolutes every time on a higher plane . . . .

A few years ago only, it was stated that:—

"The esoteric doctrine teaches, like Buddhism and Brahminism, and even the Kabala, that the one infinite and unknown Essence exists from all eternity, and in regular and harmonious successions is either passive or active. In the poetical phraseology of Manu these conditions are called the "Days" and the "Nights" of Brahmā. The latter is either "awake" or "asleep." The Svabhavikas, or philosophers of the oldest school of Buddhism (which still exists in Nepal), speculate only upon the active condition of this "Essence," which they call Svabhavat, and deem it foolish to theorise upon the abstract and "unknowable" power in its passive condition. Hence they are called atheists by both Christian theologians and modern scientists, for neither of the two are able to understand the profound logic of their philosophy. The former will allow of no other God than the personified secondary powers which have worked out the visible universe, and which became with them the anthropomorphic God of the Christians—the male Jehovah, roaring amid thunder and lightning. In its turn, rationalistic science greets the Buddhists and the Svabhavikas as the "positivists" of the archaic ages. If we take a one-sided view of the philosophy of the latter, our materialists may be right in their own way. The Buddhists maintained that there is no Creator, but an infinitude of creative powers, which collectively form the one eternal substance, the essence of which is inscrutable—hence not a subject for speculation for any true philosopher. Socrates invariably refused to argue upon the mystery of universal being, yet no one would ever have thought of charging him with atheism, except those who were bent upon his destruction. Upon inaugurating an active period, says the Secret Doctrine, an expansion of this Divine essence from without inwardly and from within outwardly, occurs in obedience to eternal and immutable law, and the phenomenal or visible universe is the ultimate result of the long chain of cosmical forces thus progressively set in motion. In like manner, when the passive condition is resumed, a contraction of the Divine essence takes place, and the previous work of creation is gradually and progressively undone. The visible universe becomes disintegrated, its material dispersed; and 'darkness' solitary and alone, broods once more over the face of the 'deep.' To use a metaphor from the Secret Books, which will convey the idea still more clearly, an outbreathing of the 'unknown essence' produces the world; and an inhalation causes it to disappear. This process has been going on from all eternity, and our present universe is but one of an infinite series, which had no beginning and will have no end."—(See *Isis Unveiled*.)[1]

This passage will be explained, as far as it is possible, in the present work. Though, as it now stands, it contains nothing new to the Orientalist, its esoteric interpretation may contain a good deal which has hitherto remained entirely unknown to the Western student.

The first illustration being a plain disc ◯ , the second one in the Archaic symbol shows ⊙ , a disc with a point in it—the first differentiation in the periodical manifestations of the ever-eternal nature, sexless and infinite "Aditi in THAT" (Rig Veda), the point in the disc, or potential Space within abstract Space. In its third stage the point is transformed into a diameter, thus ⊖ . It now symbolises a divine immaculate Mother-Nature within the all-embracing absolute Infinitude. When the diameter line is crossed by a vertical one ⊕ , it becomes the mundane cross. Humanity has reached its Third Root-Race; it is the sign for the origin of human life to begin. When the circumference disappears and leaves only the ✛ it is a sign that the fall of man into matter is accomplished, and the Fourth Race begins. The Cross within a circle symbolises pure Pantheism; when the Cross was left uninscribed, it became phallic. It had the same and yet other meanings as a TAU inscribed within a circle ⊖ or as a "Thor's hammer." the Jaina cross, so-called, or simply Svastika within a circle ⊕.

By the third symbol—the circle divided in two by the horizontal line of the diameter—the first manifestation of creative (still passive, because feminine) Nature was meant. The first shadowy perception of man connected with procreation is feminine, because man knows his mother more than his father. Hence female deities were more sacred than the male. Nature is therefore feminine, and, to a degree, objective and tangible, and the Spirit Principle which fructifies it is concealed. By adding to the circle with the horizontal line in it a perpendicular line, the Tau was formed— T —the oldest form of the letter. It was the glyph of the Third Root-Race to the day of its symbolical Fall—*i.e.*, when the separation of sexes by natural

[1] [II, pp. 264–5.]

evolution took place—when the figure became ⊕ , the circle, or sexless life modified or separated—a double glyph or symbol. With the races of our Fifth Race it became in symbology the Sacr', and in Hebrew N'cabvah, of the first-formed races; then it changed into the Egyptian ☥ (emblem of life), and still later into the sign of Venus, ♀ . Then comes the Svastika (Thor's Hammer, or the Hermetic Cross now), entirely separated from its Circle, thus becoming purely phallic. The esoteric symbol of Kali Yuga is the five-pointed star reversed, thus ⛤ —the sign of human sorcery, with its two points (horns) turned heavenward, a position every Occultist will recognize as one of the "left-hand," and used in ceremonial magic.

It is hoped that during the perusal of this work the erroneous ideas of the public in general with regard to Pantheism will be modified. It is wrong to regard the Buddhists and Advaitee Occultists as atheists. If not all of them philosophers, they are, at any rate, all logicians, their objections and arguments being based on strict reasoning. Indeed, if the Parabrahman of the Hindus may be taken as a representative of the hidden and nameless deities of other nations, this absolute Principle will be found to be the prototype from which all the others were copied. Parabrahm is not "God," because It is not *a* God. "It is that which is supreme, and not supreme (*paravara*)," explains Mandukya Upanishad (2.28). It is supreme as CAUSE, not supreme as effect. Parabrahm is simply, as a "Secondless Reality," the all-inclusive Kosmos—or, rather, the infinite Cosmic Space—in the highest spiritual sense. Brahma[2] (neuter) being the unchanging, pure, free, undecaying supreme Root, "the ONE true Existence, Paramarthika," and the absolute Chit and Chaitanya (intelligence, consciousness) cannot be a cognizer, "for THAT can have no subject of cognition." Can the flame be called the essence of Fire? This Essence is "the LIFE and LIGHT of the Universe, the visible fire and flame are destruction, death, and evil." "Fire and Flame destroy the body of an Arhat, their essence makes him immortal." (*Bodhi-mur, Book II.*) "The knowledge of the absolute Spirit, like the effulgence of the sun, or like heat in fire, is naught else than the absolute Essence itself," says Sankaracharya. IT—is "the Spirit of the Fire," not fire itself; therefore, "the attributes of the latter, heat or flame, are not the attributes of the Spirit, but of that of which that Spirit is the unconscious cause." Is not the above sentence the true key-note of later Rosicrucian philosophy? Parabrahm is, in short, the collective aggregate of Kosmos in its infinity and eternity, the "THAT" and "THIS" to which distributive aggre-

[2] [Brahman.]

gates cannot be applied. "In the beginning THIS was the Self, one only" (*Aitareya Upanishad*); the great Sankaracharya explains that "THIS" referred to the Universe (Jagat); the sense of the words, "in the beginning," meaning before the reproduction of the phenomenal Universe.

The Occultists are, therefore, at one with the Adwaita Vedantin philosophers as to the above tenet. They show the impossibility of accepting on philosophical grounds the idea of the absolute ALL creating or even evolving the "Golden—Egg," into which it is said to enter in order to transform itself into Brahmā—the Creator, who expands himself later into gods and all the visible Universe. They say that Absolute Unity cannot pass to Infinity; for Infinity presupposes the limitless extension of *something*, and the duration of that "something"; and the One All is like Space—which is its only mental and physical representation on this Earth, or our plane of existence—neither an object of, nor a subject to, perception. If one could suppose the Eternal Infinite All, the Omnipresent Unity, instead of being in Eternity, becoming through periodical manifestation a manifold Universe or a multiple personality, that Unity would cease to be one. Locke's idea that "pure Space is capable of neither resistance nor Motion" is incorrect. Space is neither a "limitless void," nor a "conditioned fulness," but both, being, on the plane of absolute abstraction, the ever-incognizable Deity, which is void only to finite minds, and on that of *mayavic* perception, the Plenum, the absolute Container of all that is, whether manifested or unmanifested: it is, therefore, that ABSOLUTE ALL. There is no difference between the Christian Apostle's "In Him we live and move and have our being," and the Hindu Rishi's "The Universe lives in, proceeds from, and will return to, Brahman (Brahmā)": for Brahman (neuter), the unmanifested, is that Universe *in abscondito*, and Brahmā, the manifested, is the Logos, made male-female in the symbolical orthodox dogmas, the God of the Apostle-Initiate and of the Rishi being both the Unseen and the Visible SPACE. Space is called in the esoteric symbolism "the Seven-Skinned Eternal Mother-Father." It is composed from its undifferentiated to its differentiated surface of seven layers.

"What is that which was, is, and will be, whether there is a Universe or not; whether there be gods or none?" asks the esoteric Senzar Catechism. And the answer made is—SPACE.

It is not the One Unknown ever-present God in Nature, or Nature *in abscondito*, that is rejected, but the God of human dogma and his *humanized* "Word." In his infinite conceit and inherent pride and vanity, man shaped it himself with his sacrilegious hand out of the material he found in his own small brain-fabric, and forced it upon mankind as a direct revelation from the one unrevealed SPACE. The Occultist accepts revelation as coming from divine yet still finite Beings, the manifested lives, never from the Unmanifestable ONE LIFE; from those entities, called Primordial Man, Dhyani-Buddhas, or Dhyan-Chohans, the Rishi-Prajapati of the Hindus, the Elohim or Sons of God, the Planetary Spirits of all nations, who have become Gods for men. He also regards the Adi-Sakti—the direct emanation of Mulaprakriti, the eternal Root of THAT, and the female aspect of the Creative Cause Brahmā, in her akasic form of the Universal Soul—as philosophically a Maya, and cause of human Maya. But this view does not prevent him from believing in its existence so long as it lasts, to wit, for one Mahamanvantara; nor from applying A'kasa, the radiation of Mulaprakriti, to practical purposes, connected as the World-Soul is with all natural phenomena, known or unknown to science.

The oldest religions of the world—exoterically, for the esoteric root or foundation is one—are the Indian, the Mazdean, and the Egyptian. Then comes the Chaldean, the outcome of these—entirely lost to the world now, except in its disfigured Sabeanism as at present rendered by the archaeologists; then, passing over a number of religions that will be mentioned later, comes the Jewish, esoterically, as in the Kabala, following in the line of Babylonian Magism; exoterically, as in Genesis and the Pentateuch, a collection of allegorical legends. Read by the light of the Zohar, the initial four chapters of Genesis are the fragment of a highly philosophical page in the World's Cosmogony. Left in their symbolical disguise, they are a nursery tale, an ugly thorn in the side of science and logic, an evident effect of Karma. To have let them serve as a prologue to Christianity was a cruel revenge on the part of the Rabbis, who knew better what their Pentateuch meant. It was a silent protest against their spoliation, and the Jews have certainly now the better of their traditional persecutors. The above-named exoteric creeds will be explained in the light of the Universal doctrine as we proceed with it.

The Occult Catechism contains the following questions and answers:

"What is it that ever is?" "Space, the eternal Anupadaka."[3] *"What is it that ever was?" "The Germ in the Root." "What is it that is ever coming and going?" "The Great Breath." "Then, there are three Eternals?" "No, the three are one. That which ever is is one, that which ever was is one, that which is ever being and becoming is also one: and this is Space."*

[3] Meaning "parentless"—see farther on.

"Explain, oh Lanoo (disciple)."—*"The One is an unbroken Circle (Ring) with no circumference, for it is nowhere and everywhere; the One is the boundless plane of the Circle, manifesting a diameter only during the manvantaric periods; the One is the indivisible point found nowhere, perceived everywhere during those periods; it is the Vertical and the Horizontal, the Father and the Mother, the summit and base of the Father, the two extremities of the Mother, reaching in reality nowhere, for the One is the Ring as also the rings that are within that Ring. Light in darkness and darkness in light: the 'Breath which is eternal.' It proceeds from without inwardly, when it is everywhere, and from within outwardly, when it is nowhere—(i.e., maya,[4] one of the centres[5]). It expands and contracts (exhalation and inhalation). When it expands the mother diffuses and scatters; when it contracts, the mother draws back and ingathers. This produces the periods of Evolution and Dissolution, Manwantara and Pralaya. The Germ is invisible and fiery; the Root (the plane of the circle) is cool; but during Evolution and Manwantara her garment is cold and radiant. Hot Breath is the Father who devours the progeny of the many-faced Element (heterogeneous); and leaves the single-faced ones (homogeneous). Cool Breath is the Mother, who conceives, forms, brings forth, and receives them back into her bosom, to reform them at the Dawn (of the Day of Brahmā, or Manvantara). . . . "*

For clearer understanding on the part of the general reader, it must be stated that Occult Science recognizes *Seven* Cosmic Elements—four entirely physical, and the fifth (Ether) semi-material, as it will become visible in the air towards the end of our Fourth Round, to reign supreme over the others during the whole of the Fifth. The remaining two are as yet absolutely beyond the range of human perception. These latter will, however, appear as presentments

[4] Esoteric philosophy, regarding as Maya (or the illusion of ignorance) every finite thing, must necessarily view in the same light every intra-Cosmic planet and body, as being something organized, hence finite. The expression, therefore, "it proceeds from without inwardly, etc." refers in the first portion of the sentence to the dawn of the Mahamanvantaric period, or the great re-evolution after one of the complete periodical dissolutions of every compound form in Nature (from planet to molecule) into its ultimate essence or element; and in its second portion, to the partial or local manvantara, which may be a solar or even a planetary one.

[5] By "centre," a centre of energy or a Cosmic focus is meant; when the so-called "Creation," or formation of a planet, is accomplished by that force which is designated by the Occultists LIFE and by Science "energy," then the process takes place from within outwardly, every atom being said to contain in itself creative energy of the divine breath. Hence, whereas after an absolute pralaya, or when the pre-existing material consists but of ONE Element, and BREATH "is everywhere," the latter acts from without inwardly: after a minor pralaya, everything having remained in *statu quo*—in a refrigerated state, so to say, like the moon—at the first flutter of manvantara, the planet or planets begin their resurrection to life from within outwardly.

during the 6th and 7th Races of this Round, and will become known in the 6th and 7th Rounds respectively. These seven elements, with their numberless Sub-Elements far more numerous than those known to Science, are simply *conditional* modifications and aspects of the one and only Element. This latter is not *Ether*, not even *A'kasa* but the *source* of these. The Fifth Element, now advocated quite freely by Science, is not the Ether hypothesised by Sir Isaac Newton —although he calls it by that name, having associated it in his mind probably with the Aether, "Father-Mother" of Antiquity. As Newton intuitionally says, "Nature is a perpetual circulatory worker, generating fluids out of solids, fixed things out of volatile, and volatile out of fixed, subtile out of gross, and gross out of subtile. ... Thus, perhaps, may all things be originated from Ether" (*Hypoth*, 1675).

The reader has to bear in mind that the Stanzas given treat only of the Cosmogony of our own planetary System and what is visible around it, after a Solar Pralaya. The secret teachings with regard to the Evolution of the Universal Kosmos cannot be given, since they could not be understood by the highest minds in this age, and there seem to be very few Initiates, even among the greatest, who are allowed to speculate upon this subject. Moreover the Teachers say openly that not even the highest Dhyani-Chohans have ever penetrated the mysteries beyond those boundaries that separate the milliards of Solar systems from the "Central Sun," as it is called. Therefore, that which is given relates only to our visible Kosmos, after a "Night of Brahmā."

Before the reader proceeds to the consideration of the Stanzas from the Book of Dzyan which form the basis of the present work, it is absolutely necessary that he should be made acquainted with the few fundamental conceptions which underlie and pervade the entire system of thought to which his attention is invited. These basic ideas are few in number, and on their clear apprehension depends the understanding of all that follows; therefore no apology is required for asking the reader to make himself familiar with them first, before entering on the perusal of the work itself.

The Secret Doctrine establishes three fundamental propositions:—

(a) An Omnipresent, Eternal, Boundless, and Immutable PRINCIPLE on which all speculation is impossible, since it transcends the power of human conception and could only be dwarfed by any human expression or similitude. It is beyond the range and reach of thought—in the words of the Mandukya Upanishad, "unthinkable and unspeakable."

To render these ideas clearer to the general reader, let him set out with the postulate that there is one absolute Reality which antecedes all manifested, conditioned, being. This Infinite and Eternal Cause —dimly formulated in the "Unconscious" and "Unknowable" of current European philosophy—is the rootless root of "all that was, is, or ever shall be." It is of course devoid of all attributes and is essentially without any relation to manifested, finite Being. It is "Be-ness" rather than Being (in Sanskrit, *Sat*), and is beyond all thought or speculation.

This "Be-ness" is symbolized in the Secret Doctrine under two aspects. On the one hand, absolute Abstract Space, representing bare subjectivity, the one thing which no human mind can either exclude from any conception, or conceive of by itself. On the other, absolute Abstract Motion representing Unconditioned Consciousness. Even our Western thinkers have shown that Consciousness is inconceivable to us apart from change, and motion best symbolizes change, its essential characteristic. This latter aspect of the one Reality is also symbolized by the term "The Great Breath," a symbol sufficiently graphic to need no further elucidation. Thus, then, the first fundamental axiom of the Secret Doctrine is this metaphysical ONE ABSOLUTE—BE-NESS—symbolized by finite intelligence as the theological Trinity.

Parabrahm (the One Reality, the Absolute) is the field of Absolute Consciousness, *i.e.*, that Essence which is out of all relation to conditioned existence, and of which conscious existence is a conditioned symbol. But once that we pass in thought from this (to us) Absolute Negation, duality supervenes in the contrast of Spirit (or consciousness) and Matter, Subject and Object.

Spirit (or Consciousness) and Matter are, however, to be regarded not as independent realities, but as the two facets or aspects of the Absolute (Parabrahm), which constitute the basis of conditioned Being whether subjective or objective.

Considering this metaphysical triad as the Root from which proceeds all manifestation, the great Breath assumes the character of precosmic Ideation. It is the *fons et origo* of force and of all individual consciousness, and supplies the guiding intelligence in the vast scheme of cosmic Evolution. On the other hand, precosmic Root-Substance (*Mulaprakriti*) is that aspect of the Absolute which underlies all the objective planes of Nature.

Just as pre-Cosmic Ideation is the root of all individual consciousness, so pre-Cosmic Substance is the substratum of matter in the various grades of its differentiation.

Hence it will be apparent that the contrast of these two aspects of the Absolute is essential to the existence of the "Manifested

Universe." Apart from Cosmic Substance, Cosmic Ideation could not manifest as individual consciousness, since it is only through a vehicle[6] of matter that consciousness wells up as "I am I," a physical basis being necessary to focus a ray of the Universal Mind at a certain stage of complexity. Again, apart from Cosmic Ideation, Cosmic Substance would remain an empty abstraction, and no emergence of consciousness could ensue.

The Manifested Universe, therefore, is pervaded by duality, which is, as it were, the very essence of its EX-istence as "manifestation." But just as the opposite poles of Subject and Object, Spirit and Matter, are but aspects of the One Unity in which they are synthesized, so, in the manifested Universe, there is "that" which links Spirit to Matter, Subject to Object.

This something, at present unknown to Western speculation, is called by the occultists Fohat. It is the "bridge" by which the "Ideas" existing in the "Divine Thought" are impressed on Cosmic Substance as the "Laws of Nature." Fohat is thus the dynamic energy of Cosmic Ideation; or, regarded from the other side, it is the intelligent medium, the guiding power of all manifestation, the "Thought Divine" transmitted and made manifest through the Dhyan Chohans,[7] the Architects of the visible World. Thus from Spirit, or Cosmic Ideation, comes our consciousness; from Cosmic Substance the several vehicles in which that consciousness is individualized and attains to self—or reflective—consciousness; while Fohat, in its various manifestations, is the mysterious link between Mind and Matter, the animating principle electrifying every atom into life.

The following summary will afford a clearer idea to the reader.

(1) THE ABSOLUTE; the *Parabrahm* of the Vedantins or the one Reality, SAT, which is, as Hegel says, both Absolute Being and Non-Being.

(2) The first manifestation, the impersonal, and, in philosophy, *unmanifested* Logos, the precursor of the "manifested." This is the "First Cause," the "Unconscious" of European Pantheists.

(3) Spirit-matter, LIFE; the "Spirit of the Universe," the Purusha and Prakriti, or the *second* Logos.

(4) Cosmic Ideation, MAHAT or Intelligence, the Universal World-Soul; the Cosmic Noumenon of Matter, the basis of the intelligent operations in and of Nature, also called MAHA-BUDDHI.

The ONE REALITY; its *dual* aspects in the conditioned Universe.

Further, the Secret Doctrine affirms:—

(*b*) The Eternity of the Universe *in toto* as a boundless plane;

[6] Called in Sanskrit *upadhi*.
[7] Called by Christian theology: Archangels, Seraphs, etc.

periodically "the playground of numberless Universes incessantly manifesting and disappearing," called "the manifesting stars," and the "sparks of Eternity." "The Eternity of the Pilgrim"[8] is like a wink of the Eye of Self-Existence (*Book of Dzyan.*) "The appearance and disappearance of Worlds is like a regular tidal ebb of flux and reflux." (See Part II., "Days and Nights of Brahmā.")

This second assertion of the Secret Doctrine is the absolute universality of that law of periodicity, of flux and reflux, ebb and flow, which physical science has observed and recorded in all departments of nature. An alternation such as that of Day and Night, Life and Death, Sleeping and Waking, is a fact so common, so perfectly universal and without exception, that it is easy to comprehend that in it we see one of the absolutely fundamental Laws of the Universe.

Moreover, the Secret Doctrine teaches:—

(*c*) The fundamental identity of all Souls with the Universal Over-Soul, the latter being itself an aspect of the Unknown Root; and the obligatory pilgrimage for every Soul—a spark of the former—through the Cycle of Incarnation (or "Necessity") in accordance with Cyclic and Karmic law, during the whole term. In other words, no purely spiritual Buddhi (Divine Soul) can have an independent (conscious) existence before the spark which issued from the pure Essence of the Universal Sixth Principle—or the OVER-SOUL—has (a) passed through every elemental form of the phenomenal world of that Manvantara, and (b) acquired individuality, first by natural impulse, and then by self-induced and self-devised efforts (checked by its Karma), thus ascending through all the degrees of intelligence, from the lowest to the highest Manas, from mineral and plant, up to the holiest archangel (Dhyani-Buddha). The pivotal doctrine of the Esoteric philosophy admits no privileges or special gifts in man, save those won by his own Ego through personal effort and merit throughout a long series of metempsychoses and re-incarnations. This is why the Hindus say that the Universe is Brahman and Brahmā, for Brahman is in every atom of the universe, the six principles in Nature being all the outcome—the variously differentiated aspects—of the SEVENTH and ONE, the only reality in the Universe whether Cosmic or micro-cosmic; and also why the

[8] "Pilgrim" is the appellation given to our *Monad* (the two in one) during its cycle of incarnations. It is the only immortal and eternal principle in us, being an indivisible part of the integral whole—the Universal Spirit, from which it emanates, and into which it is absorbed at the end of the cycle. When it is said to emanate from the One Spirit, an awkward and incorrect expression has to be used, for lack of appropriate words in English. The Vedantins call it Sutratma (Thread-Soul), but their explanation, too, differs somewhat from that of the occultists; to explain which difference, however, is left to the Vedantins themselves.

permutations (psychic, spiritual and physical), on the plane of mani-festation and form, of the SIXTH (Brahmā the vehicle of Brahman) are viewed by metaphysical antiphrasis as illusive and Mayavic. For although the root of every atom individually and of every form collectively is that Seventh Principle or the One Reality, still, in its manifested phenomenal and temporary appearance, it is no better than an evanescent illusion of our senses.

In its absoluteness, the One Principle under its two aspects (of Parabrahman and Mulaprakriti) is sexless, unconditioned and eternal. Its periodical (manvantaric) emanation—or primal radia-tion—is also One, androgynous and phenomenally finite. When the radiation radiates in its turn, all its radiations are also androgynous, to become male and female principles in their lower aspects. After Pralaya, whether the great or the minor Pralaya (the latter leaving the worlds in *statu quo*[9]), the first that re-awakes to active life is the plastic Akasa, Father-Mother, the Spirit and Soul of Ether, or the plane on the surface of the Circle. Space is called the "Mother" before its Cosmic activity, and Father-Mother at the first stage of re-awakening. . . .

Such are the basic conceptions on which the Secret Doctrine rests.

It would not be in place here to enter upon any defence or proof of their inherent reasonableness; nor can I pause to show how they are, in fact, contained—though too often under a misleading guise—in every system of thought or philosophy worthy of the name.

Once the reader has gained a clear comprehension of them and realized the light which they throw on every problem of life, they will need no further justification in his eyes, because their truth will be to him as evident as the sun in heaven. I pass on, therefore, to the subject matter of the Stanzas as given in this volume, adding a skeleton outline of them, in the hope of thereby rendering the task of the student more easy, by placing before him in a few words the general conception therein explained.

The history of cosmic evolution, as traced in the Stanzas, is, so to say, the abstract algebraical formula of that Evolution. Hence the student must not expect to find there an account of all the stages and transformations which intervene between the first beginnings of "Universal" Evolution and our present state. To give such an account would be as impossible as it would be incomprehensible to

---

[9] It is not the physical organisms that remain in *statu quo*, least of all their psychic principles, during the great Cosmic or even Solar Pralayas, but only their Akasic or astral "photographs." But during the minor pralayas, once overtaken by the "Night" the planets remain intact, though dead, as a huge animal, caught and embedded in the polar ice, remains the same for ages.

men who cannot even grasp the nature of the plane of existence next to that to which, for the moment, their consciousness is limited.

The Stanzas, therefore, give an abstract formula which can be applied, *mutatis mutandis*, to all evolution: to that of our tiny earth, to that of the chain of planets of which that earth forms one, to the Solar Universe to which that chain belongs, and so on, in an ascending scale, till the mind reels and is exhausted in the effort.

The seven Stanzas given in this volume represent the seven terms of this abstract formula. They refer to, and describe the seven great stages of the evolutionary process, which are spoken of in the *Puranas* as the "Seven Creations," and in the Bible as the "Days" of Creation.

The First Stanza describes the state of the ONE ALL during Pralaya, before the first flutter of re-awakening manifestation.

A moment's thought shows that such a state can only be symbolized; to describe it is impossible. Nor can it be symbolized except in negatives; for, since it is the state of Absoluteness *per se*, it can possess none of those specific attributes which serve us to describe objects in positive terms. Hence that state can only be suggested by the negatives of all those most abstract attributes which men feel rather than conceive as the remotest limits attainable by their power of conception.

The stage described in Stanza 2 is, to a Western mind, so nearly identical with that mentioned in the first Stanza, that to express the idea of its difference would require a treatise in itself. Hence it must be left to the intuition and the higher faculties of the reader to grasp, as far as he can, the meaning of the allegorical phrases used. Indeed it must be remembered that all these Stanzas appeal to the inner faculties rather than to the ordinary comprehension of the physical brain.

Stanza 3 describes the re-awakening of the Universe to life after Pralaya. It depicts the emergence of the "Monads" from their state of absorption within the ONE; the earliest and highest stage in the formation of "Worlds," the term Monad being one which may apply equally to the vastest Solar System or the tiniest atom.

Stanza 4 shows the differentiation of the "Germ" of the Universe into the septenary hierarchy of conscious Divine Powers, who are the active manifestations of the One Supreme Energy. They are the framers, shapers, and ultimately the creators of all the manifested Universe, in the only sense in which the name "Creator" is intelligible; they inform and guide it; they are the intelligent Beings who adjust and control evolution, embodying in themselves those manifestations of the ONE LAW, which we know as "The Laws of Nature."

Generically, they are known as the Dhyan Chohans, though each of the various groups has its own designation in the Secret Doctrine.

This stage of evolution is spoken of in Hindu mythology as the "Creation" of the Gods.

In Stanza 5 the process of world-formation is described. First, diffused Cosmic Matter, then the "fiery whirlwind," the first stage in the formation of a nebula. That nebula condenses, and after passing through various transformations forms a Solar Universe, a Planetary Chain, or a single Planet, as the case may be.

The subsequent stages in the formation of a "World" are indicated in Stanza 6, which brings the evolution of such a World down to its fourth great period, corresponding to the period in which we are now living.

Stanza 7 continues the history, tracing the descent of life down to the appearance of Man; and thus closes the First Book of *The Secret Doctrine.*

The development of "Man" from his first appearance on this earth in this Round to the state in which we now find him will form the subject of Volume Two.

The Stanzas which form the thesis of every section are given throughout in their modern translated version, as it would be worse than useless to make the subject still more difficult by introducing the archaic phraseology of the original, with its puzzling style and words. Extracts are given from the Chinese Tibetan and Sanskrit translations of the original Senzar Commentaries and Glosses on the Book of DZYAN—these being now rendered for the first time into a European language. It is almost unnecessary to state that only portions of the seven Stanzas are here given. Were they published complete they would remain incomprehensible to all save the few higher occultists. Nor is there any need to assure the reader that, no more than most of the profane, does the writer, or rather the humble recorder, understand those forbidden passages. To facilitate the reading, and to avoid the too frequent reference to footnotes, it was thought best to blend together texts and glosses, using the Sanskrit and Tibetan proper names whenever those cannot be avoided, in preference to giving the originals. The more so as th- said terms are all accepted synonyms, the former only being used between a Master and his chelas (or disciples).

As this work is written for the instruction of students of Occultism, and not for the benefit of philologists, we may well avoid foreign terms wherever it is possible to do so. The untranslateable terms alone, incomprehensible unless explained in their meanings, are left, but all such terms are rendered in their Sanskrit form. These are, in almost every case, the late developments of the later language, and pertain to the Fifth Root-Race. Sanskrit, as now known, was not spoken by the Atlanteans, and most of the philosophical terms used in the systems of the India of the post-Mahabharatan period are not found in the Vedas, nor are they to be met with in the original Stanzas, but only their equivalents. The reader is once more invited to regard all that which follows as a fairy tale, if he likes; at best as one of the yet unproven speculations of *dreamers;* and, at the worst, as an additional hypothesis to the many scientific hypotheses past, present and future, some exploded, others still lingering. It is not in any sense worse than are many of the scientific theories; and it is in every case more philosophical and probable.

PART I

COSMIC EVOLUTION

In Seven Stanzas translated from the Book of Dzyan

STANZA 1

1. "THE ETERNAL PARENT (Space), WRAPPED IN HER EVER INVISIBLE ROBES, HAD SLUMBERED ONCE AGAIN FOR SEVEN ETERNITIES (*a*)."

The "Parent Space" is the eternal, ever present Cause of all—the incomprehensible DEITY, whose "invisible Robes" are the mystic root of all Matter, and of the Universe. Space is the *one eternal thing* that we can most easily imagine, immovable in its abstraction and uninfluenced by either the presence or absence in it of an objective Universe. It is without dimension, in every sense, and self-existent. Spirit is the first differentiation from THAT, the causeless cause of both Spirit and Matter. It is, as taught in the esoteric catechism, neither limitless void, nor conditioned fulness, but both. It was and ever will be.

Thus, the "Robes" stand for the noumenon of undifferentiated Cosmic Matter. It is not matter as we know it, but the spiritual essence of matter, and is co-eternal and even one with Space in its abstract sense. Root-nature is also the source of the subtle invisible properties in visible matter. It is the Soul, so to say, of the ONE infinite Spirit. The Hindus call it Mulaprakriti, and say that it is the primordial Substance which is the basis of the Upadhi or vehicle of every phenomenon, whether physical, mental or psychic. It is the source from which Akasa radiates.

(*a*) The Seven Eternities are the seven periods, or a period answering in its duration to the seven periods, of a Manvantara, and extending throughout a Maha-Kalpa or "Great Age"—100 years of Brahmā—making a total of 311,040,000,000,000 of years; each Year of Brahmā being composed of 360 Days and of the same number of Nights of Brahmā; and a Day of Brahmā consisting of 4,320,000,000 of mortal years.

2. TIME WAS NOT, FOR IT LAY ASLEEP IN THE INFINITE BOSOM OF DURATION.

Time is only an illusion produced by the succession of our states of consciousness as we travel through eternal duration, and it does not exist where no consciousness exists in which the illusion can be produced; but "lies asleep." The present is only a mathematical line which divides that part of eternal duration which we call the future, from that part which we call the past. Nothing on earth has real duration, for nothing remains without change—or the same—for the billionth part of a second; and the sensation we have of the actuality of the division of "time" known as the present, comes from the blurring of that momentary glimpse, or succession of glimpses, of things that our senses give us, as those things pass from the region of ideals which we call the future, to the region of memories that we name the past. In the same way we experience a sensation of duration in the case of the instantaneous electric spark, by reason of the blurred and continuing impression on the retina. The real person or thing does not consist solely of what is seen at any particular moment, but is composed of the sum of all its various and changing conditions from its appearance in the material form to its disappearance from the earth. It is these "sum-totals" that exist from eternity in the "future," and pass by degrees through matter, to exist for eternity in the "past." No one could say that a bar of metal dropped into the sea came into existence as it left the air, and ceased to exist as it entered the water, and that the bar itself consisted only of that cross-section thereof which at any given moment coincided with the mathematical plane that separates, and, at the same time, joins, the atmosphere and the ocean. Even so of persons and things, which, dropping out of the to-be into the has-been, out of the future into the past—present momentarily to our senses a cross-section, as it were, of their total selves, as they pass through time and space (as matter) on their way from one eternity to another: and these two constitute that "duration" in which alone anything has true existence, were our senses but able to cognize it.

3. . . . . Universal mind was not, for there were no Ah-hi (celestial beings) to contain (hence to manifest) it.

Mind is a name given to the sum of the states of Consciousness grouped under Thought, Will, and Feeling. During deep sleep, ideation ceases on the physical plane, and memory is in abeyance; thus for the time-being "Mind is not," because the organ, through which the Ego manifests ideation and memory on the material plane, has temporarily ceased to function. A noumenon can become a phenomenon on any plane of existence only by manifesting on that plane through an appropriate basis or vehicle; and during the long night of rest called Pralaya, when all the existences are dissolved, the

"UNIVERSAL MIND" remains as a permanent possibility of mental action, or as that abstract absolute Thought of which Mind is the concrete relative manifestation. The AH-HI (Dhyan-Chohans) are the collective hosts of spiritual beings—the Angelic Hosts of Christianity, the Elohim and "Messengers" of the Jews—who are the vehicle for the manifestation of the Divine or Universal Thought and Will. They are the Intelligent Forces that give to and enact in Nature her "laws," while themselves acting according to laws imposed upon them in a similar manner by still higher Powers; but they are not "the personifications" of the powers of Nature.

4. THE SEVEN WAYS TO BLISS (Moksha or Nirvana) WERE NOT (a). THE GREAT CAUSES OF MISERY (Nidana[1] and Maya) WERE NOT, FOR THERE WAS NO ONE TO PRODUCE AND GET ENSNARED BY THEM (b).

(a) There are seven "Paths" or "Ways" to the bliss of Non-Existence, which is absolute Being, Existence, and Consciousness. They were not, because the Universe was, so far, empty, and existed only in the Divine Thought.

(b) The twelve Nidanas or causes of being. Each is the effect of its antecedent cause, and a cause, in its turn, to its successor; the sum total of the Nidanas being based on the Four Truths, a doctrine especially characteristic of the Hinayana System. They belong to the theory of the stream of catenated law which produces merit and demerit, and finally brings Karma into full sway. It is based upon the great truth that re-incarnation is to be dreaded, as existence in this world only entails upon man suffering, misery and pain; death itself being unable to deliver man from it, since death is merely the door through which he passes to another life on earth after a little rest on its threshold—Devachan. The Hinayana System, or School of the "Little Vehicle," is of very ancient growth; while the Mahayana is of a later period, having originated after the death of Buddha. Yet the tenets of the latter are as old as the hills that have contained such schools from time immemorial, and the Hinayana and Mahayana Schools (the latter, that of the "Great Vehicle") both teach the same doctrine in reality. *Yana*, or Vehicle (in Sanskrit, Vahan) is a mystic expression, both "vehicles" inculcating that man may escape the sufferings of rebirths and even the false bliss of Devachan by obtaining Wisdom and Knowledge, which alone can dispel the Fruits of Illusion and Ignorance.

Maya or illusion is an element which enters into all finite things, for everything that exists has only a relative, not an absolute, reality,

[1] The "12" Nidanas (in Tibetan, Ten-brel chug-nyi) are the chief causes of existence, effects generated by a concatenation of causes.

since the appearance which the hidden noumenon assumes for any observer depends upon his power of cognition. Nothing is permanent except the one hidden absolute existence which contains in itself the noumena of all realities. The existences belonging to every plane of being, up to the highest Dhyan-Chohans, are, in degree, of the nature of shadows cast by a magic lantern on a colourless screen; but all things are relatively real, for the cognizer is also a reflection, and the things cognized are therefore as real to him as himself. Whatever reality things possess must be looked for in them before or after they have passed like a flash through the material world; but we cannot cognize any such existence directly, so long as we have sense-instruments which bring only material existence into the field of our consciousness. Whatever plane our consciousness may be acting in, both we and the things belonging to that plane are, for the time being, our only realities. As we rise in the scale of development we perceive that during the stages through which we have passed we mistook shadows for realities, and the upward progress of the Ego is a series of progressive awakenings, each advance bringing with it the idea that now, at last, we have reached "reality"; but only when we shall have reached the absolute Consciousness, and blended our own with it, shall we be free from the delusions produced by Maya.

5. DARKNESS ALONE FILLED THE BOUNDLESS ALL (a), FOR FATHER, MOTHER AND SON WERE ONCE MORE ONE, AND THE SON HAD NOT AWAKENED YET FOR THE NEW WHEEL[2] AND HIS PILGRIMAGE THEREON (b).

(a) "Darkness is Father-Mother: light their son," says an old Eastern proverb. Light is inconceivable except as coming from some source which is the cause of it; and as, in the instance of primordial light, that source is unknown, though as strongly demanded by reason and logic, therefore it is called "Darkness" by us, from an intellectual point of view. As to borrowed or secondary light, whatever its source, it can be but of a temporary mayavic character. Darkness, then, is the eternal matrix in which the sources of light appear and disappear. Nothing is added to darkness to make of it light, or to light to make it darkness, on this our plane. They are interchangeable, and scientifically light is but a mode of darkness and *vice versa*. Yet both are phenomena of the same noumenon—

[2] That which is called "wheel" is the symbolical expression for a world or globe, which shows that the ancients were aware that our Earth was a revolving globe. The "Great Wheel" is the whole duration of our Cycle of being, or Maha Kalpa, *i.e.*, the whole revolution of our special chain of seven planets or Spheres from beginning to end; the "Small Wheels" meaning the Rounds, of which there are also Seven.

which is absolute darkness to the scientific mind, and but a grey twilight to the perception of the average mystic, though to that of the spiritual eye of the Initiate it is absolute light. When the whole universe was plunged in sleep—had returned to its one primordial element—there was neither centre of luminosity, nor eye to perceive light, and darkness necessarily filled the boundless all.

(b) The Father-Mother are the male and female principles in root-nature, the opposite poles that manifest in all things on every plane of Kosmos, or Spirit and Substance, in a less allegorical aspect, the resultant of which is the Universe, or the Son. They are "once more One" when in the Night of Brahmā, during Pralaya, all in the objective Universe has returned to its one primal and eternal cause, to reappear at the following Dawn—as it does periodically. "Karana"—eternal Cause—was alone. To put it more plainly: Karana is alone during the Nights of Brahmā. The previous objective Universe has dissolved into its one primal and eternal cause, and is, so to say, held in solution in space, to differentiate again and crystallize out anew at the following Manvantaric dawn, which is the commencement of a new Day or new activity of Brahmā—the symbol of the Universe. In esoteric parlance, Brahmā is Father-Mother-Son, or Spirit, Soul and Body at once; each personage being symbolical of an attribute, and each attribute or quality being a graduated efflux of Divine Breath in its cyclic differentiation, involutionary and evolutionary. In the cosmico-physical sense, it is the Universe, the planetary chain and the earth; in the purely spiritual, the Unknown Deity, Planetary Spirit, and Man—the Son of the two, the creature of Spirit and Matter, and a manifestation of them in his periodical appearances on Earth during the "Wheels," or the Manvantaras.

6. THE SEVEN SUBLIME LORDS AND THE SEVEN TRUTHS HAD CEASED TO BE (a), AND THE UNIVERSE, THE SON OF NECESSITY, WAS IMMERSED IN PARANISHPANNA (b) (absolute perfection, Paranirvana, which is Yong-Grüb) TO BE OUT-BREATHED BY THAT WHICH IS AND YET IS NOT. NAUGHT WAS (c).

(a) The seven sublime lords are the Seven Creative Spirits, the Dhyan-Chohans, who correspond to the Hebrew Elohim. It is the same hierarchy of Archangels to which St. Michael, St. Gabriel, and others belong, in the Christian theogony. In the Esoteric System, the Dhyanis watch successively over one of the Rounds and the great Root-races of our planetary chain. They are, moreover, said to send their Bodhisattvas, the human correspondents of the Dhyani-Buddhas (of whom vide infra) during every Round and Race.

So far "There are only Four Truths, and Four Vedas"—say the Hindus and Buddhists. For a similar reason Irenaeus insisted on the necessity of Four Gospels. But as every new Root-race at the head of a Round must have its revelation and revealers, the next Round will bring the Fifth, the following the Sixth, and so on.

(*b*) "Paranishpanna" is the absolute perfection to which all existences attain at the close of a great period of activity, or Maha-Manvantara, and in which they rest during the succeeding period of repose.

The Secret Doctrine teaches the progressive development of everything, worlds as well as atoms; and this stupendous development has neither conceivable beginning nor imaginable end. Our "Universe" is only one of an infinite number of Universes, all of them "Sons of Necessity," because links in the great Cosmic chain of Universes, each one standing in the relation of an effect as regards its predecessor, and being a cause as regards its successor.

The appearance and disappearance of the Universe are pictured as an outbreathing and inbreathing of "the Great Breath," which is eternal, and which, being Motion, is one of the three aspects of the Absolute—Abstract Space and Duration being the other two. When the "Great Breath" is projected, it is called the Divine Breath, and is regarded as the breathing of the Unknowable Deity—the One Existence—which breathes out a thought, as it were, which becomes the Kosmos. So also is it when the Divine Breath is inspired again the Universe disappears into the bosom of "the Great Mother," who then sleeps "wrapped in her invisible Robes."

(*c*) By "that which is and yet is not" is meant the Great Breath itself, which we can only speak of as absolute existence, but cannot picture to our imagination as any form of Existence that we can distinguish from Non-existence. The three periods—the Present, the Past, and the Future—are in the esoteric philosophy a compound time; for the three are a composite number only in relation to the phenomenal plane, but in the realm of noumena have no abstract validity. As said in the Scriptures: "The Past time is the Present time, as also the Future, which, though it has not come into existence, still is." Our ideas, in short, on duration and time are all derived from our sensations according to the laws of association. Inextricably bound up with the relativity of human knowledge, they nevertheless can have no existence except in the experience of the individual ego, and perish when its evolutionary march dispels the Maya of phenomenal existence. What is Time, for instance, but the panoramic succession of our states of consciousness?

7. THE CAUSES OF EXISTENCE HAD BEEN DONE AWAY WITH (a); THE
VISIBLE THAT WAS, AND THE INVISIBLE THAT IS, RESTED IN ETERNAL
NON-BEING, THE ONE BEING (b).

(a) "The Causes of Existence" mean not only the physical causes
known to science, but the metaphysical causes, the chief of which is
the desire to exist, an outcome of Nidana and Maya. This desire for
a sentient life shows itself in everything, from an atom to a sun, and
is a reflection of the Divine Thought propelled into objective existence, into a law that the Universe should exist. According to esoteric
teaching, the real cause of that supposed desire, and of all existence,
remains for ever hidden, and its first emanations are the most complete abstractions mind can conceive. These abstractions must of
necessity be postulated as the cause of the material Universe which
presents itself to the senses and intellect; and they underlie the
secondary and subordinate powers of Nature, which, anthropomorphized, have been worshipped as God and gods by the common
herd of every age. It is impossible to conceive anything without a
cause; the attempt to do so makes the mind a blank. This is virtually
the condition to which the mind must come at last when we try to
trace back the chain of causes and effects, but both science and religion jump to this condition of blankness much more quickly than is
necessary; for they ignore the metaphysical abstractions which are
the only conceivable cause of physical concretions. These abstractions become more and more concrete as they approach our plane
of existence, until finally they phenomenalize in the form of the
material Universe, by a process of conversion of metaphysics into
physics, analogous to that by which steam can be condensed into
water, and the water frozen into ice.

(b) The idea of Eternal Non-Being, which is the One Being, will
appear a paradox to anyone who does not remember that we limit
our ideas of being to our present consciousness of existence; making
it a specific, instead of a generic term.

8. ALONE, THE ONE FORM OF EXISTENCE (a) STRETCHED BOUNDLESS,
INFINITE, CAUSELESS, IN DREAMLESS SLEEP (b); AND LIFE PULSATED
UNCONSCIOUS IN UNIVERSAL SPACE, THROUGHOUT THAT ALL-PRESENCE
WHICH IS SENSED BY THE "OPENED EYE" OF THE DANGMA.[3]

[3] Dangma means a purified soul, one who has become a Jivanmukta, the highest
adept, or rather a Mahatma so-called. His "opened eye" is the inner spiritual eye
of the seer, and the faculty which manifests through it is not clairvoyance as
ordinarily understood, i.e., the power of seeing at a distance, but rather the faculty of
spiritual intuition, through which direct and certain knowledge is obtainable. This
faculty is intimately connected with the "third eye," which mythological tradition
ascribes to certain races of men. Fuller explanations will be found in Book II.

(*a*) The tendency of modern thought is to recur to the archaic idea of a homogeneous basis for apparently widely different things— heterogeneity developed from homogeneity. Biologists are now searching for their homogeneous protoplasm and chemists for their protyle, while science is looking for the force of which electricity, magnetism, heat, and so forth, are the differentiations. The Secret Doctrine carries this idea into the region of metaphysics and post-ulates a "One Form of Existence" as the basis and source of all things. But perhaps the phrase, the "One Form of Existence," is not altogether correct. The Puranic commentators explain it by Karana, "Cause," but the Esoteric Philosophy, by the *ideal spirit of that cause.* It is, in its secondary stage, the Svabhavat of the Buddhist philoso-pher, the Eternal Cause and Effect, omnipresent yet abstract, the self-existent plastic Essence and the Root of all things.

(*b*) Dreamless sleep is one of the seven states of consciousness known in Oriental esotericism. In each of these states a different portion of the mind comes into action; or as a Vedantin would express it, the individual is conscious in a different plane of his being. The term "dreamless sleep," in this case is applied allegorically to the Universe to express a condition somewhat analogous to that state of consciousness in man, which, not being remembered in a waking state, seems a blank.

9. BUT WHERE WAS THE DANGMA WHEN THE ALAYA OF THE UNI-VERSE (*Soul as the basis of all, Anima Mundi*) WAS IN PARAMARTHA (*a*) (*Absolute Being and Consciousness which are Absolute Non-Being and Unconsciousness*) AND THE GREAT WHEEL WAS ANUPADAKA (*b*)?

(*a*) Here we have before us the subject of centuries of scholastic disputations. The two terms "Alaya" and "Paramartha" have been the causes of dividing schools and splitting the truth into more different aspects than any other mystic terms. Alaya is the Soul of the World or Anima Mundi, the Over-Soul of Emerson, and accord-ing to esoteric teaching it changes periodically its nature. Alaya, though eternal and changeless in its inner essence on the planes which are unreachable by either men or Cosmic Gods (Dhyani Buddhas), alters during the active life-period with respect to the lower planes, ours included. During that time not only the Dhyani-Buddhas are one with Alaya in Soul and Essence, but even the man strong in the Yoga (mystic meditation) "is able to merge his soul with it" (Aryasanga). This is not Nirvana, but a condition next to it. Hence the disagreement. Thus, while the Yogacharyas (of the Mahayana school) say that Alaya is the personification of the Voidness, and yet Alaya is the basis of every visible and invisible thing, and that, though it is eternal and immutable in its essence, it reflects itself in every object of the Universe "like the moon in clear tranquil water," other schools dispute the statement. The same for Paramartha: the Yogacharyas interpret the term as that which is also dependent upon other things (*paratantra*); and the Madhyamikas say that Paramartha is limited to Paranishpanna or absolute perfection; i.e., in the exposition of these "two truths" (out of four), the former believe and maintain that (on this plane, at any rate) there exists only Samvritisatya or relative truth; and the latter teach the existence of Paramarthasatya, the "absolute truth."[4]

Esoteric philosophy teaches that everything lives and is conscious, but not that all life and consciousness are similar to those of human or even animal beings. Life we look upon as "the one form of existence," manifesting in what is called matter; or, as in man, what, incorrectly separating them, we name Spirit, Soul and Matter. Matter is the vehicle for the manifestation of soul on this plane of existence, and soul is the vehicle on a higher plane for the manifestation of spirit, and these three are a trinity synthesized by Life, which pervades them all. The idea of universal life is one of those ancient conceptions which are returning to the human mind in this century, as a consequence of its liberation from anthropomorphic theology. Science, it is true, contents itself with tracing or postulating the signs of universal life, and has not yet been bold enough even to whisper "Anima Mundi"! The idea of "crystalline life," now familiar to science, would have been scouted half a century ago. Botanists are now searching for the nerves of plants; not that they suppose that plants can feel or think as animals do, but because they believe that some structure, bearing the same relation functionally to plant life that nerves bear to animal life, is necessary to explain vegetable growth and nutrition. It hardly seems possible that science can disguise from itself much longer, by the mere use of terms such as "force" and "energy," the fact that things that have life are living things, whether they be atoms or planets.

(*b*) The term Anupadaka, "parentless," or without progenitors, is a mystical designation having several meanings. By this name celestial beings, the Dhyan-Chohans or Dhyani-Buddhas, are generally meant. But as these correspond mystically to the human Buddhas and Bodhisattvas, known as the "Manushi (or human)

---

[4] "Paramartha" is self-consciousness in Sanskrit, Svasamvedana, or the "self-analysing reflection"—from two words, *parama* (above everything) and *artha* (comprehension), Satya meaning absolute true being, or Esse. The opposite of this absolute reality, or actuality, is Samvritisatya—the relative truth only—"Samvriti" meaning "false conception" and being the origin of illusion, Maya.

Buddhas," the latter are also designated Anupadaka, once their whole personality is merged in their compound Sixth and Seventh Principles, or Atma-Buddhi, and they have become the "diamond-souled" (Vajra-sattvas, full Mahatmas). The "Concealed Lord," "the one merged with the Absolute," can have no parents since he is Self-existent, and one with the Universal Spirit (Svayambhu), the Svabhavat in the highest aspect. The mystery in the hierarchy of the Anupadaka is great, its apex being the universal Spirit-Soul, and the lower rung the Manushi-Buddha; and even every Soul-endowed man is an Anupadaka in a latent state. Hence, when speaking of the Universe in its formless, eternal, or absolute condition, before it was fashioned by the "Builders"—the expression, Great Wheel was Anupadaka."

STANZA 2

1. . . . . WHERE WERE THE BUILDERS, THE LUMINOUS SONS OF MANVANTARIC DAWN (a)? . . . IN THE UNKNOWN DARKNESS IN THEIR AH-HI (*Chohanic, Dhyani-Buddhic*) PARANISHPANNA. THE PRODUCERS OF FORM (*rupa*) FROM NO-FORM (*arupa*), THE ROOT OF THE WORLD— THE DEVAMATRI[1] AND SVABHAVAT, RESTED IN THE BLISS OF NON-BEING (b).

(a) The "Builders," the "Sons of Manvantaric Dawn," are the real creators of the Universe; and in this doctrine, which deals only with our Planetary System, they, as the architects of the latter, are also called the "Watchers" of the Seven Spheres, which exoterically are the Seven planets, and esoterically the seven earths or spheres (planets) of our chain also. The opening sentence of Stanza 1, when mentioning "Seven Eternities," is made to apply both to the *Maha-Kalpa* or "the (great) Age of Brahmā," as well as to the Solar Pralaya and subsequent resurrection of our Planetary System on a higher plane. There are many kinds of Pralaya (dissolution of a thing visible), as will be shown elsewhere.

(b) Paranishpanna is the Absolute, hence the same as Paranirvana. Besides being the final state it is that condition of subjectivity which has no relation to anything but the One Absolute Truth on its plane. It is that state which leads one to appreciate correctly the full meaning of Non-Being, which, as explained, is *absolute* Being. Sooner or later, all that now *seemingly* exists, will be in reality and actually in the state of Paranishpanna. But there is a great difference between *conscious* and *unconscious* "Being." The condition of Paranishpanna, without Paramartha, the Self-analysing consciousness, is no bliss, but simply extinction (for Seven Eternities). Thus, an iron ball placed under the scorching rays of the sun will get heated through, but will not feel or appreciate the warmth, while a man will.

2. . . . . WHERE WAS SILENCE? WHERE WERE THE EARS TO SENSE IT? NO! THERE WAS NEITHER ¡SILENCE, NOR SOUND (a). NAUGHT SAVE CEASELESS, ETERNAL BREATH (*Motion*) WHICH KNOWS ITSELF NOT (b).

(a) The idea that things can cease to exist and still BE, is a fundamental one in Eastern psychology. Under this apparent contradiction

---

[1] "Mother of the Gods," Aditi, or Cosmic Space. In the Zohar, she is called Sephira the Mother of the Sephiroth, and Shekinah in her primordial form, *in abscondito.*

in terms, there rests a fact of Nature to realize which in the mind, rather than to argue about words, is the important thing. A familiar instance of a similar paradox is afforded by chemical combination. The question whether hydrogen and oxygen cease to exist, when they combine to form water, is still a moot one. Existence as water may be said to be, for oxygen and hydrogen, a state of Non-being which is "more real being" than their existence as gases; and it may faintly symbolize the condition of the Universe when it goes to sleep, or ceases to be, during the Nights of Brahmā—to awaken or reappear, when the dawn of the new Manvantara recalls it to what we call existence.

(b) The "Breath" of the One Existence is used in its application only to the spiritual aspect of Cosmogony by Archaic Esotericism; otherwise, it is replaced by its equivalent on the material plane— Motion. The One Eternal Element, or element-containing Vehicle, is Space, dimensionless in every sense; co-existent with which are— endless Duration, primordial (hence indestructible) Matter, and Motion—absolute "Perpetual Motion" which is the "Breath" of the "One" Element. This Breath, as seen, can never cease, not even during the Pralayic eternities.

To know itself or oneself, necessitates consciousness and perception (both limited faculties in relation to any subject except Parabrahm), to be cognized. Hence the "Eternal Breath which knows itself not." Infinity cannot comprehend Finiteness. The Boundless can have no relation to the bounded and the conditioned. In the occult teachings, the Unknown and the Unknowable MOVER, or the Self-Existing, is the absolute divine Essence. And thus being *Absolute* Consciousness, and *Absolute* Motion—to the limited senses of those who describe this indescribable—it is unconsciousness and immoveableness. Concrete consciousness cannot be predicated of abstract Consciousness, any more than the quality wet can be predicated of water—wetness being its own attribute and the cause of the wet quality in other things. Consciousness implies limitations and qualifications; something to be conscious of, and someone to be conscious of it. But Absolute Consciousness contains the cognizer, the thing cognized and the cognition, all three in itself and all three *one*. No man is conscious of more than that portion of his knowledge that happens to have been recalled to his mind at any particular time, yet such is the poverty of language that we have no term to distinguish the knowledge not actively thought of, from knowledge we are unable to recall to memory. To forget is synonymous with not to remember. How much greater must be the difficulty of finding terms to describe, and to distinguish between, abstract metaphysical facts or differences. It must not be forgotten, also, that we give names to things according to the appearances they assume for ourselves. We call absolute consciousness "unconsciousness," because it seems to us that it must necessarily be so, just as we call the Absolute, "Darkness," because to our finite understanding it appears quite impenetrable, yet we recognize fully that our perception of such things does not do them justice. We involuntarily distinguish in our minds, for instance, between unconscious absolute consciousness, and unconsciousness, by secretly endowing the former with some indefinite quality that corresponds, on a higher plane than our thoughts can reach, with what we know as consciousness in ourselves. But this is not any kind of consciousness that we can manage to distinguish from what appears to us as unconsciousness.

3. THE HOUR HAD NOT YET STRUCK; THE RAY HAD NOT YET FLASHED INTO THE GERM (*a*); THE MATRI-PADMA (*mother lotus*) HAD NOT YET SWOLLEN (*b*).

(*a*) The Ray of the "Ever Darkness" becomes, as it is emitted, a ray of effulgent light or life, and flashes into the "Germ"—the point in the Mundane Egg represented by Matter in its abstract sense. But the term "Point" must not be understood as applying to any particular point in Space, for a germ exists in the centre of every atom, and these collectively form "the Germ"; or rather, as no atom can be made visible to our physical eye, the collectivity of these (if the term can be applied to something which is boundless and infinite) forms the noumenon of eternal and indestructible Matter.

(*b*) One of the symbolical figures for the Dual Creative Power in Nature (matter and force on the material plane) is *Padma*, the water-lily of India. The Lotus is the product of heat (fire) and water (vapour or ether); fire standing in every philosophical and religious system as a representation of the Spirit of Deity, the active, male, generative principle; and Ether, or the Soul of matter, the light of the fire, for the passive female principle from which everything in this Universe emanated. Hence, Ether or Water is the Mother, and Fire is the Father. This explains the sentence "The Mother had not yet swollen"—the form being usually sacrificed to the inner or root idea in Archaic symbology.

4. HER HEART HAD NOT YET OPENED FOR THE ONE RAY TO ENTER, THENCE TO FALL AS THREE INTO FOUR IN THE LAP OF MAYA.

The Primordial Substance had not yet passed out of its pre-cosmic latency into differentiated objectivity, or even become the (to man, so far,) invisible protyle of Science. But, as the hour strikes

and it becomes receptive of the Fohatic impress of the Divine
Thought (the Logos, or the male aspect of the Anima Mundi, Alaya)
—its "Heart" opens. It differentiates, and the THREE (Father,
Mother, Son) are transformed into Four. Herein lies the origin of
the double mystery of the Trinity and the Immaculate Conception,
The first and fundamental dogma of Occultism is Universal Unity
(or Homogeneity) under three aspects. This led to a possible conception of Deity, which as an absolute unity must remain forever
incomprehensible to finite intellects.

Thus is repeated on Earth the mystery enacted, according to the
Seers, on the divine plane. The "Son" of the Immaculate Celestial
Virgin (or the undifferentiated cosmic protyle, Matter in its infinitude) is born again on Earth as the Son of the terrestrial Eve—our
mother Earth, and becomes Humanity as a total—past, present, and
future—for Jehovah is both male and female. Above, the Son is the
whole KOSMOS; below, he is MANKIND. The Triad or Triangle be-
comes Tetraktis, the Sacred Pythagorean number, the perfect
Square, and a 6-faced Cube on Earth. The Macroprosopus (the
Great Face) is now Microprosopus (the lesser face); or, as the
Kabalists have it, the "Ancient of Days," descending on Adam
Kadmon whom he uses as his vehicle to manifest through, gets trans-
formed into Tetragrammaton. It is now in the "Lap of Maya," the
Great Illusion, and between itself and the Reality has the Astral
Light, the great Deceiver of man's limited senses, unless Knowledge
through Paramarthasatya comes to the rescue.

5. THE SEVEN (*Sons*) WERE NOT YET BORN FROM THE WEB OF
LIGHT. DARKNESS ALONE WAS FATHER-MOTHER, SVABHAVAT, AND
SVABHAVAT WAS IN DARKNESS.

The Secret Doctrine, in the Stanzas given here, occupies itself
chiefly, if not entirely, with our Solar System, and especially with
our planetary chain. The "Seven Sons," therefore, are the creators
of the latter. This teaching will be explained more fully hereafter.
(See Part II., "Theogony of the Creative Gods.")

Svabhavat, the "Plastic Essence" that fills the Universe, is the
root of all things. Svabhavat is, so to say, the Buddhist concrete
aspect of the abstraction called in Hindu philosophy Mulaprakriti.
It is the body of the Soul, and that which Ether would be to Akasa,
the latter being the informing principle of the former.

6. THESE TWO ARE THE GERM, AND THE GERM IS—ONE. THE
UNIVERSE WAS STILL CONCEALED IN THE DIVINE THOUGHT AND THE
DIVINE BOSOM.

The "Divine Thought" does not imply the idea of a Divine thinker. The Universe, not only past, present, and future—which is a human and finite idea expressed by finite thought—but in its totality, the *Sat* (an untranslatable term), the Absolute Being, with the Past and Future crystallized in an eternal Present, is that Thought itself reflected in a secondary or manifest cause. Brahman (neuter), as the Mysterium Magnum of Paracelsus, is an absolute mystery to the human mind. Brahmā, the male-female, its aspect and anthropomorphic reflection, is conceivable to the perceptions of blind faith, though rejected by human intellect when it attains its majority.

Hence the statement that during the prologue, so to say, of the drama of Creation, or the beginning of cosmic evolution, the Universe or the "Son" lies still concealed "in the Divine Thought," which had not yet penetrated "into the Divine Bosom." This idea, note well, is at the root, and forms the origin of all the allegories about the "Sons of God" born of immaculate virgins.

STANZA 3

1. THE LAST VIBRATION OF THE SEVENTH ETERNITY THRILLS THROUGH INFINITUDE (*a*). THE MOTHER SWELLS, EXPANDING FROM WITHIN WITHOUT LIKE THE BUD OF THE LOTUS (*b*).

(*a*) The seemingly paradoxical use of the sentence "Seventh Eternity," thus dividing the indivisible, is sanctified in esoteric philosophy. The latter divides boundless duration into unconditionally eternal and universal Time and a conditioned one (*Khandakala*). One is the abstraction or noumenon of infinite time (Kala); the other its phenomenon appearing periodically, as the effect of *Mahat* (the Universal Intelligence limited by Manvantaric duration).

(*b*) Therefore, the "last vibration of the Seventh Eternity" was "fore-ordained"—by no God in particular, but occurred in virtue of the eternal and changeless LAW which causes the great periods of Activity and Rest, called so graphically, and at the same time so poetically, the Days and Nights of Brahmā. The expansion "from within without" of the Mother, called elsewhere the "Waters of Space," "Universal Matrix," etc., does not allude to an expansion from a small centre or focus, but, without reference to size or limitation or area, means the development of limitless subjectivity into as limitless objectivity. "The ever (to us) invisible and immaterial Substance present in eternity threw its periodical shadow from its own plane into the lap of Maya." It implies that this expansion, not being an increase in size—for infinite extension admits of no enlargement—was a change of condition. It expanded "like the bud of the Lotus"; for the Lotus plant exists not only as a miniature embryo in its seed (a physical characteristic), but its prototype is present in an ideal form in the Astral Light from "Dawn" to "Night" during the Manvantaric period, like everything else, in this objective Universe; from man down to mite, from giant trees down to the tiniest blades of grass.

All this, teaches the Hidden Science, is but the temporary reflection, the shadow of the eternal ideal prototype in Divine Thought; the word "Eternity," note well again, standing here only in the sense of "Aeon," as lasting throughout the seemingly interminable, but still limited cycle of activity, called by us Manvantara. For what is the real esoteric meaning of Manvantara, or rather a Manu-Antara? It means, esoterically, "between two Manus," of whom there are fourteen in every Day of Brahmā, such a "Day" consisting of 1,000 aggregates of four ages, or 1,000 "Great Ages," Mahayugas. Let us now analyse the word or name Manu. Orientalists and their dictionaries tell us that the term "Manu" is from the root *Man*, "to think"; hence "the thinking man." But esoterically every Manu, as an anthropomorphized patron of his special cycle (or Round), is but the personified idea of the "Thought Divine"; each of the Manus, therefore, being the special god, the creator and fashioner of all that appears during his own respective cycle of being or Manvantara. Fohat runs the Manus' (or Dhyan-Chohans') errands, and causes the ideal prototypes to expand from within without—viz., to cross gradually, on a descending scale, all the planes from the noumenon to the lowest phenomenon, to bloom finally on the last into full objectivity—the acme of illusion, or the grossest matter.

2. The vibration sweeps along, touching with its swift wing (*simultaneously*) the whole universe, and the germ that dwelleth in darkness: the darkness that breathes (*moves*) over the slumbering waters of life.

The idea of the "Breath" of Darkness moving over "the slumbering Waters of life," which is primordial Matter with the latent Spirit in it, recalls the first chapter of Genesis. Its original is the Brahminical Narayana (the Mover on the Waters), who is the personification of the eternal Breath of the unconscious All (or Parabrahm) of the Eastern Occultists. The Waters of Life, or Chaos —the female principle in symbolism—are the vacuum (to our mental sight) in which lie the latent Spirit and Matter. In all Cosmogonies "Water" plays the same important part. It is the base and source of material existence.

3. "Darkness" radiates light, and light drops one solitary ray into the waters, into the mother deep. The ray shoots through the virgin-egg; the ray causes the eternal egg to thrill, and drop the non-eternal (*periodical*) germ, which condenses into the world egg.

The solitary ray dropping into the mother deep may be taken as meaning Divine Thought or Intelligence impregnating Chaos. This, however, occurs on the plane of metaphysical abstraction, or rather the plane whereon that which we call a metaphysical abstraction is a reality. The Virgin-egg being in one sense abstract Egg-ness, or the power of becoming developed through fecundation, is eternal and for ever the same. And just as the fecundation of an egg takes place before it is dropped; so the non-eternal periodical germ which becomes later in symbolism the mundane egg, contains in itself, when it emerges from the said symbol, "the promise and potency" of all the Universe. Though the idea *per se* is, of course, an abstraction, a symbolical mode of expression, it is a symbol truly, as it suggests the idea of infinity as an endless circle. It brings before the mind's eye the picture of Kosmos emerging from and in boundless space, a Universe as shoreless in magnitude if not as endless in its objective manifestation. The simile of an egg also expresses the fact taught in Occultism that the primordial form of everything manifested, from atom to globe, from man to angel, is spheroidal, the sphere having been with all nations the emblem of eternity and infinity—a serpent swallowing its tail. To realize the meaning, however, the sphere must be thought of as seen from its centre. The field of vision or of thought is like a sphere whose radii proceed from one's self in every direction, and extend out into space, opening up boundless vistas all around. It is the symbolical circle of Pascal and the Kabalists, "whose centre is everywhere and circumference nowhere," a conception which enters into the compound idea of this emblem.

4. (*Then*) THE THREE (*triangle*) FALL INTO THE FOUR (*quaternary*). THE RADIANT ESSENCE BECOMES SEVEN INSIDE, SEVEN OUTSIDE (*a*). THE LUMINOUS EGG (*Hiranyagarbha*), WHICH IN ITSELF IS THREE (*the triple hypostases of Brahmā, or Vishnu, the three "Avasthas"*), CURDLES AND SPREADS IN MILK-WHITE CURDS THROUGHOUT THE DEPTHS OF MOTHER, THE ROOT THAT GROWS IN THE OCEAN OF LIFE (*b*).

(*a*) The use of geometrical figures and the frequent allusions to figures in all ancient scriptures must be explained. In the "book of Dzyan", as in the Kabala, there are two kinds of numerals to be studied—the figures, often simple blinds, and the Sacred Numbers, the values of which are all known to the Occultists through Initiation. The former is but a conventional glyph, the latter is the basic symbol of all. That is to say, that one is purely physical, the other purely metaphysical, the two standing in relation to each other as Matter stands to Spirit—the extreme poles of the ONE substance.

(*b*) "The Radiant Essence curdled and spread throughout the depths of Space." From an astronomical point of view this is easy of explanation: it is the "milky way", the world-stuff, or primordial matter in its first form. It is more difficult, however, to explain it in a few words or even lines, from the standpoint of Occult Science and Symbolism, as it is the most complicated of glyphs.

5. THE ROOT REMAINS, THE LIGHT REMAINS, THE CURDS REMAIN, AND STILL OEAOHOO (*a*) IS ONE (*b*).

(*a*) OEAOHOO is rendered "*Father-Mother of the Gods*" in the Commentaries, or the SIX IN ONE, or the Septenary root from which all proceeds. All depends upon the accent given to these seven vowels, which may be pronounced as one, three, or even seven syllables by adding an *e* after the letter "o." This mystic name is given out, because without a thorough mastery of the triple pronunciation it remains for ever ineffectual.

(*b*) This refers to the Non-Separateness of all that lives and has its being, whether in active or passive state. In one sense, Oeaohoo is the "Rootless Root of All"; hence, one with Parabrahman; in another sense it is a name for the manifested ONE LIFE, the Eternal living Unity. The "Root" means, as already explained, pure knowledge, eternal unconditioned Reality or SAT, whether we call it Parabrahman or Mulaprakriti, for these are the two aspects of the ONE. The "Light" is the same Omnipresent Spiritual Ray which has entered and now fecundated the Divine Egg, and calls cosmic matter to begin its long series of differentiations. The "Curds" are the first differentiation, and probably refer also to that cosmic matter which is supposed to be the origin of the "Milky Way"—the matter we know. This "matter," which, according to the revelation received from the primeval Dhyani-Buddhas, is, during the periodical sleep of the Universe, of the ultimate tenuity conceivable to the eye of the perfect Bodhisattva—this matter, radical and cool, becomes, at the first re-awakening of cosmic motion, scattered through Space; appearing, when seen from the Earth, in clusters and lumps, like curds in thin milk. These are the seeds of the future worlds, the "Starstuff."

6. THE ROOT OF LIFE WAS IN EVERY DROP OF THE OCEAN OF IMMORTALITY AND THE OCEAN WAS RADIANT LIGHT, WHICH WAS FIRE AND HEAT AND MOTION. DARKNESS VANISHED AND WAS NO MORE. IT DISAPPEARED IN ITS OWN ESSENCE, THE BODY OF FIRE AND WATER, OF FATHER AND MOTHER.

The essence of Darkness being absolute Light, Darkness is taken as the appropriate allegorical representation of the condition of the Universe during Pralaya, or the term of absolute Rest, or Non-Being, as it appears to our finite minds. The Fire and Heat and Motion here spoken of are, of course, not the fire, heat, and motion of physical science, but the underlying abstractions, the noumena, or the soul, of the essence of these material manifestations—the "things in themselves," which, as modern science confesses, entirely elude the instruments of the laboratory, and which even the mind cannot grasp, although it can equally little avoid the conclusion that these underlying essences of things must exist. Fire and Water, or Father and Mother, may be taken here to mean the divine Ray and Chaos.

According to the Rosicrucian tenets, as handled and explained by the profane for once correctly, if only partially, "Light and Darkness are identical in themselves, being only divisible in the human mind"; and according to Robert Fludd, "Darkness adopted illumination in order to make itself visible" (*On Rosenkranz*). According to the tenets of Eastern Occultism, DARKNESS is the one true actuality, the basis and the root of Light, without which the latter could never manifest itself, nor even exist. Light is Matter, and DARKNESS pure Spirit. Darkness, in its radical, metaphysical basis, is subjective and absolute Light; while the latter in all its seeming effulgence and glory, is merely a mass of shadows, as it can never be eternal, and is simply an illusion, or Maya.

Even in the mind-baffling and science-harassing Genesis, light is created out of darkness—"and darkness was upon the face of the deep" (ch. i. v. 2.)—and not *vice versa*. "In him (in darkness) was life; and the life was the light of men" (John i. 4). A day may come when the eyes of men will be opened; and then they may comprehend better than they do now that verse in the Gospel of John that says "And the light shineth in darkness; and the darkness comprehendeth it not." They will see then that the word "darkness" does not apply to man's spiritual eyesight, but indeed to "Darkness," the absolute, that comprehendeth not (cannot cognize) transient light, however transcendent to human eyes. *Demon est Deus inversus.* The Devil is now called Darkness by the Church, whereas, in the Bible he is called the "Son of God" (see Job), the bright star of the early morning, Lucifer (see Isaiah). There is a whole philosophy of dogmatic craft in the reason why the first Archangel, who sprang from the depths of Chaos, was called Lux (Lucifer), the "Luminous Son of the Morning," or manvantaric Dawn. He was transformed by the Church into Lucifer or Satan, because he is higher and older than Jehovah, and had to be sacrificed to the new dogma. (See Book II.)

7. BEHOLD, OH LANOO![1] THE RADIANT CHILD OF THE TWO, THE UNPARALLELED REFULGENT GLORY, BRIGHT SPACE, SON OF DARK SPACE, WHO EMERGES FROM THE DEPTHS OF THE GREAT DARK WATERS. IT IS OEAOHOO, THE YOUNGER, THE * * * (*"whom thou knowest now as Kwan-Shai-Yin."—Comment*) (*a*). HE SHINES FORTH AS THE SUN. HE IS THE BLAZING DIVINE DRAGON OF WISDOM (*b*). THE EKA IS CHATUR (*four*), AND CHATUR TAKES TO ITSELF THREE, AND

[1] Lanoo is a student, a chela who studies practical Esotericism.

THE UNION PRODUCES THE SAPTA (*seven*) IN WHOM ARE THE SEVEN WHICH BECOME THE TRIDASA[2] (*the thrice ten*) THE HOSTS AND THE MULTITUDES. BEHOLD HIM LIFTING THE VEIL, AND UNFURLING IT FROM EAST TO WEST. HE SHUTS OUT THE ABOVE AND LEAVES THE BELOW TO BE SEEN AS THE GREAT ILLUSION. HE MARKS THE PLACES FOR THE SHINING ONES (*stars*) AND TURNS THE UPPER (*space*) INTO A SHORELESS SEA OF FIRE (*c*), AND THE ONE MANIFESTED (*element*) INTO THE GREAT WATERS.

"Bright Space, son of Dark Space," corresponds to the Ray dropped at the first thrill of the new "Dawn" into the great Cosmic depths, from which it re-emerges differentiated as "Oeaohoo the Younger" (the "new LIFE"), to become, to the end of the life-cycle, the Germ of all things. He is called the "Blazing Dragon of Wisdom," because, first, he is that which the Greek philosophers called the Logos, the Verbum of the Thought Divine; and secondly, because in Esoteric Philosophy this first manifestation, being the synthesis or the aggregate of Universal Wisdom, Oeaohoo, "the Son of the Son," contains in himself the Seven Creative Hosts (The Sephiroth), and is thus the essence of manifested Wisdom. "He who bathes in the light of Oeaohoo will never be deceived by the veil of Maya."

(*a*) Kwan-Shai-Yin is identical with, and an equivalent of the Sanskrit *Avalokiteshwara*, and as such is an androgynous deity, like the Tetragrammaton and all the Logoi[3] of antiquity. It is only by some sects in China that he is anthropomorphized and represented with female attributes when, under his female aspect, he becomes Kwan-Yin, the Goddess of Mercy, called the "Divine Voice." The latter is the patron deity of Tibet and of the island of Puto in China, where both deities have a number of monasteries.

(*b*) The "Dragon of Wisdom" is the One, the "Eka" (Sanskrit) or Saka. Jesus accepted the serpent as a synonym of Wisdom, and

---

[2] "Tri-dasa," or three times ten (30), alludes to the Vedic deities, in round numbers, or more accurately 33—a sacred number. They are the 12 Adityas, the 8 Vasus, the 11 Rudras, and 2 Aswins—the twin sons of the Sun and the Sky. This is the root-number of the Hindu Pantheon, which enumerates 33 crores or over three hundred millions of gods and goddesses.

[3] Hence all the higher gods of antiquity are all "Sons of the Mother" before they become those of the "Father." The Logoi, like Jupiter or Zeus, Son of Kronos-Saturn, "Infinite Time" (or Kala), in their origin were represented as male-female. Zeus is said to be the "beautiful Virgin," and Venus is made bearded. Apollo is originally bisexual, so is Brahmā-Vach in Manu and the Puranas. Osiris is interchangeable with Isis, and Horus is of both sexes. Finally St. John's vision in Revelation, that of the Logos, who is now connected with Jesus—is hermaphrodite, for he is described as having female breasts. So is the Tetragrammaton = Jehovah. But there are two Avalokiteshwaras in Esotericism; the first and the second *Logos*.

this formed part of his teaching: "Be ye wise as serpents," he says. "In the beginning, before Mother became Father-Mother, the fiery Dragon moved in the infinitudes alone" (*Book of Sarparajni.*) Before our globe became egg-shaped (and the Universe also) "a long trail of Cosmic dust (or fire mist) moved and writhed like a serpent in Space." The "Spirit of God moving on Chaos" was symbolized by every nation in the shape of a fiery serpent breathing fire and light upon the primordial waters, until it had incubated cosmic matter and made it assume the annular shape of a serpent with its tail in its mouth—which symbolizes not only Eternity and Infinitude, but also the globular shape of all the bodies formed within the Universe from that fiery mist. The Universe, as well as the Earth and Man, cast off periodically, serpent-like, their old skins, to assume new ones after a time of rest.

(*c*) The "Sea of Fire" is the Super-Astral (*i.e.*, noumenal) Light, the first radiation from the *Root*, the Mulaprakriti, the undifferentiated Cosmic Substance, which becomes *Astral* Matter. It is also called the "Fiery Serpent," as above described. If the student bears in mind that there is but One Universal Element, which is infinite, unborn, and undying, and that all the rest—as in the world of phenomena—are but so many various differentiated aspects and transformations (correlations, they are now called) of that One, from cosmic down to microcosmic effects, from super-human down to human and sub-human beings, the totality, in short, of objective existence—then the first and chief difficulty will disappear and Occult Cosmology may be mastered.[4] All the Kabalists and Occultists, Eastern and Western, recognize (*a*) the identity of "Father-Mother" with primordial *Aether* or *Akasa*, (Astral Light); and (*b*) its homogeneity before the evolution of the "Son," cosmically *Fohat*, for it is Cosmic Electricity. "Fohat hardens and scatters the seven brothers" (Book III. Dzyan); which means that the primordial Electric Entity—for the Eastern Occultists insist that Electricity is an Entity—electrifies into life, and separates primordial stuff or pregenetic matter into atoms, themselves the source of all life and consciousness. The ancients represented it by a serpent, for "Fohat hisses as he glides hither and thither" (in zigzags).

8. WHERE WAS THE GERM, AND WHERE WAS NOW DARKNESS? WHERE IS THE SPIRIT OF THE FLAME THAT BURNS IN THY LAMP, O

---

[4] In the Egyptian as in the Indian theogony there was a *concealed* deity, the ONE, and the creative, androgynous god. Thus *Shoo* is the god of creation and Osiris is, in his original primary form, the "god whose name is unknown." (See Mariette's Abydos II., p. 63, and Vol. III., pp. 413, 414, No. 1122.)

LANOO? THE GERM IS THAT, AND THAT IS LIGHT; THE WHITE BRILLIANT SON OF THE DARK HIDDEN FATHER (a).

(a) The answer to the first question, suggested by the second, which is the reply of the teacher to the pupil, contains in a single phrase one of the most essential truths of occult philosophy. It indicates the existence of things imperceptible to our physical senses which are of far greater importance, more real and more permanent, than those that appeal to these senses themselves. Before the Lanoo can hope to understand the transcendentally metaphysical problem contained in the first question he must be able to answer the second, while the very answer he gives to the second will furnish him with the clue to the correct reply to the first.

In the Sanskrit Commentary on this Stanza, the terms used for the. concealed and the unrevealed Principle are many. In the earliest MSS. of Indian literature this Unrevealed, Abstract Deity has no name. It is called generally "*That*" (*Tat* in Sanskrit), and means all that is, was, and will be, or that can be so received by the human mind.

It is useless to attempt to explain the mystery in full. Materialists and the men of modern Science will never understand it, since, in order to obtain clear perception of it, one has first of all to admit the postulate of a universally diffused, omnipresent, eternal Deity in Nature; secondly, to have fathomed the mystery of electricity in its true essence; and thirdly, to credit man with being the septenary symbol, on the terrestrial plane, of the One Great UNIT (the Logos), which is Itself the Seven-vowelled sign, the Breath crystallized into the WORD.

9. LIGHT IS COLD FLAME, AND FLAME IS FIRE, AND THE FIRE PRODUCES HEAT, WHICH YIELDS WATER, THE WATER OF LIFE IN THE GREAT MOTHER (*Chaos*).

It must be remembered that the words "Light," "Fire," and "Flame" used in the Stanzas have been adopted by the translators thereof from the vocabulary of the old "Fire philosophers,"[5] in order to render better the meaning of the archaic terms and symbols employed in the original.

All these—"Light," "Flame," "Hot," "Cold," "Fire," "Heat," "Water," and the "water of life" are all, on our plane, the progeny; or as a modern physicist would say, the correlations of ELECTRICITY. Mighty word, and a still mightier symbol! Sacred generator of a no

[5] Not the Medieval Alchemists, but the Magi and Fire-Worshippers, from whom the Rosicrucians or the Philosophers *per ignem*, the successors of the theurgists, borrowed all their ideas concerning Fire, as a mystic and divine element.

less sacred progeny; of Fire—the creator, the preserver and the destroyer; of Light—the essence of our divine ancestors; of Flame— the Soul of things. Electricity, the ONE Life at the upper rung of Being, and Astral Fluid, the Athanor of the Alchemists, at its lowest; GOD and DEVIL, GOOD and EVIL. . . .

Now, why is Light called in the Stanzas "cold flame"? Because in the order of Cosmic Evolution (as taught by the Occultist), the energy that actuates matter after its first formation into atoms is generated on our plane by Cosmic Heat; and because Kosmos, in the sense of dissociated matter, was not, before that period. The first Primordial Matter, eternal and coeval with Space, "which has neither a beginning nor an end," is "neither hot nor cold, but is of its own special nature," says the Commentary (Book II). Heat and cold are relative qualities and pertain to the realms of the manifested worlds. Primordial matter, then, before it emerges from the plane of the never-manifesting, and awakens to the thrill of action under the impulse of Fohat, is but "a cool Radiance, colourless, formless, taste- less, and devoid of every quality and aspect." Even such are her first-born, the "Four Sons," who "are One, and become Seven,"— the entities, by whose qualifications and names the ancient Eastern Occultists called the four of the seven primal "centres of Force," or atoms, that develop later into the great Cosmic "Elements," now divided into the seventy or so sub-elements, known to science. The four primal natures of the first Dhyan Chohans are the so-called (for want of better terms) Akasic, Ethereal, Watery, and Fiery, answer- ing, in the terminology of practical occultism, to scientific definitions of gases which, to convey a clear idea to both Occultists and laymen, must be defined as Parahydrogenic,[6] Paraoxygenic, Oxyhydrogenic, and Ozonic, or perhaps Nitr-ozonic; the latter forces or gases (in Occultism, supersensuous, yet atomic substances) being the most effective and active when energizing on the plane of more grossly differentiated matter.[7] These are both electro-positive and electro- negative.

10. FATHER-MOTHER SPIN A WEB WHOSE UPPER END IS FASTENED TO SPIRIT (*Purusha*), THE LIGHT OF THE ONE DARKNESS, AND THE LOWER ONE TO MATTER (*Prakriti*) ITS (*the Spirit's*) SHADOWY END; AND

[6] Para, "beyond," outside.
[7] Each of these and many more are probably the missing links of chemistry. They are known by other names in Alchemy and to the Occultists who practise in phe- nomenal powers. It is by combining and recombining in a certain way (or disso- ciating) the "Elements" by means of astral fire that the greatest phenomena are produced.

THIS WEB IS THE UNIVERSE SPUN OUT OF THE TWO SUBSTANCES MADE IN ONE, WHICH IS SWABHAVAT.

In the Mandukya Upanishad it is written, "As a spider throws out and retracts its web, as herbs spring up in the ground . . . so is the Universe derived from the undecaying one" (I. I. 7). Brahmā, as "the germ of unknown Darkness," is the material from which all evolves and develops "as the web from the spider, as foam from the water," etc. Brahmā the "Creator" is, as a term, derived from the root *brih*, to increase or expand. Brahmā "expands" and becomes the Universe woven out of his own substance.

II. IT (*the Web*) EXPANDS WHEN THE BREATH OF FIRE (*the Father*) IS UPON IT; IT CONTRACTS WHEN THE BREATH OF THE MOTHER (*the root of Matter*) TOUCHES IT. THEN THE SONS (*the Elements with their respective Powers, or Intelligences*) DISSOCIATE AND SCATTER, TO RETURN INTO THEIR MOTHER'S BOSOM AT THE END OF THE "GREAT DAY" AND RE-BECOME ONE WITH HER (*a*). WHEN IT (*the Web*) IS COOLING, IT BE-COMES RADIANT, ITS SONS EXPAND AND CONTRACT THROUGH THEIR OWN SELVES AND HEARTS; THEY EMBRACE INFINITUDE (*b*).

The expanding of the Universe under the Breath of FIRE is very suggestive in the light of the "Fire mist" period.

(*a*) Great heat breaks up the compound elements and resolves the heavenly bodies into their primeval one element, explains the commentary. "Once disintegrated into its primal constituent by getting within the attraction and reach of a focus, or centre of heat (energy), of which many are carried about to and fro in space, a body, whether alive or dead, will be vaporized and held in "the bosom of the Mother" until Fohat, gathering a few of the clusters of Cosmic matter (nebulae) will, by giving it an impulse, set it in motion anew, develop the required heat, and then leave it to follow its own new growth.

(*b*) The expanding and contracting of the Web—*i.e.*, the world stuff or atoms—expresses here the pulsatory movement; for it is the regular contraction and expansion of the infinite and shoreless Ocean of that which we may call the noumenon of matter emanated by Swabhavat, which causes the universal vibration of atoms. But it is also suggestive of something else. It shows that the ancients were acquainted with that which is now the puzzle of many scientists and especially of astronomers: the cause of the first ignition of matter or the world-stuff, the paradox of the heat produced by the refrigerative contraction and other such Cosmic riddles. For it points unmistakeably to a knowledge by the ancients of such phenomena. "There is heat internal and heat external in every atom " say the manuscript

Commentaries, to which the writer has had access; "the breath of the Father (or Spirit) and the breath (or heat) of the Mother (matter)"; and they give explanations which show that the theory of the extinction of the solar fires by loss of heat through radiation is erroneous.

12. THEN SVABHAVAT SENDS FOHAT TO HARDEN THE ATOMS. EACH (*of these*) IS A PART OF THE WEB (*Universe*). REFLECTING THE "SELF-EXISTENT LORD" (*Primeval Light*) LIKE A MIRROR, EACH BECOMES IN TURN A WORLD.[8] . . .

"Fohat hardens the atoms"; *i.e.*, by infusing energy into them: he scatters the atoms or primordial matter. "He scatters himself while scattering matter into atoms." (MSS. Commentaries.)

It is through Fohat that the ideas of the Universal Mind are impressed upon matter. Some faint idea of the nature of Fohat may be gathered from the appellation "Cosmic Electricity" sometimes applied to it; but to the commonly known properties of electricity must, in this case, be added others, including intelligence. It is of interest to note that modern science has come to the conclusion, that all cerebration and brain-activity are attended by electrical phenomena.

[8] This is said in the sense that the flame from a fire is endless, and that the lights of the whole Universe could be lit at one simple rush-light without diminishing its flame.

STANZA 4

1. LISTEN, YE SONS OF THE EARTH, TO YOUR INSTRUCTORS—THE SONS OF THE FIRE (a). LEARN THERE IS NEITHER FIRST NOR LAST; FOR ALL IS ONE NUMBER, ISSUED FROM NO NUMBER (b).

(a) These terms, the "Sons of the Fire," the "Sons of the Fire-Mist," and the like, require explanation. They are connected with a great primordial and universal mystery, and it is not easy to make it clear. These names, "Fire," "Flame," "Day," the "bright fortnight," etc.; as "Smoke," "Night," and so on, leading only to the end of the Lunar Path are incomprehensible without a knowledge of Esotericism. These are *all names of various deities* which preside over the Cosmo-psychic Powers. With these verses the mystic sense of the solar and lunar symbols are connected: the Pitris are *Lunar* Deities and our ancestors, because they *created the physical man.* The Agnishvatta, the Kumara (the seven mystic sages), are Solar Deities, though the former are Pitris also; and these are the "fashioners of the *Inner* Man." (See Book II.) They are:—

"The Sons of Fire"—because they are the first Beings (in the Secret Doctrine they are called "Minds"), evolved from Primordial Fire. "The Lord is a consuming Fire" (Deuteronomy iv. 24). Fire is Aether in its purest form, and hence is not regarded as matter, but it is the unity of Aether—the second manifested deity—in its universality. But there are two "Fires", and a distinction is made between them in the Occult teachings. The first, or the purely *formless* and *invisible* Fire concealed in the *Central Spiritual Sun*, is spoken of as "triple" (metaphysically); while the Fire of the Manifested Kosmos is Septenary, throughout both the Universe and our Solar System. "The fire or knowledge burns up all action on the plane of illusion," says the commentary. "Therefore, those who have acquired it and are emancipated, are called 'Fires.' "

(b) The expression "All is One Number, issued from No Number" relates again to that universal and philosophical tenet just explained in Stanza 3. (Comm. 4). That which is absolute is of course No-Number; but in its later significance it has an application in Space as in Time. It means that not only every increment of time is part of a larger increment, up to the most indefinitely prolonged duration conceivable by the human intellect, but also that no manifested thing can be thought of except as part of a larger whole; the total aggregate being the One Manifested Universe that issues from the Unmanifested or Absolute—called Non-Being or "No-Number," to distinguish it from BEING or "the One Number."

(2) LEARN WHAT WE, WHO DESCEND FROM THE PRIMORDIAL SEVEN, WE, WHO ARE BORN FROM THE PRIMORDIAL FLAME, HAVE LEARNED FROM OUR FATHERS.

The distinction between the "Primordial" and the subsequent Seven Builders is this: The former are the Ray and direct emanation of the first "Sacred Four," the *Tetraktis*, that is, the eternally Self-Existent One (Eternal *in Essence* note well, not in manifestation, and distinct from the universal ONE). Latent, during Pralaya, and active, during Manvantara, the "Primordial" proceed from "Father-Mother"; whereas the other manifested Quaternary and the Seven proceed from the Mother alone. It is the latter who is the immaculate Virgin-Mother, who is overshadowed, not impregnated, by the Universal MYSTERY—when she emerges from her state of Laya, or undifferentiated condition. In reality, they are, of course, all one; but their aspects on the various planes of being are different. (See Part II., "Theogony of the Creative Gods.")

The first "Primordial" are the highest Beings on the Scale of Existence. They are the Archangels of Christianity, those who refuse—as Michael did in the latter system, and as did the eldest "Mind-born sons" of Brahmā—to create or rather to multiply.

3. FROM THE EFFULGENCY OF LIGHT—THE RAY OF THE EVER-DARKNESS—SPRANG IN SPACE THE RE-AWAKENED ENERGIES (*Dhyan Chohans*): THE ONE FROM THE EGG, THE SIX AND THE FIVE (*a*); THEN THE THREE, THE ONE, THE FOUR, THE ONE, THE FIVE—THE TWICE SEVEN, THE SUM TOTAL (*b*). AND THESE ARE THE ESSENCES, THE FLAMES, THE ELEMENTS, THE BUILDERS, THE NUMBERS (*c*), THE ARUPA (*formless*), THE RUPA (*with bodies*), AND THE FORCE OR DIVINE MAN—THE SUM TOTAL. AND FROM THE DIVINE MAN EMANATED THE FORMS, THE SPARKS, THE SACRED ANIMALS, AND THE MESSENGERS OF THE SACRED FATHERS (*the Pitris*) WITHIN THE HOLY FOUR.[1]

(*a*) This relates to the sacred Science of the Numerals: It is on the Hierarchies and correct numbers of these Beings, invisible (to us) except upon very rare occasions, that the mystery of the whole

---

[1] The 4, represented in the Occult numerals by the Tetraktis, the Sacred or Perfect Square, is a Sacred Number with the mystics of every nation and race. It has one and the same significance in Brahmanism, Buddhism, the Kabala and in the Egyptian, Chaldean and other numerical systems.

Universe is built. The *Kumaras*, for instance, are called the "Four" though in reality seven in number, because Sanaka, Sananda, Sanatana and Sanat-Kumara are the chief Vaidhatra (their patronymic name), as they spring from the "four-fold mystery." "The One from the Egg, the Six and the Five," give the number 1065, the value of the first-born.

(*b*) "The Three, the One, the Four, the One, the Five" (in their totality—twice Seven) represent 31415—the numerical hierarchy of the Dhyan-Chohans of various orders, and of the inner or circumscribed world. When placed on the boundary of the great circle of "Pass not" (see Stanza V.), called also the Dhyanipasa, the "Rope of the Angels," the "rope" that hedges off the phenomenal from the noumenal Kosmos, (not falling within the range of our present objective consciousness); this number, when not enlarged by permutation and expansion, is ever 31415 anagrammatically and Kabalistically, being both the number of the circle and the mystic Svastika, the twice seven once more; for whatever way the two sets of figures are counted, when added separately, one figure after another, whether crossways, from right or from left, they will always yield fourteen. Mathematically they represent the well-known calculation that the ratio of the diameter to the circumference of a circle is as 1 to 3.1415, or the value of the π (pi), as this ratio is called—the symbol π being always used in mathematical formulae to express it. This set of figures must have the same meaning, since the 1 : 314,159, and then again 1 : 3 : 1,415,927 are worked out in the secret calculations to express the various cycles and ages of the "First-born," or 311,040,000,000,000 with fractions, and yield the same 13,415 by a process we are not concerned with at present.

Thus, while in the metaphysical world, the circle with the one central Point in it has no number, and is called Anupadaka (parentless and numberless)—viz., it can fall under no calculation—in the manifested world the mundane Egg or Circle is circumscribed within the groups called the Line, the Triangle, the Pentacle, the second Line and the Cube (or 13514); and when the Point, having generated a Line, becomes a diameter which stands for the androgynous Logos, then the figures become 31415, or a triangle, a line, a cube, the second line, and a pentacle. "When the Son separates from the Mother he becomes the Father," the diameter standing for Nature, or the feminine principle. Therefore it is said: "In the world of being, the one Point fructifies the Line—the Virgin Matrix of Kosmos (the egg-shaped zero)—and the Immaculate Mother gives birth to the Form that combines all forms." Prajapati is called the first procreating male, and "his Mother's husband." This gives the

key-note to all the later Divine Sons from "Immaculate Mothers."
It is greatly corroborated by the significant fact that Anna, the name
of the Mother of the Virgin Mary, now represented by the Roman
Catholic church as having given birth to her daughter in an immaculate way ("Mary conceived without sin"), is derived from the
Chaldean Ana, heaven, or Astral Light, Anima Mundi; whence
Anaitia, Devi-durga, the wife of Siva, is also called Annapurna,
and Kanya, the Virgin, "Uma-Kanya" being her esoteric name, and
meaning the "Virgin of light," Astral Light in one of its multitu-
dinous aspects.

(c) The Devas, Pitris, Rishis; the Suras and the Asuras; the
Daityas and Adityas; the Danavas and Gandharvas, etc., have all
their synonyms in our Secret Doctrine. Many of these may be also
found in the Christian hierarchy of divine and celestial Powers. All
those Thrones and Dominions, Virtues and Principalities, Cherubs,
Seraphs and demons, the various denizens of the Sidereal World, are
the modern copies of archaic prototypes.

The "Sacred Animals" are found in the Bible as well as in the
Kabala, and they have their meaning (a very profound one, too) on
the page of the origins of Life.

4. This was the Army of the Voice—the Divine Septenary.
The sparks of the seven are subject to, and the servants of,
the first, second, third, fourth, fifth, sixth, and the seventh
of the seven (a). These ("sparks") are called spheres, triangles,
cubes, lines, and modellers; for thus stands the Eternal
Nidana—the Oi-Ha-Hou (the permutation of Oeaohoo) (b).[a]

(a) This Sloka gives again a brief analysis of the Hierarchies of
the Dhyan Chohans, called Devas (Gods) in India, or the conscious
Intelligent Powers in Nature. To this Hierarchy correspond the
actual types into which humanity may be divided; for humanity, as
a whole, is in reality a materialized though as yet imperfect expression thereof. "The Army of the Voice" is a term closely connected with the mystery of Sound and Speech, as an effect and
corollary of the cause—Divine Thought.

"Names (and words) are either beneficent or maleficent; they are, in
a certain sense, either venomous or health-giving, according to the
hidden influences attached by Supreme Wisdom to their elements,

---

[a] The literal signification of the word is, among the Eastern Occultists of the
North, a circular wind, whirlwind; but in this instance, it is a term to denote the
ceaseless and eternal Cosmic Motion; or rather the Force that moves it, which
Force is tacitly accepted as the Deity but never named. It is the eternal Karana, the
ever-acting Cause.

that is to say, to the letters which compose them, and the *numbers* correlative to these letters."[3]

This is strictly true as an esoteric teaching accepted by all the Eastern Schools of Occultism. In the Sanskrit, as also in the Hebrew and all other alphabets, every letter has its occult meaning and its rationale; it is a cause and an effect of a preceding cause, and a combination of these very often produces the most magical effect. The vowels, especially, contain the most occult and formidable potencies. The Mantras (esoterically, magical rather than religious) are chanted by the Brahmins, and so are the Vedas and other Scriptures.

(*b*) Next we see Cosmic matter scattering and forming itself into Elements; grouped into the mystic Four within the fifth Element— Ether, the lining of Akasa, the Anima Mundi or Mother of Kosmos. "Dots, Lines, Triangles, Cubes, Circles" and finally "Spheres"— why or how? Because, says the Commentary, such is the first law of Nature, and because Nature geometrizes universally in all her manifestations. There is an inherent law—not only in the primordial, but also in the manifested matter of our phenomenal plane—by which Nature correlates her geometrical forms, and later, also, her compound elements; and in which there is no place for accident or chance. It is a fundamental law in Occultism, that there is no rest or cessation of motion in Nature. That which seems rest is only the change of one form into another; the change of substance going hand in hand with that of form—as we are taught in Occult physics, which thus seem to have anticipated the discovery of the "conservation of matter" by a considerable time. Says the ancient Commentary[4] to Stanza 4:—

"*The Mother is the fiery Fish of Life. She scatters her spawn and the Breath (Motion) heats and quickens it. The grains (of spawn) are soon attracted to each other and form the curds in the Ocean (of Space). The larger lumps coalesce and receive new spawn—in fiery dots, triangles and cubes, which ripen, and at the appointed time some of the lumps detach themselves and assume spheroidal form, a process which they effect only when not interfered with by the others. After which, law No. * * * comes into operation. Motion (the Breath) becomes the whirlwind and sets them into rotation.*"[5]

[3] P. Christian, author of *Histoire de la Magie* and *L'Homme Rouge des Tuileries*.

[4] These are ancient Commentaries attached with modern Glossaries to the Stanzas, as the Commentaries in their symbolical language are usually as difficult to understand as the Stanzas themselves.

[5] "Motion is eternal in the unmanifested, and periodical in the manifest," says an Occult teaching. It is "when heat caused by the descent of FLAME into primordial matter causes its particles to move, which motion becomes Whirlwind." A drop of liquid assumes a spheroidal form owing to its atoms moving around themselves in their ultimate, unresolvable, and noumenal essence; unresolvable for physical science, at any rate.

5. . . . WHICH IS:—
"DARKNESS," THE BOUNDLESS OR THE NO-NUMBER, ADI-NIDANA
SVA-BHAVAT: THE ◯ (*for x, unknown quantity*):

   I. THE ADI-SANAT, THE NUMBER, FOR HE IS ONE (*a*).
   II. THE VOICE OF THE WORD, SVABHAVAT, THE NUMBERS,
      FOR HE IS ONE AND NINE.[6]
   III. THE "FORMLESS SQUARE." (*Arupa.*) (*b*).

AND THESE THREE ENCLOSED WITHIN THE ◯ (*boundless circle*),
ARE THE SACRED FOUR, AND THE TEN ARE THE ARUPA (*subjective,
formless*) UNIVERSE (*c*); THEN COME THE "SONS," THE SEVEN FIGHTERS,
THE ONE, THE EIGHTH LEFT OUT, AND HIS BREATH WHICH IS THE
LIGHT-MAKER (*Bhaskara*) (*d*).

(*a*) "Adi-Sanat," translated literally, is the First or "Primeval
Ancient," which name identifies the Kabalistic "Ancient of Days"
and the "Holy Aged" (Sephira and Adam Kadmon) with Brahmā
the Creator, called also Sanat among his other names and titles.

Svabhavat is the mystic Essence, the plastic root of physical
Nature—"Numbers" when manifested; the Number, in its Unity of
Substance, on the highest plane. The name is of Buddhist use and a
synonym for the four-fold Anima Mundi, the Kabalistic "Archetypal
World," from whence proceed the "Creative, Formative, and the
Material Worlds."

(*b*) ◯ This means that the "Boundless Circle" (Zero) becomes
a figure or number only when one of the nine figures precedes it, and
thus manifests its value and potency; the Word or Logos in union
with voice and Spirit (the expression and source of Consciousness)
standing for the nine figures and thus forming, with the Cypher, the
Decade which contains in itself all the Universe. The Triad forms
within the circle the Tetraktis or Sacred Four, the Square within the
Circle being the most potent of all the magical figures.

(*c*) The "One Rejected" is the Sun of our system. The Occult
Doctrine rejects the hypothesis born out of the Nebular Theory, that
the (seven) great planets have evolved from the Sun's central mass,
not of this our visible Sun, at any rate. The first condensation of
Cosmic matter of course took place about a central nucleus, its
parent Sun; but our sun, it is taught, merely detached itself earlier
than all the others, as the rotating mass contracted, and is their
elder, bigger brother therefore, not their father.

(*d*) There is a whole poem on the pregenetic battles fought by the
growing planets before the final formation of Kosmos, thus account-

---

   [6] Which makes ten, or the perfect number applied to the "Creator," the name
given to the totality of the Creators blended by the Monotheists into One.

ing for the seemingly disturbed position of the systems of several planets, the plane of the satellites of some (of Neptune and Uranus, for instance, of which the ancients knew nothing, it is said) being tilted over, thus giving them an appearance of retrograde motion. Having evolved from Cosmic Space, and before the final formation of the primaries and the annulation of the planetary nebula, the Sun, we are taught, drew into the depths of its mass all the Cosmic vitality he could, threatening to engulf his weaker "brothers" before the law of attraction and repulsion was finally adjusted; after which he began feeding on "the Mother's refuse and sweat"; in other words, on those portions of Ether (the "Breath of the Universal Soul") of the existence and constitution of which science is as yet absolutely ignorant. Mr. W. Mattieu Williams suggested that the diffused matter or Ether which is the recipient of the heat radiations of the Universe is thereby drawn into the depths of the solar mass. Expelling thence the previously condensed and thermally exhausted Ether, it becomes compressed and gives up its heat, to be in turn itself driven out in a rarified and cooled state, to absorb a fresh supply of heat, which he supposes to be in this way taken up by the Ether, and again concentrated and redistributed by the Suns of the Universe.[7]

This is about as close an approximation to the Occult teachings as Science ever imagined; for Occultism explains it by "the dead breath" given back by Martanda and his feeding on the "sweat and refuse" of "Mother Space." What could affect Neptune,[8] Saturn and Jupiter but little, would have killed such comparatively small "Houses" as Mercury, Venus and Mars. As Uranus was not known before the end of the eighteenth century, the name of the fourth planet mentioned in the allegory must remain to us, so far, a mystery.

The "Breath" of all the "Seven" is said to be Bhaskara (light-making), because they (the planets) were all comets and suns in their origin. They evolve into Manvantaric life from primeval Chaos (now the noumenon of irresolvable nebulae) by aggregation and accumulation of the primary differentiations of the eternal Matter, according to the beautiful expression in the Commentary, "Thus the Sons of Light clothed themselves in the fabric of Darkness." They are called allegorically "the Heavenly Snails," on account of their (to us) formless INTELLIGENCES inhabiting unseen

[7] See *Comparative Geology*, by Alexander Winchell, LL.D., p. 56.

[8] When we speak of Neptune it is not as an Occultist but as a European. The true Eastern Occultist will maintain that, whereas there are many yet undiscovered planets in our system, Neptune does not belong to it, his apparent connection with our sun and the influence of the latter upon Neptune notwithstanding. This connection is *mayavic*, imaginary, they say.

their starry and planetary homes, and, so to speak, carrying them as the snails do along with themselves in their revolution. The doctrine of a common origin for all the heavenly bodies and planets, was, as we see, inculcated by the archaic astronomers before Kepler, Newton, Leibnitz, Kant, Herschel and Laplace. Heat (the Breath), attraction and repulsion—the three great factors of Motion—are the conditions under which all the members of all this primitive family are born, developed, and die, to be reborn after a "Night of Brahmā," during which eternal Matter relapses periodically into its primary undifferentiated state. The most attenuated gases can give no idea of its nature to the modern physicist. Centres of Forces at first, the invisible Sparks of[9] primordial Atoms differentiate into molecules, and become Suns—passing gradually into objectivity— gaseous, radiant, cosmic, the one "Whirlwind" (or motion) finally giving the impulse to the form, and the initial motion, regulated and sustained by the never-resting Breaths—the Dhyan Chohans.

6. . . . THEN THE SECOND SEVEN, WHO ARE THE LIPIKA, PRODUCED BY THE THREE (*Word, Voice, and Spirit*). THE REJECTED SON IS ONE, THE "SON-SUNS" ARE COUNTLESS.

The *Lipi-ka*, from the word *lipi*, "writing," means literally the "Scribes."[10] Mystically, these Divine Beings are connected with Karma, the Law of Retribution, for they are the Recorders or Annalists who impress on the (to us) invisible tablets of the Astral Light, "the great picture-gallery of eternity"—a faithful record of every act, and even thought, of man, of all that was, is, or ever will be, in the phenomenal Universe. As said in *Isis Unveiled*, this divine and unseen canvas is the BOOK OF LIFE. As it is the Lipika who project into objectivity from the passive Universal Mind the ideal plan of the Universe, upon which the "Builders" reconstruct the Kosmos after every Pralaya, it is they who stand parallel to the Seven Angels of the Presence, whom the Christians recognize in the Seven "Planetary Spirits" or the "Spirits of the Stars"; for thus it is they who are the direct amanuenses of the Eternal Ideation—or, as called by Plato, the "Divine Thought." The Eternal Record is no fantastic dream, for we meet with the same records in the world of gross matter. "A shadow never falls upon a wall without leaving thereupon a permanent trace which might be made visible by resorting to proper processes," says Dr. Draper. . . . "The portraits of our friends or landscape-views may be hidden on the sensitive surface from the

9 [? or]
10 These are the four "Immortals" which are mentioned in *Atharva Veda* as the "Watchers" or Guardians of the four quarters of the sky (see ch. lxxvi., 1-4, *et seq.*).

eye, but they are ready to make their appearance as soon as proper developers are resorted to. Upon the walls of our most private apartments, where we think the eye of intrusion is altogether shut out, and our retirement can never be profaned, there exist the vestiges of all our acts, silhouettes of whatever we have done."[11]

[11] *Conflict between Religion and Science.* Draper, pp. 132 and 133.

STANZA 5

1. THE PRIMORDIAL SEVEN, THE FIRST SEVEN BREATHS OF THE DRAGON OF WISDOM, PRODUCE IN THEIR TURN FROM THEIR HOLY CIRCUMGYRATING BREATHS THE FIERY WHIRLWIND.

This is, perhaps, the most difficult of all the Stanzas to explain. Its language is comprehensible only to him who is thoroughly versed in Eastern allegory and its purposely obscure phraseology. The question will surely be asked, "Do the Occultists believe in all these 'Builders,' 'Lipika,' and 'Sons of Light' as Entities, or are they merely imageries?" To this the answer is given as plainly: "After due allowance for the imagery of personified Powers, we must admit the existence of these Entities, if we would not reject the existence of Spiritual Humanity within physical mankind. For the hosts of these Sons of Light and 'Mind-born Sons' of the first manifested Ray of the UNKNOWN ALL are the very root of spiritual man." Unless we want to believe the unphilosophical dogma of a specially created soul for every human birth—a fresh supply of these pouring in daily, since "Adam"—we have to admit the occult teachings.

The Doctrine teaches that, in order to become a divine, fully conscious god,—aye, even the highest—the Spiritual primeval INTELLIGENCES must pass through the human stage. And when we say human, this does not apply merely to our terrestrial humanity, but to the mortals that inhabit any world, i.e., to those Intelligences that have reached the appropriate equilibrium between matter and spirit, as we have now, since the middle point of the Fourth Root Race of the Fourth Round was passed. Each Entity must have won for itself the right of becoming divine, through self-experience. Hegel, the great German thinker, must have known or sensed intuitively this truth when saying that the Unconscious evolved the Universe only "in the hope of attaining clear self-consciousness," of becoming, in other words, MAN; for this is also the secret meaning of the usual Puranic phrase about Brahmā being constantly "moved by the desire to create." This explains also the hidden Kabalistic meaning of the saying: "The Breath becomes a stone; the stone, a plant; the plant, an animal; the animal, a man; the man, a spirit; and the spirit, a god." The Mind-born Sons, the Rishis, the Builders, etc., were all men—of whatever forms and shapes—in other worlds and the preceding Manvantaras.

The "Fiery Whirlwind" is the incandescent Cosmic dust which

only follows magnetically, as the iron filings follow the magnet, the directing thought of the "Creative Forces." Yet this cosmic dust is something more; for every atom in the Universe has the potentiality of self-consciousness in it, and is, like the Monads of Leibnitz, a Universe in itself, and *for* itself. *It is an atom and an angel.*

2. THEY MAKE OF HIM THE MESSENGER OF THEIR WILL (*a*). THE DZYU BECOMES FOHAT (*b*); THE SWIFT SON OF THE DIVINE SONS, WHOSE SONS ARE THE LIPIKA, RUNS CIRCULAR ERRANDS. HE IS THE STEED, AND THE THOUGHT IS THE RIDER (*i.e., he is under the influence of their guiding thought*). HE PASSES LIKE LIGHTNING THROUGH THE FIERY CLOUDS (*cosmic mists*); TAKES THREE, AND FIVE, AND SEVEN STRIDES THROUGH THE SEVEN REGIONS ABOVE AND THE SEVEN BELOW (*the world to be*). HE LIFTS HIS VOICE, AND CALLS THE INNUMERABLE SPARKS (*atoms*) AND JOINS THEM TOGETHER (*c*).

(*a*) This shows the "Primordial Seven" using for their *Vahan* (vehicle, or the manifested subject which becomes the symbol of the Power directing it), Fohat, called in consequence, the "Messenger of their will"—the Fiery Whirlwind.

(*b*) "Dzyu becomes Fohat"—the expression itself shows it. Dzyu is the one real (magical) knowledge, or Occult Wisdom, which, dealing with eternal truths and primal causes, becomes almost omnipotence when applied in the right direction. Its antithesis is Dzyu-mi, that which deals with illusions and false appearances only, as in our exoteric modern sciences. In this case, Dzyu is the expression of the collective Wisdom of the Dhyani-Buddhas.

As the reader is supposed not to be acquainted with the Dhyani-Buddhas, it is as well to say at once that, *according to the Orientalists*, there are five Dhyanis who are the "celestial" Buddhas, of whom the human Buddhas are the manifestations in the world of form and matter. Esoterically, however, the Dhyani-Buddhas are seven, of whom five only have hitherto manifested,[1] and two are to come in the Sixth and Seventh Root-races. They are, so to speak, the eternal prototypes of the Buddhas who appear on this earth, each of whom has his particular divine prototype. So, for instance, Amitabha is the Dhyani-Buddha of Gautama Sakyamuni, manifesting through him whenever this great Soul incarnates on earth as he did in Tzon-kha-pa.[2] As the synthesis of the seven Dhyani-Buddhas, Avalokiteswara was the first Buddha (the Logos), so Amitabha is the inner "God" of

---

[1] See A. P. Sinnett's *Esoteric Buddhism*, 5th annotated edition, pp. 171–173.
[2] The first and greatest Reformer who founded the "Yellow-Caps," Gelugpas. He was born in the year 1355 A.D. in Amdo, and was the *Avatar* of Amitabha, the celestial name of Gautama Buddha.

Gautama, who, in China, is called Amita(-Buddha). They are, as Mr. Rhys Davids correctly states, "the glorious counterparts in the mystic world, free from the debasing conditions of this material life" of every earthly mortal Buddha—the liberated Manushi-Buddhas appointed to govern the Earth in this Round. They are the "Buddhas of Contemplation," and are all Anupadaka (parentless), *i.e.*, self-born of divine essence.

(*c*) Fohat, being one of the most, if not the most important character in esoteric Cosmogony, should be minutely described. Fohat is one thing in the yet unmanifested Universe and another in the phenomenal and Cosmic World. In the latter, he is that occult, electric, vital power, which, under the Will of the Creative Logos, unites and brings together all forms, giving them the first impulse which becomes in time law. But in the unmanifested Universe, Fohat is no more this than Eros is the later brilliant winged Cupid, or LOVE. Fohat has naught to do with Kosmos yet, since Kosmos is not born, and the gods still sleep in the bosom of "Father-Mother." He is an abstract philosophical idea. He produces nothing yet by himself; he is simply that potential creative power in virtue of whose action the NOUMENON of all future phenomena divides, so to speak, but to reunite in a mystic supersensuous act, and emit the creative Ray. When the "Divine Son" breaks forth, then Fohat becomes the propelling force, the active Power which causes the ONE to become Two and THREE—on the Cosmic plane of manifestation. The triple One differentiates into the Many, and then Fohat is transformed into that force which brings together the elemental atoms and makes them aggregate and combine.

Fohat is closely related to the "ONE LIFE." From the Unknown One, the Infinite TOTALITY, the manifested ONE, or the periodical, Manvantaric Deity, emanates; and this is the Universal Mind, which, separated from its Fountain-Source, is the Demiurgos or the creative Logos of the Western Kabalists, and the four-faced Brahmā of the Hindu religion. In its totality, viewed from the standpoint of manifested Divine Thought in the esoteric doctrine, it represents the Hosts of the higher creative Dhyan Chohans. Simultaneously with the evolution of the Universal Mind, the concealed Wisdom of Adi-Buddha—the One Supreme and eternal—manifests itself as Avalokiteshwara (or manifested Ishwara), which is the Osiris of the Egyptians, the Ahura-Mazda of the Zoroastrians, the Heavenly Man of the Hermetic philosopher, the Logos of the Platonists, and the Atman of the Vedantins.[3] By the action of the manifested Wisdom,

---

[3] Mr. Subba Row seems to identify him with, and to call him, the LOGOS. (See his four lectures on the "Bhagavadgita" in the Theosophist, Vol. VIII.)

or Mahat, represented by these innumerable centres of spiritual Energy in the Kosmos, the reflection of the Universal Mind, which is Cosmic Ideation and the intellectual Force accompanying such ideation, becomes objectively the Fohat of the Buddhist esoteric philosopher. Fohat, running along the seven principles of AKASHA, acts upon manifested substance or the One Element, as declared above, and by differentiating it into various centres of Energy, sets in motion the law of Cosmic Evolution, which, in obedience to the Ideation of the Universal Mind, brings into existence all the various states of being in the manifested Solar System.

The Solar System, brought into existence by these agencies, consists of Seven Principles, like everything else within these centres. Such is the teaching of the trans-Himalayan Esotericism. Every philosophy, however, has its own way of dividing these principles.

Fohat, then, is the personified electric vital power, the transcendental binding unity of all cosmic energies, on the unseen as on the manifested planes, the action of which resembles—on an immense scale—that of a living Force created by WILL, in those phenomena where the seemingly subjective acts on the seemingly objective and propels it to action. Fohat is not only the living Symbol and Container of that Force, but is looked upon by the Occultists as an Entity—the forces he acts upon being cosmic, human and terrestrial, and exercising their influence on all those planes respectively. On the earthly plane his influence is felt in the magnetic and active force generated by the strong desire of the magnetizer. On the Cosmic, it is present in the constructive power that carries out, in the formation of things—from the planetary system down to the glow-worm and simple daisy—the plan in the mind of nature, or in the Divine Thought, with regard to the development and growth of that special thing. He is, metaphysically, the objectivized thought of the gods; the "Word made flesh," on a lower scale, and the messenger of Cosmic and human ideations: the active force in Universal Life. In his secondary aspect, Fohat is the Solar Energy, the electric vital fluid, and the preserving fourth principle, the animal Soul of Nature, so to say, or—Electricity.

The Three and Seven "Strides" refer to the seven spheres inhabited by man, of the esoteric Doctrine, as well as to the Seven regions of the Earth.[4]

_____

[4] The three strides relate metaphysically to the descent of Spirit into matter, of the Logos falling as a ray into the Spirit, then into the Soul, and finally into the human physical form of man, in which it becomes LIFE.

3. He is their guiding spirit and leader. When he commences work, he separates the sparks of the lower kingdom (*mineral atoms*) that float and thrill with joy in their radiant dwellings (*gaseous clouds*), and forms therewith the germs of wheels. He places them in the six directions of space and one in the middle—the central wheel.

"Wheels," as already explained, are the centres of force around which primordial Cosmic matter expands, and, passing through all the six stages of consolidation, becomes spheroidal and ends by being transformed into globes or spheres. It is one of the fundamental dogmas of Esoteric Cosmogony, that during the Kalpas (or aeons) of life, motion, which, during the periods of Rest "pulsates and thrills through every slumbering atom" (Commentary on Dzyan), assumes an evergrowing tendency, from the first awakening of Kosmos to a new "Day," to circular movement. The "Deity becomes a whirlwind."

This law of vortical movement in primordial matter is one of the oldest conceptions of Greek philosophy, whose first historical Sages were nearly all Initiates of the Mysteries. The Greeks had it from the Egyptians, and the latter from the Chaldeans, who had been the pupils of Brahmins of the esoteric school. Leucippus, and Democritus of Abdera—the pupil of the Magi—taught that this gyratory movement of the atoms and spheres existed from eternity.

By the "Six directions of Space" is here meant the "Double Triangle," the junction and blending together of pure Spirit and Matter, of the Arupa and the Rupa, of which the Triangles are a Symbol.

4. Fohat traces spiral lines to unite the six to the seventh—the Crown (*a*); an army of the Sons of Light stands at each angle (*and*) the Lipika—in the middle wheel (*b*). They (*the Lipika*) say, "This is good." The first Divine World is ready, the first (*is now*), the second (*world*), then the "Divine Arupa" (*the formless Universe of Thought*) reflects itself in Chhayaloka (*the shadowy world of primal form, or the intellectual*) the first garment of (*the*) Anupadaka (*c*).

(*a*) This tracing of "Spiral lines" refers to the evolution of Man's as well as Nature's principles; an evolution which takes place gradually (as will be seen in Book II., on "The origin of the Human Races"), as does everything else in Nature. The Sixth principle in Man (Buddhi, the Divine Soul) though a mere breath in our conceptions, is still something material when compared with divine "Spirit" (Atma) of which it is the carrier or vehicle. Fohat, in his capacity of DIVINE LOVE (*Eros*), the electric Power of affinity and sympathy, is shown allegorically as trying to bring the pure Spirit, the Ray inseparable from the ONE Absolute, into union with the Soul, the two constituting in Man the MONAD, and in Nature the first link between the ever unconditioned and the manifested. "The First is now the Second" (World)—of the Lipikas—has reference to the same.

(*b*) The "Army" at each angle is the Host of angelic Beings (Dhyan-Chohans) appointed to guide and watch over each respective region from the beginning to the end of a Manvantara.

(*c*) The "First is the Second," because the "First" cannot really be numbered or regarded as the First, as that is the realm of noumena in its primary manifestation: the threshold to the World of Truth, or SAT, through which the direct energy that radiates from the ONE REALITY——the Nameless Deity—reaches us. It is coeval and co-existent with the One Life, "Secondless," but as a manifestation it is still a Maya—like the rest. This "World of Truth" can be described only in the words of the Commentary as "A bright star dropped from the heart of Eternity; the beacon of hope on whose Seven Rays hang the Seven Worlds of Being." Truly so; since those are the Seven Lights whose reflections are the human immortal Monads—the Atma, or the irradiating Spirit of every creature of the human family. First, this septenary Light; then:—

The "Divine World"—the countless Lights lit at the primeval Light—the Buddhis, or formless divine Souls, of the last Arupa (formless) world; the "Sum Total," in the mysterious language of the old Stanza. In the Catechism, the Master is made to ask the pupil:—

"*Lift thy head, oh Lanoo; dost thou see one, or countless lights above thee, burning in the dark midnight sky?*"

"*I sense one Flame, O Gurudeva, I see countless undetached sparks shining in it.*"

"*Thou sayest well. And now look around and into thyself. That light which burns inside thee, dost thou feel it different in anywise from the light that shines in thy Brother-men?*"

"*It is in no way different, though the prisoner is held in bondage by Karma, and though its outer garments delude the ignorant into saying, 'Thy Soul and My Soul.'*"

The radical unity of the ultimate essence of each constituent part of compounds in Nature—from star to mineral atom, from the highest Dhyan Chohan to the smallest infusoria, in the fullest acceptation of the term, and whether applied to the spiritual, intellectual, or physical worlds—this is the one fundamental law in Occult Science. "The Deity is boundless and infinite expansion," says an Occult axiom. If the Deity, the radical One, is eternal and an infinite substance ("the Lord thy God is a consuming fire") and never consumed, then it does not seem reasonable that the Occult teaching should be held as unphilosophical when it says: "Thus were the Arupa and Rupa worlds formed: from ONE Light seven lights; from each of the seven, seven times seven," etc., etc.

5. FOHAT TAKES FIVE STRIDES (*having already taken the first three*) (*a*), AND BUILDS A WINGED WHEEL AT EACH CORNER OF THE SQUARE FOR THE FOUR HOLY ONES . . . AND THEIR ARMIES (*hosts*) (*b*).

(*a*) The "Strides," as already explained (see Commentary on Stanza 4), refer to both the Cosmic and the Human Principles—the latter of which consist, in the exoteric division, of three (Spirit, Soul, and Body), and, in the esoteric calculation, of seven Principles—three Rays of the Essence and four aspects.[5] Those who have studied Mr. Sinnett's *Esoteric Buddhism* can easily grasp the nomenclature. There are two esoteric schools—or rather one school, divided into two parts—one for the inner Lanoos, the other for the outer or semi-lay chelas beyond the Himalayas; the first teaching a septenary, the other a six-fold division of human Principles.

From a Cosmic point of view, Fohat taking "Five Strides" refers here to the five upper planes of Consciousness and Being, the sixth and the seventh (counting downwards) being the astral and the terrestrial, or the two lower planes.

(*b*) "Four Winged Wheels at each corner . . . for the Four Holy Ones and their Armies (Hosts)" . . . These are the "Four Maharajahs" or great Kings of the Dhyan-Chohans, the Devas who preside, each over one of the four cardinal points. They are the Regents or Angels who rule over the Cosmic Forces of North, South, East and West, Forces having each a distinct occult property. These BEINGS are also connected with Karma, as the latter needs physical and material agents to carry out her decrees.

There are three chief groups of Builders and as many of the Planetary Spirits and the Lipika, each group being again divided into seven sub-groups. The "Builders" are the representatives of the first "Mind-Born Entities." They build or rather rebuild every "System" after the "Night." The Second group of the Builders is the Architect of our Planetary Chain exclusively; and the Third, the

[5] The four aspects are the body, its life or vitality, and the "double" of the body, the triad which disappears with the death of the person, and the Kama-rupa which disintegrates in Kama-loka.

progenitor of our Humanity—the macro-cosmic prototype of the microcosm.

The Planetary Spirits are the informing spirits of the Stars in general, and of the Planets especially. They rule the destinies of men who are all born under one or other of their constellations; the second and third groups pertaining to other systems have the same functions, and all rule various departments in Nature.

The Lipika (a description of whom is given in the Commentary on Stanza 4, No. 6) are the Spirits of the Universe, whereas the Builders are only our own planetary deities. The Lipika are connected with Karma—being its direct Recorders.

6. THE LIPIKA CIRCUMSCRIBE THE TRIANGLE, THE FIRST ONE (*the vertical line or the figure* I), THE CUBE, THE SECOND ONE, AND THE PENTACLE WITHIN THE EGG (*circle*) (*a*). IT IS THE RING CALLED "PASS NOT," FOR THOSE WHO DESCEND AND ASCEND (*as also for those*) WHO, DURING THE KALPA, ARE PROGRESSING TOWARD THE GREAT DAY "BE WITH US" (*b*). . . . THUS WERE FORMED THE ARUPA AND THE RUPA (*the Formless World and the World of Forms*); FROM ONE LIGHT SEVEN LIGHTS; FROM EACH OF THE SEVEN SEVEN TIMES SEVEN LIGHTS. THE "WHEELS" WATCH THE RING.

The Stanza proceeds with a minute classification of the Orders of Angelic Hierarchy. From the group of Four and Seven emanates the "mind-born" group of Ten, or Twelve, of Twenty-one, etc., all these divided again into sub-groups of septenaries, novems, duo-decimals, and so on, until the mind is lost in this endless enumeration of celestial Hosts and Beings, each having its distinct task in the ruling of the visible Kosmos during its existence.

(*a*) The esoteric meaning of the first sentence of the Sloka is, that those who have been called Lipikas, the Recorders of the Karmic ledger, make an impassable barrier between the personal EGO and the impersonal SELF, the Noumenon and Parent-Source of the former. Hence the allegory. They circumscribe the manifested world of matter within the RING "Pass-Not." This world is the symbol (objective) of the ONE divided into the many, on the planes of Illusion, of Adi (the "First") or of Eka (the "One"); and this One is the collective aggregate, or totality, of the principal Creators or Architects of this visible universe.

Hence the allegory. The Lipika separate the world (or plane) of pure Spirit from that of Matter. Those who "descend and ascend"— the incarnating Monads, and men striving towards purification and "ascending" but still not having quite reached the goal—may cross the "circle of the Pass-Not" only on the day "Be-With-Us", that day when man, freeing himself from the trammels of ignorance, and recognizing fully the non-separateness of the Ego within his personality—erroneously regarded as his own—from the UNIVERSAL EGO (Anima Supra-Mundi), merges thereby into the One Essence to become not only one "with us" (the manifested universal lives which are "ONE" LIFE), but that very life itself.

Astronomically, the "Ring PASS-NOT" that the Lipika trace around the Triangle, the First One, the Cube, the Second One, and the Pentacle to circumscribe these figures, is thus shown to contain the symbol of 31415 again, or the coefficient constantly used in mathematical tables (the value of π, pi), the geometrical figures standing here for numerical figures.

(*b*) No Spirit except the "Recorders" (Lipika) has ever crossed its forbidden line, nor will any do so until the day of the next Pralaya, for it is the boundary that separates the finite—however infinite in man's sight—from the truly INFINITE. The Spirits referred to, therefore, as those who "ascend and descend" are the "Hosts" of what we loosely call "Celestial Beings." But they are, in fact, nothing of the kind. They are Entities of the higher worlds in the hierarchy of Being, so immeasurably high that, to us, they must appear as Gods, and collectively—GOD.

The "Great Day of BE-WITH-US," then, is an expression the only merit of which lies in its literal translation. Its significance is not so easily revealed to a public unacquainted with the mystic tenets of Occultism, or rather of Esoteric Wisdom or "Budhism." It is an expression peculiar to the latter, and as hazy for the profane as that of the Egyptians who called the same the "Day of COME-TO-US," which is identical with the former, though the verb "be" in this sense, might be still better replaced with either of the two words "Remain" or "Rest-with-us," as it refers to that long period of REST which is called Paranirvana.

STANZA 6

1. By the power of the Mother of Mercy and Knowledge (a), Kwan-Yin,[1] the "Triple" of Kwan-Shai-Yin, residing in Kwan-Yin-Tien (b), Fohat, the breath of their progeny, the Son of the Sons, having called forth from the lower abyss (*chaos*) the illusive form of Sien-Tchan (*our Universe*) and the seven elements:—

(*a*) The Mother of Mercy and Knowledge is called "the triple" of Kwan-Shai-Yin because in her correlations, metaphysical and cosmical, she is the "Mother, the Wife and the Daughter" of the *Logos*, just as in the later theological translations she became "the Father, Son and (the female) Holy Ghost"—the *Sakti* or Energy—the Essence of the three.

(*b*) *Kwan-Yin-Tien* means the "melodious heaven of Sound," the abode of Kwan-Yin, or the "*Divine Voice*," literally. This "Voice" is a synonym of the *Verbum* or the Word: "Speech," as the expression of Thought.

2. The Swift and the Radiant One produces the seven *Laya*[2] (a) centres, against which none will prevail to the great day "Be with us"—and seats the universe on these eternal foundations, surrounding Sien-Tchan with the Elementary Germs (b).

(*a*) The seven *Laya* centres are the seven Zero points, using the term Zero in the same sense that chemists do, to indicate a point at which, in Esotericism, the scale of reckoning of differentiation begins. From the Centres—beyond which Esoteric philosophy allows us to perceive the dim metaphysical outlines of the "Seven Sons" of Life and Light, the Seven Logoi of the Hermetic and all other philosophers—begins the differentiation of the Elements which enter into the constitution of our Solar System. As well said in the

---

[1] This stanza is translated from the Chinese text, and the names, as the equivalents of the original terms, are preserved. No exoteric religious system has ever adopted a female Creator, and thus woman was regarded and treated, from the first dawn of popular religions, as inferior to man. It is only in China and Egypt that Kwan-Yin and Isis were placed on a par with the male gods. Esotericism ignores both sexes. Its highest Deity is sexless as it is formless, neither Father nor Mother; and its first manifested beings, celestial and terrestrial alike, become only gradually androgynous and finally separate into distinct sexes.

[2] From the Sanskrit *Laya*, the point of matter where every differentiation has ceased.

Bhagavadgita Lectures,[3] "The whole Kosmos must necessarily exist in the One Source of energy from which this light (*Fohat*) emanates." Whether we count the principles in Kosmos and man as seven or only as four, the forces of, and in, physical Nature are Seven." For, "just as a human being is composed of seven principles, differentiated matter in the Solar System exists in seven different conditions" (*ibid*). So does Fohat.[4] He is One and Seven, and on the Cosmic plane is behind all such manifestations as light, heat, sound, adhesion, etc., etc., and is the "spirit" of ELECTRICITY, which is the LIFE of the Universe. As an abstraction, we call it the ONE LIFE; as an objective and evident Reality, we speak of a septenary scale of manifestation, which begins at the upper rung with the One Unknowable CAUSALITY, and ends as Omnipresent Mind and Life immanent in every atom of Matter. Thus, while science speaks of its evolution through brute matter, blind force, and senseless motion, the Occultists point to *intelligent* LAW and *sentient* LIFE, and add that Fohat is the guiding Spirit of all this.

(*b*) The "Elementary Germs" with which he fills Sien-Chan (the "Universe") from Tien-Sin (the "Heaven of Mind," literally, or that which is absolute) are the Atoms of Science and the Monads of Leibnitz.

3. OF THE SEVEN (*elements*)—FIRST ONE MANIFESTED, SIX CONCEALED; TWO MANIFESTED—FIVE CONCEALED; THREE MANIFESTED—FOUR CONCEALED; FOUR PRODUCED—THREE HIDDEN; FOUR AND ONE TSAN (*fraction*) REVEALED—TWO AND ONE HALF CONCEALED; SIX TO BE MANIFESTED—ONE LAID ASIDE (*a*). LASTLY, SEVEN SMALL WHEELS REVOLVING; ONE GIVING BIRTH TO THE OTHER (*b*).

(*a*) Although these Stanzas refer to the whole Universe after a Mahapralaya (universal destruction), yet this sentence, as any student of Occultism may see, refers also by analogy to the evolution and final formation of the primitive (though compound) Seven Elements on our Earth. Of these, four elements are now fully manifested, while the fifth—Ether—is only partially so, as we are hardly in the second half of the Fourth Round, and consequently the fifth Element will manifest fully only in the Fifth Round. The Worlds, including our own, were of course, as germs, primarily evolved from the ONE Element in its second stage, whether we call it, with modern Science, Cosmic dust and Fire Mist, or with

---

[3] See *The Theosophist* of February, 1887.

[4] "Fohat" has several meanings. (See Stanza 5, Commentary *et infra*.) He is called the "Builder of the Builders," the Force that he personifies having formed our Septenary Chain.

Occultism—Akasa, Jivatma, divine Astral Light, or the "Soul of the World." But this first stage of Evolution was in due course of time followed by the next. No world, as no heavenly body, could be constructed on the objective plane, had not the Elements been sufficiently differentiated already from their primeval *Ilus*, resting in *Laya*. The latter term is a synonym of Nirvana. It is, in fact, the Nirvanic dissociation of all substances, merged after a life-cycle into the latency of their primary conditions. It is the luminous but bodiless shadow of the matter *that was*, the realm of negativeness—wherein lie latent during their period of rest the active Forces of the Universe.

Now that the conditions and laws ruling our solar system are fully developed; and the atmosphere of our earth, as of every other globe, has become, so to say, a crucible of its own, Occult Science teaches that there is a perpetual exchange taking place in space of molecules, or of atoms rather, correlating, and thus changing their combining equivalents on every planet. Some men of Science, and those among the greatest physicists and chemists, begin to suspect this fact, which has been known for ages to the Occultists. The spectroscope only shows the probable similarity (on external evidence) of terrestrial and sidereal substance; it is unable to go any farther, or to show whether atoms gravitate towards one another in the same way and under the same conditions as they are supposed to do on our planet, physically and chemically. The scale of temperature, from the highest degree to the lowest that can be conceived of, may be imagined to be one and the same in and for the whole Universe; nevertheless, its properties, other than those of dissociation and re-association, differ on every planet; and thus atoms enter into new forms of existence, undreamt of, and incognizable to, physical Science. As already expressed in *Five Years of Theosophy*,[5] the essence of Cometary matter, for instance, "is totally different from any of the chemical or physical characteristics with which the greatest chemists and physicists of the earth are acquainted" (p. 242). And even that matter, during rapid passage through our atmosphere, undergoes a certain change in its nature. Thus not alone the elements of our planets, but even those of all its sisters in the Solar System, differ as widely from each other in their combinations, as from the Cosmic elements beyond our Solar limits. Therefore, they cannot be taken as a standard for comparison with the same in other worlds.[6] En-

---

[5] [1885 edition.]

[6] "Each world has its Fohat, who is omnipresent in his own sphere of action. But there are as many Fohats as there are worlds, each varying in power and degree of manifestations. The individual Fohats make one Universal, Collective

shrined in their virgin, pristine state within the bosom of the Eternal Mother, every atom born beyond the threshold of her realm is doomed to incessant differentiation. "The Mother sleeps, yet is ever breathing." And every breath sends out into the plane of manifestation her Protean products, which, carried on by the wave of the efflux, are scattered by Fohat, and driven toward and beyond this or another planetary atmosphere. Once caught by the latter, the atom is lost; its pristine purity is gone for ever, unless Fate dissociates it by leading it to "a current of EFFLUX" (an occult term meaning quite a different process from that which the ordinary term implies); when it may be carried once more to the borderland where it had perished, and taking its flight, not into Space *above* but into Space *within*, it will be brought under a state of differential equilibrium and happily re-absorbed. Were a truly learned Occultist-Alchemist to write the "Life and Adventures of an Atom" he would secure thereby the eternal scorn of the modern chemist, perchance also his subsequent gratitude.[7] However it may be, "*The Breath of the Father-Mother issues cold and radiant and gets hot and corrupt, to cool once more, and be purified in the eternal bosom of inner Space,*" says the Commentary. Man absorbs cold pure air on the mountain-top, and throws it out impure, hot and transformed. Thus—the higher atmosphere being the mouth, and the lower one the lungs of every globe—the man of our planet breathes only the refuse of "Mother"; therefore, "he is doomed to die on it."[8]

(*b*) The process referred to as "the Small Wheels giving birth, one to the other," takes place in the sixth region from above, and on the plane of the most material world of all in the manifested Kosmos—our terrestrial plane. These "Seven Wheels" are our Planetary Chain. By "Wheels" the various spheres and centres of forces are generally meant; but in this case they refer to our septenary ring.

4. HE BUILDS THEM IN THE LIKENESS OF OLDER WHEELS (*worlds*), PLACING THEM ON THE IMPERISHABLE CENTRES (*a*). HOW DOES FOHAT

Fohat—the aspect-Entity of the one absolute Non-Entity, which is absolute Be-Ness, 'SAT.' Millions and billions of worlds are produced at every Manvantara"—it is said. Therefore there must be many Fohats, whom we consider as conscious and *intelligent* Forces. The Occultists, who have good reasons for it, consider all the forces of Nature as veritable, though supersensuous, states of Matter; and as possible objects of perception to Beings endowed with the requisite senses.

[7] Indeed, if such an imaginary chemist happened to be intuitional, and would for a moment step out of the habitual groove of strictly "Exact Science," as the Alchemists of old did, he might be repaid for his audacity.

[8] He who would allotropize sluggish oxygen into *Ozone* to a measure of alchemical activity, reducing it to its pure essence (for which there are means), would discover thereby a substitute for an "Elixir of Life" and prepare it for practical use.

BUILD THEM? HE COLLECTS THE FIERY DUST. HE MAKES BALLS OF FIRE, RUNS THROUGH THEM AND ROUND THEM, INFUSING LIFE THEREINTO; THEN SETS THEM INTO MOTION, SOME ONE, SOME THE OTHER WAY. THEY ARE COLD—HE MAKES THEM HOT. THEY ARE DRY—HE MAKES THEM MOIST. THEY SHINE—HE FANS AND COOLS THEM (b). THUS ACTS FOHAT FROM ONE *Twilight* TO THE OTHER DURING SEVEN ETERNITIES.[9]

(a) The Worlds are built "in the likeness of older Wheels"—*i.e.,* those that existed in preceding Manvantaras and went into Pralaya, because the LAW for the birth, growth, and decay of everything in Kosmos, from the Sun to the glow-worm in the grass, is ONE. It is an everlasting work of perfection with every new appearance, but the Substance-Matter and Forces are all one and the same. But this LAW acts on every planet through minor and varying laws. The "Imperishable Laya Centres" have a great importance, and their meaning must be fully understood. The worlds are built neither *upon,* nor *over,* nor *in* the *Laya* centres, the zero-point being a condition, not any mathematical point.

(b) Bear in mind that Fohat, the constructive Force of Cosmic Electricity, is said, metaphorically, to have sprung "from the brain of the Father and the bosom of the Mother," and then to have metamorphosed himself into a male and a female, *i.e.,* polarity, into positive and negative electricity. He has *seven sons* who are *his brothers;* and Fohat is forced to be born time after time whenever any two of his son-brothers indulge *in too close contact*—whether an embrace or a fight. To avoid this, he binds together and unites those of unlike nature and separates those of similar temperaments. This, of course, relates, as any one can see, to electricity generated by friction and to the law involving attraction between two objects of unlike, and repulsion between those of like polarity. The Seven "Sons-brothers," however, represent and personify the seven forms of Cosmic magnetism called in practical Occultism the "Seven Radicals," whose co-operative and active progeny are, among other energies, Electricity, Magnetism, Sound, Light, Heat, Cohesion, etc. Occult Science defines all these as Super-sensuous effects in their hidden behaviour, and as objective phenomena in the world of senses; the former requiring abnormal faculties to perceive them— the latter, our ordinary physical senses. They all pertain to, and are the emanations of, still more supersensuous spiritual qualities, not personated by, but belonging to, real and conscious CAUSES. To attempt a description of such ENTITIES would be worse than useless.

[9] A period of 311,040,000,000,000 years, according to Brahminical calculations.

The reader must bear in mind that, according to our teaching which regards this phenomenal Universe as a great *Illusion*, the nearer a body is to the UNKNOWN SUBSTANCE, the more it approaches *Reality*, as being removed the farther from this world of *Maya*. Therefore, though the molecular constitution of their bodies is not deducible from their manifestations on this plane of consciousness, they nevertheless (from the standpoint of the adept Occultist) possess a distinctive objective if not material structure, in the relatively noumenal—as opposed to the phenomenal—Universe. Men of science may term them Force or Forces generated by matter, or "modes of its motion," if they will; Occultism sees in the effects "Elemental" (forces), and, in the direct causes producing them, intelligent DIVINE Workmen. The intimate connection of those Elementals (guided by the unerring hand of the Rulers)—their correlation we might call it—with the elements of pure Matter, results in our terrestrial phenomena, such as light, heat, magnetism, etc., etc. Of course we shall never agree to call every Force and Energy—whe'her Light, Heat, Electricity or Cohesion—an "Entity"; for this would be equivalent to calling the noise produced by the rolling of the wheels of a vehicle an *Entity*—thus confusing and identifying that "noise" with the driver *outside*, and the guiding Master Intelligence *within* the vehicle. But we certainly give that name to the "drivers" and to these guiding Intelligences—the ruling Dhyan Chohans, as shown. The "Elementals," the Nature-Forces, are the acting, though invisible, or rather imperceptible, secondary Causes and in themselves the effects of primary Causes behind the Veil of all terrestrial phenomena. Electricity, light, heat, etc., have been aptly termed the "Ghost or Shadow of Matter in Motion," *i.e.*, supersensuous states of matter whose effects only we are able to cognize. To expand, then, the simile given above. The sensation of light is like the sound of the rolling wheels—a purely phenomenal effect, having no existence outside the observer; the proximate exciting cause of the sensation is comparable to the driver—a supersensuous state of matter in motion, a Nature-Force or Elemental. But, behind even this, stand—just as the owner of the carriage directs the driver from within—the higher and *noumenal* causes, the *Intelligences* from whose essence radiate these States of "*Mother*," generating the countless milliards of Elementals or psychic Nature-Spirits, just as every drop of water generates its physical infinitesimal infusoria. (See "Gods, Monads, and Atoms," in Part III.) It is Fohat who guides the transfer of the principles from one planet to the other, from one star to another—child-star. When a planet dies, its informing principles are transferred to a *laya* or sleeping centre, with potential but latent energy in it, which is thus awakened into life and begins to form itself into a new sidereal body. (*Vide infra*, "A Few Theosophical Misconceptions, etc.")

The Occultists, who do not say—if they would express themselves correctly—that *matter*, but only the *substance* or *essence* of matter, is indestructible and eternal, (*i.e.*, the Root of all, *Mulaprakriti*) assert that all the so-called Forces of Nature, Electricity, Magnetism, Light, Heat, etc., far from being modes of motion of material particles, are *in esse, i.e.*, in their ultimate constitution, the differentiated aspects of that Universal Motion which is discussed and explained in the first pages of this volume (*See Proem*). When Fohat is said to produce "Seven Laya Centres," it means that for formative or creative purposes the GREAT LAW (Theists may call it God) stops, or rather modifies its perpetual motion on seven invisible points within the area of the manifested Universe. "*The great Breath digs through Space seven holes into Laya to cause them to circumgyrate during Manvantara*" (*Occult Catechism*). We have said that Laya is what Science may call the zero-point or line; the realm of absolute negativeness, or the one real absolute Force, the NOUMENON of the Seventh State of that which we ignorantly call and recognize as "Force"; or again the Noumenon of Undifferentiated Cosmic Substance which is itself an unreachable and unknowable object to finite perception; the root and basis of all states of objectivity and subjectivity too; the neutral axis, not one of the many aspects, but its centre. It may serve to elucidate the meaning if we attempt to imagine a neutral centre—the dream of those who would discover perpetual motion. A "neutral centre" is, in one aspect, the limiting point of any given set of senses. Thus, imagine two consecutive planes of matter as already formed; each of these corresponding to an appropriate set of perceptive organs. We are forced to admit that between these two planes of matter an incessant circulation takes place; and if we follow the atoms and molecules of (say) the lower in their transformation upwards, these will come to a point where they pass altogether beyond the range of the faculties we are using on the lower plane. In fact, to us the matter of the lower plane there vanishes from our perception into nothing—or rather it passes on to the higher plane, and the state of matter corresponding to such a point of transition must certainly possess special and not readily discoverable properties. Such "Seven Neutral Centres," then, are produced by Fohat who, when, as Milton has it—

"Fair foundations (are) laid whereon to build . . . "

quickens matter into activity and evolution.

With these verses—the 4th Sloka of Stanza 6—ends that portion of the Stanzas which relates to the Universal Cosmogony after the last Mahapralaya or Universal destruction, which, when it comes, sweeps out of Space every differentiated thing, Gods as atoms, like so many dry leaves. From this verse onwards, the Stanzas are concerned only with our Solar System in general, with the Planetary Chains therein, inferentially, and with the history of our Globe (the 4th and its Chain) especially. All the Stanzas and verses which follow in this Book I. refer only to the evolution of, and on, our Earth.

Let us then make a short break between the Slokas just explained and those which follow, for the Cosmic periods which separate them are of immense duration. This will afford us ample time to take a bird's eye view of some points pertaining to the Secret Doctrine, which have been presented to the public under a more or less uncertain and sometimes mistaken light.

A FEW EARLY THEOSOPHICAL MISCONCEPTIONS CONCERNING PLANETS, ROUNDS, AND MAN

Among the eleven Stanzas omitted there is one which gives a full description of the formation of the planetary chains one after another, after the first Cosmic and Atomic differentiation had commenced in the primitive *Acosmism*. It is idle to speak of "laws arising when Deity prepares to create" for (a) laws or rather LAW is eternal and uncreated; and (b) that Deity is Law, and *vice versa*. Moreover, the one eternal LAW unfolds everything in the (to be) manifested Nature on a sevenfold principle; among the rest, the countless circular Chains of Worlds, composed of seven Globes, graduated on the four lower planes of the World of Formation (the three others belonging to the Archetypal Universe). Out of these seven only one, *the lowest and the most material of those Globes*, is within our plane or means of perception, the six others lying outside of it and being therefore invisible to the terrestrial eye. Every such Chain of Worlds is the progeny and creation of another, *lower*, and *dead* chain—its *reincarnation*, so to say. To make it clearer: we are told of the planets—of which *seven only* were held as sacred, as being ruled by the highest Regents or Gods, and not because the ancients knew nothing of the others[1]—that each, whether known or unknown, is a septenary, as is the chain to which the Earth belongs (see *Esoteric Buddhism*). For instance, all such planets as Mercury, Venus, Mars, Jupiter, Saturn,

[1] Many more planets are enumerated in the Secret Books than in modern astronomical works.

etc., or our Earth, are as visible to us as our Globe, probably, is to the inhabitants of the other planets, if any, because they are all on the same plane; while the superior fellow-globes of these planets are on other planes quite outside that of our terrestrial senses. As their relative position is given further on, and also in the diagram appended to the Comments on Verse 6 of Stanza 6., a few words of explanation is all that is needed at present. These invisible companions correspond curiously to that which we call "the Principles in Man." The seven are on three material planes and one spiritual plane, answering to the three *Upadhis* (material bases) and one spiritual vehicle (*Vahan*) of our seven Principles in the human division. If, for the sake of a clearer mental conception, we imagine the human Principles to be arranged as in the following scheme, we shall obtain the annexed diagram of correspondences:—

HUMAN PRINCIPLES.   PLANETARY DIVISION.

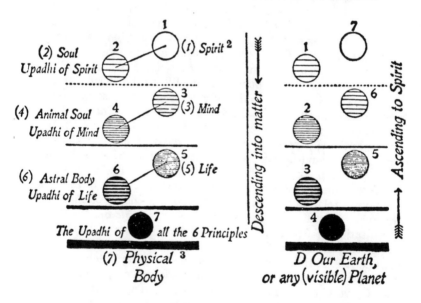

DIAGRAM I.

[2] As we are proceeding here from Universals to Particulars, instead of using the inductive or Aristotelean method, the numbers are reversed. Spirit is enumerated the first instead of seventh, as is usually done, but, in truth, *ought not to be done.*

[3] Or as usually named after the manner of *Esoteric Buddhism* and other Works: 1, Atma; 2, Buddhi (or Spiritual Soul); 3, Manas (Human Soul); 4, Kama Rupa (Vehicle of Desires and Passions); 5, Linga Sarira; 6, Prana; 7, Sthula Sarira.

The dark horizontal lines of the lower planes are the Upadhis in one case, and the planes in the case of the Planetary Chain. Of course, as regards the human Principles, the diagram does not place them quite in order, yet it shows the correspondence and analogy to which attention is now drawn. As the reader will see, it is a case of descent into matter, the adjustment—in both the mystic and the physical senses—of the two, and their interblending for the great coming "struggle of life" that awaits both the *Entities*. "Entity" may be thought a strange term to use in the case of a globe; but the ancient philosophers, who saw in the Earth a huge "animal," were wiser in their generation than our modern geologists are in theirs. It is said that the planetary chains, having their "Days" and their "Nights"—*i.e.*, periods of activity or life, and of inertia or death— behave in heaven as do men on earth: they generate their likes, get old, and become personally extinct, their spiritual principles only living in their progeny as a survival of themselves.

Without attempting the very difficult task of giving out the whole process in all its cosmic details, enough may be said to give an approximate idea of it. When a Planetary Chain is in its last Round, its Globe A, before finally *dying out*, sends all its energy and "prin-ciples" into a neutral centre of latent force, a "laya centre," and thereby informs a new nucleus of undifferentiated substance or matter, *i.e.*, calls it into activity or gives it life. Suppose such a pro-cess to have taken place in the Lunar "Planetary" Chain; suppose again, for argument's sake (though Mr. Darwin's theory quoted below has lately been upset, even if the fact has not yet been ascertained by mathematical calculation) that the Moon is far older than the Earth. Imagine the six fellow-globes of the Moon—aeons before the first globe of our seven was evolved—just in the same position in relation to each other as the fellow-globes of our Chain occupy in regard to our Earth now. (See in *Esoteric Buddhism* "The Constitution of Man," and the "Planetary Chain.") And now it will be easy to imagine further Globe A of the Lunar Chain inform-ing Globe A of the Terrestrial Chain, and—dying; Globe B of the former sending after that its energy into Globe B of the new Chain; then Globe C of the Lunar, creating its progeny sphere C of the Terrene Chain; then the Moon (our satellite[4]) pouring forth into

[4] She is the satellite, undeniably, but this does not invalidate the theory that she has given to the Earth all but her corpse. And if our Moon is but a splash from our Earth, why can no similar inference be established for the Moons of other planets? The astronomers "do not know." Why should Venus and Mercury have no satellites, and by what, when they exist, were they formed? Because, we say, Science has only one key—the key of matter—to open the mysteries of Nature withal, while Occult Philosophy has seven keys and explains that which Science

the lowest globe of our planetary ring—Globe D, our Earth—all its life, energy and powers; and, having transferred them to a new centre becoming virtually *a dead planet*, in which rotation has almost ceased since the birth of our globe.

The doctrine of the septenary Chains of Worlds in the Solar Kosmos is briefly thus:—

1. Everything in the metaphysical as in the physical Universe is septenary. Hence every sidereal body, every planet, whether visible or invisible, is credited with six companion Globes. The evolution of life proceeds on these seven Globes or bodies from the 1st to the 7th in Seven ROUNDS or Seven Cycles.

2. These Globes are formed by a process which the Occultists call the "rebirth of Planetary Chains (or Rings)." When the seventh and last Round of one of such Rings has been entered upon, the highest or first globe "A," followed by all the others down to the last, instead of entering upon a certain time of rest—or "obscuration," as in their previous Rounds—begins to die out. The "planetary" dissolution (Pralaya) is at hand, and its hour has struck; each Globe has to transfer its life and energy to another planet. (See Diagram 2, p. 80).

3. Our Earth, as the visible representative of its invisible superior fellow globes, its "Lords" or "Principles" (see Diagram 1, p. 71), has to live, as have the others, through seven Rounds. During the first three it forms and consolidates; during the fourth it settles and hardens; during the last three it gradually returns to its first ethereal form; it is spiritualized, so to say.

4. Its Humanity develops fully only in the Fourth—our present Round. Up to this Fourth Life-Cycle it is referred to as "Humanity" only for lack of a more appropriate term. Like the grub which becomes chrysalis and butterfly, Man, or rather that which becomes man, passes through all the forms and kingdoms during the First Round and through all the human shapes during the two following Rounds. Arrived on our Earth at the commencement of the Fourth in the present series of Life-Cycles and Races, MAN is the first form that appears thereon, being preceded only by the mineral and vegetable kingdoms—even the latter *having to develop and continue its further evolution through man.* During the three Rounds to come, Humanity, like the Globe on which it lives, will be ever tending to reassume its primeval form, that of a Dhyan Chohanic Host. Man

fails to see. Mercury and Venus have no satellites but they had "parents" just as the Earth had. Both are far older than the Earth and, before the latter reaches her seventh Round, her mother Moon will have dissolved into thin air, as the "Moons" of the other planets have, or have not, as the case may be, since there are planets which have *several* Moons.

tends to become *a* God and then—GOD, like every other atom in the Universe.

"Beginning so early as with the 2nd round, Evolution proceeds already on quite a different plan. It is only during the 1st Round that (heavenly) Man becomes a human being on Globe A, (rebecomes) a mineral, a plant, an animal, on globes B and C, etc. The process changes entirely from the second round . . . " (Extract from the Teacher's letters on various topics.)[5]

5. Every Life-Cycle on Globe D (our Earth)[6] is composed of seven Root-Races. They commence with the ethereal and end with the spiritual, on the double line of physical and moral evolution—from the beginning of the terrestrial Round to its close. (One is a "Planetary Round" from Globe A to Globe G, the seventh; the other, the "Globe Round," or the *terrestrial*.)

This is very well described in *Esoteric Buddhism* and needs no further elucidation for the time being.

6. The First Root-Race, *i.e.*, the first "men" on earth (irrespective of form) were the progeny of the "celestial men," called rightly in Indian philosophy the "Lunar Ancestors" or the Pitris, of which there are seven classes or Hierarchies.

From the doctrine which deals with the periodical "obscurations" and successive "Rounds" of the Globes along their circular chains, were born the first perplexities and misconceptions. One of such has reference to the *"Fifth-"* and even *"Sixth-*Rounders." Gautama Buddha, it was held, was a Sixth-Rounder, Plato and some other great philosophers and minds, "Fifth-Rounders." How could it be? One Master taught and affirmed that there were such "Fifth-Rounders" even now on Earth; and though *understood to say* that mankind was yet "in the Fourth Round," in another place he *seemed* to say that we were in the Fifth. To this an "apocalyptic answer" was returned by another Teacher:—"A few drops of rain do not make a monsoon, though they presage it." . . . "No, we are not in the Fifth Round, but Fifth Round men have been coming in for the last few thousand years."

Every "Round" brings about a new development and even an entire change in the mental, psychic, spiritual and physical constitution of man, all these principles evoluting on an ever ascending scale. Thence it follows that those persons who, like Confucius and Plato, belonged psychically, mentally and spiritually to the higher planes of evolution, were in our Fourth Round as the average man will be in the Fifth Round, whose mankind is destined to find itself, on this

---

[5] [See *The Mahatma Letters to A. P. Sinnett*. This is a paraphrase from Letter 23B.]
[6] We are not concerned with the other Globes in this work except incidentally.

scale of Evolution, immensely higher than is our present humanity. Similarly Gautama Buddha—Wisdom incarnate—was still higher and greater than all the men we have mentioned, who are called Fifth Rounders, while Buddha and Sankaracharya are termed Sixth Rounders, allegorically.

And now the truth of the remark made in *Esoteric Buddhism* by its author will be fully apparent:—

"It is impossible, *when the complicated facts of an entirely unfamiliar science are being presented to untrained minds for the first time*, to put them forward with all their appropriate qualifications . . . and abnormal developments. . . . We must be content to take the broad rules first and deal with the exceptions afterwards, and especially is this the case with occult study, in connection with which *the traditional methods of teaching, generally followed, aim at impressing every fresh idea on the memory by provoking the perplexity it at last relieves.*"

Gratuitous speculations were sometimes indulged in by European lay-chelas. Among such was the erroneous statement that two of the superior Globes of the terrestrial Chain were two of our well-known planets: "besides the Earth . . . there are *only two other worlds of our chain which are visible.* . . . Mars and Mercury. . . . " (*Esoteric Buddhism,*[7] p.136.)

This was a great mistake. But the blame for it is to be attached as much to the vagueness and incompleteness of the Master's answer as to the question of the learner itself, which was equally vague and indefinite.

It was asked: "What planets, of those known to ordinary science, besides Mercury, belong to our system worlds?" Now if by "systems of worlds" our *terrestrial Chain* or "string" was intended in the mind of the querist, instead of the "Solar System of Worlds," as it should have been, then of course the answer was likely to be misunderstood. For the reply was: "Mars and four other planets of which astronomy knows nothing. Neither A, B, nor Y, Z are known nor can they be seen through physical means however

---

[7] With the exception of course of all the planets which come *fourth* in number, as our earth, the moon, etc., etc. Copies of all the letters ever received or sent, with the exception of a few private ones—"*in which there was no teaching*" the Master says— are with the writer. As it was her duty, in the beginning, to answer and explain certain points not touched upon, it is more than likely that notwithstanding the many annotations on these copies, the writer, in her ignorance of English and her fear of saying too much, may have bungled the information given. *She takes the whole blame for it upon herself in any and every case.* But it is impossible for her to allow students to remain any longer under erroneous impressions, or to believe that the fault lies with the Esoteric system. [The*Mahatma Letters to A. P. Sinnett.* Letter 23B.]

perfected."[8] This is plain: (a) Astronomy as yet knows nothing in reality of the planets, neither the ancient ones, nor those discovered in modern times. (b) No *companion* planets from A to Z, *i.e.*, no upper globes of any chain in the Solar System, can be seen. As to Mars, Mercury, and "the four other planets," they bear a relation to Earth of which no master or high Occultist will ever speak, much less explain the nature.

Let it now be distinctly stated, then, that the theory broached is impossible, with or without the additional evidence furnished by modern astronomy. Physical Science can supply corroborative, though still very uncertain, evidence, but only as regards heavenly bodies on the same plane of materiality as our objective Universe. Mars and Mercury, Venus and Jupiter, like every hitherto discovered planet (or those still to be discovered), are all, *per se*, the representatives on our plane of such Chains. As distinctly stated in one of the numerous letters of Mr. Sinnett's Teacher, "there are other and innumerable manvantaric chains of globes which bear intelligent beings both in and outside our solar system." But neither Mars nor Mercury belong *to our Chain*. They are, along with the other planets, septenary *Units* in the great host of "Chains" of our system, and all are as visible as their *upper* Globes are invisible.

When the present work was commenced, the writer, feeling sure that the speculation about Mars and Mercury was a mistake, applied to the Teachers *by letter* for an explanation and authoritative version. Both came in due time, and *verbatim* extracts from these are now given.

" . . . *It is quite correct that Mars is in a state of obscuration at present, and Mercury just beginning to get out of it. You might add that Venus is in her last Round. . . . If neither Mercury nor Venus have satellites, it is because of the reasons* . . . (vide footnote supra, where those reasons are given), *and also because Mars has two satellites to which he has no right. . . . Phöbos, the supposed* INNER *satellite, is no satellite at all. . . . Again, both (Mars and Mercury) are septenary chains, as independent of the Earth's sidereal lords and superiors as you are independent of the 'principles' of Daumling (Tom Thumb)—which were perhaps his six brothers, with or without night-caps. . . . 'Gratification of curiosity is the end of knowledge for some men,' was said by Bacon, who was as right in postulating this truism, as those who were familiar with it before him were right in hedging off* WISDOM *from*

---

[8] In this same letter the impossibility is distinctly stated:— . . . "Try to understand that you are putting me questions pertaining to the highest initiation; that I can give you (only) a general view, but *that I dare not nor will I enter upon details.* . . ." wrote one of the Teachers to the author of *Esoteric Buddhism*. [*The Mahatma Letters to A. P. Sinnett*, Letter 23B.]

*Knowledge, and tracing limits to that which is to be given out at one time. . . .
Remember:—*

> *' . . . knowledge dwells
> In heads replete with thoughts of other men,
> Wisdom in minds attentive to their own. . . .'*

*You can never impress it too profoundly on the minds of those to whom you
impart some of the esoteric teachings. . . . "*

Again, here are more extracts from another letter written by the
same authority. This time it is in answer to some objections laid
before the Teachers.

"*Our Globe, as taught from the first, is at the bottom of the arc of descent,
where the matter of our perceptions exhibits itself in its grossest form. . . .
Hence it only stands to reason that the Globes which overshadow our Earth
must be on different and superior planes. In short, as Globes, they are in
CO-ADUNITION but not IN CONSUBSTANTIALITY WITH OUR EARTH and thus
pertain to quite another state of consciousness. Our planet (like all those we see)
is adapted to the peculiar state of its human stock, that state which enables us
to see with our naked eye the sidereal bodies which are co-essential with our
terrene plane and substance, just as their respective inhabitants, the Jovians,
Martians and others can perceive our little world: because our planes of
consciousness, differing as they do in degree but being the same in kind, are on
the same layer of differential matter. . . . What I wrote was 'The minor
Pralaya concerns only our little STRINGS OF GLOBES.' (We called Chains
'Strings' in those days of lip-confusion.) . . . 'To such a String our Earth
belongs.' This ought to have shown plainly that the other planets were also
'Strings' or CHAINS. . . . If he (meaning the objector) would perceive even
the dim silhouette of one of such 'planets' on the higher planes, he has to first
throw off even the thin clouds of the astral matter that stands between him and
the next plane. . . . "*

It becomes patent why we could not perceive, even with the help
of the best earthly telescopes, that which is outside our world of
matter. Those alone, whom we call Adepts, who know how to direct
their mental vision and to transfer their consciousness—physical and
psychic both—to other planes of being, are able to speak with
authority on such subjects. And they tell us plainly:—

"*Lead the life necessary for the acquisition of such knowledge and powers,
and Wisdom will come to you naturally. Whenever you are able to attune your
consciousness to any of the seven chords of 'Universal Consciousness,' those
chords that run along the sounding-board of Kosmos, vibrating from one
Eternity to another; when you have studied thoroughly 'the music of the
Spheres,' then only will you become quite free to share your knowledge with*

those with whom it is safe to do so. Meanwhile, be prudent. Do not give out the great Truths that are the inheritance of the future Races, to our present generation. Do not attempt to unveil the secret of Being and Non-Being to those unable to see the hidden meaning of Apollo's HEPTACHORD—*the lyre of the radiant god, in each of the seven strings of which dwelleth the Spirit, Soul and Astral body of the Kosmos, whose shell only has now fallen into the hands of modern Science. . . . Be prudent, we say, prudent and wise, and above all take care what those who learn from you believe in; lest by deceiving themselves they deceive others . . . for such is the fate of every truth with which men are, as yet, unfamiliar. . . . Let rather the Planetary Chains and other super- and sub-cosmic mysteries remain a dreamland for those who can neither see, nor yet believe that others can. . . . "*

" '*Let us imagine,*' wrote the same Master to his two 'lay chelas,' as he called the author of *Esoteric Buddhism* and another gentleman, his co-student for some time—'*let us imagine* THAT OUR EARTH IS ONE OF A GROUP OF SEVEN PLANETS OR MAN-BEARING WORLDS. . . . (*The* SEVEN *planets are the sacred planets of antiquity, and are all septenary.*) Now the life-impulse reaches A, or rather that which is destined to become A, and which so far is but cosmic dust* (a "laya centre") *. . . etc.*' "[9]

In these early letters, in which the terms had to be invented and words coined, the "Rings" very often became "Rounds," and the "Rounds" Life-Cycles, and *vice versa*. To a correspondent who called a "Round" a "World-Ring," the Teacher wrote: "I believe this will lead to a further confusion. A Round we are agreed to call the passage of a monad from Globe A to Globe G or Z. . . . The 'World-Ring' is correct. . . . Advise Mr. Sinnett strongly, to agree upon a nomenclature before going any further. . . ."[10]

Notwithstanding this agreement, many mistakes, owing to this confusion, crept into the earliest teachings. The Races even were occasionally mixed up with the "Rounds" and "Rings," and led to similar mistakes in *Man: Fragments of Forgotten Truth*. From the first the Master had written:—

"Not being permitted to give you *the whole truth*, or divulge the number of isolated fractions . . . I am unable to satisfy you."[11]

This in answer to the questions, "If we are right, then the total existence prior to the man-period is 637," etc. To all the queries relating to figures, the reply was, "Try to solve the problem of 777 incarnations. . . . *Though I am obliged to withhold information . . . yet if you should work out the problem by yourself, it will be my duty to tell you so.*"[12]

[9] [*The Mahatma Letters to A. P. Sinnett.* Letter 15.]
[10] [Ibid., Letter 14.]   [11] [Ibid.]   [12] [Ibid.]

ADDITIONAL FACTS AND EXPLANATIONS CONCERNING THE GLOBES AND THE MONADS

Two statements made in *Esoteric Buddhism* must be noticed and the author's opinions quoted. On p. 47 (fifth edition) it is said:—

"...The spiritual Monads...do not fully complete their mineral existence on Globe A, then complete it on Globe B, and so on. They pass several times round the whole circle as minerals, and then again several times round as vegetables, and several times as animals. We purposely refrain for the present from going into figures," etc., etc.

In reference to the Monads, the reader is asked to bear in mind that Eastern philsophy rejects the Western theological dogma of a newly-created soul for every baby born, as being as unphilosophical as it is impossible in the economy of Nature. There must be a limited number of Monads evolving and growing more and more perfect through their assimilation of many successive personalities, in every new Manvantara. This is absolutely necessary in view of the doctrines of Rebirth, Karma, and the gradual return of the human Monad to its source—*absolute* Deity. Thus, although the hosts of more or less progressed Monads are almost incalculable, they are still finite, as is everything in this Universe of differentiation and finiteness.

As shown in the double diagram of the human Principles and the ascending Globes of the world-chains,[1] there is an eternal concatenation of causes and effects, and a perfect analogy which runs through, and links together, all the lines of evolution. One begets the other— Globes as personalities. But, let us begin at the beginning.

The general outline of the process by which the successive Planetary Chains are formed has just been given. To prevent future misconceptions, some further details may be offered which will also throw light on the history of humanity on our own Chain, the progeny of that of the Moon.

In the diagrams on p. 80, Fig. 1 represents the Lunar Chain of seven planets[2] at the outset of its seventh or last Round; while Fig. 2 represents the "Earth Chain" which will be, but is not yet in existence. The seven Globes of each Chain are distinguished in their cyclic order by the letters A to G, the Globes of the Earth Chain being further marked by a cross ✚ , the symbol of the Earth.

Now, it must be remembered that the Monads cycling round any septenary Chain are divided into seven classes or Hierarchies

[1] p. 71.   [2] [? Globes.]

according to their respective stages of evolution, consciousness, and merit. Let us follow, then, the order of their appearance on planet A, in the first Round. The time-spaces between the appearances of these Hierarchies on any one Globe are so adjusted that when Class 7, the last, appears on Globe A, Class 1, the first, has just passed on to Globe B, and so on, step by step, all round the Chain.

Again, in the Seventh Round on the Lunar chain, when Class 7, the last, quits Globe A, that Globe, instead of falling asleep, as it had done in previous Rounds, begins to die (to go into its Planetary Pralaya)[3] and in dying it transfers successively, as just said, its "principles," or life-elements and energy, etc., one after the other to a new "laya-centre," which commences the formation of Globe A of the Earth Chain. A similar process takes place for each of the Globes of the Lunar Chain, one after the other, each forming a fresh Globe of the Earth Chain. Our Moon was the fourth Globe of the

EARTH CHAIN.   LUNAR CHAIN.

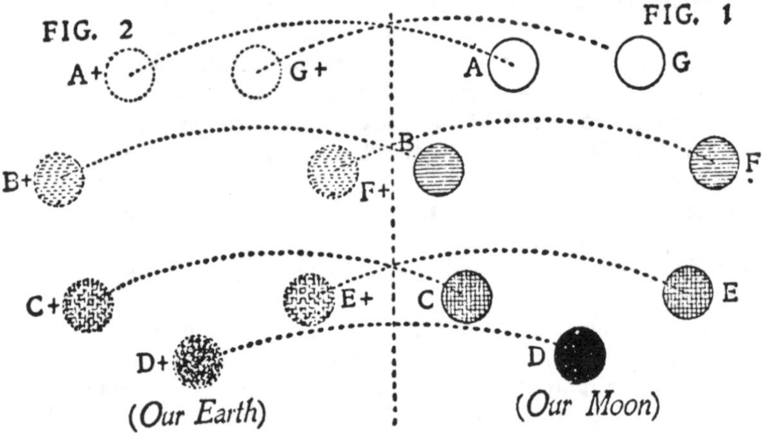

DIAGRAM II.

series, and was on the same plane of perception as our Earth. But Globe A of the Lunar Chain is not fully "dead" till the first Monads

[3] Occultism divides the periods of Rest (Pralaya) into several kinds; there is the *individual* Pralaya of each Globe, as humanity and life pass on to the next; seven minor Pralayas in each Round; the *planetary* Pralaya, when seven *Rounds* are completed; the *Solar* Pralaya, when the whole system is at an end; and finally the Universal Maha—or Brahmā—Pralaya at the close of the Age of Brahmā. These are the three chief *Pralayas* or "destruction periods." There are many other minor ones, but with these we are not concerned at present.

of the first Class have passed from Globe G or Z, the last of the Lunar Chain, into the Nirvana which awaits them between the two chains; and similarly for all the other Globes as stated, each giving birth to the corresponding Globe of the Earth Chain.

Further, when Globe A of the new Chain is ready, the first class or Hierarchy of Monads from the Lunar Chain incarnate upon it in the lowest kingdom, and so on successively. The result of this is, that it is only the first class of Monads which attains the human state of development during the first Round, since the second Class, on each planet, arriving later, has not time to reach that stage. Thus the Monads of Class 2 reach the incipient human stage only in the Second Round, and so on up to the middle of the Fourth Round. But at this point—and on this Fourth Round in which the human stage will be *fully* developed—the "Door" into the human kingdom closes; and henceforward the number of "human" Monads, *i.e.*, Monads in the human stage of development, is complete. For the Monads which had not reached the human stage by this point will, owing to the evolution of humanity itself, find themselves so far behind that they will reach the human stage only at the close of the Seventh and last Round. They will, therefore, not be men on this chain, but will form the humanity of a future Manvantara and be rewarded by becoming "Men" on a higher chain altogether, thus receiving their Karmic compensation. To this there is *but one solitary exception*, for very good reasons, of which we shall speak farther on. But this accounts for the difference in the Races.

It thus becomes apparent how perfect is the analogy between the processes of Nature in the Kosmos and in the individual man. The latter lives through his life-cycle, and dies. His "higher principles," corresponding in the development of a Planetary Chain to the cycling Monads, pass into Devachan, which corresponds to the Nirvana and states of rest intervening between two chains. The man's lower "principles" are disintegrated in time and are used by Nature again for the formation of new human principles, and the same process takes place in the disintegration and formation of Worlds. Analogy is thus the surest guide to the comprehension of the Occult teachings.

The Monadic Host may be roughly divided into three great classes:—

1. The most developed Monads (the Lunar Gods or "Spirits," called, in India, the Pitris), whose function it is to pass in the first Round through the whole triple cycle of the mineral, vegetable, and animal kingdoms in their most ethereal, filmy, and rudimentary forms, in order to clothe themselves in, and assimilate, the nature of

the newly formed Chain. They are those who first reach the human form (if there can be any form in the realm of the almost subjective) on Globe A in the first Round. It is they, therefore, who lead and represent the human element during the Second and Third Rounds, and finally evolve their shadows at the beginning of the Fourth Round for the second Class, or those who come behind them.

2. Those Monads that are the first to reach the human stage during the three and a half Rounds, and to become "men."[4]

3. The laggards; the Monads which are retarded, and which will not reach, by reason of Karmic impediments, the human stage at all during this cycle or Round, save one exception which will be spoken of elsewhere as already promised.

Now the evolution of the *external* form or body round the *astral* is produced by the terrestrial forces, just as in the case of the lower kingdoms; but the evolution of the internal or real MAN is purely spiritual. It is now no more a passage of the impersonal Monad through many and various forms of matter—endowed at best with instinct and consciousness on quite a different plane—as in the case of external evolution, but a journey of the "pilgrim-soul" through various *states* of *not only matter* but Self-consciousness and self-perception, or of *perception* from apperception. (See "*Gods, Monads and Atoms.*")

The MONAD emerges from its state of spiritual and intellectual unconsciousness; and, skipping the first two planes—too near the ABSOLUTE to permit of any correlation with anything on a lower plane—it gets direct into the plane of Mentality. But there is no plane in the whole universe with a wider margin, or a wider field of action in its almost endless gradations of perceptive and apperceptive qualities, than this plane, which has in its turn an appropriate smaller plane for every "form," from the "mineral" Monad up to the time when that Monad blossoms forth by evolution into the DIVINE MONAD. But all the time it is still one and the same Monad, differing only in its incarnations, throughout its ever succeeding cycles of partial or total obscuration of spirit, or the partial or total obscuration of matter—two polar antitheses—as it ascends into the realms of mental spirituality, or descends into the depths of materiality.

---

[4] We are forced to use here the misleading word "men." It stands to reason that these "men" did not resemble the men of to-day, either in form or nature. Why then, it may be asked, call them "men" at all? Because there is no other term in any Western language which approximately conveys the idea intended. The word "men" at least indicates that these beings were "MANUS," thinking entities, however they differed in form and intellection from ourselves. But in reality they were, in respect of spirituality and intellection, rather "gods" than "men."

To return to *Esoteric Buddhism*. It is there stated with regard to the enormous period intervening between the mineral epoch on Globe A, and the Man-epoch,[5] that: "The full development of the mineral epoch on Globe A prepares the way for the vegetable development, and, as soon as this begins, the mineral life-impulse overflows into Globe B. Then, when the vegetable development on Globe A is complete and the animal development begins, the vegetable life-impulse overflows to Globe B, and the mineral impulse passes on to Globe C. Then finally comes the human life-impulse on Globe A."

And so it goes on for three Rounds, when it slackens, and finally stops at the threshold of our Globe, at the Fourth Round; because the human period (of the true physical men to be), the seventh, is now reached. This is evident, for as said, " . . . there are processes of evolution which precede the mineral kingdom, and thus a wave of evolution, indeed several waves of evolution, precede the mineral wave in its progress round the spheres" (*ibid*).

And now we have to quote from another article, "About the Mineral Monad" in *Five Years of Theosophy*, p. 273 *et seq*.[6]

"There are seven kingdoms. The first group comprises three degrees of elementals, or nascent centres of forces—from the first stage of differentiation of (from) Mulaprakriti (or rather Pradhana, primordial homogeneous matter) to its third degree—*i.e.*, from full unconsciousness to semi-perception; the second or higher group embraces the kingdoms from vegetable to man; the mineral kingdom thus forming the central or turning point in the degrees of the "Monadic Essence," considered as an evolving energy. Three stages (sub-physical) on the elemental side; the mineral kingdom; three stages on the objective physical[7] side—these are the (first or preliminary) seven links of the evolutionary chain."

"Preliminary" because they are preparatory, and though belonging in fact to the natural, they yet would be more correctly described as sub-natural evolution. This process makes a halt in its stages at the Third, at the threshold of the Fourth stage, when it becomes, on the plane of the natural evolution, the first really manward stage,

[5] The term "Man epoch" is here used because of the necessity of giving a name to that fourth kingdom which follows the animal. But in truth the "Man" on Globe A during the First Round is no Man, but only his prototype or dimensionless image from the astral regions.

[6] [The article appears as "Question V" under the major article, "Some Impulses suggested by A. P. Sinnett's *Esoteric Buddhism*."]

[7] "Physical" here means differentiated for cosmical purposes and work; that "physical side," nevertheless, if objective to the apperception of beings from other planes, is yet quite subjective to us on our plane.

thus forming with the three elemental kingdoms, the ten, the Sephirothal number. It is at this point that begins:—

"A descent of spirit into matter equivalent to an ascent in physical evolution; a re-ascent from the deepest depths of materiality (the mineral) towards its *status quo ante*, with a corresponding dissipation of concrete organism—up to Nirvana, the vanishing point of differentiated matter." (*Five Years of Theosophy*, p. 276).

Therefore it becomes evident why that which is pertinently called in *Esoteric Buddhism* "Wave of Evolution," and "mineral-, vegetable-, animal- and man-"impulse," stops at the door of our Globe, at its Fourth Cycle or Round. It is at this point that the Cosmic Monad (Buddhi) will be wedded to and become the vehicle of the Atmic Ray, *i.e.*, it (Buddhi) will awaken to an apperception of it (Atman); and thus enter on the first step of a new septenary ladder of evolution, which will lead it eventually to the tenth (counting from the lowest upwards) of the Sephirothal tree, the Crown.

Everything in the Universe follows analogy. "As above, so below"; Man is the microcosm of the Universe. That which takes place on the spiritual plane repeats itself on the Cosmic plane. Concretion follows the lines of abstraction; corresponding to the highest must be the lowest; the material to the spiritual.

Now what is a "Monad?" And what relation does it bear to an Atom? The following reply is based upon the explanations given in answer to these questions by the author. [Ibid. p. 277.]

"None whatever," is answered to the second question, "to the atom or molecule as existing in the scientific conception at present. It can neither be compared with the microscopic organism, once classed among polygastric infusoria, and now regarded as vegetable, and classed among Algae; nor is it quite the Monas of the Peripatetics. Physically or constitutionally the mineral Monad differs, of course, from the human Monad, which is neither physical nor can its constitution be rendered by chemical symbols and elements." In short, as the Spiritual Monad is One, Universal, Boundless and Impartite, whose rays, nevertheless, form what we, in our ignorance, call the "Individual Monads" of men, so the Mineral Monad—being at the opposite point of the circle—is also One—and from it proceed the countless physical atoms which Science is beginning to regard as individualized.

"Otherwise how could one account for and explain mathematically the evolutionary and spiral progress of the Four Kingdoms? The 'Monad' is the combination of the last two 'principles' in man, the 6th and the 7th, and, properly speaking, the term 'human monad' applies only to the dual soul (Atma-Buddhi), not to its highest spiritual vivifying Principle, Atma, alone. But since the Spiritual Soul, if divorced from the latter (Atma) could have no existence, no being, it has thus been called . . . Now the Monadic, or rather Cosmic, Essence (if such a term be permitted) in the mineral, vegetable, and animal, though the same throughout the series of cycles from the lowest elemental up to the Deva Kingdom, yet differs in the scale of progression. It would be very misleading to imagine a Monad as a separate Entity trailing its slow way in a distinct path through the lower Kingdoms, and after an incalculable series of transformations flowering into a human being; in short, that the Monad of a Humboldt dates back to the Monad of an atom of horneblende. Instead of saying a 'Mineral Monad,' the more correct phraseology in physical Science, which differentiates every atom, would of course have been to call it 'the Monad manifesting in that form of Prakriti called the Mineral Kingdom.' The atom, as represented in the ordinary scientific hypothesis, is not a particle of something, animated by a psychic something, destined after aeons to blossom as a man. But it is a concrete manifestation of the Universal Energy which itself has not yet become individualized; a sequential manifestation of the one Universal Monas. The ocean (of matter) does not divide into its potential and constituent drops until the sweep of the life-impulse reaches the evolutionary stage of man-birth. The tendency towards segregation into individual Monads is gradual, and in the higher animals comes almost to the point. The Peripatetics applied the word Monas to the whole Kosmos, in the pantheistic sense; and the Occultists, while accepting this thought for convenience sake, distinguish the progressive stages of the evolution of the concrete from the abstract by terms of which the 'Mineral, Vegetable, Animal, (etc.), Monad' are examples. The term merely means that the tidal wave of spiritual evolution is passing through that arc of its circuit. The 'Monadic Essence' begins to impercept-ibly differentiate towards individual consciousness in the Vegetable Kingdom. As the Monads are uncompounded things, as correctly defined by Leibnitz, it is the spiritual essence which vivifies them in their degrees of differentiation, which properly constitutes the Monad—not the atomic aggregation, which is only the vehicle and the substance through which thrill the lower and the higher degrees of intelligence."

A few words more of the Moon.

In reality the Moon is only the satellite of the Earth in one respect, viz., that physically the Moon revolves round the Earth. But in every other respect it is the Earth which is the satellite of the Moon, and not *vice versa*. Startling as the statement may seem it is not without confirmation from scientific knowledge. It is evidenced by the tides, by the cyclic changes in many forms of disease which coincide with the lunar phases; it can be traced in the growth of plants, and is very marked in the phenomena of human gestation and conception.

It is the Moon that plays the largest and most important part in the formation of the Earth itself, as in the peopling thereof with human beings. The Lunar Monads or Pitris, the ancestors of man, become in reality man himself. They are the Monads who enter on the cycle of evolution on Globe A, and who, passing round the Chain of planets,[8] evolve the human form as has just been shown. At the beginning of the human stage of the Fourth Round on this Globe, they "ooze out" their astral doubles from the "ape-like" forms which they had evolved in Round Three. And it is this subtle, finer form, which serves as the model round which Nature builds physical man. These Monads or Divine Sparks are thus the Lunar ancestors, the Pitris themselves. For these Lunar Spirits have to become "Men" in order that their "Monads" may reach a higher plane of activity and self-consciousness, *i.e.*, the plane of the Manasa-Putras, those who endow the "senseless" shells, created and informed by the Pitris, with "mind" in the latter part of the Third Root-Race.

In the same way the "Monads" or Egos of the men of the Seventh Round of our Earth, after our own Globes A, B, C, D, *et seq.*, parting with their life-energy, will have informed and thereby called to life other laya-centres destined to live and act on a still higher plane of being—in the same way will the Terrene "Ancestors" create those who will become their superiors.

It now becomes plain that there exists in Nature a triple evolutionary scheme, for the formation of the three *periodical* Upadhis; or rather three separate schemes of evolution, which in our system are inextricably interwoven and interblended at every point. These are the Monadic (or Spiritual), the Intellectual, and the Physical evolutions. These three are the finite aspects or the reflections on the field of Cosmic Illusion of ATMA, the seventh, the ONE REALITY.

1. The Monadic is, as the name implies, concerned with the growth and development into still higher phases of activity of the Monad in conjunction with:—

2. The Intellectual, represented by the Manasa-Dhyanis (the Solar Devas, or the Agnishwatta Pitris) the "givers of intelligence and consciousness" to man and:—

3. The Physical, represented by the Chhayas of the Lunar Pitris, round which Nature has concreted the present physical body. This body serves as the vehicle for the "growth" (to use a misleading

[8] [? Globes.]

word) and the transformations through Manas and—owing to the accumulation of experiences—of the Finite into the INFINITE, of the transient into the Eternal and Absolute.

Each of these three systems has its own laws, and is ruled and guided by different sets of the highest Dhyanis or "Logoi." Each is represented in the constitution of man, the Microcosm of the great Macrocosm; and it is the union of these three streams in him which makes him the complex being he now is.

"Nature," the physical evolutionary Power, could never evolve intelligence unaided—she can only create "senseless forms," as will be seen in our "ANTHROPOGENESIS." The Lunar Monads cannot progress, for they have not yet had sufficient touch with the forms created by "Nature" to allow of their accumulating experiences through its means. It is the Manasa-Dhyanis who fill up the gap, and they represent the evolutionary power of Intelligence and Mind, the link between Spirit and Matter—in this Round.

Also it must be borne in mind that the Monads which enter upon the evolutionary cycle upon Globe A, in the first Round, are in very different stages of development. Hence the matter becomes somewhat complicated. . . . Let us recapitulate.

The most developed Monads (the Lunar) reach the human germ-stage in the First Round; become terrestrial, though very ethereal human beings towards the end of the Third Round, remaining on it (the Globe) through the "obscuration" period as the seed for future mankind in the Fourth Round, and thus become the pioneers of Humanity at the beginning of this, the Fourth Round. Others reach the Human stage only during later Rounds, i.e., in the Second, Third, or first half of the Fourth Round. And finally the most retarded of all—i.e., those still occupying animal forms after the middle turning-point of the Fourth Round—will not become men at all during this Manvantara. They will reach to the verge of humanity only at the close of the seventh Round to be, in their turn, ushered into a new chain after Pralaya, by older pioneers, the progenitors of humanity, or the Seed-Humanity (Sishta), viz., the men who will be at the head of all at the end of these Rounds.

From the preceding diagrams, which are applicable, mutatis mutandis, to Rounds, Globes or Races, it will be seen that the fourth member of a series occupies a unique position. Unlike the others, the Fourth has no "sister" Globe on the same plane as itself, and it thus forms the fulcrum of the "balance" represented by the whole Chain. It is the sphere of final evolutionary adjustments, the world of Karmic scales, the Hall of Justice, where the balance is struck which determines the future course of the Monad during the remainder of its incarnations in the cycle. And therefore it is, that, after this central turning-point has been passed in the Great Cycle—*i.e.*, after the middle point of the Fourth Race in the Fourth Round on our Globe —no more Monads can enter the human kingdom. The door is closed for this Cycle and the balance struck. For were it otherwise— had there been a new soul created for each of the countless milliards of human beings that have passed away, and had there been no re-incarnation—it would become difficult indeed to provide room for the disembodied "Spirits"; nor could the origin and cause of suffer-ing ever be accounted for. It is the ignorance of the occult tenets, and the enforcement of false conceptions under the guise of religious education, which have created materialism and atheism as a protest against the asserted divine order of things.

The only exceptions to the rule just stated are the "dumb races," whose Monads are already within the human stage, in virtue of the fact that these "animals" are later than, and even half descended from man, their last descendants being the anthropoid and other apes. These "human presentments" are in truth only the distorted copies of the early humanity. But this will receive full attention in the next Book.

As the Commentary, broadly rendered, says:—

1. "*Every form on earth, and every speck (atom) in Space strives in its efforts towards self-formation to follow the model placed for it in the* 'HEAVENLY MAN.' *. . . Its (the atom's) involution and evolution, its external and internal growth and development, have all one and the same object—man; man, as the highest physical and ultimate form on this earth; the* MONAD, *in its absolute totality and awakened condition—as the culmination of the divine incarnations on Earth.*"

2. "*The Dhyanis (Pitris) are those who have evolved their* BHUTA *(doubles) from themselves, which* RUPA *(form) has become the vehicle of Monads (seventh and sixth Principles) that had completed their cycle of transmigration in the three preceding Kalpas (Rounds). Then, they (the astral doubles) became the men of the first Human Race of the Round. But they were not complete, and were senseless.*"

Meanwhile man—or rather his Monad—has existed on the earth from the very beginning of this Round. But, up to our own Fifth Race, the external shapes which covered those divine astral doubles changed and consolidated with every sub-race; the form and physical structure of the fauna changing at the same time, as they had to be adapted to the ever-changing conditions of life on this Globe during the geological periods of its formative cycle. And thus shall they go on changing with every Root Race and *every chief sub-race* down to the last one of the Seventh in this Round.

3. "*The inner, now concealed, man, was then (in the beginnings) the external man. The progeny of the Dhyanis (Pitris), he was 'the son like unto his father.' Like the lotus, whose external shape assumes gradually the form of the model within itself, so did the form of man in the beginning evolve from within without. After the cycle in which man began to procreate his species after the fashion of the present animal kingdom, it became the reverse. The human foetus follows now in its transformations all the forms that the physical frame of man had assumed throughout the three Kalpas (Rounds) during the tentative efforts at plastic formation around the monad by senseless, because imperfect, matter, in her blind wanderings. In the present age, the physical embryo is a plant, a reptile, an animal, before it finally becomes man, evolving within himself his own ethereal counterpart, in his turn. In the beginning it was that counterpart (astral man) which, being senseless, got entangled in the meshes of matter.*"

But this "man" belongs to the fourth Round. As shown, the MONAD had passed through, journeyed and been imprisoned in, every transitional form throughout every kingdom of nature during the three preceding Rounds. But the Monad which becomes human *is not the Man*. In this Round—with the exception of the highest mammals after man, the anthropoids destined to die out in this our race, when their Monads will be liberated and pass into the astral human forms (or the highest elementals) of the Sixth[9] and the Seventh Races, and then into lowest human forms in the fifth Round—no units of either of the kingdoms are animated any longer by Monads destined to become human in their next stage, but only by the lower Elementals of their respective realms.[10]

The last human Monad incarnated before the beginning of the 5th Root-Race.[11] The cycle of metempsychosis for the Human monad

[9] Nature never repeats herself, therefore the anthropoids of our day have not existed at any time since the middle of the Miocene period; when, like all cross breeds, they began to show a tendency, more and more marked as time went on, to return to the type of their first parent, the black and yellow gigantic Lemuro-Atlantean. To search for the "Missing Link" is useless. To the scientists of the closing sixth Root-Race, millions and millions of years hence, our modern races, or rather their fossils, will appear as those of small insignificant apes—an extinct species of the *genus homo*.

[10] These "Elementals" will become human Monads, in their turn, only at the next great planetary Manvantara.

[11] Such anthropoids form an exception because they were not intended by Nature, but are the direct product and creation of "senseless" man. But though the apes descend from man, it is certainly not the fact that the human Monad, which has once reached the level of humanity, ever incarnates again in the form of an animal.

is closed, for we are in the Fourth Round and the Fifth Root-Race. The reader will have to bear in mind—at any rate one who has made himself acquainted with *Esoteric Buddhism*—that the Stanzas which follow in this Book and Book II. speak of the evolution in our Fourth Round only. The latter is the cycle of the turning-point, after which, matter, having reached its lowest depths, begins to strive onward and to get spiritualized with every new Race and with every fresh cycle. Therefore the student must take care not to see contradiction where there is none, as in *Esoteric Buddhism* Rounds are spoken of in general, while here only the Fourth, or our present Round, is meant. Then it was the work of formation; now it is that of reformation and evolutionary perfection.

Every Round repeats on a higher scale the evolutionary work of the preceding Round. With the exception of some higher anthropoids, as just mentioned, the Monadic inflow, or inner evolution, is at an end till the next Manvantara. It can never be too often repeated, that the full-blown human Monads have to be first disposed of before the new crop of candidates appears on this Globe at the beginning of the next Cycle. Thus there is a lull; and this is why, during the Fourth Round, man appears on Earth earlier than any animal creation, as will be described.

But it is still urged that the author of *Esoteric Buddhism* has "preached Darwinism" all along. Certain passages would undoubtedly seem to lend countenance to this inference. Besides which the Occultists themselves are ready to concede *partial* correctness to the Darwinian hypothesis, in later details, bye-laws of Evolution, and after the midway point of the Fourth Race. But what the Occultists have never admitted, nor will they ever admit, is that man was *an ape in this or in any other Round;* or that he ever could be one, however much he may have been "ape-like."

Thus, as the teaching stands:

"*Man in the First Round and First Race on Globe D, our Earth, was an ethereal being (a Lunar Dhyani, as man), non-intelligent but super-spiritual; and correspondingly, on the law of analogy, in the First Race of the Fourth Round. In each of the subsequent races and sub-races . . . he grows more and more into an encased or incarnate being, but still preponderatingly ethereal. . . . He is sexless, and, like the animal and vegetable, he develops monstrous bodies correspondential with his coarser surroundings.*

"*Round. 2. He (Man) is still gigantic and ethereal but growing firmer and more condensed in body, a more physical man. Yet still less intelligent than spiritual (1), for mind is a slower and more difficult evolution than is the physical frame . . .*

"Round. 3. He has now a perfectly concrete or compacted body, at first the form of a giant-ape, and now more intelligent, or rather cunning, than spiritual. For, on the downward arc, he has now reached a point where his primordial spirituality is eclipsed and overshadowed by nascent mentality (2). In the last half of the Third Round his gigantic stature decreases, and his body improves in texture, and he becomes a more rational being, though still more an ape than a Deva. . . . (All this is almost exactly repeated in the Third Root-Race of the Fourth Round.)

"Round. 4. Intellect has an enormous development in this Round. The (hitherto) dumb races acquire our (present) human speech on this globe, on which, from the Fourth Race, language is perfected and knowledge increases. At this half-way point of the Fourth Round (as of the Fourth or Atlantean Root Race) humanity passes the axial point of the minor Manvantara cycle . . . the world teeming with the results of intellectual activity and spiritual decrease . . ."[12]

This is from the authentic letter; what follows are the later remarks and additional explanations traced by the same hand in the form of footnotes.

(1.) *" . . . The original letter contained general teaching—a 'bird's-eye view'—and particularized nothing. . . . To speak of 'physical man' while limiting the statement to the early Rounds would be drifting back to the miraculous and instantaneous 'coats of skin.' . . . The first 'Nature,' the first 'body,' the first 'mind' on the first plane of perception, on the first Globe in the first Round, is what was meant.*
(2.) *"Restore: he has now reached the point (by analogy, and as the Third Root Race in the Fourth Round) where his ('the angel'-man's) primordial spirituality is eclipsed and overshadowed by nascent human mentality, and you have the true version on your thumb-nail. . . . "*

These are the words of the Teacher—text, words and sentences in brackets, and explanatory footnotes. It stands to reason that there must be an enormous difference in such terms as "objectivity" and "subjectivity," "materiality" and "spirituality," when the same terms are applied to different planes of being and perception. All this must be taken in its relative sense.

These "Men" of the Third Race—the ancestors of the Atlanteans —were just such ape-like, intellectually senseless giants as were those beings, who, during the Third Round, represented Humanity. Morally irresponsible, it was these third Race "men" who, through promiscuous connection with animal species lower than themselves,

[12] [Compare *The Mahatma Letters to A. P. Sinnett*, Letter 14.]

created that missing link which became ages later the remote
ancestor of the real ape as we find it now in the pithecoid family.[13]

And now we may return to the Stanzas.

5. AT THE FOURTH (*Round, or revolution of life and being around "the
seven smaller Wheels"*) (*a*), THE SONS ARE TOLD TO CREATE THEIR
IMAGES. ONE THIRD REFUSES. TWO (*thirds*) OBEY. THE CURSE IS PRO-
NOUNCED (*b*): THEY WILL BE BORN IN THE FOURTH (*Race*), SUFFER AND
CAUSE SUFFERING. THIS IS THE FIRST WAR (*c*).

Between this Sloka and Sloka 4 in this same Stanza extend long
ages; and there now gleams the dawn and sunrise of another aeon.
The drama enacted on our planet is at the beginning of its fourth
act, but for a clearer comprehension of the whole play the reader
will have to turn back before he can proceed onward. For this verse
belongs to the general Cosmogony given in the archaic volumes,
whereas Book II. will give a detailed account of the "Creation" or
rather the formation, of the first human beings, followed by the
second humanity, and then by the third; or, as they are called, "the
First, Second, and the Third Root-Races." As the solid Earth began
by being a ball of liquid fire, of fiery dust and its protoplasmic
phantom, so did man.

(*a*) That which is meant by the qualification the "Fourth" is
explained as the "Fourth Round" only on the authority of the Commentaries. It can equally mean Fourth "Eternity" as "Fourth
Round," or even the Fourth (our) Globe. For, as will repeatedly be
shown, it is the fourth Sphere on the fourth or lowest plane of
material life. And it so happens that we are in the Fourth Round, at
the middle point of which the perfect equilibrium between Spirit and
Matter had to take place.[14] Says the Commentary explaining the
verse:—

"*The holy youths (the Gods) refused to multiply and create species after
their likeness, after their kind. They are not fit forms (rupas) for us. They*

---

[13] And if this is found clashing with that other statement which shows the animal
later than man, then the reader is asked to bear in mind that the *placental mammal*
only is meant. In those days there were animals of which zoology does not even
dream in our own; *and the modes of reproduction were not identical* with the notions
which modern physiology has upon the subject.

[14] It was, as we shall see, at this period—during the highest point of civilization
and knowledge, as also of human intellectuality, of the Fourth, Atlantean Race—
that, owing to the final crisis of physiologico-spiritual adjustment of the races,
humanity branched off into its two diametrically opposite paths: the RIGHT- and
the LEFT-hand paths of knowledge or of Vidya. "*Thus were the germs of the White and
the Black Magic sown in those days. The seeds lay latent for some time, to sprout only during
the early period of the Fifth (our Race).*" (*Commentary.*)

*have to grow. They refuse to enter the chhayas (shadows or images) of their
inferiors. Thus had selfish feeling prevailed from the beginning, even among
the Gods, and they fell under the eye of the Karmic Lipikas."*
They had to suffer for it in later births.

It is a universal tradition that, before the physiological "Fall,"
propagation of one's kind, whether human or animal, took place
through the WILL of the Creators, or of their progeny. It was the Fall
of Spirit into generation, not the Fall of mortal man. It has already
been stated that, to become a Self-Conscious Spirit, the latter must
pass through every cycle of being, culminating in its highest point on
earth in Man. Spirit *per se* is an unconscious negative ABSTRACTION.
Its purity is inherent, not acquired by merit; hence, as already
shown, to become the highest Dhyan Chohan it is necessary for each
Ego to attain to full self-consciousness as a human, *i.e.*, conscious
Being, which is synthesized for us in Man. "A Dhyani has to be an
Atma-Buddhi; once the Buddhi-Manas breaks loose from its im-
mortal Atma of which it (Buddhi) is the vehicle, Atman passes into
NON-BEING, which is Absolute Being." This means that the purely
Nirvanic state is a passage of Spirit back to the ideal abstraction of
Be-ness which has no relation to the plane on which our Universe
is accomplishing its cycle.

(b) "The curse is pronounced" does not mean, in this instance,
that any Personal Being, God, or superior Spirit, pronounced it, but
simply that the cause which could but create bad results had been
generated, and that the effects of a Karmic cause could lead the
Beings that counteracted the laws of Nature, and thus impeded her
legitimate progress, only to bad incarnations, hence to suffering.

(c) "War" refers to struggles of adjustment, spiritual, cosmical,
and astronomical, but chiefly to the mystery of the evolution of man
as he is now.

6. THE OLDER WHEELS ROTATED DOWNWARD AND UPWARD (a)....
THE MOTHER'S SPAWN FILLED THE WHOLE (*Kosmos*).[15] THERE WERE
BATTLES FOUGHT BETWEEN THE CREATORS AND THE DESTROYERS, AND
BATTLES FOUGHT FOR SPACE; THE SEED APPEARING AND REAPPEARING
CONTINUOUSLY (b).[16]

(a) Here, having finished for the time being with our side-issues—
which, however they may break the flow of narrative, are necessary
for the elucidation of the whole scheme—the reader must return once

[15] The reader is reminded that Kosmos often means in our Stanzas only our own
Solar System, not the Infinite Universe.
[16] This is purely astronomical.

more to Cosmogony. The phrase "Older Wheels" refers to the Worlds or Globes of our Chain as they were during the "previous Rounds." The present Stanza, when explained esoterically, is found embodied entirely in the Kabalistic works. Therein will be found the very history of the evolution of those countless Globes which evolve after a periodical Pralaya, rebuilt from old material into new forms. The previous Globes disintegrate and reappear transformed and perfected for a new phase of life.

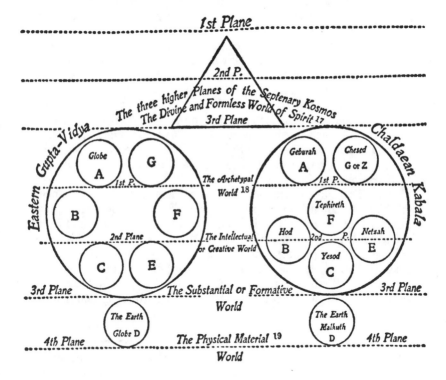

[17] The *Arupa* or "formless," there where form ceases to exist, on the objective plane.

[18] The word "Archetypal" must not be taken here in the sense that the Platonists gave to it, *i.e.*, the world as it existed *in the Mind* of the Deity; but in that of a world made as a first model, to be followed and improved upon by the worlds which succeed it physically—though deteriorating in purity.

[19] These are the four lower planes of Cosmic Consciousness, the three higher planes being inaccessible to human intellect as developed at present. The seven states of human consciousness pertain to quite another question.

The preceding comparative diagram shows the identity between the two systems, the Kabalistic and the Eastern. The three upper are the three higher planes of consciousness, revealed and explained in both schools only to the Initiates, the lower ones represent the four lower planes—the lowest being our plane, or the visible Universe.

These seven *planes* correspond to the seven *states* of consciousness in man. It remains with him to attune the three higher states in himself to the three higher planes in Kosmos. But before he can attempt to attune, he must awaken the three "seats" to life and activity.

(b) "The Seed appears and disappears continuously." Here "Seed" stands for "the World-germ," viewed by Science as material particles in a highly attenuated condition, but in Occult Physics as "spiritual particles," *i.e.*, supersensuous matter existing in a state of primeval differentiation. In theogony, every Seed is an ethereal organism, from which evolves later on a celestial being, a God.

In the "beginning," that which is called in mystic phraseology "Cosmic *Desire*" evolves into Absolute Light. Now light without any shadow would be absolute light—in other words, absolute darkness —as physical science seeks to prove. That shadow appears under the form of primordial matter, allegorized—if one likes—in the shape of the Spirit of Creative Fire or Heat. If, rejecting the poetical form and allegory, Science chooses to see in this the primordial Fire-Mist, it is welcome to do so. Whether one way or the other, whether Fohat or the famous FORCE of Science, nameless, and as difficult of definition as our Fohat himself, that Something "caused the Universe to move with circular motion," as Plato has it; or, as the Occult teaching expresses it:

"The Central Sun causes Fohat to collect primordial dust in the form of balls, to impel them to move in converging lines and finally to approach each other and aggregate." (Book of Dzyan) . . . "Being scattered in Space, without order or system, the world-germs come into frequent collision until their final aggregation, after which they become Wanderers (Comets). Then the battles and struggles begin. The older (bodies) attract the younger, while others repel them. Many perish, devoured by their stronger companions. Those that escape become worlds."

The birth of the celestial bodies in Space is compared to a crowd or multitude of "pilgrims" at the festival of the "Fires." Seven ascetics appear on the threshold of the temple with seven lighted sticks of incense. At the light of these the first row of pilgrims light their incense sticks. After which every ascetic begins whirling his stick around his head in space, and furnishes the rest with fire. Thus with the heavenly bodies. A laya-centre is lighted and awakened into life by the fires of another "pilgrim," after which the new "centre" rushes into space and becomes a comet. It is only after losing its velocity, and hence its fiery tail, that the "Fiery Dragon" settles down into quiet and steady life as a regular respectable citizen of the sidereal family. Therefore it is said:—

Born in the unfathomable depths of Space, out of the homogeneous Element called the World-Soul, every nucleus of Cosmic matter, suddenly launched into being, begins life under the most hostile circumstances. Through a series of countless ages, it has to conquer for itself a place in the infinitudes. It circles round and round between denser and already fixed bodies, moving by jerks, and pulling towards some given point or centre that attracts it, trying to avoid, like a ship drawn into a channel dotted with reefs and sunken rocks, other bodies that draw and repel it in turn; many perish, their mass disintegrating through stronger masses, and, when born within a system, chiefly within the insatiable stomachs of various Suns. (*See Comm. to Stanza 4*). Those which move slower and are propelled into an elliptic course are doomed to annihilation sooner or later. Others moving in parabolic curves generally escape destruction, owing to their velocity.

Some readers will perhaps imagine that this teaching, as to the cometary stage passed through by all heavenly bodies, is in contradiction with the statements just made as to the Moon being the mother of the Earth. They will perhaps fancy that intuition is needed to harmonize the two. But no intuition is in truth required. What does Science know of comets, their genesis, growth, and ultimate behaviour? And what is there so impossible that a laya centre—a lump of cosmic protoplasm, homogeneous and latent, when suddenly animated or fired up—should rush from its bed in Space and whirl throughout the abysmal depths in order to strengthen its homogeneous organism by an accumulation and addition of differentiated elements? And why should not such a comet settle in life, live, and become an inhabited globe?

"The abodes of Fohat are many," it is said. "He places his four fiery (electro-positive) Sons in the "Four Circles"; these *Circles* are the Equator, the Ecliptic, and the two parallels of declination, or the tropics—to preside over the *climates* of which are placed the Four mystical Entities. Then again: "Other seven (sons) are commissioned to preside over the seven hot, and seven cold *lokas* at the two ends of the Egg of Matter (our Earth and its poles). The seven *lokas* are also called the "Rings," elsewhere, and the "Circles."

The strange statement made in one of the Stanzas: "The Songs of Fohat and his Sons were *radiant* as the noon-tide Sun and the

Moon combined"; and that the Four Sons on the *middle* Four-fold Circle "*saw* their Father's songs and *heard* his Solar-selenic radiance"; is explained in the Commentary in these words: "The agitation of the *Fohatic* Forces at the two cold ends (North and South Poles) of the Earth which resulted in a multicoloured radiance at night, have in them several of the properties of Akasa (Ether), *Colour* and Sound as well." ... "Sound is the characteristic of Akasa (Ether): it generates Air, the property of which is Touch; which (by friction) becomes productive of Colour and Light." ... (*Vishnu Purana.*)

Perhaps the above will be regarded as archaic nonsense, but it will be better comprehended if the reader remembers the Aurora Borealis and Australis, both of which take place at the very centres of terrestrial electric and magnetic forces. The two poles are said to be the store-houses, the receptacles and liberators, at the same time, of Cosmic and terrestrial Vitality (Electricity); from the surplus of which the Earth, had it not been for these two natural "safety-valves," would have been rent to pieces long ago. At the same time it is now a theory that has lately become an axiom, that the phenomenon of polar lights is accompanied by, and productive of, strong sounds, like whistling, hissing, and cracking.

7. MAKE THY CALCULATIONS, O LANOO, IF THOU WOULDST LEARN THE CORRECT AGE OF THY SMALL WHEEL (*chain*). ITS FOURTH SPOKE IS OUR MOTHER (*Earth*) (*a*). REACH THE FOURTH "FRUIT" OF THE FOURTH PATH OF KNOWLEDGE THAT LEADS TO NIRVANA, AND THOU SHALT COMPREHEND, FOR THOU SHALT SEE (*b*).

(*a*) The "Small Wheel" is our Chain of Spheres, and the "fourth spoke" is our Earth, the fourth in the Chain. It is one of those on which the "hot (positive) breath of the Sun" has a direct effect.[20]

To calculate its age, however, as the pupil is asked to do in the Stanza, is rather difficult, since we are not given the figures of the Great Kalpa, and are not allowed to publish those of our small Yugas, except as to the approximate duration of these. "The older wheels rotated for one Eternity and one half of an Eternity," it says. We know that by "Eternity" the seventh part of 311,040,000,000,000 years, or an age of Brahmā is meant. But what of that? We also know that, if we take for our basis the above figures, we have first

[20] The seven fundamental transformations of the Globes or heavenly Spheres, or rather of their constituent particles of matter, is described as follows: (1) *Homogeneous*; (2) *Aeriform* and *radiant* (gaseous); (3) *Curd-like* (nebulous); (4) *Atomic, Ethereal* (beginning of motion, hence of differentiation); (5) *Germinal, fiery* (differentiated, but composed of the germs only of the Elements, in their earliest states, they having seven states, when completely developed on our earth); (6) *Four-fold, vapoury* (the future Earth); (7) *Cold and depending* (on the Sun for life and light).

of all to eliminate from the 100 years of Brahmā (or 311,040,000,000,000 years) two *years* taken up by the Sandhyas (twilights), which leaves 98, as we have to bring it to the mystical combination 14 × 7. But *we* have no knowledge at what time precisely the evolution and formation of our little Earth began. Therefore it is impossible to calculate its age, unless the time of its birth is given—which the TEACHERS refuse to do, so far. We must remember, moreover, that the law of Analogy holds good for the worlds, as it does for man; and that as "The ONE (Deity) becomes *Two* (Deva or Angel) and *Two* becomes *Three* (or Man)," etc., so we are taught that the *Curds* (world-stuff) become Wanderers, (Comets); these become stars, and the stars (the centres of vortices) *our sun and planets*—to put it briefly.

(b) There are four grades of Initiation mentioned in exoteric works, which are known respectively in Sanskrit as "Srotapanna," "Sakridagamin," "Anagamin," and "Arhat"—the Four Paths to Nirvana, in this, our Fourth Round, bearing the same appellations. The Arhat, though he can see the Past, the Present, and the Future, is not yet the highest Initiate; for the Adept himself, the *initiated* candidate, becomes chela (pupil) to a higher Initiate. Three further higher grades have to be conquered by the Arhat who would reach the apex of the ladder of Arhatship. There are those who have reached it even in this Fifth Race of ours, but the faculties necessary for the attainment of these higher grades will be fully developed in the average ascetic only at the end of this Root-Race, and in the Sixth and Seventh. Thus there will always be Initiates and the Profane till the end of this minor Manvantara, the present *Life-cycle*. The *Arhats* of the "Fire-Mist" of the 7th rung are but one remove from the Root-Base of their Hierarchy—the highest on Earth, and our Terrestrial Chain. This "Root-Base" has a name which can only be translated by several compound words into English"—"the Ever-living-human-Banyan." This "Wondrous Being" descended from a "high region," they say, in the early part of the Third Age, before the separation of the sexes of the Third Race.

This Third Race is sometimes called collectively "the Sons of *Passive* Yoga," *i.e.*, it was produced unconsciously by the Second Race, which, as it was intellectually inactive, is supposed to have been constantly plunged in a kind of blank or abstract contemplation, as required by the conditions of the Yoga state. In the first or earlier portion of the existence of this Third Race, while it was yet in its state of purity, the "Sons of Wisdom," who, as will be seen, incarnated in this Third Race, produced by *Kriyasakti* a progeny called the "Sons of Ad" or "of the Fire-Mist," the "Sons of Will and

Yoga," etc. They were a conscious production, as a portion of the Race was already animated with the divine spark of spiritual, superior intelligence. It was not a Race, this progeny. It was at first a wondrous Being, called the "Initiator," and after him a group of semi-divine and semi-human beings. "*Set apart*" in Archaic *genesis* for certain purposes, they are those in whom are said to have incarnated the highest Dhyanis, "Munis and Rishis from previous Manvantaras"—*to form the nursery for future human Adepts*, on this earth and during the present cycle. These "Sons of Will and Yoga" born, so to speak, in an immaculate way, remained, it is explained, entirely apart from the rest of mankind.

The "BEING" just referred to, which has to remain nameless, is the *Tree* from which, in subsequent ages, all the great *historically* known Sages and Hierophants, such as the Rishi Kapila, Hermes, Enoch, Orpheus, etc., etc., have branched off. As objective *man*, he is the mysterious (to the profane—the ever invisible) yet ever present Personage about whom legends are rife in the East, especially among the Occultists and the students of the Sacred Science. It is he who changes form, yet remains ever the same. And it is he again who holds spiritual sway over the *initiated* Adepts throughout the whole world. He is, as said, the "Nameless One" who has so many names, and yet whose names and whose very nature are unknown. He is *the* "Initiator," called the "GREAT SACRIFICE." For, sitting at the threshold of LIGHT, he looks into it from within the circle of Darkness, which he will not cross; nor will he quit his post till the last day of this Life-cycle. Why does the solitary Watcher remain at his self-chosen post? Why does he sit by the fountain of primeval Wisdom, of which he drinks no longer, as he has naught to learn which he does not know—aye, neither on this Earth, nor in its heaven? Because the lonely, sore-footed pilgrims on their way back to their *home* are never sure to the last moment of not losing their way in this limitless desert of illusion and matter called Earth-Life. Because he would fain show the way to that region of freedom and light, from which he is a voluntary exile himself, to every prisoner who has succeeded in liberating himself from the bonds of flesh and illusion. Because, in short, he has sacrificed himself for the sake of mankind, though but a few Elect may profit by the GREAT SACRIFICE.

It is under the direct, silent guidance of this MAHA GURU that all the other less divine Teachers and instructors of mankind became, from the first awakening of human consciousness, the guides of early Humanity. It is through these "Sons of God" that infant humanity got its first notions of all the arts and sciences, as well as of spiritual knowledge; and it is they who have laid the first

foundation-stone of those ancient civilizations that puzzle so sorely
our modern generation of students and scholars.[21]

[21] It is the pupils of those incarnated Rishis and Devas of the third Root Race,
who handed their knowledge from one generation to another, to Egypt and Greece
with its now lost *canon of proportion;* as it is the Disciples of the Initiates of the 4th,
the Atlanteans, who handed it over to their *Cyclopes,* the "Sons of Cycles" or of the
"Infinite," from whom the name passed to the still later generations of Gnostic
priests. "It is owing to the divine perfection of those architectural proportions that
the Ancients could build those wonders of all the subsequent ages, their Fanes,
Pyramids, Cave-Temples, Cromlechs, Cairns, Altars, proving they had the powers
of machinery and a knowledge of mechanics to which modern skill is like a child's
play, and which that *skill* refers to itself as the 'works of hundred-handed giants.' "
(See *The Book of God,* Kenealy.) Modern architects may not altogether have neglected
those rules, but they have superadded enough empirical innovations to destroy
those just proportions. It is Vitruvius who gave to posterity the rules of construction
of the Grecian temples erected to the immortal Gods; and the ten books of Marcus
Vitruvius Pollio on Architecture, of one, in short, *who was an Initiate,* can only be
studied esoterically. The Druidical circles, the Dolmens, the Temples of India,
Egypt and Greece, the Towers and the 127 towns in Europe which were found
"Cyclopean in origin" by the French Institute, are all the work of initiated Priest-
Architects, the descendants of those primarily taught by the "Sons of God," justly
called "The Builders." This is what appreciative posterity says of those descendants.
"They used neither mortar nor cement, nor steel nor iron to cut the stones with;
and yet they were so artfully wrought that in many places the joints are not seen,
though many of the stones, as in Peru, are 18 ft. thick, and in the walls of the
fortress of Cuzco there are stones of a still greater size." (*Acosta,* vi., 14.)

STANZA 7.

1. BEHOLD THE BEGINNING OF SENTIENT FORMLESS LIFE (*a*). FIRST, THE DIVINE (*vehicle*) (*b*), THE ONE FROM THE MOTHER-SPIRIT (*Atman*); THEN THE SPIRITUAL—(*Atma-Buddhi, Spirit-soul*)[1] (*c*); (*again*) THE THREE FROM THE ONE (*d*), THE FOUR FROM THE ONE (*e*), AND THE FIVE (*f*), FROM WHICH THE THREE, THE FIVE AND THE SEVEN (*g*)— THESE ARE THE THREE-FOLD AND THE FOUR-FOLD DOWNWARD; THE "MIND-BORN SONS OF THE FIRST LORD (*Avalokiteshwara*) THE SHINING SEVEN (*the "Builders"*).[2] IT IS THEY WHO ARE THOU, ME, HIM, O LANOO; THEY WHO WATCH OVER THEE AND THY MOTHER, BHUMI (*the Earth*).

(*a*) The Hierarchy of Creative Powers is divided into Seven (or 4 and 3) esoterically, within the Twelve great Orders, recorded in the twelve Signs of the Zodiac; the Seven of the manifesting scale being connected, moreover, with the Seven Planets. All this is subdivided into numberless groups of divine spiritual, semi-spiritual, and ethereal Beings.

(*b*) As in the Japanese system, in the Egyptian, and every old cosmogony—at this divine FLAME, the "One," are lit the three descending groups.

(*c*) The second Order of Celestial Beings, those of Fire and Aether (corresponding to Spirit and Soul, or the Atma-Buddhi) whose names are legion, are still formless, but more definitely "substantial." They are the first differentiation in the Secondary Evolution or "Creation"—a misleading word. As the name shows, they are the prototypes of the incarnating Jivas or Monads, and are composed of the Fiery Spirit of Life. It is through these that passes, like a pure solar beam, the Ray which is furnished by them with its future vehicle, the Divine Soul, Buddhi. These are directly concerned with the Hosts of the higher World of *our* system. From these Twofold *Units* emanate the *Threefold*.

Turning back to the esoteric explanations in every cosmogony:—

(*d*) The *Third* Order corresponds to *Atma-Buddhi-Manas*: Spirit, Soul and Intellect, and is called the "Triads."

(*e*) The *Fourth* are substantial Entities. This is the highest Group

---

[1] This relates to the Cosmic principles.

[2] The seven creative Rishis now connected with the constellation of the Great Bear.

among the *Rupas* (Atomic Forms). It is the nursery of the human, conscious, spiritual Souls. They are called the "Imperishable Jivas," and constitute, through the Order below their own, the first group of the first Septenary Host—the great mystery of human conscious and intellectual Being. For the latter is the field wherein lies concealed *in its privation* the Germ *that will fall into generation.* That Germ will become the spiritual potency in the physical cell that guides the development of the embryo, and which is the cause of the hereditary transmission of faculties and all the inherent qualities in man. The Darwinian theory, however, of the transmission of acquired faculties, is neither taught nor accepted in Occultism. Evolution, in it, proceeds on quite other lines; the physical, according to Esoteric teaching, evolving gradually from the spiritual, mental, and psychic. This inner soul of the physical cell—this "spiritual plasm" that dominates the germinal plasm—is the key that must open one day the gates of the *terra incognita* of the biologist, now called the dark mystery of embryology.

(*f*) The Fifth Group is a very mysterious one, as it is connected with the Microcosmic Pentagon, the five-pointed star representing man. The Fifth Group of the celestial Beings is supposed to contain in itself the dual attributes of both the spiritual and physical aspects of the Universe; the two poles, so to say, of Mahat, the Universal Intelligence, and the dual nature of man, the spiritual and the physical. Hence its number Five, multiplied and made into Ten, connecting it with *Makara,* the 10th sign of the Zodiac.

(*g*) The Sixth and Seventh Groups partake of the lower qualities of the Quaternary. They are conscious, ethereal Entities, as invisible as Ether, which are shot out like the boughs of a tree from the first central Group of the Four, and shoot out in their turn numberless side Groups, the lower of which are the Nature-Spirits, or Elementals of countless kinds and varieties; from the formless and unsubstantial—the ideal THOUGHTS of their creators—down to atomic, though, to human perception, invisible organisms. The latter are considered as the "Spirits of Atoms" for they are the first remove (backwards) from the physical Atom—sentient, if not intelligent creatures. They are all subject to Karma, and have to work it out through every cycle. A Dhyan Chohan has to become one; he cannot be born or appear suddenly on the plane of life as a full-blown Angel. The Celestial Hierarchy of the present Manvantara will find itself transferred in the next Cycle of life into higher, superior worlds, and will make room for a new Hierarchy, composed of the elect ones of our mankind. Being is an endless cycle within the one Absolute Eternity, wherein move numberless inner cycles finite and conditioned. Gods, created as such, would evince no personal merit in being Gods. Therefore the "Four" and the "Three" have to incarnate as all other beings have. This Sixth Group, moreover, remains almost inseparable from man, who draws from it all but his highest and lowest principles, or his Spirit and body, the five middle human principles being the very essence of those Dhyanis.

2. THE ONE RAY MULTIPLIES THE SMALLER RAYS. LIFE PRECEDES FORM, AND LIFE SURVIVES THE LAST ATOM (*of Form, Sthula-sarira, external body*). THROUGH THE COUNTLESS RAYS THE LIFE-RAY, THE ONE, LIKE A THREAD THROUGH MANY BEADS (*pearls*) (*a*).

(*a*) This Sloka expresses the conception of a life-thread, *Sutratma*, running through successive generations.[3] Now to the simile. Complete the physical plasm, mentioned in the last footnote, the "Germinal Cell" of man with all its material potentialities, with the "Spiritual Plasm," so to say, or the fluid that contains the five lower principles of the six-principled Dhyani—and you have the secret.

"When the seed of the animal man is cast into the soil of the animal woman, that seed cannot germinate unless it has been fructified by the five virtues (the fluid of, or the emanation from the principles) of the six-fold Heavenly Man. Wherefore the Microcosm is represented as a Pentagon, within the Hexagon Star, the "Macrocosm." Then: "The functions of *Jiva* on this Earth are of a five-fold character. In the mineral atom it is connected with the lowest principles

[3] Professor Weissmann—at one time a fervent Darwinist—shows—thus stepping over the heads of the Greek Hippocrates and Aristotle, right back into the teachings of the old Aryans—one infinitesimal cell, out of millions of others at work in the formation of an organism, determining alone and unaided, by means of constant segmentation and multiplication, the correct image of the future man (or animal) in its physical, mental, and psychic characteristics. It is that cell which impresses on the face and form of the new individual the features of the parents or of some distant ancestor; it is that cell again which transmits to him the intellectual and mental idiosyncracies of his sires, and so on. This Plasm is the immortal portion of our bodies—simply through the process of successive assimilations. Darwin's theory, viewing the embryological cell as an essence or the extract from all other cells, is set aside; it is incapable of accounting for hereditary transmission. There are but two ways of explaining the mystery of heredity; either the substance of the germinal cell is endowed with the faculty of crossing the whole cycle of transformations that lead to the construction of a separate organism and then to the reproduction of identical germinal cells; or, *those germinal cells do not have their genesis at all in the body of the individual, but proceed directly from the ancestral germinal cell passed from father to son through long generations.* It is the latter hypothesis that Weissmann accepted and has worked upon; and it is to this cell that he traces the immortal portion of man. So far, so good; and when this almost correct theory is accepted, how will biologists explain the first appearance of this everlasting cell? Unless man "grew," and was not born at all, but fell from the clouds, how was that embryological cell born in him?

of the Spirits of the Earth (the Six-fold Dhyanis); in the vegetable particle, with their second—the *Prana* (life); in the animal, with all these plus the third and the fourth; in man, the germ must receive the fruition of all the five. Otherwise he will be born no higher than an animal"; namely, a congenital idiot. Thus in man alone the Jiva is complete. As to his seventh principle, it is but one of the Beams of the Universal Sun. Each rational creature receives only the temporary loan of that which has to return to its source; while his physical body is shaped by the lowest terrestrial Lives, through physical, chemical, and physiological evolution.

It comes to this: Mankind in its first prototypal, shadowy form, is the offspring of the Elohim of Life (or Pitris); in its qualitative and physical aspect it is the direct progeny of the "Ancestors," the lowest Dhyanis, or Spirits of the Earth; for its moral, psychic, and spiritual nature, it is indebted to a group of divine Beings, the name and characteristics of which will be given in Book II. Collectively, men are the handiwork of Hosts of various Spirits; distributively, the tabernacles of those Hosts; and occasionally and singly, the vehicles of some of them. In our present all-material Fifth Race, the earthly Spirit of the Fourth is still strong in us; but we are approaching the time when the pendulum of evolution will direct its swing decidedly upwards, bringing Humanity back on a parallel line with the primitive Third Root-Race in Spirituality. During its childhood, mankind was composed wholly of that Angelic Host, who were the indwelling Spirits that animated the monstrous and gigantic tabernacles of clay of the Fourth Race—built by (as they are now also) and composed of countless myriads of Lives.[4]

3. WHEN THE ONE BECOMES TWO, THE "THREE-FOLD" APPEARS (*a*). THE THREE ARE (*linked into*) ONE; AND IT IS OUR THREAD, O LANOO, THE HEART OF THE MAN-PLANT, CALLED SAPTAPARNA (*b*).

(*a*) "When the ONE becomes Two, the Three-fold appears": to wit, when the One Eternal drops its reflection into the region of Manifestation, that reflection, "the Ray," differentiates the "Water of Space."

This is the metaphysical explanation, and refers to the very beginning of Evolution. In order to form a clear conception of what is meant by the One becoming Two, and then being transformed into

[4] Science, dimly perceiving the truth, may find bacteria and other infinitesimals in the human body, and see in them but occasional and abnormal visitors to which diseases are attributed. Occultism—which discerns a Life in every atom and molecule, whether in a mineral or human body, in air, fire or water—affirms that our whole body is built of such Lives, the smallest bacteria under the miscroscope being to them in comparative size like an elephant to the tiniest infusoria.

the "Three-fold," the student has to make himself thoroughly acquainted with what we call "Rounds." If he refers to *Esoteric Buddhism*—the first attempt to sketch out an approximate outline of archaic Cosmogony—he will find that by a "Round" is meant the serial evolution of nascent material Nature, of the seven Globes of our Chain with their mineral, vegetable, and animal kingdoms (man being there included in the latter and standing at the head of it) during the whole period of a Life-Cycle. The latter would be called by the Brahmins "a Day of Brahmā." It is, in short, one revolution of the "Wheel" (our Planetary Chain), which is composed of seven Globes (or seven separate "Wheels," in another sense this time). When evolution has run downward into matter from planet A to planet G,[5] it is one Round. In the middle of the Fourth revolution, which is our present "Round," "Evolution has reached its acme of physical development, crowned its work with the perfect physical man, and, from this point, begins its work spirit-ward."

Now every Round (on the descending scale) is but a repetition in a more concrete form of the Round which preceded it, as every Globe—down to our fourth Sphere (the actual Earth)—is a grosser and more material copy of the more shadowy Sphere which precedes it in their successive order, on the three higher planes. (See diagram in Stanza 6. Comm. 6). On its way upwards on the ascending arc, Evolution spiritualizes and etherealizes, so to speak, the general nature of all, bringing it on to a level with the plane on which the twin Globe on the opposite side is placed; the result being, that when the seventh Globe is reached (in whatever Round) the nature of everything that is evolving returns to the condition it was in at its starting point—*plus*, every time, a new and superior degree in the states of consciousness. Thus it becomes clear that the "origin of man," so-called, on this our present Round, or Life-cycle on this Planet, must occupy the same place in the same order—save details based on local conditions and time—as in the preceding Round. Again, it must be explained and remembered that, as the work of each Round is said to be apportioned to a different Group of so-called "Creators" or "Architects," so is that of every Globe; *i.e.*, it is under the supervision and guidance of special "Builders" and "Watchers"—the various Dhyan-Chohans.

The Group of the Hierarchy which is commissioned to "create"[6]

[5] [This should surely be Globe A to Globe G.]

[6] Creation is an incorrect word to use, as no religion, not even the sect of the Visishta Adwaitees in India—one which anthropomorphizes even Parabrahman—believes in creation out of *nihil* as Christians and Jews do, but in evolution out of pre-existing materials.

men is a special Group, then; yet it evolved shadowy man in this Cycle just as a higher and still more spiritual Group evolved him in the Third Round. But as it is the Sixth—on the downward scale of Spirituality—the last and Seventh being the terrestrial Spirits (Elementals) which gradually form, build, and condense his physical body—this Sixth Group evolves no more than the future man's shadowy form, a filmy, hardly visible transparent copy of themselves. It becomes the task of the fifth Hierarchy—the mysterious Beings that preside over the constellation Capricornus, Makara, or "Crocodile," in India as in Egypt—to inform the empty and ethereal animal form and make of it the Rational Man. This is one of those subjects upon which very little may be said to the general public. It is a MYSTERY, truly, but only to him who is prepared to reject the existence of intellectual and conscious spiritual Beings in the Universe, limiting full Consciousness to man alone, and that only as a "function of the brain." Many are those among the Spiritual Entities who have incarnated bodily in man, since the beginning of his appearance, and who, for all that, still exist as independently as they did before, in the infinitudes of Space. . . .

To put it more clearly, the invisible Entity may be bodily present on earth without abandoning, however, its status and functions in the supersensuous regions. If this needs explanation, we can do no better than remind the reader of like cases in Spiritualism, though such cases are very rare, at least as regards the nature of the Entity incarnating,[7] or taking temporary possession of a medium.

(b) The concluding sentence of this Sloka shows how archaic is the belief and the doctrine that man is seven-fold in his constitution. The Thread of Being which animates man and passes through all his personalities, or rebirths on this Earth (an allusion to Sutratma), the Thread on which moreover all his "Spirits" are strung—is spun from the essence of the "Three-fold," the "Four-fold" and the "Five-fold"; which contain all the preceding.

4. It is the root that never dies, the three-tongued flame of the four wicks (a). . . . The wicks are the sparks, that draw from the three-tongued flame (their upper triad) shot out by the seven, their flame; the beams and sparks of one moon reflected in the running waves of all the rivers of the earth ("Bhumi," or "Prithivi") (b).

(a) The "Three-tongued flame" that never dies is the immortal

---

[7] The so-called "Spirits" that may occasionally possess themselves of the bodies of mediums are not the Monads or Higher Principles of disembodied personalities. Such a "Spirit" can only be either an Elementary, or—a Nirmanakaya.

spiritual Triad—the Atma-Buddhi and Manas—the fruition of the latter assimilated by the first two after every terrestrial life. The "Four Wicks" that go out and are extinguished, are the four lower principles, including the body.

(*b*) Just as milliards of bright sparks dance on the waters of an ocean above which one and the same moon is shining, so our evanescent personalities—the illusive envelopes of the immortal MONAD-EGO—twinkle and dance on the waves of Maya. They last and appear, as the thousands of sparks produced by the moon-beams, only so long as the Queen of the Night radiates her lustre on the "Running Waters" of Life: the period of a Manvantara; and then they disappear, the "Beams"—symbols of our eternal Spiritual Egos —alone surviving, re-merged in, and being as they were before, one with the Mother-Source.

5. THE SPARK HANGS FROM THE FLAME BY THE FINEST THREAD OF FOHAT. IT JOURNEYS THROUGH THE SEVEN WORLDS OF MAYA (*a*). IT STOPS IN THE FIRST (*Kingdom*), AND IS A METAL AND A STONE; IT PASSES INTO THE SECOND (*Kingdom*), AND BEHOLD—A PLANT; THE PLANT WHIRLS THROUGH SEVEN FORMS AND BECOMES A SACRED ANIMAL; (*the first Shadow of the physical Man*) (*b*). FROM THE COMBINED ATTRI-BUTES OF THESE, MANU (*man*), THE THINKER, IS FORMED. WHO FORMS HIM? THE SEVEN LIVES; AND THE ONE LIFE (*c*). WHO COMPLETES HIM? THE FIVE-FOLD LHA. AND WHO PERFECTS THE LAST BODY? FISH, SIN, AND SOMA (*the Moon*) (*d*).

(*a*) The phrase "through the Seven Worlds of Maya" refers here to the seven Globes of the Planetary Chain and the seven Rounds, or the 49 stations of active existence that are before the "Spark" or Monad, at the beginning of every Great Life-Cycle or Manvantara. The "Thread of Fohat" is the thread of life before referred to.

This relates to the greatest problem of philosophy—the physical and substantial nature of Life, the independent nature of which is denied by modern science because that science is unable to com-prehend it. The reincarnationists and believers in Karma alone dimly perceive that the whole secret of Life is in the unbroken series of its manifestations: whether in, or apart from, the physical body. Because if—

> "Life, like a dome of many-coloured glass,
> Stains the white radiance of Eternity"—

yet it is itself part and parcel of that Eternity; for Life alone can understand Life.

What is that "Spark" which "hangs from the Flame?" It is JĪVA, the MONAD in conjunction with MANAS, or rather its aroma—that which remains from each personality, when worthy, and hangs from Atma-Buddhi, the Flame, by the Thread of life. In whatever way interpreted, and into whatever number of principles the human being is divided, it may easily be shown that this doctrine is supported by all the ancient religions, from the Vedic to the Egyptian, from the Zoroastrian to the Jewish.

(b) The well-known Kabalistic aphorism runs:—"A stone becomes a plant; a plant, a beast; a beast, a man; a man, a spirit; and the spirit a god." The "Spark" animates all the kingdoms in turn before it enters into and informs Divine Man, between whom and his predecessor, animal man, there is all the difference in the world.

The Monad or Jiva is, first of all, shot down by the law of Evolution into the lowest form of matter—the mineral. After a seven-fold gyration encased in the stone (or that which will become mineral and stone in the Fourth Round), it creeps out of it, say, as a lichen. Passing thence, through all the forms of vegetable matter, into what is termed animal matter, it has now reached the point in which it has become the germ, so to speak, of the animal, that will become the physical man. All this, up to the Third Round, is formless, as matter, and senseless, as consciousness. For the Monad or Jiva *per se* cannot be even called Spirit: it is a Ray, a breath of the ABSOLUTE, or the Absoluteness rather, and the Absolute Homogeneity, having no relations with the conditioned and relative finiteness, is unconscious on our plane. Therefore, besides the material which will be needed for its future human form, the Monad requires (a) a spiritual model, or prototype, for that material to shape itself into; and (b) an intelligent consciousness to guide its evolution and progress, neither of which is possessed by the homogeneous Monad, or by senseless though living matter. The Adam of dust requires the *Soul of Life* to be breathed into him; the two middle Principles, which are the *sentient* Life of the irrational animal and the Human Soul, for the former is irrational without the latter. It is only when, from a potential androgyne, man has become separated into male and female, that he will be endowed with this conscious, rational, individual Soul, (*Manas*) "the principle, or the intelligence, of the Elohim," to receive which he has to eat of the fruit of Knowledge from the Tree of Good and Evil. How is he to obtain all this? The Occult Doctrine teaches that while the Monad is cycling on downward into matter, these very Elohim—or Pitris, the lower Dhyan-Chohans—are evolving *pari passu* with it on a higher and more spiritual plane, descending also relatively into matter on their own plane of consciousness, when, after having reached a certain point, they will meet the incarnating senseless Monad, encased in the lowest matter, and blending the two potencies, Spirit and Matter, the union will produce that terrestrial symbol of the "Heavenly Man" in space—PERFECT MAN. Though one and the same thing in their origin, Spirit and Matter, when once they are on the plane of differentiation, begin each of them their evolutionary progress in contrary directions—Spirit falling gradually into matter, and the latter ascending to its original condition, that of a pure Spiritual Substance. Both are inseparable, yet ever separated. In polarity, on the physical plane, two like poles will always repel each other, while the negative and the positive are mutually attracted, so do Spirit and Matter stand to each other—the two poles of the same homogeneous Substance, the Root-Principle of the Universe.

Therefore, when the hour strikes for Purusha to mount on Prakriti's shoulders for the formation of the Perfect Man—rudimentary man of the first 2½ Races being only the *first*, gradually evolving into *the most perfect of mammals*—the Celestial "Ancestors" step in on this our plane, as the Pitris had stepped in before them for the formation of the physical or animal-man, and incarnate in the latter. Thus the two processes for the two *creations*—the animal and the divine man—differ greatly. The Pitris shoot out from their ethereal bodies still more ethereal and shadowy similitudes of themselves, or what we should now call "doubles," or "astral forms," in their own likeness.[8] This furnishes the Monad with its first dwelling, and blind matter with a model around and upon which to build henceforth. But *Man is still incomplete.*

"Who forms Manu (the Man) and who forms his body? The LIFE and the LIVES. Sin[9] and the MOON." Here Manu stands for the spiritual, heavenly Man, the real and non-dying EGO in us, which is the direct emanation of the "One Life" or the Absolute Deity.

It has been stated before now that Occultism does not accept anything inorganic in the Kosmos. The expression employed by Science, "inorganic substance," means simply that the latent life slumbering in the molecules of so-called "inert matter" is incognizable. ALL IS LIFE, and every atom of even mineral dust is a LIFE.

"*The Worlds, to the profane,*" says a Commentary, "*are built up of the known Elements. To the conception of an Arhat, these Elements are themselves collectively a Divine Life; distributively, on the plane of manifestations, the*

---

[8] Read in *Isis Unveiled*, vol. ii., pp. 297–303, the doctrine of the Codex Nazaraeus —every tenet of our teaching is found there under a different form and allegory.

[9] The word "Sin" is curious, but has a particular Occult relation to the Moon, besides being its Chaldean equivalent.

numberless and countless crores of Lives. Fire alone is ONE, on the plane of the One Reality: on that of manifested, hence illusive, Being, its particles are fiery Lives which live and have their being at the expense of every other Life that they consume. Therefore they are named the "DEVOURERS." . . . "Every visible thing in this Universe was built by such LIVES, from conscious and divine primordial man down to the unconscious agents that construct matter." . . . "From the ONE LIFE, formless and Uncreate, proceeds the Universe of Lives. First was manifested from the Deep (Chaos) cold luminous Fire (gaseous light?) which formed the curds in Space." (Irresolvable nebulae, perhaps?) . . . . . . " . . . These fought, and a great heat was developed by the encountering and collision, which produced rotation. Then came the first manifested MATERIAL FIRE, the hot Flames, the wanderers in heaven (comets); heat generates moist vapour; that forms solid water (?); then dry mist, then liquid mist, watery, that puts out the luminous brightness of the pilgrims (comets?) and forms solid watery Wheels (MATTER Globes). Bhumi (the EARTH) appears with six sisters. These produce by their continuous motion the inferior fire, heat, and an aqueous mist, which yields the third World-Element—WATER; and from the breath of all (atmospheric) AIR is born. These four are the four Lives of the first four periods (Rounds) of Manvantara. The three last will follow."

This means that every new Round develops one of the Compound Elements, as now known to Science,—which rejects the primitive nomenclature, preferring to subdivide them into constituents. If Nature is the "Ever-becoming" on the manifested plane, then those Elements are to be regarded in the same light: they have to evolve, progress, and increase to the Manvantaric end. Thus the First Round, we are taught, developed but one Element, and a nature and humanity in what may be called one aspect of Nature—called by some, very unscientifically, though it may be so *de facto*, "One-dimensional Space." The Second Round brought forth and developed two Elements—Fire and Earth—and *its* humanity, adapted to this condition of Nature, if we can give the name Humanity to beings living under conditions unknown to men, was—to use again a familiar phrase in a strictly figurative sense (the only way in which it can be used correctly)—"a two-dimensional species." The processes of natural development which we are now considering will at once elucidate and discredit the fashion of speculating on the attributes of the *two*, *three*, and *four* or more "dimensional Space"; but in passing, it is worth while to point out the real significance of the sound but incomplete intuition that has prompted—among Spiritualists and Theosophists, and several great men of Science, for the matter of that—the use of the modern expression, "the fourth dimension of Space." To begin with, of course, the superficial absurdity of assuming that Space itself is measurable in any direction is of little consequence. The familiar phrase can only be an abbreviation of the fuller form—the *"Fourth dimension of* MATTER *in Space."* But it is an unhappy phrase even thus expanded, because while it is perfectly true that the progress of evolution may be destined to introduce us to new characteristics of matter, those with which we are already familiar are really more numerous than the three dimensions. The faculties, or what is perhaps the best available term, the characteristics of matter, must clearly bear a direct relation always to the senses of man. Matter has extension, colour, motion (molecular motion), taste, and smell, corresponding to the existing senses of man, and by the time that it fully develops the next characteristic— let us call it for the moment PERMEABILITY—this will correspond to the next sense of man—let us call it "NORMAL CLAIRVOYANCE"; thus, when some bold thinkers have been thirsting for a fourth dimension to explain the passage of matter through matter, and the production of knots upon an endless cord, what they were really in want of was a *sixth characteristic of matter.* The three dimensions belong really but to one attribute or characteristic of matter—extension; and popular common sense justly rebels against the idea that under any condition of things there can be more than three of such dimensions as length, breadth, and thickness. These terms, and the term "dimension" itself, all belong to one plane of thought, to one stage of evolution, to one characteristic of matter. So long as there are foot-rules within the resources of Kosmos, to apply to matter, so long will they be able to measure it three ways and no more; and from the time the idea of measurement first occupied a place in the human understanding, it has been possible to apply measurement in three directions and no more. But these considerations do not militate in any way against the certainty that in the progress of time —as the faculties of humanity are multiplied—so will the characteristics of matter be multiplied also.

We now return to the consideration of material evolution through the Rounds. Matter in the *second* Round, it has been stated, may be figuratively referred to as two-dimensional. But here another *caveat* must be entered. That loose and figurative expression may be regarded—in one plane of thought, as we have just seen—as equivalent to the second characteristic of matter corresponding to the second perceptive faculty or sense of man. But these two linked scales of evolution are concerned with the processes going on within the limits of a single Round. The succession of primary aspects of Nature with which the succession of Rounds is concerned, has to do, as already indicated, with the development of the "Elements" (in the Occult sense)—Fire, Air, Water,[10] Earth. We are only in the Fourth Round, and our catalogue so far stops short. The centres of consciousness (destined to develop into humanity as we know it) of the Third Round arrived at a perception of the third Element, Water. Those of the Fourth Round have added Earth as a state of matter to their stock as well as the three other elements in their present transformation. In short, none of the so-called elements were, in the three preceding Rounds, as they are now. FIRE may have been *pure* AKASA, Nitrogen.

The Elements, whether simple or compound, could not have remained the same since the commencement of the evolution of our Chain. Everything in the Universe progresses steadily in the Great Cycle, while incessantly going up and down in the smaller cycles. Nature is never stationary during Manvantara, as it is ever *becoming*, not simply *being;* and mineral, vegetable, and human life are always adapting their organisms to the then reigning Elements, and therefore *those* Elements were then fitted for them, as they are now for the life of present humanity. It will only be in the next, or Fifth Round that the fifth Element, *Ether*—the gross body of Akasa, if it can be called even that—will, by becoming a familiar fact of Nature to all men, as Air is familiar to us now, cease to be as at present hypothetical, and also an "agent" for so many things. And only during that Round will those higher senses, the growth and development of which Akasa subserves, be susceptible of a complete expansion. As already indicated, a *partial* familiarity with the characteristic of matter—Permeability—which should be developed concurrently with the sixth sense, may be expected to develop at the proper period in this Round. But with the next Element added to our resources in the next Round, *Permeability* will become so manifest a characteristic of matter that the densest forms of this will seem to man's perceptions as obstructive to him as a thick fog, and no more.

Let us return to the Life-Cycle now. Without entering at length upon the description given of the *higher* LIVES, we must direct our attention at present simply to the earthly Beings and the Earth itself.

---

[10] The order in which these Elements are placed above is the correct one for esoteric purposes and in the Secret Teachings. Milton was right when he spoke of the "Powers of Fire, Air, Water, Earth"; the Earth, such as we know it now, had no existence before the 4th Round, hundreds of million years ago, the commencement of our geological Earth. The globe was "*fiery, cool and radiant* as its ethereal men and animals during the first Round," says the Commentary, uttering a contradiction or paradox in the opinion of our present Science; "*luminous* and more dense and heavy—during the second Round; *watery* during the Third!" Thus are the elements reversed.

The latter, we are told, is built up for the First Round by the "Devourers" which disintegrate and differentiate the germs of other Lives in the Elements; pretty much, it must be supposed, as in the present stage of the world, the *aerobes* do, when, undermining and loosening the chemical structure in an organism, they transform animal matter and generate substances that vary in their constitutions. Wherever there is an atom of matter, a particle or a molecule, even in its most gaseous condition, there is life in it, however latent and unconscious. "*Whatsoever quits the Laya State, becomes active Life; it is drawn into the vortex of MOTION (the alchemical solvent of Life); Spirit and Matter are the two States of the ONE, which is neither Spirit nor Matter, both being the Absolute Life, latent.*" (*Book of Dzyan, Comm. III., par.* 18). . . . "*Spirit is the first differentiation of (and in) SPACE; and Matter the first differentiation of Spirit. That, which is neither Spirit nor matter—that is IT—the Causeless CAUSE of Spirit and Matter, which are the Cause of Kosmos. And THAT we call the ONE LIFE or the Intra-Cosmic Breath.*"

Once more we will say—*like must produce like*. Absolute Life cannot produce an inorganic atom, whether single or complex, and there is life even in *Laya*, just as a man in a profound cataleptic state—to all appearance a corpse—is still a living being.

When the "Devourers" (in whom the men of science are invited to see, with some show of reason, atoms of the Fire-Mist, if they will, as the Occultist will offer no objection to this); when the "Devourers," we say, have differentiated "the Fire-Atoms" by a peculiar process of segmentation, the latter become Life-Germs, which aggregate according to the laws of cohesion and affinity. Then the Life-Germs produce Lives of another kind, which work on the structure of our Globes.

Thus, in the First Round, the Globe, having been built by the primitive Fire-Lives, *i.e.*, formed into a sphere—had no solidity, no qualifications, save a cold brightness, no form nor colour; it is only towards the end of the First Round that it developed one Element which from its inorganic, so to say, or simple Essence became now in our Round the fire we know throughout the System.

The Second Round brings into manifestation the second Element —AIR, that element the purity of which would ensure continuous life to him who would use it. "*From the second Round, Earth—hitherto a foetus in the matrix of Space—began its real existence: it had developed individual sentient Life, its second Principle. The second corresponds to the sixth (Principle); the second is Life continuous; the other, temporary.*"

The *Third* Round developed the *third* Principle—WATER; while the Fourth transformed the gaseous fluids and plastic form of our globe into the hard, crusted, grossly material sphere we are living on. Bhumi has reached her *fourth* Principle. To this it may be objected that the law of analogy, so much insisted upon, is broken. Not at all. Earth will reach her true ultimate form—(inversely in this to man)—her body shell—only towards the end of the Manvantara after the Seventh Round.

It is not molecularly constituted matter—least of all the human Body (*Sthulasarira*)—that is the grossest of all our "Principles," but verily the *middle* Principle, the real animal centre; whereas our Body is but its shell, the irresponsible factor and medium through which the beast in us acts all its life. Thus the idea that the human tabernacle is built by countless *Lives*, just in the same way as the rocky crust of our Earth was, has nothing repulsive in it for the true mystic. Nor can Science oppose the Occult teaching, for it is not because the microscope will ever fail to detect the ultimate living atom or life that it can reject the doctrine.

(*c*) Science teaches us that the living as well as the dead organism of both man and animal are swarming with bacteria of a hundred various kinds. But Science never yet went so far as to assert with the Occult doctrine that our bodies, as well as those of animals, plants, and stones, are themselves altogether built up of such beings; which, except larger species, no microscope can detect. So far, as regards the purely animal and material portion of man, Science is on its way to discoveries that will go far towards corroborating this theory. Chemistry and physiology are the two great magicians of the future, which are destined to open the eyes of mankind to the great physical truths. With every day, the identity between the animal and physical man, between the plant and man, and even between the reptile and its nest, the rock, and man—is more and more clearly shown. The physical and chemical constituents of all being found to be identical, chemical science may well say that there is no difference between the matter which composes the ox and that which forms man. But the Occult doctrine is far more explicit. It says:—Not only the chemical compounds are the same, but the same infinitesimal *invisible Lives* compose the atoms of the bodies of the mountain and the daisy, of man and the ant, of the elephant, and of the tree which shelters him from the sun. Each particle—whether you call it organic or inorganic —*is a Life*. Every atom and molecule in the Universe is both *life-giving* and *death-giving* to that form, inasmuch as it builds by aggregation universes and the ephemeral vehicles ready to receive the transmigrating soul, and as eternally destroys and changes the *forms* and expels those souls from their temporary abodes. It creates and kills; it is self-generating and self-destroying; it brings into being, and annihilates, that mystery of mysteries, the *living body* of man, animal, or plant, every second in time and space; and it generates equally life and death, beauty and ugliness, good and bad, and even the agreeable and disagreeable, the beneficent and maleficent sensations. It is that mysterious LIFE, represented collectively by countless myriads of Lives, that follows in its own sporadic way the hitherto incomprehensible law of Atavism; that copies family resemblances as well as those it finds impressed in the aura of the generators of every future human being. Thus, having discovered the effects, Science has to find their PRIMARY causes; and this it can never do without the help of the old sciences, of Alchemy, Occult Botany and Physics. We are taught that every physiological change, in addition to pathological phenomena; diseases—nay, life itself—or rather the objective phenomena of life, produced by certain conditions and changes in the tissues of the body which allow and force life to act in that body; that all this is due to those unseen CREATORS and DESTROYERS that are called in such a loose and general way, microbes.[11]

(*d*) But what has the Moon to do in all this? we may be asked. What have "Fish, Sin and Moon," in the apocalyptic saying of the Stanza, to do in company with the "Life-microbes"? With the latter nothing, except availing themselves of the tabernacle of clay prepared by them; with divine perfect Man everything, since "Fish, Sin and Moon" make conjointly the three symbols of the immortal Being.

6. FROM THE FIRST-BORN (*Primitive, or the First Man*) THE THREAD

[11] It might be supposed that these "Fiery Lives" and the microbes of science are identical. This is not true. The Fiery Lives are the seventh and highest subdivision of the plane of matter, and correspond in the individual with the One Life of the Universe, though only on that plane. The microbes of science are the first and lowest subdivision on the second plane—that of material *Prana* (or Life). The physical body of man undergoes a complete change of structure every seven years, and its destruction and preservation are due to the alternate function of the Fiery Lives as "Destroyers" and "Builders." They are Builders by sacrificing themselves in the form of vitality to restrain the destructive influence of the microbes, and, by supplying the microbes with what is necessary, they compel them under that restraint to build up the material body and its cells. They are Destroyers also when that restraint is removed and the microbes, unsupplied with vital constructive energy, are left to run riot as destructive *agents*. Thus during the first half of a man's life (the first *five* periods of seven years each) the Fiery Lives are indirectly engaged in the process of building up man's material body; Life is on the ascending scale, and the force is used in construction and increase. After this period is passed the age of retrogression commences, and, the work of the Fiery Lives exhausting their strength, the work of destruction and decrease also commences.

BETWEEN THE SILENT WATCHER AND HIS SHADOW BECOMES MORE
STRONG AND RADIANT WITH EVERY CHANGE (*Re-incarnation*) (*a*). THE
MORNING SUN-LIGHT HAS CHANGED INTO NOON-DAY GLORY . . . .

(*a*) This sentence: "The Thread between the *Silent Watcher* and
his *Shadow* (Man) becomes stronger"—with every re-incarnation—is
another psychological mystery, that will find its explanation in Book
II. For the present it will suffice to say that the "Watcher" and his
"Shadows"—the latter numbering as many as there are re-incarnations for the Monad—are one. The Watcher, or the Divine Prototype, is at the upper rung of the ladder of Being; the Shadow, at the
lower. Withal, the *Monad* of every living being, unless his moral
turpitude breaks the connection and [he] runs loose and "astray into
the Lunar Path"—to use the Occult expression—*is an individual
Dhyan Chohan, distinct from others, a kind of spiritual Individuality of its
own*, during one special Manvantara. Its *Primary*, the Spirit (Atman)
is one, of course, with *Paramatma* (the one Universal Spirit), but the
vehicle (Vahan) it is enshrined in, the *Buddhi*, is part and parcel of
that Dhyan-Chohanic Essence; and it is in this that lies the mystery
of that *ubiquity*, which was discussed a few pages back. "My Father,
that is in Heaven, and I—are one,"—says the Christian Scripture;
in this, at any rate, it is the faithful echo of the esoteric tenet.

7. "THIS IS THY PRESENT WHEEL"—SAID THE FLAME TO THE SPARK.
"THOU ART MYSELF, MY IMAGE AND MY SHADOW. I HAVE CLOTHED
MYSELF IN THEE, AND THOU ART MY VAHAN (*Vehicle*) TO THE DAY, "BE
WITH US," WHEN THOU SHALT RE-BECOME MYSELF AND OTHERS, THY-
SELF AND ME" (*a*). THEN THE BUILDERS, HAVING DONNED THEIR FIRST
CLOTHING, DESCEND ON RADIANT EARTH, AND REIGN OVER MEN—WHO
ARE THEMSELVES (*b*).

(*a*) The day when "the Spark will re-become the Flame (Man
will merge into his Dhyan Chohan), "myself and others, thyself and
me," as the Stanza has it—means this: In *Paranirvana*—when *Pralaya*
will have reduced not only material and psychical bodies, but even
the spiritual *Ego(s)* to their original principle—the Past, Present, and
even Future Humanities, like all things, will be one and the same.
Everything will have re-entered the *Great Breath*. In other words,
everything will be "merged in Brahma"[12] or the Divine Unity.

Is this annihilation, as some think? Or *Atheism*, as other critics—
the worshippers of a *personal* deity and believers in an unphilosophical
paradise—are inclined to suppose? Neither. It is worse than useless
to return to the question of implied atheism in that which is *spirituality*
of a most refined character. To see in Nirvana annihilation amounts

[12] [? Brahman.]

to saying of a man plunged in a sound *dreamless* sleep—*one that leaves no impression on the physical memory and brain, because the sleeper's Higher Self is in its original state of Absolute Consciousness*—that he, too, is annihilated. The latter simile answers only to one side of the question—the most material; since *re-absorption* is by no means such a "dreamless sleep," but, on the contrary, *Absolute* Existence, an unconditioned unity, or a state, to describe which human language is absolutely and hopelessly inadequate. The only approach to anything like a comprehensive conception of it can be attempted solely in the panoramic visions of the soul, through spiritual ideations of the divine Monad. Nor is the individuality—*nor even the essence of the personality*, if any be left behind—lost, because re-absorbed. For, however limitless—from a human standpoint—the paranirvanic state, it has yet a limit in Eternity. Once reached, the same Monad will *re-emerge* therefrom, as a still higher being, on a far higher plane, to recommence its cycle of perfected activity. The human mind cannot in its present stage of development transcend, scarcely reach this plane of thought. It totters here, on the brink of incomprehensible Absoluteness and Eternity.

(*b*) The "Watchers" reign over man during the whole period of *Satya Yuga* and the smaller subsequent yugas, down to the beginning of the Third Root Race; after which it is the Patriarchs, Heroes, and the Manes, the incarnated Dhyanis of a lower order, up to King Menes and the human kings of other nations.

Dhyani-Buddhas of the two higher Groups, namely, the "Watchers" or the "Architects," furnished the many and various races with divine kings and leaders. It is the latter who taught humanity their arts and sciences, and the former who revealed to the incarnated Monads that had just shaken off their vehicles of the lower Kingdoms—and who had, therefore, lost every recollection of their divine origin—the great spiritual truths of the transcendental worlds.

Thus, as expressed in the Stanza, the Watchers descended on Earth and reigned over men—"*who are themselves.*" The reigning kings had finished their cycle on Earth and other worlds, in the preceding Rounds. In the future manvantaras they will have risen to higher systems than our planetary World; and it is the Elect of our Humanity, the Pioneers on the hard and difficult path of Progress, who will take the places of their predecessors. The next great Manvantara will witness the men of our own life-cycle becoming the instructors and guides of a mankind whose Monads may now yet be imprisoned—semi-conscious—in the most intellectual of the animal kingdom, while their lower principles will be animating, perhaps, the highest specimens of the vegetable world.

Thus proceed the cycles of the septenary evolution, in Septennial nature; the Spiritual or divine; the psychic or semi-divine; the intellectual, the passional, the instinctual, or *cognitional;* the semi-corporeal and the purely material or physical natures. All these evolve and progress cyclically, passing from one into another, in a double, centrifugal and centripetal way, *one* in their ultimate essence, *seven* in their aspects. The lowest, of course, is the one depending upon and subservient to our five physical senses.[13] Thus far, for individual, human, sentient, animal and vegetable life, each the microcosm of its higher macrocosm. The same for the Universe, which manifests periodically, for purposes of the collective progress of the countless *Lives*, the outbreathings of the One *Life;* in order that through the *Ever-Becoming*, every cosmic atom in this infinite Universe, passing from the formless and the intangible, through the mixed natures of the semi-terrestrial, down to matter in full generation, and then back again, reascending at each new period higher and nearer the final goal; that each atom, we say, *may reach through individual merits and efforts*, that plane where it re-becomes the one unconditioned ALL. But between the Alpha and the Omega there is the weary "Road" hedged in by thorns, that goes down first, then—

> Winds uphill all the way
> Yes, to the very end. . . ."

Starting upon the long journey immaculate; descending more and more into sinful matter, and having connected himself with every atom in manifested *Space*—the *Pilgrim*, having struggled through and suffered in every form of life and being, is only at the bottom of the valley of matter, and half through his cycle, when he has identified himself with collective Humanity. This, *he has made in his own image.* In order to progress upwards and homewards, the "God" has now to ascend the weary uphill path of the Golgotha of Life. It is the martyrdom of self-conscious existence. Like Visvakarman he has to sacrifice *himself to himself* in order to redeem all creatures, to resurrect from the many into the *One Life*. Then he ascends into heaven indeed; where, plunged into the incomprehensible absolute Being and Bliss of Paranirvana, he reigns unconditionally, and whence he will re-descend again at the next "Coming," which one portion of humanity expects as the *Second Advent*, and the other as the last "Kalki Avatar."

[13] Which are in truth *seven* as shown later.

SUMMING UP

Let us recapitulate and show, by the vastness of the subjects expounded, how difficult, if not impossible, it is to do them full justice.

(1) The Secret Doctrine is the accumulated Wisdom of the Ages, and its cosmogony alone is the most stupendous and elaborate system. But such is the mysterious power of Occult symbolism, that the facts which have actually occupied countless generations of initiated seers and prophets to marshal, to set down and explain, in the bewildering series of evolutionary progress, are all recorded on a few pages of geometrical signs and glyphs. It is useless to say that the system in question is no fancy of one or several isolated individuals. That it is the uninterrupted record covering thousands of generations of Seers whose respective experiences were made to test and to verify the traditions passed orally by one early race to another, of the teachings of higher and exalted Beings, who watched over the childhood of Humanity. That for long ages, the "Wise Men" of the Fifth Race, of the stock saved and rescued from the last cataclysm and shifting of continents, had passed their lives *in learning, not teaching.* How did they do so? It is answered: by checking, testing, and verifying in every department of nature the traditions of old by the independent visions of great Adepts; *i.e.,* men who have developed and perfected their physical, mental, psychic, and spiritual organizations to the utmost possible degree. No vision of one Adept was accepted till it was checked and confirmed by the visions—so obtained as to stand as independent evidence—of other Adepts, and by centuries of experience.

(2) The fundamental Law in that system, the central point from which all emerged, around and toward which all gravitates, and upon which is hung the philosophy of the rest, is the One homogeneous divine SUBSTANCE-PRINCIPLE, the one radical cause.

It is called "Substance-Principle," for it becomes "Substance" on the plane of the manifested Universe, an illusion, while it remains a "Principle" in the beginningless and endless abstract, visible and invisible SPACE. It is the omnipresent Reality: impersonal, because it contains all and everything. *Its impersonality is the fundamental conception* of the System. It is latent in every atom in the Universe, and is the Universe itself.

(3) The Universe is the periodical manifestation of this unknown Absolute Essence. IT is best described as neither Spirit nor Matter, but both. "Parabrahman and Mulaprakriti" are One, in reality, yet Two in the Universal conception of the manifested, even in the

conception of the One Logos, its first manifestation, to which IT appears from the objective standpoint of the One Logos as Mulaprakriti and not as Parabrahman; as its *veil* and not the One REALITY hidden behind, which is unconditioned and absolute.

(4) The Universe is called, with everything in it, MAYA, because all is temporary therein, from the ephemeral life of a fire-fly to that of the Sun. Yet, the Universe is real enough to the conscious beings in it, which are as unreal as it is itself.

(5) Everything in the Universe, throughout all its kingdoms, is CONSCIOUS: *i.e.*, endowed with a consciousness of its own kind and on its own plane of perception. Because *we* do not perceive any signs—which we can recognize—of consciousness, say, in stones, we have no right to say that *no consciousness exists there*. There is no such thing as either "dead" or "blind" matter, as there is no "blind" or "unconscious" Law. These find no place among the conceptions of Occult philosophy.

(6) The Universe is worked and *guided* from *within outwards*. As above so it is below, as in heaven so on earth; and man—the microcosm and miniature copy of the macrocosm—is the living witness to this Universal Law and to the mode of its action. We see that every *external* motion, act, gesture, whether voluntary or mechanical, organic or mental, is produced and preceded by *internal* feeling or emotion, will or volition, and thought or mind. As no outward motion or change, when normal, in man's external body can take place unless provoked by an inward impulse, given through one of the three functions named, so with the external or manifested Universe. The whole Kosmos is guided, controlled, and animated by almost endless series of Hierarchies of sentient Beings, each having a mission to perform, and who—whether we give to them one name or another, and call them Dhyan-Chohans or Angels—are "messengers" in the sense only that they are the agents of Karmic and Cosmic Laws. They vary infinitely in their respective degrees of consciousness and intelligence; and to call them all pure Spirits is only to indulge in poetical fancy. Each of these Beings either *was*, or prepares to become, a man, if not in the present, then in a past or a coming cycle (Manvantara). They are *perfected*, when not *incipient*, men; and differ morally from the terrestrial human beings on their higher (less material) spheres, only in that they are devoid of the feeling of personality and of the *human* emotional nature—two purely earthly characteristics. The former, or the "perfected," have become free from those feelings, because (*a*) they have no longer fleshly bodies—an ever-numbing weight on the Soul; and (*b*) the pure spiritual element being left untrammelled and more free, they are less influenced

by *maya* than man can ever be, unless he is an Adept who keeps his
two personalities—the spiritual and the physical—entirely separated.

The incipient Monads, having never had terrestrial bodies yet,
can have no sense of personality or EGO-ism. None of these Beings,
high or low, has either individuality or personality as separate
Entities, *i.e.*, they have no individuality in the sense in which a man
says, "*I am myself* and no one else"; in other words, they are conscious
of no such distinct separateness as men and things have on earth.
Individuality is the characteristic of their respective Hierarchies, not
of their units; and these characteristics vary only with the degree of
the plane to which those hierarchies belong. They are "Living
Ones," because they are the streams projected on the Kosmic screen
of Illusion from the ABSOLUTE LIFE; Beings in whom life cannot become extinct, before the fire of ignorance is extinct in those who
sense these "Lives." They are neither "ministering" nor "protecting" Angels; nor are they "Harbingers of the Most High," still less
the "Messengers of wrath" of any God such as man's fancy has
created. To appeal to their protection is as foolish as to believe that
their sympathy may be secured by any kind of propitiation; for they
are, as much as man himself is, the slaves and creatures of immutable
Karmic and Kosmic law. Man, as shown in Book II., being a compound of the essences of all those celestial Hierarchies, may succeed in
making himself, as such, superior, in one sense, to any Hierarchy or
Class, or even combination of them. "Man can neither propitiate
nor command the *Devas*," it is said. But, by paralysing his lower
personality, and arriving thereby at the full knowledge of the *non-
separateness* of his higher SELF from the One absolute SELF, man can,
even during his terrestrial life, become as "One of Us."

(7) In sober truth, every "Spirit" so-called is either a *disembodied
or a future man.* As from the highest Archangel (Dhyan Chohan)
down to the last conscious "Builder" (the inferior Class of Spiritual
Entities), all such are *men*, having lived aeons ago, in other Manvantaras, on this or other Spheres; so the inferior, semi-intelligent
and non-intelligent Elementals—are all *future* men. That fact alone
—that a Spirit is endowed with intelligence—is a proof to the
Occultist that that Being must have been a **man**, and acquired his
knowledge and intelligence throughout the human cycle. There is
but one indivisible and absolute Omniscience and Intelligence in the
Universe, and this thrills throughout every atom and infinitesimal
point of the whole finite Kosmos which hath no bounds, and which
people call SPACE, considered independently of anything contained
in it. But the first differentiation of its *reflection* in the manifested
World is purely Spiritual, and the Beings generated in it are not

endowed with a consciousness that has any relation to the one we conceive of. They can have no human consciousness or Intelligence before they have acquired such, personally and individually.

The whole order of nature evinces a progressive march towards *a higher life*. The whole process of evolution with its endless adaptations is a proof of this. The very *fact* that adaptations *do* occur, that the fittest *do* survive in the struggle for existence, shows that what is called "unconscious Nature"[1] is in reality an aggregate of forces manipulated by semi-intelligent beings (Elementals) guided by High Planetary Spirits (Dhyan Chohans), whose collective aggregate forms the manifested *verbum* of the unmanifested LOGOS, and constitutes at one and the same time the MIND of the Universe and its immutable LAW.

Whatever may be the destiny of these actual writings in a remote future, we hope to have proven so far the following facts:

(1) The Secret Doctrine teaches no *Atheism*, except in the Hindu sense of the word *nastika*, or the rejection of *idols*, including every anthropomorphic God. In this sense every Occultist is a *Nastika*.

(2) It admits a Logos or a collective "Creator" of the Universe; a *Demi-urgos*—in the sense implied when one speaks of an "Architect" as the "Creator" of an edifice, whereas that architect has never touched one stone of it, but, while furnishing the plan, left all the manual labour to the masons; in our case the plan was furnished by the Ideation of the Universe, and the constructive labour was left to the Hosts of intelligent Powers and Forces. But that *Demiurgos* is no *personal* Deity,—*i.e.*, an imperfect *extra-cosmic God*,—but only the aggregate of the Dhyan-Chohans and the other forces.

As to the latter—

(3) They are dual in their character; being composed of (*a*) the irrational *brute Energy*, inherent in matter, and (*b*) the intelligent Soul or Cosmic Consciousness which directs and guides that energy, and which is the *Dhyan-Chohanic thought reflecting the Ideation of the Universal Mind*. This results in a perpetual series of physical manifestations and *moral effects* on Earth, during manvantaric periods, the whole being subservient to Karma. As that process is not always perfect it still shows gaps and flaws, and even results very often in evident failures—therefore, neither the collective Host (Demiurgos), nor any of the working powers individually, are proper subjects for

---

[1] Nature, taken in its abstract sense, *cannot* be "unconscious," as it is the emanation from, and thus an aspect (on the manifested plane) of the ABSOLUTE consciousness. Where is that daring man who would presume to deny to vegetation and even to minerals *a consciousness of their own*. All he can say is, that this consciousness is beyond his comprehension.

divine honours or worship. The ever unknowable and incognizable *Karana* alone, the *Causeless* Cause of all causes, should have its shrine and altar on the holy and ever untrodden ground of our heart— invisible, intangible, unmentioned, save through "the still small voice" of our spiritual consciousness. Those who worship before it, ought to do so in the silence and the sanctified solitude of their Souls;[2] making their Spirit the sole mediator between them and the *Universal Spirit*, their good actions the only priests, and their sinful intentions the only visible and objective sacrificial victims to the *Presence*.

(4) Matter is *Eternal*. It is the *Upadhi* (the physical basis) for the One infinite Universal Mind to build thereon its ideations. There- fore, the Esotericists maintain that there is no inorganic or *dead* matter in nature.

(5) The Universe was evolved out of its ideal plan, upheld through Eternity in the Unconsciousness of that which the Vedantins call Parabrahm. This is practically identical with the conclusions of the highest Western Philosophy—"the innate, eternal, and self- existing Ideas" of Plato, now reflected by Von Hartmann.

The active Power, the "Perpetual Motion of the great Breath" only awakens Kosmos at the dawn of every new Period, setting it into motion by means of the two contrary Forces, and thus causing it to become objective on the plane of Illusion. In other words, that dual motion transfers Kosmos from the plane of the Eternal Ideal into that of finite manifestation, or from the *Noumenal* to the *phe- nomenal* plane. Everything that *is*, *was*, and *will be*, eternally is, even the countless forms, which are finite and perishable only in their objective, not in their *ideal* Form. They existed as Ideas, in the Eternity,[3] and, when they pass away, will exist as reflections. Neither the form of man, nor that of any animal, plant or stone has ever been *created*, and it is only on this plane of ours that it commenced "becoming," *i.e.*, objectivizing into its present materiality, or ex- panding *from within outwards*, from the most sublimated and super- sensuous essence into its grossest appearance. Therefore *our* human

[2] "When thou prayest, thou shalt not be as the hypocrites are . . . but enter into *thine inner chamber and having shut thy door, pray to thy Father which is in secret.*" *Matt. vi.*) Our Father is *within us* "in Secret," our 7th principle, in the "inner chamber" of our Soul perception. "The Kingdom of Heaven" and of God "*is within us*" says Jesus, not *outside*. Why are Christians so absolutely blind to the self-evident meaning of the words of wisdom they delight in mechanically repeating?

[3] Occultism teaches that no form can be given to anything, either by nature or by man, whose ideal type does not already exist on the subjective plane. More than this; that no such form or shape can possibly enter man's consciousness, or evolve in his imagination, which does not exist in prototype, at least as an approximation.

forms have existed in the Eternity as astral or ethereal prototypes; according to which models, the Spiritual Beings (or Gods) whose duty it was to bring them into objective being and terrestrial Life, evolved the protoplasmic forms of the future *Egos* from *their own essence*. After which, when this human *Upadhi*, or basic mould was ready, the natural terrestrial Forces began to work on those super-sensuous moulds *which contained, besides their own, the elements of all the past vegetable and future animal forms of this Globe in them*. Therefore, man's *outward* shell passed through every vegetable and animal body before it assumed the human shape.

PART II

THE EVOLUTION OF SYMBOLISM IN ITS APPROXIMATE ORDER

1. SYMBOLISM AND IDEOGRAPHS

THE study of the hidden meaning in every religious and profane legend, of whatsoever nation, large or small—pre-eminently the traditions of the East—has occupied the greater portion of the present writer's life. She is one of those who feel convinced that no mythological story, no traditional event in the folk-lore of a people has ever been, at any time, pure fiction, but that every one of such narratives has an actual, historical lining to it.

The proofs brought forward in corroboration of the old teachings are scattered widely throughout the old scriptures of ancient civilizations. The Puranas, the Zendavesta, and the old classics are full of them; but no one has ever gone to the trouble of collecting and collating together those facts. The reason for this is that all such events were recorded symbolically. Even a parable is a spoken symbol: a fiction or a fable, as some think; an allegorical representation, we say, of life-realities, events, and facts. And, as a moral was ever drawn from a parable, that moral being an actual truth and fact in human life, so an historical, real event was deduced—by those versed in the hieratic sciences—from certain emblems and symbols recorded in the ancient archives of the temples. The religious and esoteric history of every nation was embedded in symbols; it was never expressed in so many words. All the thoughts and emotions, all the learning and knowledge, revealed and acquired, of the early races, found their pictorial expression in allegory and parable. Why? Because *the spoken word has a potency unknown to, unsuspected and disbelieved in,* by the modern "sages," because sound and rhythm are closely related to the four Elements of the Ancients; and because such or another vibration in the air is sure to awaken corresponding powers, union with which produces good or bad results, as the case may be.

2. THE MYSTERY LANGUAGE AND ITS KEYS

RECENT discoveries made by great mathematicians and Kabalists prove that every theology, from the earliest and oldest down to the latest, has sprung not only from a common source of abstract beliefs, but from one universal esoteric, or "Mystery" language. These scholars hold the key to the universal language of old, and have turned it successfully, though only *once*, in the hermetically closed door leading to the Hall of Mysteries. The great archaic system known from prehistoric ages as the sacred Wisdom Science, one that is contained and can be traced in every old as well as in every new religion, had and still has, its universal language—the language of the Hierophants, which has seven "dialects," so to speak, each referring, and being specially appropriated, to one of the seven mysteries of Nature. Each had its own symbolism. Nature could thus be either read in its fullness, or viewed from one of its special aspects.

The proof of this lies, to this day, in the extreme difficulty which the Orientalists experience in interpreting the allegorical writings of the Aryans and the hieratic records of old Egypt. This is because they will never remember that all the ancient records were written in a language which was universal and known to all nations alike in days of old, but which is now intelligible only to the few.

It is maintained that India (not in its present limits, but including its ancient boundaries) is the only country in the world which still has among her sons Adepts who have the knowledge of all the seven *sub-systems* and the key to the entire system. Since the fall of Memphis, Egypt began to lose those keys one by one, and Chaldea had preserved only three in the days of Berosus. As for the Hebrews, in all their writings they show no more than a thorough knowledge of the astronomical, geometrical and numerical systems of symbolizing all the human, and especially the *physiological* functions. They never had the higher keys.

3. PRIMORDIAL SUBSTANCE AND DIVINE THOUGHT

ETHER is one of the lower "principles" of what we call PRIMORDIAL SUBSTANCE (Akasa, in Sanskrit), one of the *dreams* of old, which has now become again the dream of modern science. It is the greatest, just as it is the boldest, of the surviving speculations of ancient philosophers. For the Occultists, however, both ETHER and the Primordial Substance are a reality. To put it plainly, ETHER is the Astral Light, and the Primordial Substance is AKASA, the *Upadhi* of DIVINE THOUGHT.

In modern language, the latter would be better named COSMIC IDEATION—Spirit; the former, COSMIC SUBSTANCE, Matter. These, the Alpha and the Omega of Being, are but the two *facets* of the one Absolute Existence.

Divine Thought cannot be defined, or its meaning explained, except by the numberless manifestations of Cosmic Substance in which the former *is sensed* spiritually by those who can do so. Its place is found in the old primitive Symbolic charts, in which, as shown in the text, it is represented by a boundless darkness, on the ground of which appears the first central point in white—thus symbolizing coeval and co-eternal SPIRIT-MATTER making its appearance in the phenomenal world, before its first differentiation. When "the One becomes two," it may then be referred to as Spirit *and* matter. To "Spirit" is referable every manifestation of consciousness, reflective or direct, and of *unconscious purposiveness* (to adopt a modern expression), as evidenced in the Vital Principle, and Nature's submission to the majestic sequence of immutable Law. "Matter" must be regarded as objectivity in its purest abstraction—the self-existing basis whose septenary manvantaric differentiations constitute the objective reality underlying the phenomena of each phase of conscious existence. During the period of Universal Pralaya, Cosmic Ideation is non-existent; and the variously differentiated states of Cosmic Substance are resolved back again into the primary state of abstract potential objectivity.

Manvantaric impulse commences with the re-awakening of Cosmic Ideation (the "Universal Mind") concurrently with the emergence of Cosmic Substance—the latter being the manvantaric vehicle of the former—from its undifferentiated pralayic state. Then, Absolute Wisdom mirrors itself in its Ideation, which, by a transcendental process, superior to and incomprehensible by human Consciousness, results in Cosmic Energy (*Fohat*). Thrilling through the bosom of inert Substance, *Fohat* impels it to activity, and guides its primary differentiations on all the Seven planes of Cosmic Consciousness. There are thus *Seven Protyles* or Natures, serving severally as the *relatively* homogeneous basis, which in the course of the increasing heterogeneity (in the evolution of the Universe) differentiate into the marvellous complexity presented by phenomena on the planes of perception. The term "relatively" is used designedly, because the very existence of such a process compels us to regard the *protyle*[1] of each plane as only a *mediate* phase assumed by Substance in its passage from abstract, into full objectivity.

[1] The term *Protyle* is due to Mr. Crookes, the eminent chemist, who has given that name to *pre-Matter*, if one may so call primordial and purely homogeneous substances, suspected, if not actually yet found, by Science in the ultimate composition of the atom. But the incipient segregation of primordial matter into atoms and molecules takes its rise subsequent to the evolution of the Seven *Protyles*. It is the last of these that Mr. Crookes is seeking.

What, then, is the "primordial Substance"? We touch and do not feel it; we look at it without seeing it; we breathe it and do not perceive it; we hear and smell it without the smallest cognition that it is there; for it is in every molecule of that which in our illusion and ignorance we regard as Matter in any of its states, or conceive as a feeling, a thought, an emotion.

Spirit, then, or Cosmic Ideation, and Cosmic Substance—one of whose *principles* is Ether—are *one*, and include the ELEMENTS, in the sense St. Paul attaches to them. These Elements are the veiled Synthesis standing for Dhyan Chohans, Devas, Sephiroth, Archangels, etc. The Ether of science—the *Protyle* of chemistry—constitutes, so to speak, the *rude* material (relatively) out of which the above-named "Builders," following the plan traced out for them eternally in the DIVINE THOUGHT, fashion the systems in the Cosmos. They are "myths," we are told. "No more so than Ether and the Atoms," we answer. The two latter are *absolute* necessities of physical science; the "Builders" are as absolute a necessity of metaphysics.

The one prevailing, most distinct idea—found in all ancient teaching, with reference to Cosmic Evolution and the first "creation" of our Globe with all its products, organic and *inorganic* (strange word for an Occultist to use)—is that the whole Kosmos has sprung from the DIVINE THOUGHT. This Thought impregnates Matter, which is co-eternal with the ONE REALITY; and all that lives and breathes evolves from the emanations of the ONE *Immutable* Parabrahm—Mulaprakriti, the eternal One-Root. The former of these is, so to say, the aspect of the central Point turned inward into regions quite inaccessible to human intellect, and is absolute abstraction; whereas, in its aspect as *Mulaprakriti*—the eternal Root of all,—it gives one some hazy comprehension at least of the Mystery of Being.

No one can study ancient philosophies seriously without perceiving that the striking similitude of conception between all—in their exoteric form very often, in their hidden spirit invariably—is the result of no mere coincidence, but of a concurrent design: and that there was, during the youth of mankind, one language, one knowledge, one universal religion, when there were no churches, no creeds or sects, but when every man was a priest unto himself. And, if it is shown that already in those ages which are shut out from our sight by the exuberant growth of tradition, human religious thought developed in uniform sympathy in every portion of the globe, it becomes evident that that thought was inspired by the same revelations, and man was nurtured under the protecting shadow of the same TREE OF KNOWLEDGE.

4. CHAOS—THEOS—KOSMOS

DEMOCRITUS, with his instructor Leucippus, taught that the first principles of all things contained in the Universe were atoms and a *vacuum*. The latter means simply *latent* Deity or force; which, before its first manifestation when it became WILL—communicating the first impulse to these atoms—was the great *Nothingness*, Ain-Soph, or NO-THING; was, therefore, to every sense, a Void—or CHAOS.

Chaos-Theos-Kosmos, the triple deity, is *all in all*. Therefore, it is said to be male and female, good and evil, positive and negative; the whole series of contrasted qualities. When latent (in pralaya) it is incognizable and becomes the *unknowable Deity*. It can be known only in its active functions; hence as *matter-Force* and *living Spirit*, the correlations and outcome, or the expression, on the visible plane, of the ultimate and ever-to-be unknown UNITY.

7. THE DAYS AND NIGHTS OF BRAHMĀ

THIS is the name given to the Periods called MANVANTARA (*Manuantara*, or between the Manus) and PRALAYA (Dissolution); one referring to the active periods of the Universe, the other to its times of relative and complete *rest*—according to whether they occur at the end of a "Day," or an "Age" (a life) of Brahmā. These periods, which follow each other in regular succession, are also called *Kalpas*, small and great, the minor and the *Maha Kalpa;* though, properly speaking, the Maha Kalpa is never a "day," but a whole life or age of Brahmā.

There are many kinds of *Pralaya*, but three chief ones are specially mentioned in old Hindu books:—The first is called Naimittika caused by the intervals of "Brahmā's Days"; it is the destruction of creatures, of all that lives and has a form, but not of the substance which remains *in statu quo* till the new DAWN in that "Night." The second is called Prakritika—and occurs at the end of the *Age* or Life of Brahmā, when everything that exists is resolved into the primal Element, to be remodelled at the end of that longer Night. But the third, Atyantika, does not concern the Worlds or the Universe, but only the individualities of some people; it is thus individual pralaya or NIRVANA; after which there is no more future existence possible, no rebirth till after the *Maha Pralaya*. The latter Night, lasting as it does 311,040,000,000,000 years, and having the possibility of being almost doubled in case the lucky *Jivanmukti* reaches Nirvana at an early period of a Manvantara, is long enough to be regarded as *eternal*, if not endless. The *Bhagavata* (XII., iv, 35) speaks of a fourth kind of pralaya, the Nitya or constant dissolution, the change which takes place imperceptibly in everything in this Universe from the globe down to the atom—without cessation. It is growth and decay, life and death.

The final PRALAYA[1]—the Death of Kosmos—after which its Spirit rests in Nirvana, or in THAT for which there is neither Day nor Night. All the other pralayas are periodical and follow, in regular succession, the Manvantaras, as the night follows the day of every human creature, animal, and plant. The cycle of creation of the *lives* of Kosmos is run down, the energy of the manifested "Word" having its growth, culmination, and decrease, as have all things temporary, however long their duration. The Creative Force is Eternal as Noumenon; as a phenomenal manifestation in its aspects, it has a *beginning* and must, therefore, have an end. During that interval it has its periods of activity and its periods of rest. And these are the "Days and the Nights of Brahmā." But Brahman, the Noumenon, never rests, as IT never changes and ever IS, though IT cannot be said to be anywhere. . . .

[1] As it is the *Maha*, the Great, or so-called *final* PRALAYA which is here described, everything is re-absorbed into its original ONE Element—the "Gods themselves, Brahmā and the rest" being said to die and disappear during that long NIGHT.

PART III

SCIENCE AND THE SECRET DOCTRINE CONTRASTED

1. REASONS FOR THESE ADDENDA

MANY of the doctrines contained in the foregoing seven Stanzas and Commentaries, having been studied and critically examined by some Western Theosophists, have been found wanting from the stand-point of modern scientific knowledge. They seemed to encounter insuperable difficulties in the way of their acceptance, and to require reconsideration in view of scientific criticism. Some friends have already been tempted to regret the necessity of so often calling in question the assertions of modern Science. It appeared to them that "to run counter to the teachings of its most eminent exponents, was to court a premature discomfiture in the eyes of the Western World."

So far as Science remains, in the words of Prof. Huxley, "organized common sense"; so far as its inferences are drawn from accurate premises—its generalizations resting on a purely inductive basis— every Theosophist and Occultist welcomes respectfully its contributions to the domain of cosmological law. There can be no possible conflict between the teachings of Occult and so-called exact Science, where the conclusions of the latter are grounded on a sub-stratum of unassailable fact. It is only when its more ardent exponents, overstepping the limits of observed phenomena, attempt to wrench the formation of Kosmos and its *living* Forces from Spirit, and attribute all to blind matter, that the Occultists claim the right to dispute their theories. Science cannot, owing to the very nature of things, unveil the mystery of the Universe around us. Science can, it is true, collect, classify, and generalize upon phenomena; but the Occultist, arguing from admitted metaphysical data, declares that the daring explorer, who would probe the inmost secrets of Nature, must transcend the narrow limitations of sense, and transfer his consciousness into the region of noumena and the sphere of Primal Causes. To do this, he must develop faculties which are absolutely dormant —save in a few rare and exceptional cases—in the constitution of the off-shoots of our present Fifth Root-race in Europe and America. He can in no other conceivable manner collect the facts on which to base his speculations.

To offer the reader a systematic and uninterrupted version of the Archaic Stanzas is impossible. A gap of 43 verses has to be left between the 7th (already given) and the 51st, which is the subject of Book II., though the latter are made to run from 1 *et seq.* for easier reading and reference.

Another good reason for these Addenda is this. Since only a certain portion of the Secret Teachings can be given out in the present age, if they were published without any explanations or commentary, the doctrines would never be understood even by Theosophists. Therefore they must be contrasted with the speculations of modern science. Archaic axioms must be placed side by side with modern hypotheses and comparison left to the sagacious reader.

4. IS GRAVITATION A LAW?

THE corpuscular theory has been unceremoniously put aside; but gravitation—the principle that all bodies attract each other with a force proportional directly to their masses, and inversely to the squares of the distances between them—survives to this day and reigns, supreme as ever, in the alleged ethereal waves of Space. Astronomers who see in gravitation an easy-going solution for many things, and a *universal* force which allows them to calculate thereby planetary motions, care little about the Cause of Attraction. They call Gravity a law, a *cause* in itself. We call the forces acting under that name *effects*, and very secondary effects, too. One day it will be found that the scientific hypothesis does not answer after all; and then it will follow the corpuscular theory of light and be consigned to rest for many scientific *aeons* in the archives of exploded speculations. At the outset of his "Principia," Sir Isaac Newton took the greatest care to impress upon his school that he did not use the word "attraction" with regard to the mutual action of bodies in a physical sense. To him it was, he said, a purely mathematical conception involving no consideration of real and primary physical causes. In one of the passages of his "Principia" (*Defin.* 8, *B. I. Prop.* 69, "*Scholium*"), he tells us plainly that, physically considered, attractions are rather *impulses*. In section XI. (*Introduction*) he expresses the opinion that "there *is some subtle spirit by the force and action of which* all movements of matter are determined" (see *Mod. Mater.*, by Rev. *W. F. Wilkinson*); and in his third Letter to Bentley he says: "It is inconceivable that inanimate brute matter should, without the mediation of something else *which is not material*, operate upon and affect other matter, without mutual contact, as it must do if gravitation, in the sense of Epicurus, be essential and inherent in it. . . . That gravity should be innate, inherent and essential to matter, so that one body may act upon another at a distance, through a vacuum, without the mediation of anything else by and through which their action may be conveyed from one to another, is to me so great an absurdity that I believe no man, who has in philosophical matters a competent faculty of thinking, can ever fall into it. Gravity must be caused by an agent acting constantly according to certain laws; but *whether this agent* be *material or immaterial* I have left to the consideration of my readers."

When an Occultist speaks of Fohat—the energizing and guiding intelligence in the Universal Electric or *Vital* Fluid,—he is laughed at. Withal, as now shown, neither the nature of electricity, nor of Life nor even of Light, are to this day understood. The Occultist sees, in the manifestation of every force in Nature, the action of the quality, or the special characteristic of its Noumenon; which *Noumenon* is a distinct and intelligent Individuality *on the other side of the manifested mechanical Universe.* Now the Occultist does not deny —on the contrary he will support the claim—that light, heat, electricity and so on are *affections* (not properties or qualities) of matter. To put it more clearly: Matter is the condition—the necessary basis or vehicle—for the manifestation of these Forces, or Agents, on this plane.

Let us remember Sir William Grove's wise "concluding remarks," on the ultimate structure of matter.

The learned gentleman states a purely occult tenet:—

"The term perpetual motion, which I have not infrequently used in these pages, is itself equivocal. If the doctrines here advanced be well founded, *all motion is, in one sense, perpetual.* In masses, whose motion is stopped by mutual concussion, heat or motion of the particles is generated; and thus the motion continues, so that if we could venture to extend such thoughts to the universe, we should assume the same amount of motion affecting the same amount of matter for ever."[1]

Thus, supposing attraction or gravitation should be given up in favour of the Sun being a *huge magnet*—which is a theory already accepted by some physicists—a magnet that acts on the planets as attraction is now supposed to do, whereto, or how much farther would it lead the astronomers from where they are now? That such magnetism exists in nature is as certain as that gravitation does not;

[1] *"Correl. Phys. Forces,"* p. 173. This is precisely what Occultism maintains, and on the same principle that "where force is made to oppose force, and produce static equilibrium, the balance of pre-existing equilibrium is affected, and *fresh motion is started* equivalent to that which is withdrawn into a state of abeyance." This process finds intervals in the Pralaya, but is eternal and ceaseless as the 'Breath," even when the manifested Kosmos rests.

not at any rate, in the way in which it is taught by Science, which never took into consideration the different modes in which the dual Force that Occultism calls attraction and repulsion may act within our Solar System, the Earth's atmosphere, and *beyond* in the Kosmos.

The ideas of Kepler, weeded from their theological tendencies, are purely Occult. He saw that:

(I) The Sun is a great Magnet. This is what some eminent modern scientists and also the Occultists believe in.

(II) The Solar substance is immaterial.[1] (See *Isis Unveiled*, *Vol. I., pp.* 270 *to* 271.)

(III) He provided, for the constant motion and restoration of the Sun's energy and planetary motion, the perpetual care of a Spirit, or Spirits. The whole of Antiquity believed in this idea. The Occultists do not use the word Spirit, but say *Creative* Forces, which they *endow with intelligence*. But we may call them Spirits also.

9. THE SOLAR THEORY

The origin of the LIFE ESSENCE, Occultism locates in the same centre as the nucleus of *prima materia* (for they are one) of our Solar system.

"*The Sun is the heart of the Solar World (System) and its brain is hidden behind the (visible) Sun. Thence, sensation is radiated into every nerve-centre of the great body, and the waves of the life-essence flow into each artery and vein. . . . The planets are its limbs and pulses. . . .*" (*Commentary.*)

Occult philosophy denies that the Sun is a globe in combustion, but defines it simply as a world, a glowing sphere, the *real* Sun being hidden behind, and the visible being only its reflection, its *shell*. The Nasmyth willow leaves, mistaken by Sir J. Herschell for "Solar inhabitants," are the reservoirs of solar vital energy, "the vital electricity that feeds the whole system. . . . The Sun *in abscondito* being thus the storehouse of our little Kosmos, self-generating its vital fluid, and ever receiving as much as it gives out," and the *visible* Sun only a *window cut into the real* Solar palace and presence, which reflects, however, faithfully the interior work.

Thus, there is a regular circulation of the vital fluid throughout our system of which the Sun is the heart—the same as the circulation of the blood in the human body—during the manvantaric solar period, or life; the Sun contracting as rhythmically at every return of it, as the human heart does. Only, instead of performing the round

[1] In the sense, of course, of Matter existing in states unknown to Science.

in a second or so, it takes the solar blood ten of its years [to circulate] and a whole year to pass through its *auricles* and *ventricles*, before it washes the *lungs* and passes thence to the great veins and arteries of the system.

This, Science will not deny, since astronomy knows of the fixed cycle of eleven years when the number of solar spots increases *which is due to the contraction* of the Solar HEART. The Universe (our World in this case) breathes, just as man and every living creature, plant, and even mineral does upon the earth; and as our globe itself breathes every twenty-four hours. It is similar to the regular and healthy pulsation of the heart, as the life fluid passes through its hollow muscles. Could the human heart be made luminous, and the living and throbbing organ be made visible, so as to have it reflected upon a screen, such as used by the astronomers in their lectures— say for the moon—then every one would see the Sun-spot phenomenon repeated every second—due to its contraction and the rushing of the blood.

It is said in a work on geology that it is the *dream of Science* that "all the recognized chemical elements will one day be found *but modifications of a single material element.*"

Occult Philosophy has taught this since the existence of human speech and languages, adding only, on the principle of the immutable law of analogy—"as it is above, so it is below"—that there is neither Spirit nor Matter, in reality, but only numberless aspects of the One ever-hidden IS (or *Sat*). The homogeneous primordial Element is *simple* and *single only on the terrestrial plane* of consciousness and sensation, since Matter, after all, is nothing else than the sequence of our own states of consciousness, and Spirit an idea of psychic intuition. Even on the next higher plane, that *single element* which is defined on our earth by current science as the ultimate undecomposable constituent of some kind of matter, would be pronounced in the world of a higher spiritual perception as something very complex indeed.

Surely, then, the elements now known to us are not, nor can they be, the *primordial* elements. Those were formed from "*the curds of the cold radiant Mother*" and "*the fire-seed* of the hot Father" who "*are one,*" or, to express it in the plainer language of modern science, those elements had their genesis in the depths of the primordial Fire-mist—the masses of incandescent vapour of the *irresolvable* nebulae.

The elements now known have arrived at their state of permanency in this 4th Round and 5th Race. They have a short period of rest before they are propelled once more on their upward spiritual evolution, when the "living fire of Orcus" will dissociate the most irresolvable and scatter them again into the primordial ONE.

Meanwhile the Occultist goes further, as has been shown in the Commentaries on the Seven Stanzas. He maintains that Spirit and Matter are two FACETS of the unknowable UNITY, their apparently contrasted aspects depending, (a) on the various degrees of differentiation of the latter, and (b) on the grades of consciousness attained by man himself.

"Matter is eternal," says the Esoteric Doctrine. But the Matter the Occultists conceive of in its *laya*, or *zero state*, is not the matter of modern science; not even in its most rarefied gaseous state. Mr. Crookes' "radiant matter" would appear matter of the grossest kind in the realm of the beginnings, as it becomes pure Spirit before it has returned back even to its first point of differentiation. Therefore, when the Adept or alchemist adds that, though matter is eternal, for it is PRADHANA, yet atoms *are born at every new Manvantara*, or reconstruction of the universe, it is no such contradiction as a materialist, who believes in nothing beyond the atom, might think. There is a difference between *manifested* and *unmanifested* Matter, between *Pradhana*, the beginningless and endless cause, and *Prakriti*, or the manifested effect.

That which in modern phraseology is respectively referred to as Spirit and Matter is ONE in eternity as the perpetual Cause, and it is neither Spirit nor Matter, but IT—rendered in Sanskrit TAT ("THAT"),—all that is, was, or will be.

Occultism, which knows of the existence and presence in Nature of the One Eternal Element at the first differentiation of which the roots of the Tree of Life are periodically struck, needs no scientific proofs. It says:—Ancient Wisdom has solved the problem ages ago. Science is slowly but as surely approaching our domains of the Occult. Chemical Science is now compelled, by the very force of things, to accept even our illustration of the evolution of the Gods and Atoms, so suggestively and undeniably figured in the caduceus of Mercury, the God of Wisdom, and in the allegorical language of the Archaic Sages. Says a Commentary in the Esoteric Doctrine:—

... *The trunk of the* ASVATTHA (*the tree of Life and Being, the* ROD *of the Caduceus*) *grows from and descends at every Beginning* (*every new Manvantara*) *from the two dark wings of the Swan* (HANSA) *of Life. The two Serpents, the ever-living and its illusion* (*Spirit and matter*) *whose two heads grow from the one head between the wings, descend along the trunk, interlaced in close embrace. The two tails join on earth* (*the manifested Universe*) *into one, and this is the great illusion, O Lanoo!*"

Everyone knows what the caduceus is, already modified by the Greeks. Yet it is as good an illustration as can be for our purpose, this laya rod entwined by two serpents. A *lemniscate*[2] for the evolution downward, from Spirit into Matter, another form of a *spiral*, perhaps, in its *reinvolutionary* path onward, from Matter into Spirit, and the necessary gradual and final reabsorption into the *laya* state, that which Science calls in her own way "the point neutral as to electricity" etc., or the *zero* point. Such are the Occult facts and statement. They may be left with the greatest security and confidence to Science, to be justified some day.

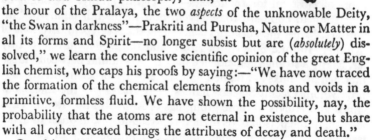

As if to prove the postulate of Occult Science and Hindu philosophy, that, at the hour of the Pralaya, the two *aspects* of the unknowable Deity, "the Swan in darkness"—Prakriti and Purusha, Nature or Matter in all its forms and Spirit—no longer subsist but are (*absolutely*) dissolved," we learn the conclusive scientific opinion of the great English chemist, who caps his proofs by saying:—"We have now traced the formation of the chemical elements from knots and voids in a primitive, formless fluid. We have shown the possibility, nay, the probability that the atoms are not eternal in existence, but share with all other created beings the attributes of decay and death."

Occultism says *amen* to this, as the scientific "possibility" and "probability" are for it facts demonstrated beyond the necessity of further proof or any extraneous physical evidence. Nevertheless, it repeats with as much assurance as ever: "MATTER IS ETERNAL, becoming atomic (its aspect) only periodically." This is as sure as that the other proposition, which is almost unanimously accepted by astronomers and physicists—namely, that the wear and tear of the body of the Universe is steadily going on, and that it will finally lead to the extinction of the Solar Fires and the destruction of the Universe—is quite erroneous on the lines traced by men of science. There will be, as there ever were in time and eternity, periodical dissolutions of the manifested Universe, but (*a*) a partial Pralaya after every "Day of Brahmā"; and (*b*) a Universal Pralaya—the MAHA-PRALAYA—only after the lapse of every Brahmā's Age.

By a strong and curious coincidence even our "Septenary"

[2] [Closed curves, having resemblance to the figure 8.]

doctrine seems to force the hand of Science. If we understand rightly, chemistry speaks of fourteen groupings of primitive atoms—lithium, beryllium, boron, carbon, nitrogen, oxygen, fluorine, sodium, magnesium, aluminium, silicon, phosphorus, sulphur and chlorine; and Mr. Crookes, speaking of the "dominant atomicities," enumerates seven groups of these, for he says:—

"As the mighty focus of creative energy goes round, we see it in successive cycles sowing in one tract of space seeds of lithium, potassium, rubidium, and caesium; in another tract, chlorine, bromine, and iodine; in a third, sodium, copper, silver, and gold; in a fourth, sulphur, selenium, and tellurium; in a fifth, beryllium, calcium, strontium, and barium; in a sixth, magnesium, zinc, cadmium, and mercury; in a seventh, phosphorus, arsenic, antimony, and bismuth"—which makes seven groupings on the one hand. And after showing "in other tracts the other elements—namely, aluminium, gallium, indium, and thallium; silicon, germanium, and tin; carbon, titanium, and zirconium."

He adds: "While a natural position near the neutral axis is found for the three groups of elements relegated by Professor Mendeleeff to a sort of Hospital for Incurables—his eighth family." It might be interesting to compare these seven, and the eighth family of "incurables," with the allegories concerning the seven primitive sons of "Mother, Infinite Space," or Aditi, and the *eighth* son rejected by her. Many a strange coincidence may thus be found between "those intermediate links . . . named 'meta-elements or elementoids and those whom Occult Science names their *Noumenoi*,' the intelligent Minds and Rulers of those groupings of Monads and Atoms. Thus Science, in the person of its highest representatives, in order to make itself clearer to the profane, adopts the phraseology of such old adepts as Roger Bacon, and returns to the "protyle." All this is hopeful and suggestive of the "signs of the times."

Indeed these "signs" are many and multiply daily; but none are more important than those just quoted. One, at least, of the few eminent chemists of the day is in the realm of the infinite possibilities of Occultism. Every new step he will take will bring him nearer and nearer to that mysterious Centre, from which radiate the innumerable paths that lead down Spirit into Matter, and which transform the Gods and the living Monads into man and sentient Nature.

11. ON THE ELEMENTS AND ATOMS

In Occultism the word *Element* means "rudiment" in every case. When we say "Elementary Man," we mean either the proëmial, incipient sketch of man, in its unfinished and undeveloped condition, hence in that form which now lies latent in physical man during his life-time, and takes shape only occasionally and under certain conditions; or that form which for a time survives the material body, and which is better known as an "Elementary." With regard to "Element," when the term is used metaphysically, it means, in distinction to the mortal, the incipient *Divine* Man; and, in its physical usage, inchoate Matter in its first undifferentiated condition, or in the *Laya* state, which is the eternal and the *normal* condition of Substance, differentiating only periodically, and is during that differentiation in an *abnormal* state—in other words, a transitory illusion of the senses.

As to the "Elemental Atoms," so called, the Occultists refer to them by that name with a meaning analogous to that which is given by the Hindu to Brahmā when he calls him ANU, the "Atom." Every Elemental *Atom*, in search of which more than one chemist has followed the path indicated by the Alchemists, is, in their firm belief (when not *knowledge*), a SOUL; not necessarily a disembodied Soul, but a *Jiva*, as the Hindus call it, a centre of POTENTIAL VITALITY, with latent intelligence in it, and, in the case of compound Souls, an intelligent active EXISTENCE, from the highest to the lowest order, a form composed of more or less differentiations. All those Atom-Souls are differentiations from the ONE, and in the same relation to it as the *divine Soul*—Buddhi—to its informing and inseparable Spirit, or *Atman.*

The star under which a human Entity is born, says the Occult Teaching, will remain for ever its star, throughout the whole cycle of its incarnations in one Manvantara. But *this is not his astrological star.* The latter is concerned and connected with the *personality*, the former with the INDIVIDUALITY. The "Angel" of that Star, or the Dhyani-Buddha will be either the guiding or simply the presiding "Angel," so to say, in every new rebirth of the Monad, *which is part of his own essence*, though his vehicle, man, may remain for ever ignorant of this fact. The Adepts have each their Dhyani-Buddha, their elder "Twin Soul," and they know it, calling it "Father-Soul," and "Father-Fire." It is only at the last and supreme initiation, however, that they learn it when placed face to face with the bright "Image." How much has Bulwer Lytton known of this mystic fact when describing, in one of his highest inspirational moods, Zanoni face to face with his *Augoeides?*

The *Logos*, or both the unmanifested and the manifested WORD, is called by the Hindus, Isvara, "the Lord," though the Occultists give it another name. Isvara, say the Vedantins, is the highest consciousness in Nature. "This highest consciousness," answer the Occultists, "is only a *synthetic unit* in the world of the manifested Logos—or on the *plane of illusion;* for it is the sum total of Dhyan-Chohanic *consciousnesses.*" Atma is *not-Spirit* in its final Parabrahmic state; *Isvara* or *Logos* is Spirit; or, as Occultism explains, it is a compound unity of manifested living Spirits, the parent-source and nursery of all the mundane and terrestrial Monads, *plus* their *divine* reflection, which emanate from, and return into, the Logos, each in the culmination of its time. There are seven chief Groups of such Dhyan Chohans, which Groups will be found and recognized in every religion, for they are the primeval SEVEN Rays. Humanity, Occultism teaches us, is divided into seven distinct Groups and their sub-divisions, mental, spiritual, and physical.[1] The Monad, then, viewed as ONE, is above the seventh principle in Kosmos and man, and as a triad, it is the direct radiant progeny of the said *compound* UNIT, not the Breath (and special *creation* out of *nihil*) of God, as that unit is called; for such an idea is quite unphilosophical, and degrades Deity, dragging it down to a finite, attributive condition. As well expressed by the translator of the "Crest-Jewel of Wisdom"—though *Isvara* is God "unchanged in the profoundest depths of *pralaya* and in the intensest activity of the *manvantaras*" . . . , still "*beyond*" (him) is ATMA, round whose pavilion is the darkness of eternal MAYA."[2] The "Triads" born under the same Parent-planet, or rather the *radiations* of one and the same Planetary Spirit (Dhyani Buddha) are, in all their after lives and rebirths, sister, or "*twin*" souls, on this Earth.[3]

[1] Hence the seven chief planets, the *spheres* of the indwelling seven Spirits, under each of which is born one of the human Groups which is guided and influenced thereby. There are only seven planets *specially* connected with Earth, and twelve houses, but the possible combinations of their aspects are countless. As each planet can stand to each of the others in twelve different aspects, their combinations must be almost infinite; as infinite, in fact, as the spiritual, psychic, mental, and physical capacities in the numberless varieties of the *genus homo*, each of which varieties is born under one of the seven planets and one of the said countless planetary combinations. See *The Theosophist*, for August, 1886.

[2] The now universal error of attributing to the ancients the knowledge of only seven planets, simply because they mentioned no others, is based on the same general ignorance of their occult doctrines. The question is not whether they were, or were not, aware of the existence of the later discovered planets; but whether the reverence paid by them to the four exoteric and three secret Great Gods—the Star-Angels, had not some special reason. The writer ventures to say there was such a reason, and it is this. Had they known of as many planets as we do now (and this question can hardly be decided at present, either way), they would have still connected with their religious worship only the seven, because these seven are directly and specially connected with our earth, or, using esoteric phraseology, with our septenary Ring of Spheres.

[3] It is the same, only still more metaphysical idea, as that of the Christian Trinity—"Three in One"—*i.e.*, the Universal "over-Spirit," manifesting on the two higher planes, those of Buddhi and Mahat; and these are the three hypostases, metaphysical, but *never personal*.

This was known to every high Initiate in every age and in every country: "I and my Father are one," said Jesus (John x. 30).[4] When He is made to say, elsewhere (xx. 17): "I ascend to *my* Father and your Father," it meant that which has just been stated. It was simply to show that the group of his disciples and followers attracted to him belonged to the same Dhyani Buddha, Star, or Father, again of the same planetary realm and division as he did. It is the *knowledge* of this occult doctrine that found expression in the review of *The Idyll of the White Lotus*, when Mr. T. Subba Row wrote: "Every Buddha meets at his last Initiation all the great Adepts who reached Buddhahood during the preceding ages . . . every class of Adepts has its own bond of spiritual communion which knits them together. . . . The only possible and effectual way of entering into such brotherhood . . . is by bringing oneself within the influence of the Spiritual light which radiates *from one's own Logos*. I may further point out here . . . that such communion is only possible *between persons whose souls derive their life and sustenance from the same divine* RAY, and that, as seven distinct Rays radiate from the 'Central Spiritual Sun,' *all Adepts and Dhyan Chohans are divisible into seven classes*, each of which is guided, controlled, and overshadowed *by one of the seven forms* or manifestations of the divine Wisdom." (*The Theosophist*, Aug., 1886.)

14. FORCES—MODES OF MOTION OR INTELLIGENCES?

MODERN Science is secure only in its own domain and region; within the physical boundaries of our Solar System, beyond which everything, every particle of matter, is different from the matter it knows, which matter exists in states of which Science can form no idea. *That* Matter, which is truly homogeneous, is beyond human perceptions, if perception is tied merely to the five senses. We feel its effects through those INTELLIGENCES which are the results of its primeval differentiation, whom we name Dhyan-Chohans.

From *Gods* to men, from Worlds to atoms, from a star to a rushlight, from the Sun to the vital heat of the meanest organic being—the world of Form and Existence is an immense chain, whose links are all connected. The law of Analogy is the first key to the world-problem, and these links have to be studied co-ordinately in their Occult relations to each other.

[4] The identity, and at the same time the illusive differentiation of the *Angel*-Monad and the *Human*-Monad is shown by the following sentences: "My Father is *greater* than I" (John xiv. 26); "Glorify *your* Father *who is in Heaven*" (Matt. v. 16); "The righteous will *shine* in the kingdom of *their* Father" (not *our* Father) (Matt. xiii. 43) "Know ye not ye are *a temple* of God, and that the *Spirit of God dwelleth* in you? (I Cor. iii. 16); "I *ascend* to my Father," etc., etc.

How long has it taken the world, as it is now, to become what it is? If it can be said of cosmic dust that some of it comes to the present day *"which had never belonged to the earth before"* (*"World-Life"*), how much more logical to believe—as the Occultists do—that through the countless ages and millions of years that have rolled away, since that dust aggregated and formed the Globe we live in around its *nucleus* of *intelligent* Primeval Substance—many humanities, differing from our present mankind, as greatly as the one which will evolve millions of years hence will differ from our races, appeared but to disappear from the face of the Earth, as our own will. Those primitive and far-distant humanities, having, as geologists think, left no tangible relics of themselves, are denied. All trace of them is swept away, and therefore they have never existed. Yet their relics—a very few of them, truly—are to be found, and they have to be discovered by geological research. Though, even if they were never to be met with, there is no reason to say that no men could have ever lived in those geological times, to which the period of their presence on earth is assigned. For their organisms needed no warm blood, no atmosphere, no feeding.

When we speak, therefore, of men who inhabited this Globe 18,000,000 years back, we have in mind neither the men of our present races, nor the present atmospheric laws, thermal conditions, etc. The Earth and Mankind, like the Sun, Moon, and Planets, have all their growth, changes, developments, and gradual evolution in their life-periods; they are born, become infants, then children, adolescents, grown-up bodies, grow old, and finally die. Why should not *Mankind* be also under this universal law? Says Uriel to Enoch: "Thou seest the Sun, Moon, and those which conduct the stars of heaven, *which cause all their operations*, seasons, and arrivals to return. . . . *In the days of sinners* the years shall be shortened . . . everything done on earth shall be subverted . . . the moon shall change its laws" . . . etc. (*The Book of Enoch*, Ch. *lxxix*.)

The "days of Sinners" meant the days when matter would be in its full sway on Earth, and man would have reached the apex of physical development in stature and animality. That came to pass during the period of the Atlanteans, about the middle point of their Race (the 4th) which was drowned as prophesied by Uriel. Since then man began decreasing in physical stature, strength, and years. But as we are in the mid-point of our *sub-race* of the Fifth Root Race —the acme of materiality in each—therefore the animal propensities, though more refined, are not the less developed for that: and they are so chiefly in civilized countries.

15. GODS, MONADS, AND ATOMS

"EVERY atom becomes a visible complex unit (a molecule), and once attracted into the sphere of terrestrial activity, the Monadic Essence, passing through the mineral, vegetable, and animal kingdoms, becomes man." (*Esot. Catechism.*) Again, "God, Monad, and Atom are the correspondences of Spirit, Mind, and Body (*Atma, Manas* and *Sthula Sarira*) in man." In their septenary aggregation they are the "Heavenly Man" (see *Kabala* for the latter term); thus, terrestrial man is the provisional reflection of the Heavenly. . . . "The Monads (*Jivas*) are the Souls of the Atoms; both are the fabric in which the Chohans (Dhyanis, *gods*) clothe themselves when a form is needed." (*Esot. Cat.*)

This relates to Cosmic and sub-planetary Monads. The Monads of the present dissertation are treated from the standpoint of their individuality, as *Atomic Souls*, before these atoms descend into pure terrestrial form. For this descent into *concrete* Matter marks the medial point of their own individual pilgrimage. Here, losing in the mineral kingdom their individuality, they begin to ascend through the seven states of terrestrial evolution to that point where a correspondence is firmly established between the human and *Deva* (divine) consciousness.

This evolution—viewed as the *universal* and the *individualized* Monad, and the chief aspects of the Evolving Energy, after differentiation—the purely Spiritual, the Intellectual, the Psychic and the Physical—may be thus formulated as an invariable law; a descent of Spirit into Matter, equivalent to an ascent in physical evolution; a re-ascent from the depths of materiality towards its *status quo ante*, with a corresponding dissipation of concrete form and substance up to the LAYA state, or what Science calls "the zero-point," and beyond. . .

To the eye of the Seer, the higher Planetary Powers appear under two aspects, the subjective as *influences*, and the objective as mystic FORMS, which, under Karmic law, become a *Presence*, Spirit and Matter being One, as repeatedly stated. Spirit is matter *on the seventh plane;* matter is Spirit—on the lowest point of its cyclic activity; and both—are MAYA. . .

Atoms fill the immensity of Space, and by their continuous vibration *are* that MOTION which keeps the wheels of Life perpetually going. It is that inner work that produces the natural phenomena called the correlation of Forces. Only, at the origin of every such "force," there stands the *conscious* guiding noumenon thereof—Angel or God, Spirit or Demon—ruling powers, yet the same.

16. CYCLIC EVOLUTION AND KARMA

IT IS the Spiritual evolution of the *inner*, immortal Man that forms the fundamental tenet in the Occult Sciences. To realize even distantly such a process, the student has to believe (*a*) in the ONE Universal Life, independent of matter (or what Science regards as matter); and (*b*) in the individual Intelligences that animate the various manifestations of this Principle.

The ONE LIFE is closely related to *the one* law which governs the World of Being—KARMA. Exoterically, this is simply and literally "action," or rather an "effect-producing cause." Esoterically it is quite a different thing in its far-fetching moral effects. It is the unerring LAW OF RETRIBUTION.

At the first flutter of renascent life, Svabhavat, "the mutable radiance of the Immutable Darkness unconscious in Eternity," passes, at every new rebirth of Kosmos, from an inactive state into one of intense activity; it differentiates, and then begins its work through that differentiation. This work is KARMA.

The Cycles are also subservient to the effects produced by this activity. "The one Cosmic Atom becomes seven atoms on the plane of Matter, and each is transformed into a centre of energy; that same Atom becomes seven Rays on the plane of Spirit, and the seven creative Forces of Nature, radiating from the Root-Essence . . . follow, one the right, the other the left path, separate till the end of the Kalpa, and yet are in close embrace. What unites them? KARMA." The Atoms emanated from the Central Point emanate in their turn new centres of energy, which, under the potential breath of *Fohat*, begin their work from within without, and multiply other minor centres. These, in the course of evolution and involution, form in their turn the roots or developing causes of new effects, from worlds and "man-bearing" globes, down to the genera, species, and classes of all the *seven* kingdoms.[1]

The true Buddhist, recognizing no "personal God," nor any "Father" and "*Creator* of Heaven and Earth," still believes in an *Absolute Consciousness*, "Adi-Buddhi"; and the Buddhist philosopher *knows* that there are Planetary Spirits, the "Dhyan Chohans." But though he admits of "Spiritual Lives," yet, as they are temporary in eternity, even they, according to his philosophy, are "the *Maya* of the *Day*," the *illusion* of a "day of Brahmā," a short manvantara of 4,320,000,000 years. If the Dhyan Chohans and all the invisible Beings—the *Seven* Centres and their direct Emanations, the *minor* centres of Energy—are the direct reflex of the ONE Light, yet men

[1] Vide Stanza 6. (Book I.) and Commentary.

are far removed from these, since the whole of the *visible* Kosmos consists of "*self-produced* beings, the creatures of *Karma*." Thus regarding a personal God "as only a gigantic shadow thrown upon the void of space by the imagination of ignorant men,"[2] they teach that only "two things are (objectively) eternal, namely *Akasa* and *Nirvana*"; and that these are ONE in reality, and but a *maya* when divided. "Buddhists deny creation and cannot conceive of a *Creator*." "Everything has come out of Akasa (or Svabhavat on our earth) in obedience to a law of motion inherent in it, and after a certain existence passes away. Nothing ever came out of nothing." (*Buddhist Catechism*.)

If a Vedantic Brahmin of the Advaita Sect, when asked whether he believes in the existence of God, is always likely to answer, as Jacolliot was answered—"I am myself 'God' "; a Buddhist (a Sinhalese especially) would simply laugh, and say in reply, "There is no God; no Creation." Yet the root philosophy of both Advaita and Buddhist scholars is *identical*, and both have the same respect for animal life, for both believe that every creature on earth, however small and humble, "is an immortal portion of the immortal matter"—for matter with them has quite another significance than it has with either Christian or materialist—and that every creature is subject to Karma.

The answer of the Brahmin is one which would suggest itself to every ancient philosopher, Kabalist, and Gnostic of the early days. It contains the very spirit of the Delphic and Kabalistic commandments, for Esoteric Philosophy solved, ages ago, the problem of what man *was*, *is*, and *will be*; of man's origin, life-cycle—interminable in its duration of successive incarnations or rebirths—and finally of his absorption into the source from which he started.

To make the working of Karma, in the periodical renovations of the Universe, more evident and intelligible to the student when he arrives at the origin and evolution of man, he has now to examine with us the esoteric bearing of the Karmic Cycles upon Universal Ethics.

The question is, do those mysterious divisions of time, called Yugas and Kalpas by the Hindus, have any bearing upon, or any direct connection with, human life? Even exoteric philosophy explains that these perpetual circles of time are ever returning on themselves, periodically, and intelligently in Space and Eternity. There are "Cycles of Matter"[3] and there are "Cycles of Spiritual evolution." Racial, national, and individual cycles.

---

[2] *Buddhist Catechism*, by H. S. Olcott, President of the Theosophical Society.

[3] "The Cycles of Matter," a name given by Professor Winchell to an Essay of his written in 1860.

According to the teachings, Maya, or the illusive appearance of the marshalling of events and actions on this earth, changes, varying with nations and places. But the chief features of one's life are always in accordance with the "Constellation" one is born under, or, we should say, with the characteristics of its animating principle or the Deity that presides over it, whether we call it a *Dhyan Chohan*, as in Asia, or an Archangel, as with the Greek and Latin churches. In ancient Symbolism it was always the SUN (though the Spiritual, not the visible, Sun was meant), that was supposed to send forth the chief Saviours and Avatars. Hence the connecting link between the Buddhas, the Avatars, and so many other incarnations of the highest SEVEN. The closer the approach to one's *Prototype*, "in Heaven," the better for the mortal whose personality was chosen, by his own *personal* Deity (the Seventh Principle), as its terrestrial abode. For, with every effort of will toward purification and unity with that "Self-god," one of the lower rays breaks and the spiritual entity of man is drawn higher and ever higher to the ray that supersedes the first, until, from ray to ray, the inner man is drawn into the one and highest beam of the Parent-SUN.

Yes; "our destiny *is* written in the stars!" Only, the closer the union between the mortal reflection MAN and his celestial PROTO-TYPE, the less dangerous the external conditions and subsequent re-incarnations—which neither Buddhas nor Christs can escape. This is not superstition, least of all is it *Fatalism*. The latter implies a blind course of some still blinder power, and man is a free agent during his stay on earth. He cannot escape his *ruling* Destiny, but he has the choice of two paths that lead him in that direction, and he can reach the goal of misery—if such is decreed to him, either in the snowy white robes of the martyr, or in the soiled garments of a volunteer in the iniquitous course; for, there are *external and internal conditions* which affect the determination of our will upon our actions, and it is in our power to follow either of the two. Those who believe in *Karma* have to believe in *Destiny*, which, from birth to death, every man is weaving thread by thread around himself, as a spider does his cobweb; and this Destiny is guided either by the heavenly voice of the invisible *prototype* outside of us, or by our more intimate *astral*, or inner man, who is but too often the evil genius of the embodied entity called man. Both these lead on the outward man, but one of them must prevail; and from the very beginning of the invisible affray the stern and implacable *Law of Compensation* steps in and takes its course, faithfully following the fluctuations. When the last strand is woven, and man is seemingly enwrapped in the net-work of his own doing, he finds himself completely under the empire of this *self-made* Destiny. It then either fixes him like the inert shell against the immovable rock, or carries him away like a feather in a whirlwind raised by his own actions, and this is—KARMA.

Karma-Nemesis is the synonym of PROVIDENCE, minus *design*, goodness, and every other *finite* attribute and qualification, so unphilosophically attributed to the latter. An Occultist or a philosopher will not speak of the goodness or cruelty of Providence; but, identifying it with Karma-Nemesis, he will teach that nevertheless it guards the good and watches over them in this, as in future lives; and that it punishes the evil-doer—aye, even to his seventh rebirth, so long, in short, as the effect of his having thrown into perturbation even the smallest atom in the Infinite World of harmony has not been finally readjusted. For the only decree of Karma—an eternal and immutable decree—is absolute Harmony in the world of matter as it is in the world of Spirit. It is not, therefore, Karma that rewards or punishes, but it is we, who reward or punish ourselves according to whether we work with, through and along with nature, abiding by the laws on which that Harmony depends, or—break them.

Nor would the ways of Karma be inscrutable were men to work in union and harmony, instead of disunion and strife. For our ignorance of those ways—which one portion of mankind calls the ways of Providence, dark and intricate; while another sees in them the action of blind Fatalism; and a third, simple Chance, with neither gods nor devils to guide them—would surely disappear, if we would but attribute all these to their correct cause. With right knowledge, or at any rate with a confident conviction that our neighbours will no more work to hurt us than we would think of harming them, two-thirds of the World's evil would vanish into thin air. Were no man to hurt his brother, Karma-Nemesis would have neither cause to work for, nor weapons to act with. It is the constant presence in our midst of every element of strife and opposition, and the division of races, nations, tribes, societies and individuals into Cains and Abels, wolves and lambs, that is the chief cause of the "ways of Providence." We cut these numerous windings in our destinies daily with our own hands, while we imagine that we are pursuing a track on the royal high road of respectability and duty, and then complain of those ways being so intricate and so dark. We stand bewildered before the mystery of our own making, and the riddles of life that *we will not* solve, and then accuse the great Sphinx of devouring us. But verily there is not an accident in our lives, not a mis-shapen day, or a misfortune, that could not be traced back to our own doings in this or in another life. If one breaks the laws of Harmony, or, as a theosophical writer expresses it, "the laws of life," one must be prepared to fall into the chaos one has oneself produced. For, according to the same writer, "the only conclusion one can come to is that these laws of life are their own avengers; and consequently that every avenging Angel is only a typified representation of their re-action."

Therefore, if anyone is helpless before these immutable laws, it is not ourselves, the artificers of our destinies, but rather those Angels, the guardians of harmony. Karma-Nemesis is no more than the (spiritual) dynamical effect of causes produced and forces awakened into activity by our own actions. It is a law of Occult dynamics that "a given amount of energy expended on the spiritual or astral plane is productive of far greater results than the same amount expended on the physical objective plane of existence."

This state will last till man's spiritual intuitions are fully opened, which will not happen before we fairly cast off our thick coats of matter; until we begin acting from *within*, instead of ever following impulses from *without*; namely, those produced by our physical senses and gross selfish body. Until then the only palliative to the evils of life is union and harmony—a Brotherhood IN ACTU, and *altruism* not simply in name.

VOLUME SECOND
ANTHROPOGENESIS

PRELIMINARY NOTES

ON THE ARCHAIC STANZAS, AND THE FOUR PREHISTORIC CONTINENTS

THE Stanzas, with the Commentaries thereon, in this Volume are drawn from the same Archaic Records as the Stanzas on Cosmogony. As regards the evolution of mankind, the Secret Doctrine postulates three new propositions: (*a*) the simultaneous evolution of seven human groups on seven different portions of our globe; (*b*) the birth of the *astral* before the *physical* body, the former being a model for the latter; and (*c*) that man, in this Round, preceded every mammalian—the anthropoids included—in the animal kingdom. . . .

Before we turn to the *Anthropogenesis* of the prehistoric Races, it may be useful to agree upon the names to be given to the Continents on which the four great Races, which preceded our *Adamic* Race, were born, lived, and died. Their archaic and esoteric names were many, and varied with the language of the nationality which mentioned them in its annals and scriptures.

Therefore, in view of the possible confusion that may arise, it is considered more convenient to adopt, for each of the four Continents referred to, a name more familiar to the cultured reader. It is proposed to call the first continent, or rather the first *terra firma* on which the first Race was evolved by the divine progenitors:—

I. The Imperishable Sacred Land.

The reasons for this name are explained as follows: This "Imperishable Sacred Land" is stated never to have shared the fate of the other continents; because it is the only one whose destiny it is to last from the beginning to the end of the Manvantara throughout each Round. It is the cradle of the first man and the dwelling of the last *divine* mortal. Of this mysterious and sacred land very little can be said, except, perhaps, according to a poetical expression in one of the Commentaries, that the "pole-star has its watchful eye upon it, from the dawn to the close of the twilight of 'a day' of the GREAT BREATH."

II. The Hyperborean will be the name chosen for the second Continent, the land which stretched out its promontories southward and westward from the North Pole to receive the Second Race, and comprised the whole of what is now known as Northern Asia.

III. The third Continent we propose to call Lemuria. The name is an invention of Mr. P. L. Sclater, who asserted, between 1850 and

1860, on zoological grounds the actual existence, in prehistoric times, of a Continent which he showed to have extended from Madagascar to Ceylon and Sumatra. It included some portions of what is now Africa; but otherwise this gigantic Continent, which stretched from the Indian ocean to Australia, has now wholly disappeared beneath the waters of the Pacific, leaving here and there only some of its highland tops which are now islands.

IV. "Atlantis" is the fourth Continent. The famous island of Plato of that name was but a fragment of this great Continent. (See *Esoteric Buddhism.*)

V. The fifth Continent was America; but, as it is situated at the Antipodes, it is Europe and Asia Minor, almost coeval with it, which are generally referred to by the Indo-Aryan Occultists as the fifth. If their teaching followed the appearance of the Continents in their geological and geographical order, this classification would have to be altered. But as the sequence of the Continents is made to follow the order of evolution of the Races, from the First to the Fifth, our Aryan Root-race, Europe must be called the fifth great Continent. Since the destruction of the great Atlantis the face of the earth has changed more than once. There was a time when the delta of Egypt and Northern Africa belonged to Europe, before the formation of the Straits of Gibraltar, and a further upheaval of the continent, changed entirely the face of the map of Europe. The last serious change occurred some 12,000 years ago, and was followed by the submersion of Plato's little Atlantic island, which he calls Atlantis after its parent continent. Geography was part of the mysteries, in days of old.

The claim that physical man was originally a colossal pre-tertiary giant, and that he existed 18,000,000 years ago, must of course appear preposterous to admirers of modern learning. The whole *posse comitatus* of biologists will turn away from the conception of this third race Titan of the Secondary age, a being fit to fight as successfully with the then gigantic monsters of the air, sea, and land, as his forefathers—the ethereal prototype of the Atlantean—had little need to fear that which could not hurt him. . . .

But the main point for us lies not in the agreement or disagreement of the naturalists as to the duration of geological periods, but rather in their perfect accord on one point. They all agree that during "The Miocene Age"—whether one or ten million years ago—Greenland and even Spitzbergen, the remnants of our Second or Hyperborean Continent, "had *almost a tropical climate.*"

STANZA I[1]

BEGINNINGS OF SENTIENT LIFE

1. The Lha (a) which turns the fourth (*Globe, or our Earth*) is servant to the Lha(s) of the seven (*the planetary Spirits*) (b), they who revolve, driving their chariots around their Lord, the one eye (*Loka-Chakshub*) of our world. His breath gave life to the seven (*gives light to the planets*). It gave life to ᵀhe first (c). "They are all dragons of Wisdom," adds the Commentary (d).

(a) Lha is the ancient word in trans-Himalayan regions for "Spirit," any celestial or *superhuman* Being, and it covers the whole series of heavenly hierarchies, from Archangel, or Dhyani, down to an angel of darkness, or terrestrial Spirit.

(b) This expression shows in plain language that the Spirit-Guardian of our Globe, which is the fourth in the Chain, is subordinate to the chief Spirit (or God) of the Seven Planetary Genii or Spirits.

"The Seven Higher make the Seven Lhas create the world," states a Commentary; which means that our Earth was *created* or fashioned by terrestrial Spirits, the "Regents" being simply the supervisors.

(c) "His Breath gave life to the Seven," refers as much to the Sun, who gives life to the Planets, as to the "High One," the *Spiritual Sun*, who gives life to the whole Kosmos.

The summation of the Stanzas in Book I. showed the genesis of Gods and men taking rise in, and from, one and the same Point, which is the One Universal, Immutable, Eternal, and absolute Unity. In its primary manifested aspect we have seen it become: (1) in the sphere of objectivity and physics, Primordial Substance and Force (centripetal and centrifugal, positive and negative, male and female, etc., etc.); (2) in the world of Metaphysics, the Spirit of the Universe, or Cosmic Ideation, called by some the Logos.

At the commencement of a great Manvantara, Parabrahm

---

[1] All the words and sentences placed in brackets in the Stanzas and Commentaries are the writer's. In some places they may be incomplete and even inadequate from the Hindu standpoint; but in the meaning attached to them in Trans-Himalayan Esotericism they are correct. The teaching is offered as it is understood; and as there are seven keys of interpretation to every symbol and allegory, that which may not fit a meaning, say from the psychological or astronomical aspect, will be found quite correct from the physical or metaphysical.

manifests as Mulaprakriti and then as the Logos. This Logos is equivalent to the "Unconscious Universal Mind," etc., of Western Pantheists. It constitutes the Basis of the SUBJECT-side of manifested Being,
and is the source of all manifestations of individual consciousness.
Mulaprakriti or Primordial Cosmic Substance is the foundation of the
OBJECT-side of things—the basis of all objective evolution and Cosmogenesis. Force, then, does not emerge with Primordial Substance
from Parabrahmic latency. It is *the transformation into energy of the
supra-conscious thought of the Logos*, infused, so to speak, into the objectivation of the latter out of potential latency in the One Reality.
Hence spring the wondrous laws of matter. Force thus is *not syn-
chronous with the first objectivation of Mulaprakriti*. But as, apart from it,
the latter is absolutely and necessarily inert—*a mere abstraction*—it is
unnecessary to weave too fine a cobweb of subtleties as to the order
of succession of the Cosmic Ultimates. Force *succeeds* Mulaprakriti;
but, *minus* Force, Mulaprakriti is for all practical intents and purposes non-existent.

The esoteric meaning of the word *Logos* (speech or word, *Verbum*)
is the rendering in objective expression, as in a photograph, of the
concealed thought. The *Logos* is the mirror reflecting DIVINE MIND,
and the Universe is the mirror of the Logos, though the latter is the
esse of that Universe. As the *Logos* reflects *all* in the Universe of
Pleroma, so man reflects in himself all that he sees and finds in *his*
Universe, the Earth.

(*d*) In China the men of Fohi (or the "Heavenly Man") are called
the twelve *Tien-Hoang*, the twelve hierarchies of Dhyanis or Angels,
with human faces, and dragon bodies; the Dragon standing for
Divine Wisdom or Spirit.

All these allegories point to one and the same origin—to the dual
and the triple nature of man; dual, as male and female; triple, as
being of spiritual and psychic essence *within*, and of a material fabric
without.

2. SAID THE EARTH, "LORD OF THE SHINING FACE (*the Sun*) MY
HOUSE IS EMPTY. . . . SEND THY SONS TO PEOPLE THIS WHEEL (*Earth*).
THOU HAST SENT THY SEVEN SONS TO THE LORD OF WISDOM (*a*).
SEVEN TIMES DOTH HE SEE THEE NEARER TO HIMSELF; SEVEN TIMES
MORE DOTH HE FEEL THEE. THOU HAST FORBIDDEN THY SERVANTS,
THE SMALL RINGS, TO CATCH THY LIGHT AND HEAT, THY GREAT BOUNTY
TO INTERCEPT ON ITS PASSAGE (*b*). SEND NOW TO THY SERVANT THE
SAME!" (*c*).

(*a*) The "Lord of Wisdom" is Mercury, or *Budha*.

(*b*) The modern Commentary explains the words as a reference to a well-known astronomical fact, "that Mercury receives seven times more light and heat from the Sun than Earth, or even the beautiful Venus, which receives but twice that amount more than our insignificant Globe."

In the words of the Commentary:—

"The Globe, propelled onward by the Spirit of the Earth and his six assistants, gets all its vital forces, life, and powers through the medium of the seven planetary Dhyanis from the Spirit of the Sun. They are his messengers of Light and Life."

"Like each of the seven Regions of the Earth, each of the seven[2] First-born (the primordial human Groups) *receives its light and life from its own especial Dhyani—spiritually, and from the Palace* (house, the Planet) *of that Dhyani physically; so with the seven great Races to be born on it. The First is born under the Sun; the Second under Brihaspati* (Jupiter); *the Third under Lohitanga* (the "fiery-bodied," Venus, or Sukra); *the Fourth, under Soma* (the Moon, our Globe also, the Fourth Sphere being born under and from the Moon) *and Sani, Saturn, the Krura-lochana* (evil-eyed) *and the Asita* (the dark); *the Fifth, under Budha* (Mercury)."

"So also with man and every 'man' in man (every principle). *Each gets its specific quality from its primary* (the Planetary Spirit); *therefore every man is a septenate* (or a combination of principles, each having its origin in a quality of that special Dhyani). *Every active power or force of the earth comes to her from one of the seven Lords. Light comes through Sukra* (Venus), *who receives a triple supply, and gives one-third of it to the Earth.[3] Therefore the two are called 'Twin-sisters,' but the Spirit of the Earth is subservient to the 'Lord' of Sukra. Our wise men represent the two Globes, one over, the other under the double Sign* (the primeval Svastika bereft of its four arms, or the cross+)."[4]

The "double sign" is, as every student of Occultism knows, the symbol of the male and the female principles in Nature, of the positive and the negative, for the Svastika or 卐 is all that and much

[2] "As it is above so it is below" is the fundamental axiom of occult philosophy. As the logos is seven-fold, *i.e.*, throughout Kosmos it appears as seven logoi under seven different forms, or, as taught by learned Brahmins, "each of these is the central figure of one of the seven main branches of the ancient wisdom religion"; and, as the seven principles which correspond to the seven distinct states of *Prajna*, or consciousness, are allied to seven states of matter and the seven forms of force, the division must be the same in all that concerns the earth.

[3] Science teaches that Venus receives from the sun twice as much light and heat as the earth. Thus the planet, precursor of the dawn and the twilight, the most radiant of all the planets, said to give the earth one-third of the supply she receives, has two parts left for herself. This has an occult as well as an astronomical meaning.

[4] Venus is thus ♀ the Earth ♁

more. All antiquity, ever since the birth of Astronomy—imparted to the Fourth Race by one of its divine kings of the Divine Dynasty— and also of Astrology, represented Venus in its astronomical tables as a *Globe poised over a Cross*, and the Earth, as a *Globe under a Cross*. The esoteric meaning of this is: "Earth fallen into generation, or into the production of its species through sexual union." Venus is the most occult, powerful, and mysterious of all the planets; the one whose influence upon, and relation to the Earth is most prominent. The whole history of Sukra in the Puranas refers to the Third and to the Fourth Races.

"*It is through Sukra that the 'double ones' (the Hermaphrodites) of the Third* (Root-Race) *descended from the first 'Sweat-born,'* " says the Commentary. *Therefore it is represented under the symbol of ⊖ (the circle and diameter) during the Third (Race) and of ⊕ during the Fourth.*

This needs explanation. The *diameter*, when found isolated in a circle, stands for female nature, for the first *ideal* World, *self-generated and self-impregnated* by the universally diffused Spirit of Life—referring thus to the primitive Root-Race also. It becomes androgynous as the Races and all on Earth develop into their physical forms, and the symbol is transformed into a circle with a diameter from which runs a vertical line: expressive of male and female, not separated as yet— the first and earliest *Tau* ⊤ ; after which it becomes ✝, or male-female separated (See first pp. of Book I) and fallen into generation. Venus (the Planet) is symbolized by the sign of a globe over the cross, which shows it as presiding over the natural generation of man. The Egyptians symbolized *Ankh*, "life," by the ansated cross, or ♀ , which is only another form of Venus (Isis) ♀ , and meant, esoterically, that mankind and all animal life had stepped out of the divine spiritual circle and fallen into physical male and female generation. This sign, from the end of the Third Race, has the same phallic significance as the "*Tree* of Life" in Eden.

"*Every world has its parent Star and sister Planet. Thus Earth is the adopted child and younger brother of Venus, but its inhabitants are of their own kind. . . . All sentient complete beings* (full septenary men or higher beings) *are furnished, in their beginnings, with forms and organisms in full harmony with the nature and state of the sphere they inhabit.*"

"*The Spheres of Being, or Centres of Life, which are isolated nuclei breeding their men and their animals, are numberless; not one has any resemblance to its sister-companion or to any other in its own special progeny.*"

"*All have a double physical and spiritual nature.*"

"*The nucleoles are eternal and everlasting; the nuclei periodical and finite. The nucleoles form part of the Absolute. They are the embrasures of that black impenetrable fortress, which is for ever concealed from human or even Dhyanic sight. The nuclei are the light of eternity escaping therefrom."*

"*It is that* LIGHT *which condenses into the forms of the 'Lords of Being'—the first and the highest of which are, collectively,* JIVATMA. (It is the Logos of the Greek philosophers—appearing at the beginning of every new Manvantara). *From these downwards—formed from the ever-consolidating waves of that Light, which becomes on the objective plane gross Matter—proceed the numerous hierarchies of the Creative Forces, some formless, others having their own distinctive form, others, again, the lowest (Elementals), having no form of their own, but assuming every form according to the surrounding conditions.*"

"*Thus there is but one Absolute Upadhi (basis) in the spiritual sense, from, on, and in which, are built for Manvantaric purposes the countless basic centres on which proceed the Universal, cyclic, and individual Evolutions during the active period.*"

"*The informing Intelligences, which animate these various centres of Being, are referred to indiscriminately by men beyond the Great Range as the Manus, the Rishis, the Pitris,*[5] *the Prajapati, and so on; and as Dhyani Buddhas, the Chohans, Melhas* (Fire-Gods), *Bodhisattvas, and others, on this side. The truly ignorant call them gods; the learned profane, the One God; and the wise, the Initiates, honour in them only the Manvantaric manifestations of* THAT *which neither our Creators* (the Dhyan Chohans) *nor their creatures can ever discuss or know anything about. The* ABSOLUTE *is not to be defined, and no mortal or immortal has ever seen or comprehended it during the periods of Existence. The mutable cannot know the Immutable, nor can that which lives perceive Absolute Life.*"

"Therefore, man cannot know higher beings than his own "progenitors." "*Nor shall he worship them,*" but he ought to learn *how* he came into the world.

(c) Number Seven, the fundamental figure among all other figures in every national religious system, from Cosmogony down to man, must have its *raison d'être.*

The ancient symbols are based upon and start from the figures given from the Archaic Manuscript in the Proem of Book I. The mystic system contains the • , the central point; the three or△ ; the five, ✩ , and the seven or ▣ , or again ✡ ; the triangle in the square and the synthesizing point in the interlaced double triangles. This for the world of the archetypes. The phenomenal world receives its culmination and the reflex of all in MAN. Therefore he is

[5] The term Pitris is used by us in these Slokas to facilitate their comprehension, but it is not so used in the original Stanzas, where they have distinct appellations of their own, besides being called "Fathers" and "Progenitors."

the mystic square—in his metaphysical aspect—the *Tetraktis*; and becomes the *Cube* on the creative plane. His symbol is the cube unfolded, and 6 becoming 7, or the ☩ *three* crossways (the female) and *four* vertically; and this is man, the culmination of the deity on Earth, whose body is the cross of flesh, *on, through*, and *in* which he is ever crucifying and putting to death the divine Logos or his HIGHER SELF...

Now there are three kinds of light in Occultism: (1) The Abstract and Absolute Light, which is Darkness; (2) The Light of the Manifested-Unmanifested, called by some the Logos and (3) The latter light reflected in the Dhyan Chohans, the minor *logoi* (the Elohim, collectively), who, in their turn, shed it on the objective Universe.

Nature (in man) must become a compound of Spirit and Matter before he becomes what he is; and the Spirit latent in Matter must be awakened to life and consciousness gradually. The Monad has to pass through its mineral, vegetable and animal forms before the Light of the Logos is awakened in the animal man. Therefore, till then, the latter cannot be referred to as "MAN," but has to be regarded as a Monad imprisoned in ever changing forms. *Evolution,* not *creation*, by means of WORDS is recognized in the philosophies of the East, even in their exoteric records. *Ex oriente lux.*

There is frequent confusion in the attributes and genealogies of the Gods in their theogonies, as given to the world by the half-initiated writers, Brahmanical and Biblical, the Alpha and the Omega of the records of that symbolical science. Yet there could be no such confusion made by the earliest nations, the descendants and pupils of the Divine Instructors: for both the attributes and the genealogies were inseparably linked with cosmogonical symbols, the "Gods" being the life and animating "soul-principle" of the various regions of the Universe. Nowhere and by no people was speculation allowed to range *beyond* those *manifested* Gods. The boundless and infinite UNITY remained with every nation a virgin forbidden soil, untrodden by man's thought, untouched by fruitless speculation. The only reference made to it was the brief conception of its diastolic and systolic property, of its periodical expansion or dilatation, and contraction. In the Universe with all its incalculable myriads of systems and worlds disappearing and re-appearing in eternity, the anthropomorphized Powers, or Gods, their Souls, had to disappear from view with their bodies:—"The Breath returning to the eternal Bosom which exhales and inhales them," says our Catechism.

In every Cosmogony, behind and higher than the *Creative* Deity, there is a superior Deity, a Planner, an Architect, *of whom* the Creator is but the executive agent. And still higher, *over* and *around*, *within* and *without*, there is the UNKNOWABLE and the *Unknown*, the Source and Cause of all these Emanations. . . .

3. SAID THE LORD OF THE SHINING FACE, "I SHALL SEND THEE A FIRE WHEN THY WORK IS COMMENCED. RAISE THY VOICE TO OTHER LOKAS, APPLY TO THY FATHER THE LORD OF THE LOTUS (*Kumuda-Pati*) (*a*) FOR HIS SONS. . . . THY PEOPLE SHALL BE UNDER THE RULE OF THE FATHERS (*Pitri-pati*). THY MEN SHALL BE MORTALS. THE MEN OF THE LORD OF WISDOM (*Budha, Mercury*) NOT THE SONS OF SOMA (*the Moon*) ARE IMMORTAL. CEASE THY COMPLAINTS (*b*). THY SEVEN SKINS ARE YET ON THEE. . . . THOU ART NOT READY. THY MEN ARE NOT READY (*c*).

(*a*) *Kumuda-Pati* is the Moon, the Earth's parent, in his region of Soma-loka. Though the Pitris (or "Fathers") are sons of the Gods, elsewhere sons of Brahmā and even Rishis, they are generally known as the "Lunar" Ancestors.

(*b*) Pitri-pati is the lord or king of the *Pitris*, Yama, the God of Death and the Judge of mortals. The men of Budha (Mercury) are metaphorically *immortal* through their Wisdom. Such is the common belief of those who credit every star or planet with being inhabited. The Moon being an inferior body even to the Earth, to say nothing of other planets, the terrestrial men produced by her sons—the Lunar Men or "Ancestors"—from her shell or body, cannot be immortal. They cannot hope to become real, self-conscious and intelligent men unless they are *finished*, so to say, by other creators. Thus Mercury is the elder brother of the Earth, metaphorically—his step-brother, so to say, the offspring of *Spirit*—while she (the Earth) is the progeny of the *body*. These allegories have a deeper and more scientific meaning (astronomically and geologically) than our modern physicists are willing to admit.

Here the word "men" refers to the celestial men, or what are called in India *Pitris*, the Fathers, the progenitors of men. This does not remove the seeming difficulty, in view of modern hypotheses, of the teaching, which shows these progenitors or ancestors creating the first human Adams out of their sides: as astral shadows. Such, however, is the teaching of Occultism.

(*c*) Man's organism was adapted in every Race to its surroundings. The first Root-Race was as ethereal as ours is material. The progeny of the seven Creators, who evolved the seven primordial Adams, surely required no purified gases to breathe and live upon. Therefore the Occultist maintains that the case was as stated *aeons of years* before even the evolution of the Lemurian, the first physical man, which itself took place 18,000,000 years ago.

Archaic Scripture teaches that at the commencement of every local Kalpa, or Round, the earth is reborn; "as the human *Jiva* (monad), when passing into a new womb, gets re-covered with a new body, so does the Jiva of the Earth; it gets a more perfect and solid covering with each Round after re-emerging once more from the matrix of space into objectivity." This process is attended, of course, by the throes of the new birth or geological convulsions.

The only reference to it is contained in one verse of the volume of the *Book of Dzyan* before us, where it says:—

4. AND AFTER GREAT THROES SHE (*the Earth*) CAST OFF HER OLD THREE AND PUT ON HER NEW SEVEN SKINS, AND STOOD IN HER FIRST ONE (*a*).

(*a*) This refers to the growth of the Earth, whereas in the Stanza treating of the First Round it is said (in the Commentary):—

"*After the changeless* (avikara) *immutable Nature* (Essence, sadaikarupa) *had awakened and changed* (differentiated) *into* (a state of) *causality* (avyakta), *and from cause* (karana) *had become its own discrete effect* (vyakta), *from invisible it became visible. The smallest of the small* (the most atomic of atoms, or aniyansam aniyasam) *became one and the many* (ekanekarupa); *and producing the Universe produced also the Fourth Loka* (our Earth) *in the garland of the seven lotuses. The Achyuta then became the Chyuta.*[6]

The Earth is said to cast off her old *three* skins, because this refers to the three preceding Rounds she has already passed through; the present being the *fourth* Round out of the seven. At the beginning of every new ROUND, after a period of "obscuration," the Earth (as do also the other six "earths") casts off, or is supposed to cast off, her old skins as the Serpent does. The "Seven Skins," in the first of which she now stands, refer to the seven geological changes which accompany and correspond to the evolution of the Seven Root-Races of Humanity.

Stanza 2, which speaks of this Round, begins with a few words of information concerning the age of our Earth.

---

[6] Achyuta is an almost untranslatable term. It means that which is not subject to fall or change for the worse: the *Unfalling*; and it is the reverse of *chyuta*, "the Fallen." The Dhyanis who incarnate in the human forms of the *Third* Root-Race and endow them with intellect (Manas) are called the *chyuta*, for they fall into generation.

STANZA 2

NATURE UNAIDED FAILS

5. THE WHEEL WHIRLED FOR THIRTY CRORES (*of years, or* 300,000,000). IT CONSTRUCTED RUPAS (*forms*). SOFT STONES, THAT HARDENED (*minerals*); HARD PLANTS, THAT SOFTENED (*vegetation*). VISIBLE FROM INVISIBLE, INSECTS AND SMALL LIVES (*sarisripa, swapada*). SHE (*the Earth*) SHOOK THEM OFF HER BACK, WHENEVER THEY OVER-RAN THE MOTHER (*a*). AFTER THIRTY CRORES OF YEARS, SHE TURNED ROUND. SHE LAID ON HER BACK; ON HER SIDE. . . . SHE WOULD CALL NO SONS OF HEAVEN, SHE WOULD ASK NO SONS OF WISDOM. SHE CREATED FROM HER OWN BOSOM. SHE EVOLVED WATER-MEN TERRIBLE AND BAD.

(*a*) This relates to an inclination of the axis—of which there were several—to a consequent deluge and chaos on Earth (having, how-ever, no reference to primeval chaos), in which monsters, half-human, half-animal, were generated.

"The water-men terrible and bad," who were the production of physical Nature alone, a result of the "evolutionary impulse" and the first attempt to create *man* the "crown," and the aim and goal of all animal life on Earth—are shown to be failures in our Stanzas.

6. THE WATER-MEN TERRIBLE AND BAD SHE HERSELF CREATED. FROM THE REMAINS OF OTHERS (*from the mineral, vegetable and animal remains*) FROM THE FIRST, SECOND, AND THIRD (*Rounds*) SHE FORMED THEM. THE DHYANI CAME AND LOOKED. . . . THE DHYANI FROM THE BRIGHT FATHER-MOTHER, FROM THE WHITE (*Solar-lunar*) REGIONS THEY CAME, FROM THE ABODES OF THE IMMORTAL-MORTALS.

Thus physical Nature, when left to herself in the creation of animal and man, is shown to have failed. She can produce the first two and the lower animal kingdoms, but when it comes to the turn of man, spiritual, independent and intelligent powers are required for his creation, besides the "coats of skin" and the "breath of animal life." The human Monads of preceding Rounds need something higher than purely physical materials to build their personalities with, under the penalty of remaining even below any "Frankenstein" animal.

7. DISPLEASED THEY WERE. OUR FLESH IS NOT THERE (*they said*). THIS IS NO FIT RUPA FOR OUR BROTHERS OF THE FIFTH. NO DWELLINGS FOR THE LIVES.[1] PURE WATERS, NOT TURBID, THEY MUST DRINK (*a*). LET US DRY THEM (*the waters*).

(*a*) Says the Catechism (Commentaries):—

"*It is from the material Worlds that descend they who fashion physical man at the new Manvantaras. They are inferior Lha* (Spirits), *possessed of a dual body* (an astral within an ethereal form). *They are the fashioners and creators of our body of illusion.*" . . .

"*Into the forms projected by the Lha* (Pitris) *the two letters*[2] (the Monad, called also 'the Double Dragon') *descend from the spheres of expectation.*[3] *But they are like a roof with no walls, nor pillars to rest upon.*" . . .

"*Man needs four Flames and three Fires to become one on Earth, and he requires the essence of the forty-nine Fires to be perfect. It is those who have deserted the Superior Spheres, the Gods of Will,*[4] *who complete the Manu of illusion. For the 'Double Dragon' has no hold upon the mere form. It is like the breeze where there is no tree or branch to receive and harbour it. It cannot affect the form where there is no agent of transmission* (Manas, "Mind") *and the form knows it not.*"

"*In the highest worlds, the three are one;*[5] *on Earth* (at first) *the one becomes two. They are like the two* (side) *lines of a triangle that has lost its bottom line—which is the third Fire.*"

8. THE FLAMES CAME. THE FIRES WITH THE SPARKS; THE NIGHT FIRES AND THE DAY FIRES (*a*). THEY DRIED OUT THE TURBID DARK WATERS. WITH THEIR HEAT THEY QUENCHED THEM. THE LHAS (*Spirits*) OF THE HIGH; THE LHAMAYIN (*those*) OF BELOW, CAME (*b*). THEY SLEW THE FORMS, WHICH WERE TWO- AND FOUR-FACED. THEY FOUGHT THE GOAT-MEN, AND THE DOG-HEADED MEN, AND THE MEN WITH FISHES' BODIES.

(*a*) The "Flames" are a Hierarchy of Spirits parallel to, if not identical with, the "burning" fiery *Saraph* (Seraphim) mentioned by Isaiah (vi. 2–6).

---

[1] The Monads of the *presentments* of men of the *Third* Round, the huge Ape-like forms.

[2] In the esoteric system the seven principles in man are represented by seven letters. The first two are *more* sacred than the four letters of the Tetragrammaton.

[3] The intermediate spheres, wherein the Monads, which have not reached Nirvana, are said to slumber in unconscious inactivity between the Manvantaras.

[4] The *Suras*, who become later the A-Suras.

[5] Atma, Buddhi and Manas. In Devachan the higher element of the Manas is needed to make it a state of perception and consciousness for the disembodied *Monad*.

(b) The word "Below" must not be taken to mean infernal regions, but simply a spiritual, or rather ethereal, Being of a lower grade, because nearer to the Earth, or one step higher than our terrestrial sphere; while the Lhas are Spirits of the highest Spheres—whence the name of the capital of Tibet, *Lha-ssa*.

Besides a statement of a purely physical nature and belonging to the evolution of life on Earth, there may be another allegorical meaning attached to this Sloka, or indeed, as is taught, several. The FLAMES, or "Fires," represent Spirit, or the male element, and "Water," matter, or the opposite element. And here again we find, in the action of the Spirit slaying the purely material form, a reference to the eternal struggle, on the physical and psychic planes, between Spirit and Matter, besides a scientific cosmic fact. For, as said in the next verse:—

9. MOTHER-WATER, THE GREAT SEA WEPT. SHE AROSE, SHE DISAPPEARED IN THE MOON, WHICH HAD LIFTED HER, WHICH HAD GIVEN HER BIRTH.

Now what can this mean? Is it not an evident reference to tidal action in the early stage of the history of our planet in its Fourth Round? Mr. Darwin's theory was that not less than 52,000,000 years ago—and probably much more—the Moon originated from the Earth's plastic mass.

The Occult teaching is the reverse of this. The Moon is far older than the Earth; and it is the latter which owes its being to the former, however astronomy and geology may explain the fact. Hence, the tides and the attraction to the Moon, as shown by the liquid portion of the Globe ever striving to raise itself towards its parent. This is the meaning of the sentence that "the Mother-Water arose and disappeared in the Moon, which had lifted her, which had given her birth."

10. WHEN THEY (*the Rupas*) WERE DESTROYED, MOTHER-EARTH REMAINED BARE. SHE ASKED TO BE DRIED.

The time for its incrustation had arrived. The waters had separated and the process was started. It was the beginning of a new life.

STANZA 3

ATTEMPTS TO CREATE MAN

11. THE LORD OF THE LORDS CAME. FROM HER BODY HE SEPARATED THE WATERS, AND THAT WAS HEAVEN ABOVE, THE FIRST HEAVEN (*the atmosphere, or the air, the firmament*).

12. THE GREAT CHOHANS (*Lords*), CALLED THE LORDS OF THE MOON, OF THE AIRY BODIES (*a*). "BRING FORTH MEN, (*they were told*), MEN OF YOUR NATURE. GIVE THEM (*i.e., the Jivas or Monads*) THEIR FORMS WITHIN. SHE (*Mother Earth or Nature*) WILL BUILD COVERINGS WITHOUT (*external bodies*). (*For*) MALES-FEMALES WILL THEY BE. LORDS OF THE FLAME, ALSO."

(*a*) Who are the Lords of the Moon? In India they are called *Pitris* or "Lunar Ancestors," but in the Hebrew scrolls it is Jehovah himself who is the "Lord of the Moon," collectively as the Host, and also as one of the Elohim.

13. THEY (*the Moon-gods*) WENT, EACH ON HIS ALLOTTED LAND: SEVEN OF THEM, EACH ON HIS LOT. THE LORDS OF THE FLAME REMAINED BEHIND. THEY WOULD NOT GO, THEY WOULD NOT CREATE.

The Secret Teachings show the divine Progenitors creating men on seven portions of the Globe "each on his lot"—*i.e.*, each a different Race of men externally and internally, and on different zones. This polygenistic claim is considered elsewhere (*vide* Stanza 7.). But who are "They" who create, and the "Lords of the Flame," "who would not"? Occultism divides the "Creators" into twelve classes; of which four have reached *liberation* to the end of the "Great Age," the fifth is ready to reach it, but still remains active on the intellectual planes, while seven are still under direct Karmic law. These last act on the man-bearing Globes of our Chain.

Exoteric Hindu books mention seven classes of Pitris, and among them two distinct kinds of Progenitors or Ancestors: the *Barhishad* and the *Agnishvatta;* or those possessed of the "sacred fire" and those devoid of it.

Esoteric philosophy explains the original qualifications as being due to the difference between the natures of the two classes: the *Agnishvatta* Pitris are devoid of "fire" (*i.e.*, of creative passion), because too divine and pure; whereas the Barhishad, being the Lunar Spirits more closely connected with Earth, became the creative Elohim of form, or the Adam of dust.

It thus becomes clear why the *Agnishvatta*, devoid of the grosser *creative fire*, hence unable to create physical man, having no *double*, or Astral body, to project, since they were without any *form*, are shown in exoteric allegories as Yogis, Kumaras (chaste youths), who became "rebels," *Asuras*, fighting and opposing Gods,[1] etc. Yet it is they alone who could complete man, *i.e.*, make of him a self-conscious, almost a divine Being—a God on Earth. The *Barhishad*, though possessed of creative fire, were devoid of the higher MAHAT-ic element. Being on a level with the lower Principles—those which precede gross objective matter—they could only give birth to the outer man, or rather to the model of the physical, the astral man. Thus, though we see them intrusted with the task by Brahmā (the collective *Mahat* or Universal Divine Mind), the "Mystery of Creation" is repeated on Earth, only in an inverted sense, as in a *mirror*. It is those who are unable to create the spiritual immortal man, who project the senseless model (the *Astral*) of the physical Being; and it was those who would not multiply who sacrificed themselves to the good and salvation of *Spiritual Humanity*. For, to complete the *septenary man*, to add to his three lower Principles and cement them with the Spiritual Monad—which could never dwell in such a form otherwise than in an *absolutely latent state*—two connecting principles are needed: *Manas* and *Kama*. This requires a living *Spiritual Fire* of the middle Principle from the *fifth* and *third states* of Pleroma. But this Fire is the possession of the *Triangles*, not of the (perfect) *Cubes*, which symbolize the Angelic Beings,[2] the former having from the first Creation got hold of it and being said to have appropriated it for themselves, as in the allegory of Prometheus. These are the active, and therefore—in Heaven—no longer "pure" Beings. They have become the independent and free Intelligences, shown in every Theogony as fighting for that independence and

---

[1] Because, as the allegory shows, the Gods who had no personal merit of their own, dreading the sanctity of those self-striving incarnated Beings who had become *ascetics* and Yogis, and thus threatened to upset the power of the former by their *self-acquired* powers—denounced them. All this has a deep philosophical meaning and refers to the evolution and acquirement of divine powers through *self-exertion*. Some Rishi-Yogis are shown in the Puranas to be far more powerful than the gods. Secondary gods or temporary powers in Nature (the Forces) are doomed to disappear; it is only the spiritual potentiality in man which can lead him to become one with the INFINITE and the ABSOLUTE.

[2] See Volume I., Stanzas 3 to 5. The triangle becomes a Pentagon (five-fold) on Earth.

freedom, and hence—in the ordinary sense—"rebellious to the divine passive law." These are then those "Flames" (the *Agnishvatta*) who, as shown in Sloka 13, "remain behind" instead of going along with the others to create men on Earth. But the true esoteric meaning is that most of them were destined to incarnate as the *Egos* of the forthcoming crop of Mankind. The human *Ego* is neither Atman nor Buddhi, but the higher *Manas*, the intellectual fruition and the efflorescence of the intellectual self-conscious *Egotism*—in the higher spiritual sense. The ancient works refer to it as *Karana Sarira* on the plane of *Sutratma*, which is the golden thread on which, like beads, the various personalities of this higher *Ego* are strung.

Hence, as the higher Pitris or Dhyanis had no hand in his physical creation, we find primeval man, issued from the bodies of his *spiritually fireless* Progenitors, described as aeriform, devoid of compactness, and MINDLESS. He had no middle Principle to serve him as a medium between the *highest* and the *lowest*, the Spiritual Man and the physical brain, for he lacked *Manas*. The Monads which incarnated in those *empty* Shells remained as unconscious as when separated from their previous incomplete forms and vehicles. There is no potentiality for Creation, or Self-Consciousness, in a *pure* Spirit on this our plane, unless its too homogeneous, perfect, because divine, nature is, so to say, mixed with, and strengthened by, an essence already differentiated. It is only the lower line of the Triangle—representing the first triad that emanates from the Universal MONAD—that can furnish this needed consciousness on the plane of differentiated Nature. But how could these pure Emanations, which, on this principle, must have originally been themselves *unconscious* (in our sense), be of any use in supplying the required Principle, as they could hardly have possessed it themselves?

The answer is difficult to comprehend, unless one is well acquainted with the philosophical metaphysics of a beginningless and endless series of Cosmic Re-births; and becomes well impressed and familiarized with that immutable law of Nature which is ETERNAL MOTION, cyclic and spiral, therefore progressive even in its seeming retrogression. The one Divine Principle, the nameless THAT of the Vedas, is the Universal Total, which, neither in its spiritual aspects and emanations, nor in its physical atoms, can ever be at "*absolute rest*" except during the "Nights" of Brahmā. Hence, also, the "First-Born" are those who are first set in motion at the beginning of a Manvantara, and thus the first to fall into the lower spheres of materiality. They who are called in theology the "Thrones," and are the "Seat of God," must be the first incarnated men on Earth; and it becomes comprehensible, if we think of the endless series of past Manvantaras, to find that the last had to come first, and the first last. We find, in short, that the higher Angels had broken, countless aeons before, through the "Seven Circles," and thus *robbed* them of the Sacred fire; which means in plain words, that they had assimilated during their past incarnations, in lower as well as in higher worlds, all the wisdom therefrom—the reflection of MAHAT in its various degrees of intensity. No Entity, whether angelic or human, can reach the state of Nirvana, or of absolute purity, except through aeons of suffering and the *knowledge* of EVIL as well as of good, as otherwise the latter remains incomprehensible.

Between man and the animal—whose Monads (or Jivas) are fundamentally identical—there is the impassable abyss of Mentality and Self-consciousness. What is human mind in its higher aspect, whence comes it, if it is not a portion of the essence—and, in some rare cases of incarnation, the *very essence*—of a higher Being; one from a higher and divine plane? Can man—a God in the animal form—be the product of Material Nature by evolution alone, even as is the animal, which differs from man in external shape, but by no means in the materials of its physical fabric, and is informed by the same, though undeveloped, Monad—seeing that the intellectual potentialities of the two differ as the Sun does from the glow-worm? And what is it that creates such difference, unless man is an animal *plus* a *living God* within his physical shell?

STANZA 4

CREATION OF THE FIRST RACES

14. THE SEVEN HOSTS, THE "WILL (*or Mind*)-BORN" LORDS, PRO-PELLED BY THE SPIRIT OF LIFE-GIVING (*Fohat*), SEPARATE MEN FROM THEMSELVES, EACH ON HIS OWN ZONE.

They threw off their "shadows" or *astral bodies*—if such an ethereal being as a "Lunar Spirit" may be supposed to rejoice in an astral, besides a hardly tangible body. In another Commentary it is said that the "Ancestors" *breathed* out the first man as Brahmā is explained to have breathed out the *Suras* (Gods), when they became "*Asuras*" (from *Asu*, breath). In a third it is said that they, the newly-created men, "were the shadows of the Shadows."

With regard to this sentence—"They were the shadows of the Shadows"—a few more words may be said and a fuller explanation attempted. This first process of the evolution of mankind is far easier to accept than the one which follows it. An "Adam" made of the dust of the ground will always be found preferable, by a certain class of students, to one projected out of the ethereal body of his creator; though the former process has never been heard of, while the latter is familiar, as all know, to many Spiritualists in Europe and America, who, of all men, ought to understand it. For who of those who have witnessed the phenomenon of a materializing form oozing out of the pores of a medium or, at other times, out of his *left side*, can fail to credit the possibility, at least, of such a *birth?* If there are in the Universe such beings as Angels or Spirits, whose *incorporeal* essence may constitute an intelligent Entity notwithstanding the absence of any (to us) solid organism; and if there are those who believe that a God made the first man out of dust, and breathed into him a living Soul—and there are millions upon millions who believe both—what does this doctrine of ours contain that is so impossible? Occult philosophy teaches that the first human stock was projected by higher and semi-divine Beings out of their own essences. If the latter process is to be considered as abnormal or even inconceivable—because obsolete in Nature at this point of evolution—it is yet proven possible on the authority of certain "Spiritualistic" FACTS. Which, then, we ask of the three hypotheses or theories is the most reasonable and the least absurd? Certainly no one—provided he is not a soul-blind materialist—can ever object to the occult teaching.

Now, as shown, we gather from the latter that man was not "created" the complete being he is now, however imperfect he still remains. There was a spiritual, a psychic, an intellectual, and an animal evolution, from the highest to the lowest, as well as a physical development—from the simple and homogeneous up to the more complex and heterogeneous; though not quite on the lines traced for us by the modern evolutionists. This double evolution in two contrary directions required various ages, of divers natures and degrees of spirituality and intellectuality, to fabricate the being now known as man. Furthermore, the one absolute, ever acting and never erring law, which proceeds on the same lines from one eternity (or Manvantara) to the other—ever furnishing an ascending scale for the manifested, or that which we call the great Illusion (*Maha-Maya*), but plunging Spirit deeper and deeper into materiality, and then *redeeming it through flesh* and liberating it—this law, we say, uses for these purposes the Beings from other and higher planes, men, or *Minds* (Manus), in accordance with their Karmic exigencies.

At this juncture, the reader is again asked to turn to the Indian philosophy and religion. The Esotericism of both is at one with our Secret Doctrine, however much the form may differ and vary.

15. Seven times Seven Shadows (*chhayas*) of Future Men (*or Amanasas*) (*a*) were (*thus*) Born, each of his own colour (*complexion*) and kind (*b*). Each (*also*) inferior to his Father (*creator*). The Fathers, the Boneless, could give no Life to Beings with Bones. Their Progeny were Bhuta (*phantoms*) with neither Form nor Mind, therefore they were called the Chhaya (*image or shadow*) Race.

(*a*) The Pitris being divided into *seven classes*, we have here the mystic number again. Nearly all the Puranas agree that three of these are *arupa*, formless, while four are corporeal; the former being intellectual and spiritual, the latter material and devoid of intellect.

"*Having projected their shadows and made men of one element* (ether), *the Progenitors re-ascend to Maha-loka, whence they descend periodically, when the world is renewed, to give birth to new men.*"

"*The subtle bodies remain without understanding* (Manas) *until the advent of the Suras* (Gods) *now called Asuras* (not Gods)," says the Commentary.

"*Not-gods,*" for the Brahmins, perhaps, but the highest *Breaths*, for the Occultist; since those Progenitors (*Pitar*), the formless and the intellectual, refuse to build man, but endow him with mind; the four corporeal classes creating only his body.

Esoteric philosophy teaches that *one third* of the Dhyanis—*i.e.*, the three classes of the *Arupa* Pitris, endowed with intelligence, "which is a formless breath, composed of *intellectual* not elementary substances", was simply *doomed by the law of Karma and evolution to be reborn* (or incarnated) on Earth. Some of these were *Nirmanakayas* from other Manvantaras. Hence we see them, in all the Puranas, reappearing on this globe, as Kings, Rishis and Heroes in the Third Root-Race.

The supposed "rebels," then, were simply those who, compelled by Karmic law to drink the cup of gall to its last bitter drop, *had to incarnate* anew, and thus make responsible thinking entities of the astral statues projected by their inferior brethren. Some are said to have refused, because they had not in them the requisite materials—*i.e.*, an astral body—since they were *Arupa*. The refusal of others had reference to their having been Adepts and Yogis of long preceding Manvantaras; another mystery. But, later on, as *Nirmanakayas*, they sacrificed themselves for the good and salvation of the Monads which were waiting for their turn, and which otherwise would have had to linger for countless ages in irresponsible, animal-like, though in appearance human, forms.

As to their fashioners or "Ancestors"—those Angels who, in the exoteric legends, obeyed the law—they must be identical with the Barhishad Pitris, or the Pitar-Devata, *i.e.*, those *possessed of the physical creative fire*. They could only create, or rather clothe, the human Monads with their own astral Selves, but they could not make man in their image and likeness. Their creating the semblance of men out of their own divine Essence means, esoterically, that it is they who became the first Race, and thus shared its destiny and further evolution. They *would* not, simply because they *could* not, give to man that sacred spark which burns and expands into the flower of human reason and self-consciousness, for they had it not to give. This was left to that class of Devas who became symbolized in Greece under the name of Prometheus, to those who had nought to do with the physical body, yet everything with the purely spiritual man.

Each class of Creators endows man with what it has to give: the one builds his external form; the other gives him its essence, which later on becomes the Human *Higher Self* owing to the *personal exertion of the individual;* but they could not make men as they were themselves—perfect, because sinless. Where there is no struggle, there is no merit. Humanity, "of the Earth earthy," was not destined to be created by the angels of the first divine Breath: therefore they are said to *have refused* to do so, and man had to be formed by more material creators, who, in their turn, could give only what they had in their own natures, and no more. Subservient to eternal law, the pure Gods could only project out of themselves *shadowy* men, a little less ethereal and spiritual, less *divine and perfect* than themselves— shadows still. The first humanity, therefore, was a pale copy of its Progenitors; too material, even in its ethereality, to be a hierarchy of Gods; too spiritual and pure to be MEN, endowed as it is with every *negative* perfection. Perfection, to be fully such, must be born out of imperfection, the *incorruptible* must grow out of the corruptible, having the latter as its vehicle and basis and contrast. Absolute light is absolute darkness, and *vice versa*. In fact, there is neither light nor darkness in the realms of truth. Good and Evil are twins, the progeny of Space and Time, under the sway of Maya. Separate them, by cutting off one from the other, and they will both die. Neither exists *per se*, since each has to be generated and created out of the other, in order to come into being; both must be known and appreciated before becoming objects of perception; hence, in mortal mind, they must be divided.

(*b*) These "Shadows" were born "each of his own colour and kind," each also "inferior to his Creator," because the latter was a complete being of his kind. The Commentaries refer the first sentence to the colour or complexion of each human race thus evolved.

16. HOW ARE THE (*real*) MANUSHYAS BORN? THE MANUS WITH MINDS, HOW ARE THEY MADE? (*a*) THE FATHERS (*Barhishad* (?)) CALLED TO THEIR HELP THEIR OWN FIRE (*the Kavyavahana, electric fire*), WHICH IS THE FIRE WHICH BURNS IN EARTH. THE SPIRIT OF THE EARTH CALLED TO HIS HELP THE SOLAR FIRE (*Suchi, the spirit in the Sun*). THESE THREE (*the Pitris and the two Fires*) PRODUCED IN THEIR JOINT EFFORTS A GOOD RUPA. IT (*the form*) COULD STAND, WALK, RUN, RECLINE AND FLY. YET IT WAS STILL BUT A CHHAYA, A SHADOW WITH NO SENSE (*b*). . . .

(*a*) The "*Manushyas*" (men) and the *Manus* are here equivalent to the Chaldean "Adam" or *mankind* collectively. It is the four Orders or Classes of Dhyan Chohans out of the seven, says the Commentary, "who were the progenitors of the *concealed* man," *i.e.*, the subtle inner man. The "Lha" of the Moon, the Lunar Spirits, were, as already stated, only the *ancestors of his form, i.e.*, of the model according to which Nature began her external work upon him. Thus primitive man was, when he appeared, only a senseless "phantom." This "creation" was a failure.

(*b*) This attempt was again a failure. It allegorizes the vanity of *physical* nature's unaided attempts to construct even a perfect *animal* —let alone man. For the "Fathers," the lower Angels, are all Nature-Spirits, and the higher Elementals also possess an intelligence of their own; but this is not enough to construct a THINKING man. *"Living* Fire" was needed, that Fire which gives the human mind its self-perception and self-consciousness, or *Manas;* and the progeny of *Parvaka* and *Suchi* are the *animal electric* and solar fires, which create animals, and could thus furnish but a physical living constitution to that first astral model of man. The first creators, then, were the Pygmalions of primeval man: they failed to animate the statue— *intellectually.*

This Stanza is very suggestive. It explains the mystery of, and fills the gap between, the informing Principle in man—the HIGHER SELF or human Monad—and the animal Monad, both one and the same, although the former is endowed with *divine* intelligence, the latter with *instinctual* faculty alone. How is the difference to be explained, and the presence of that HIGHER SELF in man accounted for?

"The Sons of MAHAT *are the quickeners of the human Plant. They are the Waters falling upon the arid soil of latent life, and the Spark that vivifies the human animal. They are the Lords of Spiritual Life eternal."* . . . *"In the beginning* (in the Second Race) *some* (of the Lords) *only breathed of their essence into Manushya* (men); *and some took in man their abode."*

This shows that not all men became incarnations of the "divine Rebels," but only a few among them. The remainder had their fifth Principle simply quickened by the spark thrown into it, which accounts for the great difference between the intellectual capacities of men and races. Had not the "sons of Mahat," speaking allegorically, skipped the intermediate worlds, in their impulse toward intellectual freedom, the animal man would never have been able to reach upward from this earth, and attain through self-exertion his ultimate goal. The cyclic pilgrimage would have to be performed through all the planes of existence half unconsciously, if not entirely so, as in the case of the animals. It is owing to this rebellion of intellectual life against the morbid inactivity of pure spirit, that we are what we are—self-conscious, thinking men, with the capabilities and attributes of Gods in us, for good as much as for evil. Hence the REBELS are our saviours. Let the philosopher ponder well over this, and more than one mystery will become clear to him. It is only by the attractive force of the contrasts that the two opposites—Spirit and Matter —can be cemented on Earth, and, smelted in the fire of self-conscious experience and suffering, find themselves wedded in Eternity.

17. THE BREATH (*human Monad*) NEEDED A FORM; THE FATHERS GAVE IT. THE BREATH NEEDED A GROSS BODY; THE EARTH MOULDED IT. THE BREATH NEEDED THE SPIRIT OF LIFE; THE SOLAR LHAS BREATHED IT INTO ITS FORM. THE BREATH NEEDED A MIRROR OF ITS

BODY (*astral shadow*); "WE GAVE IT OUR OWN," SAID THE DHYANIS.
THE BREATH NEEDED A VEHICLE OF DESIRES (*Kama Rupa*); "IT HAS
IT," SAID THE DRAINER OF WATERS (*Suchi, the fire of passion and animal
instinct*). THE BREATH NEEDS A MIND TO EMBRACE THE UNIVERSE;
"WE CANNOT GIVE THAT," SAID THE FATHERS. "I NEVER HAD IT,"
SAID THE SPIRIT OF THE EARTH. "THE FORM WOULD BE CONSUMED
WERE I TO GIVE IT MINE," SAID THE GREAT (*solar*) FIRE ... (*Nascent*)
MAN REMAINED AN EMPTY, SENSELESS BHUTA.... THUS HAVE THE
BONELESS GIVEN LIFE TO THOSE WHO BECAME (*later*) MEN WITH BONES
IN THE THIRD (*Race*).

As a full explanation is found in Stanza 5, a few remarks will now
suffice. The "Father" of primitive physical man, or of his body, is the
vital electric Principle residing in the Sun. The Moon is its "Mother,"
because of that mysterious power in the Moon which has as decided
an influence upon human gestation and generation, which it regulates, as it has on the growth of plants and animals. The "Wind" or
Ether, standing in this case for the agent of transmission by which
those influences are carried down from the two luminaries and
diffused upon Earth, is referred to as the "nurse"; while "Spiritual
Fire" alone makes of man a divine and perfect entity.

Now what is that "Spiritual Fire"? In alchemy it is HYDROGEN,
in general; while in esoteric actuality it is the emanation or the Ray
which proceeds from its *noumenon*, the "Dhyan of the first Element."
Hydrogen is *gas* only on our terrestrial plane. It is the father and
generator, so to say, or rather the *Upadhi* (basis), of both AIR and
WATER, and is "fire, air and water," in fact: *one* under three aspects;
hence the chemical and alchemical trinity. In the world of manifestation or matter it is the objective symbol and the material emanation from the subjective and purely spiritual entitative Being in
the region of *noumena*.

The following order on parallel lines may be found in the evolution of the Elements and the Senses; or in Cosmic terrestrial "MAN"
or "Spirit," and mortal physical man:—

1. Ether   Hearing Sound.
2. Air   Touch   Sound and Touch.
3. Fire, or Light Sight   Sound, Touch and Colour.
4. Water   Taste   Sound, Touch, Colour and Taste.
5. Earth   Smell   Sound, Touch, Colour, Taste and Smell.

As seen, each Element adds to its own characteristics those of its
predecessor; as each Root-Race adds the characterizing sense of the
preceding Race. The same is true in the *septenary* creation of man,
who evolves gradually in seven stages, and on the same principles.

THE EVOLUTION OF THE SECOND RACE

18. The first (*Race*) were the Sons of Yoga. Their sons, the children of the Yellow Father and the White Mother.

In the later Commentary, the sentence is translated:—

"*The Sons of the Sun and of the Moon, the nursling of Ether* (or the Wind) (*a*) . . .

"*They were the shadows of the Shadows of the Lords* (*b*). *They* (the shadows) *expanded. The Spirits of the Earth clothed them; the solar Lhas warmed them* (*i.e.* preserved the vital Fire in the nascent physical forms). *The Breaths had life, but had no understanding. They had no fire nor water of their own* (*c*).

(*a*) Remember in this connection the *Tabula Smaragdina* of Hermes, the esoteric meaning of which has seven keys to it. The "One thing" mentioned in it is MAN. It is said: "The Father of THAT ONE ONLY THING is the Sun; its Mother the Moon; the Wind carries it in his bosom, and its nurse is the Spirituous Earth." In the occult rendering of the same it is added: "and *Spiritual* Fire is its instructor (Guru)."

This Fire is the higher Self, the Spiritual Ego, or that which is eternally reincarnating under the influence of its lower personal Selves, changing with every re-birth, full of *Tanha* or desire to live. It is a strange law of Nature that, on this plane, the higher (Spiritual) Nature should be, so to say, in bondage to the lower. Unless the Ego takes refuge in the Atman, the ALL-SPIRIT, and merges entirely into the essence thereof, the personal Ego may goad it to the bitter end. This cannot be thoroughly understood unless the student makes himself familiar with the mystery of evolution, which proceeds on triple lines—spiritual, psychic and physical.

That which propels towards, and forces evolution, *i.e.*, compels the growth and development of Man towards perfection, is (a) the Monad, or that which acts in it unconsciously through a force inherent in itself; and (b) the lower astral body or the *personal* SELF. Owing to its identity with the ALL-FORCE, which, as said, is inherent in the Monad, it is all-potent on the *Arupa*, or formless plane. On our plane, its essence being too pure, it remains all-potential, but individually inactive: *e.g.*, the rays of the Sun, which contribute to the growth of vegetation, do not select this or that plant to shine upon. Uproot the plant and transfer it to a piece of soil where the sunbeam cannot reach it, and the latter will not follow it. So with the Atman: unless the higher Self or EGO gravitates towards its Sun— the Monad—the lower *Ego*, or *personal* Self, will have the upper hand in every case. For it is this Ego, with its fierce Selfishness and animal desire to live a senseless life (*Tanha*), which is "the maker of the tabernacle," as Buddha calls it in *Dhammapada* (153 and 154). Hence the expression, "the Spirits of the Earth clothed the shadows and expanded them." To these "Spirits" belong temporarily the human astral selves; and it is they who build the physical tabernacle of man, for the Monad and its conscious principle, Manas, to dwell in. But the "Solar" *Lhas*, Spirits, warm them, the shadows. This is physically and literally true; metaphysically, or on the psychic and spiritual plane, it is equally true that the Atman alone *warms* the inner man; *i.e.*, it enlightens it with the ray of Divine Life and alone is able to impart to the inner man, or the reincarnating Ego, its immortality. Thus, as we shall find, for the first three and a half Root-Races, up to the middle or turning point, it is the astral shadows of the "Progenitors," the lunar Pitris, which are the formative powers in the Races, and which build and gradually force the evolution of the physical form towards perfection—this, at the cost of a proportionate loss of spirituality. Then, from the turning point, it is the Higher Ego, or incarnating principle, the *nous* or *Mind*, which reigns over the animal Ego, and rules it whenever it is not carried down by the latter. In short, Spirituality is on its ascending arc, and the animal or physical impedes it from steadily progressing on the path of its evolution only when the selfishness of the *personality* has so strongly infected the real *inner* man, that the upward attraction has lost all its power on the thinking reasonable man.

(*b*) The sentence: "They were the shadows of the Shadows of the Lords," *i.e.*, the Progenitors created man out of their own astral bodies, explains a universal belief. The *Devas* are credited in the East with having no shadows of their own. "The devas cast no shadows," and this is the sure sign of a *good holy Spirit*.

(*c*) Why had they "no fire or water of their own"? Because:—

That which Hydrogen is to the elements and gases on the objective plane, its noumenon is in the world of mental or subjective phenomena; since its trinitarian latent nature is mirrored in its three active emanations from the three higher principles in man, namely, "Spirit, Soul, and Mind," or *Atma, Buddhi*, and *Manas*. It is the spiritual and also the material human basis. Rudimentary man, having been nursed by the "Air" or the "Wind," becomes the perfect man later on; when, with the development of "Spiritual Fire," the *noumenon* of the "Three in One" within his Self, he acquires from his inner Self, or Instructor, the Wisdom of Self-Consciousness, which he does not possess in the beginning.

19. THE SECOND RACE (*was*) THE PRODUCT BY BUDDING AND EXPANSION; THE A-SEXUAL (*form*) FROM THE SEXLESS (*shadow*). THUS WAS, O LANOO, THE SECOND RACE PRODUCED (*a*).

(*a*) What will be most contested by scientific authorities is this a-sexual Race, the Second, the fathers of the "Sweat-born" so-called, and perhaps still more the Third Race, the "Egg-born" androgynes. It is not denied that in the beginning of physical evolution there must have been processes in Nature, spontaneous generation, for instance, now extinct, which are repeated in other forms. Thus we are told that microscopic research shows no permanence of any particular mode of reproducing life. For "it shows that the same organism may run through various metamorphoses in the course of its life-cycle, during some of which it may be *sexual,* and in others *a-sexual*; *i.e.,* it may reproduce itself alternately by the co-operation of two beings of opposite sex, and also by fissure or *budding* from one being only, which is of no sex."[1] "Budding" is the very word used in the Stanza. How could these Chhayas reproduce themselves otherwise; viz., procreate the Second Race, since they were ethereal, a-sexual, and even devoid, as yet, of the vehicle of desire, or Kama Rupa, which evolved only in the Third Race? They evolved the Second Race unconsciously, as do some plants. Or, perhaps, as the *Amoeba,* only on a more ethereal, impressive, and larger scale. If, indeed, the microscopic cells are looked upon by physical science as independent living beings—just as Occultism regards the "Fiery Lives"—there is no difficulty in the conception of the primitive process of procreation.

Consider the first stages of the development of a germ-cell. Its *nucleus* grows, changes, and forms a double cone or spindle, thus, $\times$ *within* the cell. This spindle approaches the surface of the cell, and one half of it is *extruded* in the form of what are called the "*polar cells.*" These polar cells *now* die, and the embryo develops from the growth and segmentation of the remaining part of the nucleus which is *nourished* by the substance of the cell. Then why could not beings have lived thus, and been created in *this* way—at the very beginning of *human and mammalian evolution?*

This may, perhaps, serve as an analogy to give some idea

[1] See Laing's *Modern Science and Modern Thought,* p. 90.

of the process by which the Second Race was formed from the First.

The astral form clothing the Monad was surrounded, as it still is, by its egg-shaped sphere of *aura*, which here corresponds to the substance of the germ-cell or *ovum*. The astral form itself is the nucleus, now, as then, instinct with the principle of life.

When the season of reproduction arrives, the *sub*-astral "*extrudes*" a miniature of itself from the egg of surrounding aura. This germ grows and feeds on the aura till it becomes fully developed, when it gradually separates from its parent, carrying with it its own sphere of aura.

The analogy with the "*polar cells*" would seem to hold good, since their death would *now* correspond to the change introduced by the separation of the sexes, when gestation *in utero, i.e., within the cell,* became the rule.

"*The early Second* (Root) *Race were the Fathers of the 'Sweat-born'; the later Second* (Root) *Race were 'Sweat-born' themselves.*"

This passage from the Commentary refers to the work of evolution from the beginning of a Race to its close. The "Sons of Yoga," or the primitive astral race, had seven stages of evolution *racially*, or collectively; as every individual Being in it had, and has now. Thus the first sub-races of the Second Race were born at first by the process described on the law of analogy; while the last began gradually, *pari passu* with the evolution of the human body, to be formed otherwise. The process of reproduction had seven stages also in each Race, each covering aeons of time.

Primeval human hermaphrodites are a fact in Nature well known to the ancients, and form one of Darwin's greatest perplexities. Yet there is certainly no impossibility, but, on the contrary, a great probability that hermaphroditism existed in the evolution of the early races; while on the grounds of analogy, and on that of the existence of one universal law in physical evolution, acting indifferently in the construction of plant, animal, and man, it must be so. The mistaken theories of monogenesis, and the descent of man from the mammals instead of the reverse, are fatal to the completeness of evolution as taught in modern schools on Darwinian lines, and they will have to be abandoned in view of the insuperable difficulties which they encounter. Occult tradition can alone reconcile the inconsistencies and fill the gap.

In the *Descent of Man* occurs the following passage; which shows how near Darwin came to the acceptance of this ancient teaching.

"It has been known that in the vertebrate kingdom one sex bears rudiments of various accessory parts appertaining to the reproductive system, which properly belong to the opposite sex. . . . Some re-mote progenitor of the whole vertebrate kingdom appears to have been hermaphrodite or androgynous[2] . . . But here we encounter a *singular difficulty*. In *the mammalian class the males possess rudiments of a uterus with the adjacent passages in the Vesiculae prostaticae; they bear also rudiments of mammae, and some male marsupials have traces of a marsupial sac*. Other analogous facts could be added. Are we then to suppose that some extremely ancient mammal continued androgynous after it had acquired the chief distinctions of its class, and therefore after it had diverged from the lower classes of the vertebrate kingdom? This seems very improbable,[3] for *we have to look to fishes, the lowest of all the classes, to find any still existent androgynous forms*."

Why not candidly admit the argument in favour of the herma-phroditism which characterises the old fauna? Occultism proposes a solution which embraces the facts in a most comprehensive and simple manner. These relics of a prior androgyne stock must be placed in the same category as the pineal gland, and other organs as mysterious, which afford us silent testimony as to the reality of functions which have long since become atrophied in the course of animal and human progress, but which once played a signal part in the general economy of primeval life.

20. THEIR FATHERS WERE THE SELF-BORN. THE SELF-BORN, THE CHHAYA FROM THE BRILLIANT BODIES OF THE LORDS, THE FATHERS, THE SONS OF TWILIGHT.

The "Shadows," or *Chhayas*, are called the sons of the "Self-born," as the latter name is applied to all the Gods and Beings born through the WILL, whether of Deity or Adept.

21. WHEN THE RACE BECAME OLD, THE OLD WATERS MIXED WITH THE FRESHER WATERS (*a*); WHEN THE DROPS BECAME TURBID, THEY VANISHED AND DISAPPEARED, IN THE NEW STREAM, IN THE HOT STREAM OF LIFE. THE OUTER OF THE FIRST BECAME THE INNER OF THE SECOND (*b*). THE OLD WING BECAME THE SHADOW, AND THE SHADOW OF THE WING (*c*).

(*a*) The old (primitive) Race merged in the Second Race, and became one with it.

(*b*) This is the mysterious process of transformation and evolution of mankind. The material of the first forms—shadowy, ethereal, and

---

[2] And why not all the progenitive first Races, human as well as animal; and why *one* "remote progenitor"?

[3] Obviously so, on the lines of Evolutionism, which traces the mammalia to some amphibian ancestor.

negative—was drawn or absorbed into, and thus became the com-
plement of the forms of the Second Race. The *Commentary* explains
this by saying that, as the First Race was simply composed of the
astral shadows of the creative Progenitors, having of course neither
astral nor physical bodies of their own—this Race *never died*. Its
"men" melted gradually away, becoming absorbed in the bodies of
their own "sweat-born" progeny, more solid than their own. The
old form vanished and was absorbed by, disappeared in, the new
form, more human and physical. There was no death in those days
of a period more blissful than the Golden Age; but the first, or
parent material was used for the formation of the new being, to form
the body and even the inner or *lower* principles or bodies of the
progeny.

(c) When the "shadow" retires, *i.e.*, when the astral body becomes
covered with more solid flesh, man develops a physical body. The
"wing," or the ethereal form that produced its shadow and image,
became the shadow of the astral body and its own progeny.

THE DIVINE HERMAPHRODITE

An impenetrable veil of secrecy was thrown over the occult and
religious mysteries taught after the submersion of the last remnant
of the Atlantean race, some 12,000 years ago, lest they should be
shared by the unworthy, and so desecrated.

It is this secrecy which led the Fifth Race to the establishment, or
rather the re-establishment of the religious Mysteries, in which
ancient truths might be taught to the coming generations under the
veil of allegory and symbolism.

In the Book of Enoch we have Adam, the first divine androgyne,
separating into man and woman, and becoming JAH-HEVA in one
form, or *Race*, and Cain and Abel[4] (male and female) in its other form
or *Race*—the double-sexed Jehovah[5]—an echo of its Aryan prototype, Brahmā-Vach. After which come the Third and Fourth Root-
Races of mankind[6]—that is to say, Races of men and women, or
individuals of opposite sexes, no longer sexless semi-spirits and
androgynes, as were the two Races which precede them.

[4] Abel is Chebel, meaning "Pains of Birth," conception.

[5] See *Isis Unveiled*, Vol. II., p. 398, where Jehovah is shown to be Adam and Eve
blended, and *Hevah*, and Abel, the *feminine serpent*.

[6] See *Isis Unveiled*, Vol. I., p. 305: "The union of the two create a *third* Race, etc."

STANZA 6

THE EVOLUTION OF THE "SWEAT-BORN"

22. THEN THE SECOND EVOLVED THE SWEAT-BORN, THE THIRD
(*Race*). THE SWEAT GREW, ITS DROPS GREW, AND THE DROPS BECAME
HARD AND ROUND. THE SUN WARMED IT; THE MOON COOLED AND
SHAPED IT; THE WIND FED IT UNTIL ITS RIPENESS. THE WHITE SWAN
FROM THE STARRY VAULT (*the Moon*), OVERSHADOWED THE BIG DROP.
THE EGG OF THE FUTURE RACE, THE MAN-SWAN (*Hamsa*) OF THE
LATER THIRD (*a*). FIRST MALE-FEMALE, THEN MAN AND WOMAN (*b*).

(*a*) The text of the Stanza clearly implies that the human embryo
was nourished *ab extra* by Cosmic forces, and that the "Father-
Mother" furnished apparently the germ that ripened; in all probability a "sweat-born egg," to be hatched out, in some mysterious
way, disconnected from the "double" parent. It is comparatively
easy to conceive of an oviparous humanity, since even now man is,
in one sense, "egg-born."

(*b*) This is a very curious statement as explained in the Commentaries. To make it clear: The First Race having created the Second
by "budding," as just explained, the Second Race gives birth to the
Third—which itself is separated into three distinct divisions, consisting of men differently procreated. The first two of these are
produced by an oviparous method. While the early sub-races of the
Third Humanity procreated their species by a kind of exudation of
moisture or vital fluid, the drops of which coalescing formed an ovi-
form ball—or shall we say egg?—which served as an extraneous
vehicle for the generation therein of a *foetus* and child, the mode of
procreation by the later races changed, in its results at all events.
The little ones of the earlier races were entirely sexless; but those of
the later races were born androgynous. It is in the Third Race that
the separation of sexes occurred. From being previously a-sexual,
Humanity became distinctly hermaphrodite or bi-sexual; and finally
the man-bearing eggs began to give birth, gradually and almost imperceptibly in their evolutionary development, first, to beings in
which one sex predominated over the other, and, finally, to distinct
men and women.

The point most insisted upon at present is that, whatever origin
be claimed for man, his evolution took place in this order: (1) Sex-

less, as all the earlier forms are; (2) then, by a natural transition, he became "a solitary hermaphrodite," a bi-sexual being; and (3) finally separated and became what he is now.

The humanities developed coordinately, and on parallel lines with the four Elements, every new Race being physiologically adapted to meet the additional element. Our Fifth Race is rapidly approaching the Fifth Element—call it interstellar ether, if you will—which has more to do, however, with psychology than with physics. We men have learned to live in every climate, whether frigid or tropical, but the first two Races had nought to do with climate, nor were they subservient to any temperature or change therein. And thus, we are taught, men lived down to the close of the Third Root-Race, when eternal spring reigned over the whole globe, such as is now enjoyed by the inhabitants of Jupiter. It must, however, be always borne in mind that the "eternal spring" referred to is only a condition *cognized as such by the Jovians.* It is not "spring" *as we know it.*

23. THE SELF-BORN WERE THE CHHAYAS, THE SHADOWS FROM THE BODIES OF THE SONS OF TWILIGHT. NEITHER WATER NOR FIRE COULD DESTROY THEM. THEIR SONS WERE (*so destroyed*).

This verse cannot be understood without the help of the Commentaries. It means that the First Root-Race, the "Shadows" of the Progenitors, could not be injured, or destroyed by death. Being so ethereal and so little human in constitution, they could not be affected by any element—flood or fire. But their "Sons," the Second Root-Race, could be and were so destroyed. As the "Progenitors" merged wholly in their own astral bodies, which were their progeny, so that progeny was absorbed in its descendants, the "Sweat-born." These were the Second Humanity—composed of the most heterogeneous gigantic semi-human monsters—the first attempts of material nature at building human bodies. The ever-blooming lands of the Second Continent (Greenland, among others) were transformed from Edens with their eternal spring into hyperborean Hades. This transformation was due to the displacement of the great waters of the globe, to oceans changing their beds; and the bulk of the Second Race perished in this first great throe of the evolution and consolidation of the globe during the human period. Of such great cataclysms there have already been four. And we may expect a fifth for ourselves in due course of time...

The "Deluge" is undeniably a *universal tradition.* "Glacial periods" were numerous, and so were the "Deluges," for various reasons. Stockwell and Croll enumerate some half dozen Glacial Periods and subsequent Deluges—the earliest of all being dated by them 850,000, and the last about 100,000 years ago.[1] But which was *our* Deluge? Assuredly the former, the one which to this date remains recorded in the traditions of all the peoples, from the remotest antiquity; the one that finally swept away the last peninsulas of Atlantis, beginning with Ruta and Daitya and ending with the (comparatively) small island mentioned by Plato. This is shown by the agreement of certain details in all the legends. It was the last of its gigantic character. The little deluge, the traces of which Baron Bunsen found in Central Asia, and which he places at about 10,000 years B.C., had nothing to do with either the *semi*-universal Deluge, or Noah's flood —the latter being a purely mythical rendering of old traditions—nor even with the submersion of the last Atlantean island; at least, only a moral connection.

Our Fifth Race (the non-initiated portions), hearing of many Deluges, confused them, and now know of but one. This one altered the whole aspect of the globe in its interchange and shifting of land and sea.

The *semi*-universal deluge known to geology (first Glacial Period) must have occurred just at the time allotted to it by the Secret Doctrine, namely, 200,000 years (in round numbers) after the commencement of our FIFTH RACE, or about the time assigned by Messrs. Croll and Stockwell for the first Glacial Period: *i.e.*, about 850,000 years ago. Thus, as the latter disturbance is attributed by geologists and astronomers to "an extreme eccentricity of the Earth's orbit," and as the Secret Doctrine attributes it to the same source, but with the addition of another factor, the shifting of the Earth's axis, all this should tend to show that the ancients knew something of the "modern discoveries" of Science.

COULD MEN EXIST 18,000,000 YEARS AGO?

To this Occultism answers in the affirmative, notwithstanding all scientific objectors. Moreover, this duration covers only the Vaivasvata-Manu *Man*, *i.e.*, the male and female entity already separated into distinct sexes. The two and a half Races that preceded that event may have lived 300,000,000 years ago for all that science can tell. For the geological and physical difficulties in the way of the theory could not exist for the *primeval, ethereal* man of the Occult teachings. *The whole issue of the quarrel between the profane and the esoteric sciences depends upon the belief in, and demonstration of, the existence*

---

[1] "*Smithsonian Contributions to Knowledge*," xviii.; "*American Journal of Science*," III., xi., 456; and Croll's "*Climate and Time*." Lemuria was not submerged by a flood, but was destroyed by volcanic action, and afterwards sank.

of an astral body within the physical, the former independent of the latter.

The Secret Doctrine maintains that, notwithstanding the general cataclysms and disturbances of our Globe, which—owing to its being the period of its greatest physical development, for the Fourth Round is the middle-point of the life allotted to it—were far more terrible and intense than during any of the three preceding Rounds (the cycles of its earlier psychic and spiritual life and of its semi-ethereal conditions) physical Humanity has existed upon it for the last 18,000,000 years. This period was preceded by 300,000,000 years of the mineral and vegetable development. To this, all those who refuse to accept the theory of a "boneless," purely ethereal, man, will object.

The Occultists maintain, on their side, that, during those periods when there must have been insufferable heat, even at the two poles, successive floods, upheaval of the valleys and constant shifting of the great waters and seas, none of these circumstances could form an impediment to human life and organization, such *as is assigned by them to the early mankind.* Neither the heterogeneity of ambient regions, full of deleterious gases, nor the perils of a crust hardly consolidated, could prevent the First and Second Races from making their appearance even during the Carboniferous, or the Silurian age itself.

Thus the *Monads* destined to animate future Races were ready for the new transformation. They had passed their phases of immetalization, of plant and animal life, from the lowest to the highest, and were waiting for their human, more intelligent form. Yet, what could the plastic Modellers do but follow the laws of evolutionary Nature? ...

If "spontaneous generation" has changed its methods now, owing perhaps to accumulated material on hand, so as to almost escape detection, it was in full swing in the genesis of terrestrial life. Even the simple physical form and the evolution of species show how Nature proceeds. The scale-bound, gigantic sauria, the winged pterodactyl, the megalosaurus, and the hundred-feet long iguanodon of the later period, are the transformations of the earliest representatives of the animal kingdom found in the sediments of the primary epoch. There was a time when all those above enumerated "antediluvian" monsters appeared as filamentoid infusoria without shell or crust, with neither nerves, muscles, organs nor sex, and reproduced their kind by gemmation; as do microscopical animals also, the architects and builders of our mountain ranges, agreeably to the teachings of science. Why not man in this case? Why should he not have followed the same law in his growth, *i.e.,* gradual condensation?

Every unprejudiced person would prefer to believe that primeval
humanity had at first an ethereal—or, if so preferred, a huge filamentoid, jelly-like form, evolved by gods or natural "forces," which
grew, condensed throughout millions of ages, and became gigantic
in its physical impulse and tendency, until it settled into the huge,
physical form of the Fourth Race Man,—rather than believe him
created of the dust of the Earth (*literally*), or from some unknown
anthropoid ancestor.

Analogy is the guiding law in Nature. Nature, as a creative potency,
is infinite, and no generation of physical scientists can ever boast of
having exhausted the list of her ways and methods, however uniform
the laws upon which she proceeds. If we can conceive of a ball of
Fire-mist becoming gradually—as it rolls through aeons of time in
the interstellar spaces—a Planet, a self-luminous Globe, to settle into
a *man-bearing* world or Earth, thus having passed from a soft plastic
body into a rock-bound Globe; and if we see on it everything evolving from the non-nucleated jelly-speck that becomes the sarcode[2] of
the *moneron*, then passes from its *protistic* state[3] into the form of an
animal, to grow into a gigantic reptilian monster of the Mesozoic
times; then dwindles again into the (comparatively) dwarfish
crocodile, now confined solely to tropical regions, and the universally
common lizard[4]—how can man alone escape the general law?
"There were giants on earth in those days," says *Genesis*, repeating
the statement of all the other Eastern Scriptures; and the *Titans* are
founded on anthropological and physiological fact.

And, as the hard-shelled crustacean was once upon a time a jelly-
speck, "a thoroughly homogeneous particle of albumen in a firmly
adhesive condition," so was the outward covering of primitive man,
his early "coat of skin," *plus* an immortal spiritual Monad, and a
psychic temporary form and body within that shell. The modern,
hard, muscular man, almost impervious to any climate, was, perhaps, some 25,000,000 years ago, just what the Haeckelian Moneron
is, strictly "an organism without organs," an entirely homogeneous

[2] Or what is more generally known as *Protoplasm*. This substance received its
name of "*Sarcode*" from Prof. Dujardin Beaumetz far earlier.

[3] The Monera are indeed *Protista*. They are neither animals "nor plants," writes
Haeckel; " . . . the whole body of the Moneron represents nothing more than a
single thoroughly homogeneous particle of albumen in a firmly adhesive condition."
("*Journal of Microscopical Science*," Jan., 1869, p. 28.)

[4] Behold the *Iguanodon* of the Mesozoic ages — the monster 100 feet long — now
transformed into the small Iguana lizard of South America. Popular traditions
about *giants* in days of old, and their mention in every mythology, including the
Bible, may some day be shown to be founded on fact. In nature, the logic of analogy
alone ought to make us accept these *traditions* as scientific verities.

substance with a structureless albumen body within, and a human form only outwardly.

Therefore even the Stanza which says:—

"The mind-born, the boneless, gave being to the will-born with bones"; adding that this took place in the middle of the *Third* Race 18,000,000 years ago—has yet a chance of being accepted by future scientists.

As far as XIXth century thought is concerned, we shall be told that such a statement is absurd. How much more improbable will appear our further assertion, to the effect that the antiquity of the *First* Race dates back millions of years beyond this again. For, although the exact figures are withheld, and it is out of the question to refer the incipient evolution of the primeval Divine Races with *certainty* to either the early Secondary, or the Primary ages of geology, one thing is clear, that the figures 18,000,000 of years, which embrace the duration of *sexual, physical,* man, have to be enormously increased if the whole process of spiritual, astral and physical development is taken into account. Such terrestrial conditions as were then operative had no touch with the plane on which the evolution of the *ethereal astral Races* proceeded. Only in relatively recent geological periods has the spiral course of cyclic law swept mankind into the lowest grade of physical evolution—the plane of gross material causation. In those early ages, *astral* evolution was alone in progress, and the two planes, the astral and the physical,[5] though developing on parallel lines, had no direct point of contact with one another. It is obvious that a shadow-like *ethereal* man is related by virtue of his organization—if such it can be called—only to that plane from which the substance of his *Upadhi* is derived.

Again, to take up the question of "spontaneous generation"; life—as science shows—has not always reigned on this terrestrial plane. There was a time when even the Haeckelian Moneron—that simple globule of Protoplasm—had not yet appeared at the bottom of the seas. Whence came the *Impulse* which caused the molecules of Carbon, Nitrogen, Oxygen, etc., to group themselves into that organic "slime," now christened protoplasm. What were the prototypes of the Monera? They, at least, could not have fallen in meteorites from other globes already formed. And if *they have* so fallen; if our Earth got its supply of life-germs from other planets;

[5] It must be noted that, though the astral and physical planes of matter ran parallel with one another even in the earliest geological ages, yet they were not in the same phases of manifestation in which they are *now*. The Earth did not reach its present *grade of density* till 18,000,000 years ago. Since then *both* the physical and astral planes have become grosser.

who, or *what*, had carried them into those planets? Here, again, unless the Occult Teaching is accepted, we are compelled once more to face a *miracle;* to accept the theory of a *personal, anthropomorphic Creator*, the attributes and definitions of whom, as formulated by the Monotheists, clash as much with philosophy and logic as they degrade the ideal of an infinite Universal Deity, before whose incomprehensible awful grandeur the highest human intellect feels dwarfed.

The conditions that were necessary for the earliest Race of mankind require no elements, whether simple or compound. The spiritual ethereal Entity which lived in Spaces unknown to Earth, before the first sidereal "jelly-speck" evolved in the ocean of crude Cosmic Matter—billions and trillions of years before our globular speck in infinity, called Earth, came into being and generated the *Moneron* in its drops, called Oceans—needed no "elements." The "Manu with soft bones" could well dispense with calcium phosphate, as he had no bones, save in a figurative sense. And while even the Monera, however homogeneous their organism, still required physical conditions of life that would help them toward further evolution, the being which became primitive Man and the "Father of man," after evolving on planes of existence undreamt of by science, could well remain impervious to any state of atmospheric conditions around him.

FROM THE SEMI-DIVINE DOWN TO THE FIRST HUMAN RACES

24. THE SONS OF WISDOM, THE SONS OF NIGHT (*issued from the body of Brahmā when it became Night*), READY FOR RE-BIRTH, CAME DOWN. THEY SAW THE (*intellectually*) VILE FORMS OF THE FIRST THIRD (*still senseless Race*) (*a*). "WE CAN CHOOSE," SAID THE LORDS, "WE HAVE WISDOM." SOME ENTERED THE CHHAYAS. SOME PROJECTED A SPARK. SOME DEFERRED TILL THE FOURTH (*Race*). FROM THEIR OWN ESSENCE THEY FILLED (*intensified*) THE KAMA (*the vehicle of desire*). THOSE WHO RECEIVED BUT A SPARK REMAINED DESTITUTE OF (*higher*) KNOWLEDGE. THE SPARK BURNT LOW (*b*). THE THIRD REMAINED MINDLESS. THEIR JIVAS (*Monads*) WERE NOT READY. THESE WERE SET APART AMONG THE SEVEN (*primitive human species*). THEY (*became the*) NARROWHEADED. THE THIRD WERE READY. IN THESE SHALL WE DWELL, SAID THE LORDS OF THE FLAME AND OF THE DARK WISDOM (*c*).

This Stanza contains, in itself, the whole key to the mysteries of evil. It solves the secret of the subsequent inequalities of intellectual capacity, of birth or social position, and gives a logical explanation to the incomprehensible Karmic course throughout the aeons which followed.

(*a*) Up to the Fourth Round, and even to the later part of the Third Race in this Round, *Man*—if the ever-changing forms that clothed the Monads during the first three Rounds and the first two and a half Races of the present one can be given that misleading name—was only an animal intellectually. It is only in the present *midway* Round that he himself has entirely developed the Fourth Principle as a fit vehicle for the Fifth. But Manas will be relatively *fully* developed only in the following Round, when it will have an opportunity of becoming entirely divine until the end of the Rounds.

(*b*) "*They were not ready*" signifies that the *Karmic* development of these Monads had not yet fitted them to occupy the forms of men destined for incarnation in higher intellectual Races.

(*c*) The *Zohar* speaks of "Black Fire," which is *Absolute* Light-Wisdom.

Esoteric philosophy identifies the pre-Brahmanical Asuras, Rudras, Rakshasas and all the "Adversaries" of the Gods in the allegories, with the Egos, which, by incarnating in the still witless man of the Third Race, made him *consciously* immortal. They are, then, during the cycle of Incarnations, the true *dual Logos*—the conflicting and two-faced Divine Principle in Man. The Commentary that follows, and the next Stanzas may throw more light on this very difficult tenet, but the writer does not feel competent to give it out fully. Of the succession of Races, however, they say:—

"*First come the SELF-EXISTENT on this Earth. They are the 'Spiritual Lives' projected by the absolute WILL and LAW, at the dawn of every rebirth of the Worlds. These LIVES are the divine 'Sishta,'* (the Seed-Manus, or the Prajapati and the Pitris).''

From these proceed—

1. *The First Race, the "Self-born," which are the* (astral) *shadows of their Progenitors. The body was devoid of all understanding* (mind, intelligence, and will). *The Inner Being* (the higher Self or Monad), *though within the earthly frame, was unconnected with it. The link, the Manas, was not there as yet.*

2. *From the First* (race) *emanated the Second, called the "Sweat-born" and the "Boneless." This is the Second Root-Race, endowed by the Preservers* (Rakshasas) *and the incarnating Gods* (Asuras and the Kumaras) *with the first primitive and weak Spark* (the germ of intelligence) . . . *And from these in turn proceeds:—*

3. *The Third Root-Race, the "Two-fold"* (Androgynes). *The first Races hereof are shells, till the last is "inhabited"* (i.e., informed) *by the Dhyanis.*

The Second Race, as stated above, being also sexless, evolved out of itself, at its beginning, the Third Androgyne Race by an analogous, but already more complicated process. As described in the Commentary, the very earliest of that race were:—

"*The 'Sons of Passive Yoga.'*[1] *They issued from the second Manushyas* (human race), *and became oviparous. The emanations that came out of their bodies during the seasons of procreation were ovulary; the small spheroidal nuclei developing into a large soft, egg-like vehicle, gradually hardened, when, after a period of gestation, it broke and the young human animal issued from it unaided, as the fowls do in our race.*"

---

[1] The gradual evolution of man in the Secret Doctrine shows that all the later (to the profane the earliest) Races have their *physical* origin in the early Fourth Race. But it is the sub-race which preceded the one that separated sexually, that is to be regarded as the *spiritual* ancestors of our present generations, and especially of the Eastern Aryan Races.

This must seem to the reader ludicrously absurd. Nevertheless, it is strictly on the lines of evolutionary analogy, which science perceives in the development of the living animal species. First the *moneron*-like procreation by self-division (*vide Haeckel*); then, after a few stages, the oviparous, as in the case of reptiles, which are followed by the birds; then, finally, the mammals with their *ovoviviparous* modes of producing their young ones.

The *progressive* order of the methods of reproduction, as unveiled by science, is a brilliant confirmation of esoteric ethnology. It is only necessary to tabulate the data in order to prove our assertion.

I. *Fission:*—

(*a*) As seen in the division of the homogeneous speck of protoplasm, known as Moneron or Amoeba, into two.

(*b*) As seen in the division of the nucleated cell, in which the cell-nucleus splits into two sub-nuclei, which either develop within the original cell-wall or burst it, and multiply outside as independent entities. (*Cf., the First Root-Race.*)

II. *Budding:*—

A small portion of the parent structure swells out at the surface and finally parts company, growing to the size of the original organism; *e.g.*, many vegetables, the sea-anemone, etc. (*Cf., the Second Root-Race*).[2]

III. *Spores:*—

A single cell thrown off by the parent organism, which develops into a multicellular organism reproducing the features of the latter, *e.g.*, bacteria and mosses.

IV. *Intermediate Hermaphroditism:*—

Male and female organs inhering in the same individual; *e.g.*, the majority of plants, worms, and snails, etc.; allied to budding. (*Cf., Second and early Third Root-Races.*)

V. *True sexual union:*—

(*Cf., later Third Root-Race.*)

We now come to an important point with regard to the double evolution of the human race. The Sons of Wisdom, or the *spiritual* Dhyanis, had become "intellectual" through their contact with matter, because they had already reached, during previous cycles of incarnation, that degree of intellect which enabled them to become independent and self-conscious entities, *on this plane* of matter. They were reborn only by reason of Karmic effects. They *entered* those who

---

[2] Every process of healing and cicatrization in the higher animal groups—even in the case of reproduction of mutilated limbs with the Amphibians—is effected by *fission* and *gemmation* of the elementary morphological elements.

were "ready," and became the Arhats, or *sages,* alluded to above. This needs explanation.

It does not mean that *Monads* entered forms in which other Monads already were. They were "Essences," "Intelligences," and *Conscious Spirits;* entities seeking to become still more conscious by uniting with more developed matter. Their essence was too pure to be distinct from the universal Essence; but their "Egos," or *Manas* (since they are called *Manasaputra,* born of "Mahat," or Brahmā) had to pass through earthly human experiences to become *all-wise,* and be able to start on the returning ascending cycle. The *Monads* are not *discrete* principles, limited or conditioned, but rays from that one universal *absolute* Principle. It is not in the course of natural law that man should become a *perfect* septenary Being before the Seventh Race in the seventh Round. Yet he has all these principles latent in him from his birth. Nor is it part of the evolutionary law that the Fifth Principle (*Manas*), should receive its complete development before the *Fifth* Round. All such prematurely developed intellects (on the *spiritual* plane) in our Race are *abnormal*; they are those whom we call the "Fifth-Rounders." Even in the coming Seventh Race, at the close of this Fourth Round, while our four lower principles will be fully developed, that of *Manas* will be only proportionately so. This limitation, however, refers solely to the spiritual development. The intellectual, on the physical plane, was reached during the Fourth Root-Race. Thus, those who were "half ready," who received "but a spark," constitute the average humanity which has to acquire its intellectuality during the present Manvantaric evolution, after which they will be ready in the next for the full reception of the "Sons of Wisdom." While those which "were not ready" at all, the latest Monads, which had hardly evolved from their last transitional and lower animal forms at the close of the Third Round, remained the "narrow-brained" of the Stanza. This explains the otherwise unaccountable degrees of intellectuality among the various races of men—the savage Bushman and the European—even now. Those tribes of savages are not the unjustly disinherited, or the *unfavoured,* as some may think. They are simply those *latest arrivals* among the human Monads which *were not ready;* which have to evolve during the present Round, as on the three remaining Globes (hence on four different planes of being) so as to arrive at the level of the average class when they reach the Fifth Round. One remark may prove useful, as food for thought in this connection. The MONADS *had no Karma to work out when first born as men, as their more favoured brethren in intelligence had.* The former are spinning out Karma only now; the latter are burdened with past, present, and future Karma. In this respect the poor savage is more fortunate than the greatest genius of *civilized countries.*

Recapitulating that which has been said we find:—That the Secret Doctrine claims for man, (1) a polygenetic origin; (2) A variety of modes of procreation before humanity fell into the ordinary method of generation; (3) That the evolution of animals—of the mammalians at any rate—follows that of man instead of preceding it.

As regards the priority of man to the animals in the order of evolution, the answer is promptly given. If man is really the Microcosm of the Macrocosm, then the teaching is but logical. For, man becomes that Macrocosm for the three lower kingdoms under him. Arguing from a physical standpoint, all the lower kingdoms, save the mineral—which is light itself, crystallized and immetallized—from plants to the creatures which preceded the first mammalians, all have been consolidated in their physical structures by means of the "cast-off dust" of those minerals, and *the refuse of the human matter, whether from living or dead bodies, on which they fed and which gave them their outer bodies.* In his turn, man grew more physical, by reabsorbing into his system that which he had given out, and which became transformed in the living animal crucibles through which it had passed. There were animals in those days of which our modern naturalists have never dreamed; and the stronger became physical material man, the giants of those times, the more powerful were his emanations. Once that Androgyne "Humanity" separated into sexes, transformed by Nature into child-bearing engines, it ceased to procreate its like through drops of vital energy oozing out of the body. But while man was still ignorant of his procreative powers on the human plane, all this vital energy, scattered far and wide from him, was used by Nature for the production of the first mammal-animal forms. Evolution is *an eternal cycle of becoming,* we are taught; and Nature never leaves an atom unused. Moreover, from the beginning of the Round, all in Nature tends to become Man. All the impulses of the dual, centripetal and centrifugal Force are directed towards one point—MAN.

25. HOW DID THE MANASA, THE SONS OF WISDOM ACT? THEY REJECTED THE SELF-BORN, (*the boneless*). THEY ARE NOT READY. THEY SPURNED THE (*First*) SWEAT-BORN. THEY ARE NOT QUITE READY. THEY WOULD NOT ENTER THE (*First*) EGG-BORN.

26. WHEN THE SWEAT-BORN PRODUCED THE EGG-BORN, THE TWO-FOLD (*androgyne Third Race*), THE MIGHTY, THE POWERFUL WITH BONES, THE LORDS OF WISDOM SAID: "NOW SHALL WE CREATE" (*a*).

Why "now"—and not earlier? This the following Sloka explains.

27. (*Then*) THE THIRD (*race*) BECAME THE VAHAN (*vehicle*) OF THE LORDS OF WISDOM. IT CREATED SONS OF WILL AND YOGA, BY KRIYASAKTI (*b*), IT CREATED THEM, THE HOLY FATHERS, ANCESTORS OF THE ARHATS. . . .

(*a*) How did they *create*, since the "Lords of Wisdom" are identical with the Hindu Devas, who refused "to create"? Clearly they are the *Kumaras* of the Hindu Pantheon and Puranas, those elder sons of Brahmā, who, previously created by him "without desire or passion, remained chaste, full of holy wisdom and un-desirous of progeny?"

The power, by which they first created, is just that which has since caused them to be degraded from their high status to the position of evil spirits, of Satan and his Host, created in their turn by the unclean fancy of exoteric creeds. It was by *Kriyasakti*, that mysterious and divine power latent in the will of every man, and which, if not called to life, quickened and developed by Yogi-training, remains dormant in 999,999 men out of a million, and gets atrophied. This power is explained in the "Twelve Signs of the Zodiac,"[3] as follows:

(*b*) "*Kriyasakti*—the mysterious *power of thought* which enables it to produce external, perceptible, phenomenal results by its own inherent energy. The ancients held that any idea will manifest itself *externally*, if one's attention (and Will) is deeply concentrated upon it; similarly, an intense volition will be followed by the desired result. A Yogi generally performs his wonders by means of Itchasakti (Will-power) and Kriyasakti."

The Third Race had thus created the so-called SONS OF WILL AND YOGA, or the "Ancestors" (the *spiritual* Forefathers) of all the subse-quent and present Arhats, or Mahatmas, in a truly *immaculate* way. They were indeed *created*, not *begotten*, as were their brethren of the Fourth Race, who were generated sexually after the separation of sexes, the *Fall of Man*. For creation is but the result of will acting on phenomenal matter, the calling forth out of it the primordial divine *Light* and eternal *Life*. They were the "holy seed-grain" of the future Saviours of Humanity.

The order of the evolution of the human Races stands thus in the Fifth Book of the Commentaries, and has been already given:—

[3] See *Five Years of Theosophy*, p. 111. [The article is by T. Subba Row.]

The First men were Chhayas; the second, the "Sweat-born;" the Third, "Egg-born," and the holy Fathers born by the power of Kriyasakti; the Fourth were the children of the Padmapani (Chenresi).

The meaning of the last sentence in the above-quoted Commentary on Stanza 27, namely, that the Fourth Race were the children of Padmapani, may find its explanation in a certain letter from the Inspirer of *Esoteric Buddhism* quoted on p. 68. "The majority of mankind belongs to the seventh sub-race of the Fourth Root-Race—the above-mentioned Chinamen and their off-shoots and branchlets; (Malayans, Mongolians, Tibetans, Hungarians, Finns, and even the Esquimaux are all remnants of this last offshoot)."

Padmapani, or Avalokiteswara in Sanskrit, is, in Tibetan, Chenresi. Now, Avalokiteswara is the great *Logos* in its higher aspect and in the divine regions. But in the manifested planes, he is, like Daksha, the progenitor (in a spiritual sense) of men. He is considered now as the greatest protector of Asia in general, and of Tibet in particular. In order to guide the Tibetans and Lamas in holiness, and preserve the great Arhats in the world, this heavenly Being is credited with manifesting himself from age to age in human form. A popular legend has it that whenever faith begins to die out in the world, Padmapani Chenresi, the "lotus-bearer," emits a brilliant ray of light, and forthwith incarnates himself in one of the two great Lamas—the Dalai and Teschu Lamas; finally, it is believed that he will incarnate as "the most perfect Buddha" in Tibet, instead of in India, where his predecessors, the great Rishis and Manus had appeared in the beginning of our Race, but now appear no longer. He is evidently, like Daksha, the synthesis of all the preceding Races and the progenitor of all the *human* Races after the Third.

STANZA 8

EVOLUTION OF THE ANIMAL MAMMALIANS—
THE FIRST FALL

28. From the drops of sweat; from the residue of the substance; matter from dead bodies and animals of the wheel before (*previous, Third Round*); and from cast-off dust, the first animals (*of this Round*) were produced.

The Occult Doctrine maintains that, in this Round, the mammalians were a later work of evolution than man. Evolution proceeds in cycles. The great Manvantaric cycle of Seven Rounds, beginning in the First Round with mineral, vegetable, and animal, brings its evolutionary work on the descending arc to a dead stop in the middle of the Fourth *Race*, at the close of the first half of the Fourth *Round*. It is on our Earth, then, (the Fourth Sphere and the lowest) and in the present *Round*, that this middle point has been reached. And since the Monad has passed, after its "first immetallization" on Globe A, through the mineral, vegetable, and animal worlds in every degree of the three states of matter, except the last degree of the third or solid state, which it reached only at the "*mid-point of evolution*," it is but logical and natural that at the beginning of the Fourth Round on Globe D, Man should be the first to appear; and also that his frame should be of the most tenuous matter that is compatible with objectivity. To make it still clearer: if the Monad begins its cycle of incarnations through the three objective kingdoms on the descending curved line, it has necessarily to enter on the re-ascending curved line of the sphere as a man also. On the descending arc it is the spiritual which is gradually transformed into the material. On the middle line of the base, Spirit and Matter are equilibrized in Man. On the ascending arc, Spirit is slowly re-asserting itself at the expense of the physical, or matter, so that, at the close of the seventh Race of the Seventh Round, the Monad will find itself as free from matter and all its qualities as it was in the beginning; having gained in addition the experience and wisdom, the fruition of all its personal lives, without their evil and temptations.

This order of evolution is found also in *Genesis* (*ch.* 1 *and* 2) if one reads it in its true esoteric sense, for chapter 1 contains the history of

the first Three Rounds, as well as that of the first Three Races of the
Fourth, up to that moment when Man is called to conscious life by
the Elohim of Wisdom. In the first chapter, animals, whales and
fowls of the air are created before the androgyne Adam.[1] In the second,
Adam (the sexless) comes first, and the animals only appear after him.
Even the state of mental torpor and unconsciousness of the first two
races, and of the first half of the Third Race, is symbolized, in the
second chapter of *Genesis*, by the *deep sleep of Adam*. It was the dreamless sleep of mental inaction, the slumber of the Soul and Mind,
which was meant by that "sleep."

In the Secret Doctrine, the first *Nagas*—Beings wiser than Serpents—are the "Sons of Will and Yoga," born before the complete
separation of the sexes, "matured in the man-bearing eggs produced
by the power (Kriyasakti) of the holy sages" of the early Third
Race.

Some of the descendants of the primitive Nagas, the Serpents of
Wisdom, peopled America, when its continent arose during the
palmy days of the great Atlantis.

29. ANIMALS WITH BONES, DRAGONS OF THE DEEP AND FLYING
SARPAS (*serpents*) WERE ADDED TO THE CREEPING THINGS. THEY THAT
CREEP ON THE GROUND GOT WINGS. THEY OF THE LONG NECKS IN THE
WATER BECAME THE PROGENITORS OF THE FOWLS OF THE AIR.

This is a point on which the teachings and modern biological
speculation are in perfect accord. The missing links representing this
transition process between reptile and bird are apparent to the
veriest bigot, especially in the *ornithoscelidae, hesperornis,* and the
archaeopteryx of Vogt.

30. DURING THE THIRD (*Race*), THE BONELESS ANIMALS GREW AND
CHANGED: THEY BECAME ANIMALS WITH BONES, THEIR CHHAYAS
BECAME SOLID (*also*).

31. THE ANIMALS SEPARATED THE FIRST (*into male and female*) (*a*)
. . . THEY (*the animals*) BEGAN TO BREED. THE TWO-FOLD MAN
(*then*) SEPARATED ALSO. HE (*man*), SAID "LET US AS THEY; LET US
UNITE AND MAKE CREATURES." THEY DID. . . .

(*a*) Vertebrates, and after that mammalians. Before that the
animals were also ethereal proto-organisms, just as man was.

32. AND THOSE WHICH HAD NO SPARK (*the "narrow-headed"*[2]) TOOK
HUGE SHE-ANIMALS UNTO THEM. THEY BEGAT UPON THEM DUMB RACES.

[1] An allegorical reference to the "Sacred Animals" of the Zodiac and other
heavenly bodies. Some Kabalists see in them the prototypes of the animals.
[2] See Sloka 24.

DUMB THEY WERE (*the "narrow-headed"*) THEMSELVES. BUT THEIR
TONGUES UNTIED. THE TONGUES OF THEIR PROGENY REMAINED STILL.
MONSTERS THEY BRED. A RACE OF CROOKED, RED-HAIR-COVERED
MONSTERS, GOING ON ALL FOURS.[3] A DUMB RACE, TO KEEP THE SHAME
UNTOLD.[4]

The animals "separated the first," says Sloka 31. Bear in mind
that at that period men were different, even physiologically, from
what they are now, having passed the middle point of the Fifth
Race. We are not told what the "huge she-animals" were; but they
certainly were as different from any we know now as were the men.

This was the first physical "fall into matter" of some of the then
existing and lower races. Bear in mind Sloka 24. The "Sons of
Wisdom" had spurned the early *Third* Race, *i.e.*, the non-developed,
and are shown incarnating in, and thereby endowing with intellect,
the *later* Third Race. Thus the sin of the brainless or "mindless"
Races, who had no "spark" and were irresponsible, fell upon those
who failed to do by them their Karmic duty.

WHAT MAY BE THE OBJECTIONS TO THE FOREGOING

Thus Occultism rejects the idea that Nature developed man from
the ape, or even from an ancestor common to both, but traces, on
the contrary, some of the most anthropoid species to the Third Race
man of the early Atlantean period. As this proposition will be maintained and defended elsewhere, a few words more are all that are
needed at present. For greater clearness, however, we shall repeat
in brief what was said previously in Book I., Stanza 6.

Our teachings show that, while it is quite correct to say that
Nature had built, at one time, around the human astral form an *ape-
like external* shape, yet this shape was no more that of the "missing
link" than were the coverings of that astral form during the course
of its natural evolution through all the kingdoms of Nature. Nor was
it on this Fourth Round planet that such evolution took place, but
only during the First, Second, and Third Rounds, when MAN was, in
turn, "a stone, a plant, and an animal" until he became what he
was in the First Root-Race of present humanity. The real line of
evolution differs from the Darwinian, and the two systems are irre-
concilable, except when the latter is divorced from the dogma of
"Natural Selection" and the like. Indeed, between the *Monera* of
Haeckel and the *Sarisripa*[5] of Manu, there lies an impassable chasm

---

[3] These "animals," or monsters, are not the anthropoid or any other apes, but
what the anthropologists might call the "missing link," the primitive lower man.

[4] The shame of their animal origin.

[5] [Lit. Serpent].

in the shape of the *Jiva;* for the "human" Monad, whether *im-metallized* in the stone-atom, or *invegetallized* in the plant, or *inanima-lized* in the animal, is still and ever a divine, hence also a HUMAN Monad. It ceases to be human only when it becomes *absolutely divine.* The terms "mineral," "vegetable" and "animal" *Monad* are meant to create a superficial distinction: there is no such thing as a Monad (jiva) other than divine, and consequently having been, or having to become, human. And the latter term has to remain meaningless unless the difference is well understood. The Monad is a drop out of the shoreless Ocean beyond, or, to be correct, *within* the plane of primeval differentiation. It is divine in its higher and *human* in its lower condition—the adjectives "higher" and "lower" being used for lack of better words—and a Monad it remains at all times, save in the Nirvanic state, under whatever conditions, or whatever ex-ternal forms. As the Logos reflects the Universe in the Divine Mind, and the manifested Universe reflects itself in each of its Monads, so the MONAD has, during the cycle of its incarnations, to reflect in itself every *root-form* of each kingdom. Therefore, the Kabalists say correctly that "MAN becomes a stone, a plant, an animal, a man, a Spirit, and finally God, thus accomplishing his cycle or circuit and returning to the point from which he had started as the *heavenly* MAN." But by "Man" the divine Monad is meant, and not the Thinking Entity, much less his physical body. In truth, all the present fauna are the descendants of those primordial monsters of which the Stanzas speak. The animals—the creeping beasts and those in the waters that preceded man in this Fourth Round, as well as those contemporary with the Third Race, and again the mamma-lia that are posterior to the Third and Fourth Races—all are either directly or indirectly the mutual and correlative product (physic-ally) of man. It is correct to say that the man of this Manvantara, *i.e.,* during the three preceding Rounds, has passed through all the kingdoms of nature. That he was "a stone, a plant, an animal." But (*a*) these stones, plants, and animals were the prototypes, the filmy presentments of those of the Fourth Round; and (*b*) even those at the beginning of the Fourth Round were the astral shadows of the present, as the Occultists express it. And finally the forms and *genera* of neither man, animal, nor plant were what they became later. Thus the astral prototypes of the lower beings of the animal kingdom of the Fourth Round, which *preceded* the Chhayas of *Men,* were the consolidated, though still very ethereal *sheaths* of the still more ethereal forms or models produced at the close of the Third Round on Globe D.[6] "Produced from the residue of the substance

[6] Vide *Esoteric Buddhism.*

matter; from dead bodies of men and (other *extinct*) animals of the wheel before," or the previous *Third* Round—as Sloka 28 tells us. Hence, while the nondescript "animals" that preceded the astral man at the beginning of this life-cycle on our Earth were still, so to speak, the progeny of the man of the Third Round, the mammalians of this Round owe their existence, in a great measure, to man again. Moreover, the "ancestor" of the present anthropoid animal, the ape, is the direct production of the yet mindless *Man*, who desecrated his human dignity by putting himself physically on the level of an animal.

The above accounts for some of the alleged physiological proofs, brought forward by the anthropologists as a demonstration of the descent of man from the animals.

The point most insisted upon by the Evolutionists is that "The history of the embryo is an epitome of that of the race." That "every organism, in its development from the egg, runs through a series of forms, through which, in like succession, its ancestors have passed in the long course of Earth's history. The history of the embryo . . . is a picture in little, and outline of that of the race. *This conception forms the gist of our fundamental biogenetic law, which we are obliged to place at the head of the study of the fundamental law of organic development.*"[7]

This modern theory was known as a fact to, and far more philosophically expressed by, the Sages and Occultists from the remotest ages.

But how is the chasm between the mind of man and animal to be bridged in this case? How, if the anthropoid and *Homo primigenius* had, *argumenti gratia*, a common ancestor, did the two groups diverge so widely from one another as regards mental capacity? True, the Occultist may be told that in every case Occultism does what Science repeats; it gives a *common* ancestor to ape and man, since it makes the former issue from primeval man. Ay, but that "primeval man" was *man* only in external form. He was *mindless* and *soulless* at the time he begot, with a female animal monster, the forefather of a series of apes. This speculation is at least logical, and fills the chasm between the mind of man and animal. Thus it accounts for and explains the hitherto unaccountable and inexplicable. The fact that, in the present stage of evolution, Science is almost certain that no issue can follow from the union of man and animal, is considered and explained elsewhere.

[7] "*The Proofs of Evolution*," a lecture by Haeckel.

STANZA 9

THE FINAL EVOLUTION OF MAN

33. SEEING WHICH (*the sin committed with the animals*), THE LHAS (*the Spirits, the "Sons of Wisdom"*) WHO HAD NOT BUILT MEN (*who had refused to create*), WEPT, SAYING:—

34. "THE AMANASA (*the 'mindless'*) HAVE DEFILED OUR FUTURE ABODES (*a*). THIS IS KARMA. LET US DWELL IN THE OTHERS. LET US TEACH THEM BETTER, LEST WORSE SHOULD HAPPEN." THEY DID. . . .

35. THEN ALL BECAME ENDOWED WITH MANAS (*minds*). THEY SAW THE SIN OF THE MINDLESS.

But they had already *separated* before the ray of divine reason had enlightened the dark region of their hitherto slumbering minds, and had *sinned*. That is to say, they had committed evil unconsciously, by producing an effect which was unnatural. But we must see whether the "animals" tampered with were of the same kind as those known to zoology.

(*a*) The "Fall" occurred, according to the testimony of ancient Wisdom and the old records, as soon as Daksha (the reincarnated Creator of men and things in the early Third Race) disappeared to make room for that portion of mankind which had "separated." This is how the Commentary explains the details that preceded the "Fall":—

"In the initial period of man's Fourth evolution, the human kingdom branched off in several and various directions. The outward shape of its first specimens was not uniform, for the vehicles (the egg-like, external shells, in which the future fully physical man gestated) *were often tampered with, before they hardened, by huge animals, of species now unknown, and which belonged to the tentative efforts of Nature. The result was that intermediate races of monsters, half animals, half men, were produced. But as they were failures, they were not allowed to breathe long and live, though the intrinsically paramount power of psychic over physical nature being yet very weak, and hardly established, the 'Egg-Born' Sons had taken several of their females unto themselves as mates, and bred other human monsters. Later, animal species and human races becoming gradually equilibrized, they separated and mated no longer. Man created no more—he begot. But he also*

begot animals, as well as men in days of old. Therefore the Sages (or wise men), who speak of males who had no more will-begotten offspring, but begat various animals along with Danavas (giants) on females of other species— animals being as (or in a manner of) sons putative to them; and they (the human males) *refusing in time to be regarded as* (putative) *fathers of dumb creatures—spoke truthfully and wisely. Upon seeing this* (state of things), *the Kings and Lords of the Last Races* (of the Third and the Fourth) *placed the seal of prohibition upon the sinful intercourse. It interfered with Karma, it developed new* (Karma). *They* (the divine Kings) *struck the culprits with sterility. They destroyed the Red and Blue Races.*[1]

In another we find:—

"There were blue and red-faced animal-men even in later times; not from actual intercourse (between the human and animal species), *but by descent."*

And still another passage mentions:—

"Red-haired swarthy men going on all-fours, who bend and unbend (stand erect and fall on their hands again) *who speak as their forefathers, and run on their hands as their giant fore-mothers."*

Perchance in these specimens Haeckelians might recognize, not the *Homo primigenius*, but some of the lower tribes, such as some tribes of the Australian savages. Nevertheless, even these are not descended from the anthropoid apes, but from human fathers and semi-human mothers, or, to speak more correctly, from human monsters—those "failures" mentioned in the first Commentary. The real anthropoids, Haeckel's *Catarrhini* and *Platyrrhini*, came far later, in the closing times of Atlantis. The orang-outang, the gorilla, the chimpanzee and cynocephalus are the latest and purely physical evolutions from lower anthropoid mammalians. They have a spark of the purely human essence in them; man on the other hand, has not one drop of pithecoid blood in his veins. Thus saith old Wisdom and universal tradition.

How was the separation of sexes effected? it is asked. Are we to believe in the old Jewish fable of Adam yielding Eve? The rib is bone, and when we read in Genesis that Eve was made out of the rib, it only means that the *Race with bones* was produced out of a previous Race and Races, which were "boneless."

To return to the history of the Third Race, the "Sweat-Born," the "Egg-bearing," and the "Androgyne." Almost sexless, in its early beginnings, it became bisexual or androgynous; very gradually of course. The passage from the former to the latter transformation

[1] Rudra, as a Kumara, is *Lilalohita*—red and blue.

required numberless generations, during which the simple cell that issued from the earliest parent (the two in one), first developed into a bisexual being; and then the cell, becoming a regular egg, gave forth a unisexual creature. The Third-Race-mankind is the most mysterious of all the hitherto developed five Races. But it is evident that the units of the Third Race humanity began to separate in their pre-natal shells, or eggs, and to issue out of them as distinct male and female babes, ages after the appearance of its early progenitors. And, as time rolled on its geological periods, the newly born sub-races began to lose their natal capacities. Toward the end of the fourth *sub-race*, the babe lost its faculty of walking as soon as liberated from its shell, and by the end of the fifth, mankind was born under the same conditions and by the same identical process as our historical generations. This required, of course, millions of years.

We are approaching the turning-point of the evolution of the Races. Let us see what Occult philosophy says on the origin of language.

36. The Fourth Race developed Speech.

The Commentaries explain that the First Race—the ethereal or astral Sons of Yoga, also called "Self-born"—was, in our sense, speechless, as it was devoid of mind on our plane. The Second Race had a "Sound-language," to wit, chant-like sounds composed of vowels alone. The Third Race developed in the beginning a kind of language which was only a slight improvement on the various sounds in Nature, on the cry of gigantic insects and of the first animals, which, however, were hardly nascent in the day of the "Sweat-born" (the *early* Third Race). In its second half, when the "Sweat-born" gave birth to the "Egg-born" (the *middle* Third Race); and when these, instead of "hatching out" as androgynous beings, began to evolve into separate males and females; and when the same law of evolution led them to reproduce their kind sexually, an act which forced the creative Gods, compelled by Karmic law, to incarnate in *mindless* men; then only was speech developed. But even then it was still no better than a tentative effort. The whole human race was at that time of "one language and of one lip." This did not prevent the last two Sub-Races of the Third Race from building cities, and sowing far and wide the first seeds of civilization under the guidance of their Divine Instructors, and their own already awakened minds. Let the reader also bear in mind that, as each of the seven Races is divided into four Ages—the Golden, Silver, Bronze, and Iron Age—so is every smallest division of such races. Speech then developed, according to occult teaching, in the following order:—

I. *Monosyllabic speech;* that of the first approximately fully developed human beings at the close of the Third Root-Race, the "golden-coloured," yellow-complexioned men, after their separation into sexes, and the full awakening of their minds. Before that, they communicated through what would now be called "thought-transference," though, with the exception of the Race called the "Sons of Will and Yoga"—the first in whom the "Sons of Wisdom" had incarnated—thought was but very little developed in nascent physical man. Their physical bodies belonging to the Earth, their Monads remained on a higher plane altogether. Language could not be well developed before the full acquisition and development of their reasoning faculties. This monosyllabic speech was the vowel parent, so to speak, of the monosyllabic languages mixed with hard consonants, still in use amongst the yellow races which are known to the anthropologist.[2]

II. *Agglutinative languages.* These were spoken by some Atlantean races, while other parent stocks of the Fourth Race preserved the mother-language. And as languages have their cyclic evolution, their childhood, purity, growth, *fall into matter,* admixture with other languages, maturity, decay and finally death, so the primitive speech of the most civilized Atlantean races decayed and almost died out. While the "cream" of the Fourth Race gravitated more and more toward the apex of physical and intellectual evolution, thus leaving as an heirloom to the nascent Fifth (the Aryan) Race the inflectional, highly developed languages, the agglutinative decayed and remained as a fragmentary fossil idiom, scattered now, and nearly limited to the aboriginal tribes of America.

III. *Inflectional speech*—the root of Sanskrit was the first language (now the mystery tongue of the Initiates, of the Fifth Race). At any rate, the "Semitic" languages are the bastard descendants of the first phonetic corruptions of the eldest children of the early Sanskrit. The occult doctrine admits of no such divisions as the Aryan and the Semite, accepting even the Turanian with ample reservations. The Semites, especially the Arabs, are later Aryans—degenerate in spirituality and perfected in materiality. To these belong all the Jews and the Arabs. The former are a tribe descended from the

---

[2] The present yellow races are the descendants of the early branches of the Fourth Race. Of the Third, the only *pure and direct* descendants are, as said above, a portion of the fallen and degenerated Australians, whose far distant ancestors belonged to a division of the seventh Sub-race of the Third. The rest are of mixed Lemuro-Atlantean descent. They have since then entirely changed in stature and intellectual capacities.

Chandalas of India, the outcasts, many of them ex-Brahmins, who sought refuge in Chaldea, in Scinde, and Iran, and were truly born from their father A-bram (No Brahmin) some 8,000 years B.C. The latter, the Arabs, are the descendants of those Aryans who would not go into India at the time of the dispersion of nations, some of whom remained on the borderlands thereof, in Afghanistan and Kabul, and along the Oxus, while others penetrated into and invaded Arabia.

37. THE ONE (*androgyne*) BECAME TWO; ALSO ALL THE LIVING AND CREEPING THINGS, THAT WERE STILL ONE, GIANT-FISH, BIRDS, AND SERPENTS WITH SHELL-HEADS.

This relates evidently to the so-called age of the amphibious reptiles, during which ages science maintains that *no man existed!* Nevertheless, in Book VI. of the Commentaries is found a passage which says, freely translated:—

"*When the Third separated and fell into sin by breeding men-animals, these* (the animals) *became ferocious, and men and they mutually destructive. Till then, there was no sin, no life taken. After* (the separation) *the Satya* (Yuga) *was at an end. The eternal spring became constant change and seasons succeeded. Cold forced men to build shelters and devise clothing. Then man appealed to the superior Fathers* (the higher Gods or Angels). *The Nirmanakaya of the Nagas, the wise Serpents and Dragons of Light came, and the precursors of the Enlightened* (Buddhas). *Divine Kings descended and taught men sciences and arts, for man could live no longer in the first land* (Adi-Varsha, the Eden of the first Races), *which had turned into a white frozen corpse.*"

THE HISTORY OF THE FOURTH RACE

38. THUS TWO BY TWO, ON THE SEVEN ZONES, THE THIRD (*Race*) GAVE BIRTH TO THE FOURTH (*Race men*). THE GODS BECAME NO-GODS (*Sura became a-Sura*) (*a*).

39. THE FIRST (*Race*) ON EVERY ZONE WAS MOON-COLOURED (*yellow-white*); THE SECOND, YELLOW, LIKE GOLD; THE THIRD, RED; THE FOURTH, BROWN, WHICH BECAME BLACK WITH SIN.[1] THE FIRST SEVEN (*human*) SHOOTS WERE ALL OF ONE COMPLEXION IN THE BEGINNING. THE NEXT (*seven, the sub-races*) BEGAN MIXING THEIR COLOURS (*b*).

(*a*) To understand Sloka 38, it must be read together with the three Slokas of Stanza 9. Up to this point of evolution man belongs more to metaphysical than physical nature. It is only after the so-called FALL that the races began to develop rapidly into a purely human shape.

The archaic Commentaries explain, as the reader must remember, that of the Host of Dhyanis whose turn it was to incarnate as the *Egos* of the immortal, but, *on this plane, senseless* Monads, some "obeyed" (the law of evolution) immediately when the men of the Third Race became physiologically and physically ready, *i.e.*, when they had separated into sexes. These were those early conscious Beings who, now adding conscious knowledge and will to their inherent Divine purity, *created* by *Kriyasakti* the semi-Divine man, who became the seed on Earth for future Adepts. Those, on the other hand, who, jealous of their intellectual freedom (unfettered as it then was by the bonds of Matter), said:—"We can choose . . . we have wisdom" (*See Sloka* 24), and incarnated far later—these had their first Karmic punishment prepared for them. They got bodies (physiologically) inferior to their astral models, because their *chhayas* had belonged to Progenitors of an inferior degree in the seven Classes. As to those "Sons of Wisdom" who had "deferred" their incarnation till the Fourth Race, which was already tainted (physiologically) with sin and impurity, they produced a terrible cause, the

---

[1] Strictly speaking, it is only from the time of the Atlantean, brown and yellow giant Races, that one ought to speak of MAN, since it was the Fourth race only which was the first *completely human species*, however much larger in size than we are now.

Karmic result of which weighs on them to this day. (*See Sloka* 32.) This was the "Fall of the Angels," because of their rebellion against Karmic Law. The "fall of *man*" was no fall, *for he was irresponsible.*

There is an eternal cyclic Law of Re-births, and the series is headed at every new Manvantaric dawn by those who had enjoyed their rest from re-incarnations in previous Kalpas for incalculable *Aeons*—by the highest and the earliest *Nirvanees.* It was the turn of those "Gods" to incarnate in the present Manvantara; hence their presence on Earth, and the ensuing allegories; hence, also, the perversion of the original meaning. The Gods who had *fallen* into generation, whose mission it was to complete *divine* man, are found represented later on as Demons, evil Spirits, at war with Gods, or the irresponsible agents of the one Eternal law. But no conception of such creatures as the Devils and Satan of the Christian, Jewish, and Mahomedan religions was ever intended under those thousand and one Aryan allegories.[2]

Now, as everything proceeds cyclically, the evolution of man like everything else, the order in which he is generated is described fully in the Eastern teachings, whereas it is only hinted at in the Kabala. Says the *Book of Dzyan* with regard to primeval man when first projected by the "Boneless," the incorporeal Creato:: "*First, the Breath, then Buddhi, and the Shadow-Son* (the Body) *were* 'CREATED.' *But where was the pivot* (the middle Principle, Manas)? *Man is doomed. When alone, the indiscrete* (undifferentiated Element) *and the Vahan* (Buddhi)—*the Cause of the Causeless*—*break asunder from manifested life*"—"*Unless cemented and held together by the middle principle, the vehicle of the personal consciousness of* JIVA"; explains the Commentary. In other words, the two higher principles *can have no individuality on Earth,* cannot be *man,* unless there is (*a*) the Mind, the *Manas-Ego,* to cognize itself, and (*b*) the terrestrial *false* Personality, or the body of egotistical desires and personal Will, to cement the whole, as if

---

[2] We have a passage from a Master's letter which has a direct bearing upon these incarnating Angels. Says the letter: "Now there are, and there *must be*, failures in the ethereal races of the many classes of Dhyan-Chohans, or Devas (*progressed entities of a previous* planetary period), as well as among men. But still, as the *failures* are too far progressed and spiritualized to be thrown back forcibly from Dhyan-Chohanship into the vortex of a new primordial evolution through the lower Kingdoms, this then happens. Where a new solar system has to be evolved these Dhyan-Chohans are borne in by influx 'ahead' of the Elementals (Entities . . . to be developed into humanity at a *future* time) and remain as a latent or inactive spiritual force, in the aura of a nascent world . . . until the stage of human evolution is reached. . . . Then they *become an active force* and commingle with the Elementals, to *develop little by little the full type of humanity.*" That is to say, to develop in, and endow man with his Self-conscious mind, or *Manas.* [See *The Mahatma Letters to A. P. Sinnett,* Letter 14.]

round a pivot (which it is, truly), to the physical form of man. It is the *Fifth* and the *Fourth* principles[3]—*Manas* and *Kama rupa*—that contain the dual personality; the real immortal Ego (*if it assimilates itself to the two higher*) and the false and transitory personality, the *mayavi* or astral body, so-called, or the *animal-human* Soul—the two having to be closely blended for purposes of a *full* terrestrial existence. Incarnate the Spiritual Monad of a Newton grafted on that of the greatest saint on earth—in a physical body the most perfect you can think of—*i.e.*, in a two or even a three-principled body composed of its *Sthula Sarira*, *Prana* (life principle), and *Linga Sarira*—and, if it lacks its middle and fifth principles you will have created *an idiot*—at best a beautiful, soul-less, empty and unconscious appearance. "*Cogito—ergo sum*"—can find no room in the brain of such a creature, not on this plane, at any rate.

As said in the text:—

"*Like produces like and no more at the genesis of Being, and evolution with its limited conditioned laws comes later. The Self-Existent*[4] *are called* CREATIONS, *for they appear in the Spirit Ray, manifested through the potency inherent in its* UNBORN *Nature, which is beyond Time and* (limited or conditioned) *Space. Terrene products, animate and inanimate, including mankind, are falsely called creation and creatures: they are the development* (evolution) *of the discrete elements.*" Again:—

"*The Heavenly Rupa* (Dhyan Chohan) *creates* (man) *in his own form; it is a spiritual ideation consequent on the first differentiation and awakening of the universal* (manifested) *Substance; that form is the ideal Shadow of Itself: and this is* THE MAN OF THE FIRST RACE."

To express it in still clearer form, limiting the explanation to this Earth only, it was the duty of the first "differentiated Egos"—the Church calls them Archangels—to imbue primordial matter with the evolutionary impulse and guide its formative powers in the fashioning of its productions. This it is which is referred to in the sentences both in the Eastern and Western tradition—"the Angels were *commanded to create*." After the Earth had been made ready by the *lower* and more material powers, and its three Kingdoms fairly started on their way to be "fruitful and multiply" the higher Powers, the Archangels or Dhyanis, were compelled by the evolutionary Law to descend on Earth and construct the crown of its evolution—MAN. Thus the "Self-created" and the "Self-existent"

---

[3] The Fourth, and the Fifth from *below* beginning with the physical body; the Third and the Fourth, if we reckon from *Atma*.

[4] Angelic, Spiritual Essences, immortal in their being because unconditioned in Eternity; periodical and conditioned in their Manvantaric manifestations.

projected their pale Shadows; but Group the Third, the Fire-Angels, *rebelled and refused* to join their Fellow Devas.

Hindu exotericism represents them all as *Yogis*, whose piety inspired them to refuse *creating*, as they desired to remain eternally *Kumaras*, "Virgin Youths," in order, if possible, to anticipate their fellows in progress towards Nirvana—the final liberation. But, agreeably to esoteric interpretation, it was a self-sacrifice for the benefit of mankind. The "Rebels" would not create will-less irresponsible men, as the "obedient" Angels did; nor could they endow human beings with only the temporary reflections of their own attributes; for even the latter, belonging to another and a so-much higher plane of consciousness, would leave man still irresponsible, hence interfere with any possibility of a higher progress. No spiritual and psychic evolution is possible on earth—the lowest and most material plane—for one who on that plane, at all events, is inherently *perfect* and cannot accumulate either merit or demerit. Man, remaining the pale shadow of the inert, immutable, and motionless Perfection, the one negative and passive attribute of the real *I am that I am*, would have been doomed to pass through life on earth as in a heavy dreamless sleep; hence a failure on this plane.

The Secret Doctrine teaches that the Fire-Devas, the Rudras, and the Kumaras, the "Virgin-Angels," (to whom Michael and Gabriel, the Archangels, both belong), the divine "Rebels," preferred the *curse of incarnation* and the long cycles of terrestrial existence and rebirths, to seeing the misery (even if *unconscious*) of the beings evolved as shadows out of their Brethren through the semi-passive energy of their *too spiritual* Creators. Hence, tradition shows the celestial *Yogis* offering themselves as voluntary victims in order to redeem Humanity—created god-like and perfect at first—and to endow him with human affections and aspirations. To do this they had to give up their natural status and, descending on our Globe, take up their abode on it for the whole cycle of the Mahayuga, thus exchanging their impersonal Individualities for individual Personalities—the bliss of sidereal existence for the curse of terrestrial life. This voluntary sacrifice of the Fiery Angels, whose nature was *Knowledge* and *Love*, was construed by the exoteric theologies into a statement that shows "the rebel angels hurled down from Heaven into the darkness of Hell"—our Earth.

"*Our earth and man,*" says the Commentary, "*being the products of the three Fires*"—whose three names answer, in Sanskrit, to "*the Electric fire, the Solar fire, and the fire produced by Friction,*"—these three Fires, explained on the Cosmic and human planes, are Spirit, Soul, and Body, the three great Root Groups, with their four additional divisions. In the metaphysical sense the "Fire of Friction" means the Union between *Buddhi*, the sixth, and *Manas*, the fifth, principles, which thus are united or cemented together; the fifth merging partially into and becoming part of the *Monad;* in the physical, it relates to the *creative spark*, or germ, which fructifies and generates the human being.

(*b*) This Sloka 39 relates exclusively to the racial divisions. Strictly speaking, esoteric philosophy teaches a modified polygenesis. For, while it assigns to humanity a oneness of origin, in so far that its forefathers or "Creators" were all divine beings—though of different degrees of perfection in their hierarchy—men were nevertheless born on seven different centres of the continent of that period. Though all of one common origin, yet for reasons given their potentialities and mental capabilities, outward or physical forms, and future characteristics, were very different.

Esotericism now classes these seven variations, with their four great divisions, into only *three* distinct primeval Races—as it does not take into consideration the First Race, which had neither type nor colour, and hardly an objective, though colossal form. The evolution of these races, their formation and development, went *pari passu* and on parallel lines with the evolution, formation, and development of three geological strata, from which the human complexion was as much derived as it was determined by the climates of those zones. It names three great divisions, namely, the RED-YELLOW, the BLACK, and the BROWN-WHITE.[5] The Aryan races, for instance, now varying from dark brown, almost black, red-brown-yellow, down to the whitest creamy colour, are yet all of one and the same stock—the Fifth Root-Race—and spring from one single Progenitor, called in Hindu *exotericism* by the generic name of Vaivasvata Manu; the latter, remember, being that generic personage, the Sage, who is said to have lived over 18,000,000 years ago, and also 850,000 years ago—at the time of the sinking of the last remnants of the great continent of Atlantis,[6] and who is said to live even *now* in his mankind. The light yellow is the colour of the first SOLID human race, which

[5] Some superior, others inferior, to suit the Karma of the various reincarnating Monads, which could not be all of the same degree of purity in their last births in other worlds. This accounts for the difference of races, the inferiority of the savage, and other human varieties.

[6] It must be remembered that the "last remnants" here spoken of, refer to those portions of the "Great Continent" which still remained, and not to any of the numerous islands which existed contemporaneously with the continent. Plato's "island" was, for instance, one of such remnants; the others having sunk at various periods previously. An occult "tradition" teaches that such submersions occur whenever there is an eclipse of the "Spiritual Sun."

appeared after the middle of the Third Root Race (*after its fall* into generation—as just explained), bringing on the final changes. For it is only at that period that the last transformation took place, which brought forth man as he is now, only on a magnified scale. This Race gave birth to the Fourth Race; "Siva" gradually transforming that portion of Humanity which became "black with sin" into *red-yellow* (the red Indians and the Mongolians being the descendants of these) and finally into brown-white races—which now, together with the yellow races, form the great bulk of Humanity.

When reading of "the last transformation," let the reader consider at this juncture, if that took place 18,000,000 years ago, how many millions more it must have required to reach that final stage? And if man, in his gradual consolidation, developed *pari passu* with the Earth, how many millions of years must have elapsed during the *First*, *Second*, and the first half of the *Third* Race? For the Earth was in a comparatively ethereal condition before it reached its last consolidated state; the archaic teachings, moreover, telling us that, during the middle period of the Lemuro-Atlantean Race, three and a half Races after the Genesis of man, the Earth, man, and everything on the Globe was of a still grosser and more material nature, while such things as corals and some shells were still in a semi-gelatinous, astral state. The cycles that intervened since then, have already carried us onward, on the opposite ascending arc, some steps towards *our dematerialization*. The Earth, ourselves, and all things have softened since then—aye, even our brains. But it has been objected by some Theosophists that an ethereal Earth even some 15, or 20,000,000 years ago, *does not square with geology*, which teaches us that winds blew, rains fell, waves broke on the shore, sands shifted and accumulated, etc., that, in short, all natural causes now in operation were then in force, "*in the very earliest ages of geological time, aye, that of the oldest palaeozoic rocks.*" To this the following answers are given. *First*, what is the date assigned by geology to those "oldest palaeozoic rocks"? And *secondly*, why could not the winds blow, rain fall, and waves (*of carbonic acid* apparently, as science seems to imply) break on the shore, on an Earth semi-astral, *i.e.*, viscid? The word "astral" does not necessarily mean as thin as smoke, in occult phraseology, but rather "starry," shining or pellucid, in various and numerous degrees, from a quite filmy to a viscid state, as just observed. But it is further objected: How could an astral *Earth* have affected the other planets in this system? Would not the whole process get out of gear now if the attraction of one planet was suddenly removed? The objection is evidently invalid, since our system is composed of older and younger planets, some dead (like the moon), others in process of formation, for all astronomy knows to the contrary. Nor has the latter ever affirmed, so far as we know, that all the bodies of our system have sprung into existence and developed simultaneously. The Cis-Himalayan Secret Teachings differ from those of India in this respect. Hindu Occultism teaches that the Vaivasvata Manu Humanity is eighteen million and odd years old. We say, yes; but only so far as *physical*, or approximately physical, man is concerned, who dates from the close of the Third Root-Race. Beyond that period MAN, or his filmy image, may have existed for 300 million years, for all we know; *since we are not taught figures* which are and will remain secret with the Masters of Occult Science.

ARCHAIC TEACHINGS IN THE PURANAS AND GENESIS

Having been in all the so-called "Seven creations," allegorizing the seven evolutionary changes, or the *sub-races*, we may call them, *of the First Root-race of Mankind*—MAN was on earth in this Round from the beginning. Having passed through all the kingdoms of nature in the previous *three* Rounds, his *physical* frame—one adapted to the thermal conditions of those early periods—was ready to receive the *divine Pilgrim* at the first dawn of human life, *i.e.*, 18,000,000 years ago. It is only at the mid-point of the 3rd Root Race that man was endowed with *Manas*. Once united, the *Two* and then the *Three* made One; for though the lower animals, from the amoeba to man, received *their* Monads, in which all the higher qualities are potential, all have to remain dormant till each reaches its human form, before which stage *Manas* (mind) has no development in them.

The Monads have passed through all these forms of being up to man, on every Globe, in the three *preceding* Rounds; every Round, as well as every subsequent Globe, from A to G, having been, and still having to be the arena of the same evolution, only repeated each time on a more solid material basis. Therefore the question:—"What relation is there between the Third Round astral prototypes and ordinary physical development in the course of the origination of pre-mammalian organic species?"—is easily answered. One is the shadowy prototype of the other, the preliminary, hardly defined, and evanescent sketch on the canvas, of objects which are destined to receive the final and vivid form under the brush of the painter. The fish evolved into an amphibian—a frog—in the *shadows* of ponds, and man passed through all his metamorphoses on this Globe in the Third Round as he did in this, his Fourth Cycle. The Third Round types contributed to the formation of the types in this one. On strict analogy, the cycle of Seven Rounds in their work of the gradual formation of man through every kingdom of Nature is repeated on a microscopical scale in the first seven months of gestation of a future human being. Let the student think over and work out this analogy. As the seven months old unborn baby, though quite ready, yet needs two months more in which to acquire strength and consolidate; so man, having perfected his evolution during seven Rounds, remains two periods more in the womb of mother-Nature before he is born, or rather reborn a Dhyani, still more perfect than he was before he launched forth as a Monad on the newly built chain of worlds. Let the student ponder over this mystery, and then he will easily convince himself that, as there are also physical links between many classes, so there are precise domains wherein the astral merges into physical evolution.

That man originates like other animals in a cell and develops "through stages undistinguishable from those of fish, reptile, and mammal until the cell attains the highly specialized development of the quadrumanous and *at last the human type*," is an Occult axiom thousands of years old. The Kabalistic axiom: "A stone becomes a plant; a plant a beast; a beast a man; a man a God," holds good throughout the ages.

Believing as we do that man has evolved from, and passed through, (during the preceding Rounds) the lowest forms of every life, vegetable and animal, on earth, there is nothing very degrading in the idea of having the orang-outang as an ancestor of our physical form. Quite the reverse; as it would forward the Occult Doctrine with regard to the final evolution of everything in terrestrial nature into man, most irresistibly. One may even inquire how it is that biologists and anthropologists, having once firmly accepted the theory of the descent of man from the ape—how it is that they have hitherto left untouched the future evolution of the existing apes into man? This is only a logical sequence of the first theory, unless Science would make of man a privileged being, and his evolution a *non*-precedent in nature, quite a *special* and unique case. And that is what all this leads physical Science to. The reason, however, why the Occultists reject the Darwinian, and especially the Haeckelian, hypothesis is because it is the ape which is, in sober truth, a special and unique instance, not man. The pithecoid is *an accidental creation*, a forced growth, the result of an unnatural process.

The Occult Doctrine, is, we think, more logical. It teaches a cyclic, never varying law in Nature, the latter having no personal, "special design," but acting on a uniform plan that prevails through the whole Manvantaric period and deals with the land worm as it deals with man. Neither the one nor the other have sought to come into being, hence both are under the same evolutionary Law, and both have to progress according to Karmic law. Both have started from the same neutral centre of Life and both have to re-emerge into it at the consummation of the cycle.

Furthermore, we are taught that the transformations through which man passed on the descending arc—which is centrifugal for Spirit and centripetal for Matter—and those he prepares to go through, henceforward, on his ascending path, which will reverse the direction of the two forces—viz., Matter will become centrifugal and Spirit centripetal—that all such transformations *are next in store for the anthropoid ape also,* all those, at any rate, who have reached the remove next to man in this Round—and these will all be men in the Fifth Round, as present men inhabited ape-like forms in the Third, the preceding Round.

The apes are millions of years later than the speaking human being, and are the latest contemporaries of our Fifth Race. Thus, it is most important to remember that the *Egos* of the apes are entities compelled by their Karma to incarnate in the animal forms which resulted from the bestiality of the *latest* Third and the earliest Fourth Race men. They are entities who had already reached the "human stage" before this Round. Consequently, they form an exception to the general rule. They are truly "speechless men," and will become speaking animals (or men of a lower order) in the Fifth Round, while the adepts of a certain school hope that some of the Egos of the apes of a higher intelligence will reappear at the close of the Sixth Root-race. What their form will be is of secondary consideration. The form means nothing. Species and genera of the flora, fauna, and the highest animal, its crown—man, change not only with every Round, but every Root-Race, as well as after every geological cataclysm that puts an end to, or produces a turning point in the latter. In the Sixth Root-Race the fossils of the orang, the gorilla and the chimpanzee will be those of extinct quadrumanous mammals; and new forms—though fewer and ever wider apart as ages pass on and the close of the Manvantara approaches—will develop from the "cast off" types of the human races as they revert once again to astral, out of the mire of physical, life. There were none before man, and they will be extinct before the Seventh Race develops. Karma will lead on the Monads of the unprogressed men of our race and lodge them in the newly evolved human frames of the thus physiologically regenerated baboon.

This will take place, of course, millions of years hence. But the picture of this cyclic precession of all that lives and breathes now on

Earth, of each species in its turn, is a true one, and needs no "special creation" or miraculous formation of man, beast, and plant *ex nihilo.*

This is how Occult Science explains the absence of any link between ape and man, and shows the former evolving from the latter.

40. Then the third and fourth (*Races*) became tall with pride. We are the kings, we are the gods (*a*).

41. They took wives fair to look at. Wives from the "mindless," the narrow-headed. They bred monsters, wicked demons, male and female. Also Khado (*Dakini*) with little minds (*b*).

42. They built temples for the human body. Male and female they worshipped (*c*). Then the third eye acted no longer (*d*).

(*a*) Such were the first truly physical men, whose first characteristic was—pride! It is the Third Race and the gigantic Atlanteans, the memory of whom lingered from one generation and race to another.

What was the religion of the Third and Fourth Races? In the common acceptation of the term, neither the Lemurians, nor yet their progeny, the Lemuro-Atlanteans, had any, as they knew no dogma, nor had they to believe *on faith.* No sooner had the mental eye of man been opened to understanding than the Third Race felt itself one with the ever-present as the ever to be unknown and invisible ALL, the One Universal Deity. Endowed with divine powers, and feeling in himself his *inner* God, each felt he was a Man-God in his nature, though an animal in his physical self. The struggle between the two began from the very day they tasted of the fruit of the Tree of Wisdom; a struggle for life between the spiritual and the psychic, the psychic and the physical. Those who conquered the lower principles by obtaining mastery over the body, joined the "Sons of Light." Those who fell victims to their lower natures became the slaves of Matter. From "Sons of Light and Wisdom" they ended by becoming the "Sons of Darkness." They had fallen in the battle of mortal life with Life Immortal, and all those so fallen became the seed of the future generations of Atlanteans.[7]

At the dawn of his consciousness, the man of the Third Root Race

---

[7] The name is used here in the sense of, and as a synonym of "sorcerers." The Atlantean races were many, and lasted in their evolution for millions of years; all were not bad. They became so toward their end, as we (the Fifth) are fast becoming now.

had thus no beliefs that could be called *religion*. But if the term is to be defined as the binding together of the masses in one form of reverence paid to those we feel higher than ourselves, of piety—as a feeling expressed by a child toward a loved parent—then even the earliest Lemurians had a religion—and a most beautiful one—from the very beginning of their intellectual life. Had they not their bright Gods of the Elements around them, and even within themselves.[8] We are assured it was so, and we believe it. For the evolution of Spirit into Matter could never have been achieved, nor would it have received its first impulse, had not the bright Spirits sacrificed their own respective super-ethereal essences to animate the man of clay, by endowing each of his inner principles with a portion, or rather, a reflection of that essence. The Dhyanis of the Seven Heavens (the seven planes of Being) are the NOUMENA of the actual and future Elements, just as the Angels of the Seven Powers of Nature—the grosser effects of which are perceived by us in what Science is pleased to call the "modes of motion"—the imponderable forces and what not—are the still higher Noumena of still higher Hierarchies.

It was the "Golden Age" in those days of old, the age when the "gods walked the earth, and mixed freely with the mortals." Since then, the gods departed (*i.e.*, became invisible), and later generations ended by worshipping their kingdoms—the Elements.

It was the Atlanteans, the first progeny of *semi-divine* man after his separation into sexes—hence the first-begotten and humanly-born mortals—who became the first "Sacrificers" to the *God of matter*. They stand in the dim past as the prototype on which the great symbol of Cain was built as the first anthropomorphists who worshipped form and matter. That worship degenerated very soon into *self-worship*, thence led to phallicism, or that which reigns supreme to this day in the symbolisms of every exoteric religion of ritual, dogma, and form.

Thus the first Atlantean races, born on the Lemurian Continent, separated into those who worshipped the one unseen Spirit of Nature, the ray of which man feels within himself, and those who offered fanatical worship to the Spirits of the Earth, the dark Cosmic, anthropomorphic Powers, with whom they made alliance.

The legend of the "Fallen Angels," in its esoteric signification, contains the key to the manifold contradictions of human character; it points to the secret of man's self-consciousness; it is the history of his evolution and growth.

On a firm grasp of this doctrine depends the correct understand-

[8] The "Gods of the Elements" are by no means the Elementals. The latter are at best used by them as vehicles and materials in which to clothe themselves.

ing of esoteric anthropogenesis. It gives a clue to the vexed question of the Origin of Evil; and shows how man himself is the separator of the ONE into various contrasted aspects.

The Divine Man dwelt in the animal, and, therefore, when the physiological separation took place in the natural course of evolution—when also "all the animal creation was *untied*," and males were attracted to females—*that race fell*: not because they had eaten of the fruit of Knowledge and knew good from evil, but because they knew no better. Propelled by the sexless creative instinct, the early sub-races had evolved an intermediate race in which, as hinted in the Stanzas, the higher Dhyan-Chohans had incarnated. "When we have ascertained the extent of the Universe and learnt to know all that there is in it, we will multiply our race," answer the *Sons of Will and Yoga* to their brethren of the same race, who invite them to do as they do. This means that the great Adepts and Initiated Ascetics will "multiply," *i.e.*, once more produce *Mind-born* immaculate Sons —in the Seventh Root-Race.

(*b*) The first war that Earth knew, the first human gore shed, was the result of man's eyes and senses being opened; which made him see that the daughters of his brethren were fairer than his own, and their wives also . . .

ARE GIANTS A FICTION?

Not being in a position to give out a full and detailed history of the Third and Fourth Races, as many isolated facts concerning them as are permitted must be now collated together. As the "coats of skin" of men thickened, and they fell more and more into physical sin, the intercourse between physical and ethereal *divine* man was stopped. The veil of matter between the two planes became too dense for even the inner man to penetrate. The mysteries of Heaven and Earth, revealed to the Third Race by their celestial Teachers in the days of their purity, became a great focus of light, the rays from which became necessarily weakened as they were diffused and shed upon an uncongenial, because too material soil. With the masses they degenerated into Sorcery, taking later on the shape of exoteric religions, of idolatry full of superstitions, and man-, or hero-worship. Alone a handful of primitive men—in whom the spark of divine Wisdom burnt bright, and only strengthened in its intensity as it got dimmer and dimmer with every age in those who turned it to bad purposes—remained the elect custodians of the Mysteries revealed to mankind by the divine Teachers. There were those among them, who remained in their *Kumaric* condition from the beginning; and tradition whispers, what the Secret Teachings affirm, that these Elect were the germ of a Hierarchy *which never died since that period:*—

"*The Inner Man of the first* * * * *only changes his body from time to time; he is ever the same, knowing neither rest nor Nirvana, spurning Devachan and remaining constantly on Earth for the salvation of mankind. . . .*" "*Out of the seven Virgin-men* (Kumara) *four sacrificed themselves for the sins of the world and the instruction of the ignorant, to remain till the end of the present Manvantara. Though unseen, they are ever present.*" (Catechism of the inner Schools.)

It is these sacred "Four" who have been allegorized and symbolized in the "*Linga Purana.*" Higher than the "Four" is only ONE on Earth as in Heavens—that still more mysterious and solitary Being described in Volume I.

With the Fourth Race we reach the purely human period. Those who were hitherto semi-divine Beings, self-imprisoned in bodies which were human only in appearance, became physiologically changed and took unto themselves wives who were entirely human and fair to look at, but in whom *lower, more material,* though sidereal, Beings had incarnated.

(c) This is the beginning of a worship which, ages later, was doomed to degenerate into phallicism and sexual worship. It began by the worship of the human body—that "miracle of miracles," as an English author calls it—and ended by that of its respective sexes.

Yet the "Lemurians" and the Atlanteans, "those children of Heaven and Earth," were indeed marked with a character of SORCERY; for the Esoteric Doctrine charges them precisely with that, which, if believed, would put an end to the difficulties of science with regard to the origin of man, or rather, his anatomical similarities to the *Anthropoid Ape.* It accuses them of·having committed the (*to us*) abominable crime of breeding with so-called "animals," and thus producing a truly pithecoid species, now extinct.

A careful perusal of the Commentaries would make one think that the Being that the new "*Incarnate*" bred with was called an "animal," not because he was no human being, but rather because he was so dissimilar physically and mentally to the more perfect races, which had developed physiologically at an earlier period. Remember Stanza 7 and what is said in Sloka 24:—that when the "Sons of

Wisdom" came to incarnate the first time, some of them incarnated fully, others projected into the forms only *a Spark*, while some of the Shadows were left over from being *filled* and perfected, till the Fourth Race. Those races, then, which "remained destitute of knowledge," which were left "mindless," remained as they were, even after the natural separation of the sexes. It is these who committed the first cross-breeding, so to speak, and bred monsters; and it is from the descendants of these that the Atlanteans chose their wives. The Commentary says, in describing that species (or race) of animals "fair to look at" as a biped:—"*Having human shape, but having the lower extremities, from the waist down, covered with hair.*" Hence the race of the *satyrs*, perhaps.

If men existed two million years ago, they must have been—just as the animals were—quite different physically and anatomically from what they have become; and they were nearer then to the type of pure mammalian animal than they are now. Anyhow, we learn that the animal world breeds strictly *inter se, i.e.*, in accordance with genus and species—only since the appearance *on this earth* of the Atlantean race.

(*d*). ... *Then*, "*the third eye acted no longer,*" says the Stanza, because MAN had sunk too deep into the mire of matter.

THE RACES WITH THE "THIRD EYE"

The evidence for the Cyclopes—a race of giants—will be pointed out in forthcoming Sections, in the Cyclopean remnants, so called to this day. An indication that, during its evolution and before the final adjustment of the human organism—which became perfect and symmetrical only in the Fifth Race—the early Fourth Race may have been three-eyed, without having necessarily a third eye in the middle of the brow like the legendary Cyclops, is also furnished by Science.

To the Occultists who believe that spiritual and psychic *involution* proceeds on parallel lines with physical *evolution;* that the *inner* senses—innate in the first human races—atrophied during racial growth and the material development of the outer senses; to the student of Esoteric symbology, finally, this statement is no conjecture or possibility, but simply *a phase of the law of growth, a proven fact*, in short. They understand the meaning of this passage in the *Commentaries* which says:—

"*There were four-armed human creatures in those early days of the male-females* (hermaphrodites); *with one head, yet three eyes. They could see before them and behind them.*[9] *A Kalpa later* (after the separation of the sexes) *men having fallen into matter, their spiritual vision became dim; and coordinately the third eye commenced to lose its power. . . . When the Fourth* (Race) *arrived at its middle age, the inner vision had to be awakened, and* acquired by artificial stimuli, *the process of which was known to the old sages. . . . The third eye, likewise, getting gradually* PETRIFIED,[10] *soon disappeared. The double-faced became the one-faced, and the eye was drawn deep into the head and is now buried under the hair. During the activity of the Inner Man* (during trances and spiritual visions) *the eye swells and expands. The Arhat sees and feels it, and regulates his action accordingly. . . . The undefiled Lanoo* (disciple) *need fear no danger; he who keeps himself not in purity* (who is not chaste) *will receive no help from the 'deva eye.'* "

The "deva-eye" exists no more for the majority of mankind. The *third eye is dead*, and acts no longer; but it has left behind a witness to its existence. This witness is now the PINEAL GLAND.

The development of the *Human eye* gives more support to the occult anthropology than to that of the physiologists. "The eyes in the human embryo *grow from within without*" out of the brain, instead of being part of the skin, as in the insects and cuttlefish.

The allegorical expression of the Hindu mystics when speaking of the "Eye of Siva," the *Tri-lochana* ("three-eyed"), thus receives its justification and *raison d'être*—the transference of the pineal gland (once that "third eye") to the forehead, being an exoteric licence. This throws also a light on the mystery—incomprehensible to some—of the connection between *abnormal*, or Spiritual Seership, and the physiological purity of the Seer. The question is often asked, "Why should celibacy and chastity be a *sine quâ non* rule and condition of regular *chelaship*, or the development of psychic and occult powers? The answer is contained in the Commentary. When we learn that the "third eye" was once a physiological organ, and that later on, owing to the gradual disappearance of spirituality and increase of materiality (Spiritual nature being extinguished by the physical), it became an atrophied organ, the connection will become clear. During human life the greatest impediment in the way of spiritual development, and especially to the acquirement of *Yoga* powers, is

[9] Viz., the third eye was at the back of the head. The statement that the latest hermaphrodite humanity was "four-armed," unriddles probably the mystery of all the representations and idols of the exoteric gods of India.

[10] This expression "petrified" instead of "ossified" is curious. The "back eye," which is of course the *pineal gland*, now so-called, the small pea-like mass of grey nervous matter attached to the back of the third ventricle of the brain, is said to almost invariably contain *mineral concretions* and *sand*, and "nothing more." (*Vide Infra.*)

the activity of our physiological senses. Sexual action being closely connected, by interaction, with the spinal cord and the grey matter of the brain, it is useless to give any longer explanation. Of course, the normal and abnormal state of the brain, and the degree of active work in the *medulla oblongata*, reacts powerfully on the pineal gland, for, owing to the number of "centres" in that region which control by far the greater majority of the physiological actions of the animal economy, and also owing to the close and intimate neighbourhood of the two, there must be exerted a very powerful "inductive" action by the *medulla* on the pineal gland.

It is asserted upon the authority of Science that many of the animals—especially among the lower orders of the vertebrata—have a *third* eye, now atrophied, but necessarily active in its origin. There were and are palaeontologists who feel convinced to this day that this "third eye" has functioned in its origin, and they are certainly right.

In the beginning, every class and family of living species was hermaphrodite and objectively one-eyed. In the animal, whose form was as ethereal (astrally) as that of man, before the bodies of both began to evolve their coats of skin, viz., to evolve from *within without* the thick coating of physical substance or matter with its internal physiological mechanism—the third eye was primarily, as in man, the only seeing organ. The two physical front eyes developed later on in both brute and man, whose organ of physical sight was, at the commencement of the Third Race, in the same position as that of some of the blind vertebrata, in our day, *i.e.*, beneath an opaque skin. Only the stages of the *odd*, or primeval eye, in man and brute, are now inverted, as the former has already passed that animal *non-rational* stage in the Third Round, and is ahead of mere brute creation by a whole plane of consciousness. Therefore, while the "Cyclopean" eye was, and still *is*, in man the organ of *spiritual* sight, in the animal it was that of objective vision. And this eye, having performed its function, was replaced, in the course of physical evolution from the simple to the complex, by two eyes, and thus was stored and laid aside by nature for further use in aeons to come.

This explains why the pineal gland reached its highest development proportionately with the lowest physical development. It is the vertebrata in which it is the most prominent and objective, and in man it is most carefully hidden and inaccessible, except to the anatomist. No less light is thrown thereby on the future physical, spiritual, and intellectual state of mankind, in periods corresponding on parallel lines with other past periods, and always on the lines of ascending and descending cyclic evolution and development. Thus, a few centuries before the *Kali yuga*—the "black age" which began nearly 5,000 years ago—it was said (paraphrased into comprehensible sentences):

"*We* (the Fifth Root-Race) *in our first half* (of duration) *onward* (on the now ASCENDING arc of the cycle) *are on the mid point of* (or between) *the First and the Second Races—falling downward* (*i.e.*, the races were then on the descending arc of the cycle).... *Calculate for thyself*, Lanoo, *and see.*"

Calculating as advised, we find that during that transitional period—namely, in the second half of the First spiritual ethereo-astral race—nascent mankind was devoid of the intellectual brain element. As it was on its *descending* line, and as we are parallel to it,

EVOLUTION OF ROOT-RACES IN THE FOURTH ROUND

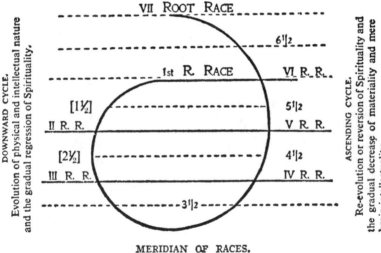

MERIDIAN OF RACES.

on the *ascending*, we are, therefore devoid of the Spiritual element, which is now replaced by the intellectual. For, remember well, as we are in the *manasa* period of our cycle of races, or in the Fifth, we have, therefore, crossed the meridian point of the perfect adjustment of Spirit and Matter—or that equilibrium between brain intellect and Spiritual perception. One important point has, however, to be borne in mind.

We are only in the Fourth Round, and it is in the Fifth that the full development of *Manas*, as a direct ray from the Universal

MAHAT—a ray unimpeded by Matter—will be finally reached. Our race then has, as a Root-race, crossed the equatorial line and is cycling onward on the Spiritual side; but some of our sub-races still find themselves on the shadowy descending arc of their respective national cycles; while others again—the oldest—having crossed their crucial point, which alone decides whether a race, a nation, or a tribe will live or perish, are at the apex of spiritual development as sub-races.

The "Third Eye" is indissolubly connected with Karma.

The "Eye of Siva" did not become entirely atrophied before the close of the Fourth Race. When spirituality and all the divine powers and attributes of the Deva-man of the Third had been made the hand-maidens of the newly-awakened physiological and psychic passions of the physical man, instead of the reverse, the Eye lost its powers. But such was the law of Evolution, and it was, in strict accuracy, no FALL. The sin was not in using those newly-developed powers, but in *misusing* them; in making of the tabernacle, designed to contain a god, the fane of every *spiritual* iniquity. And if we say "sin" it is merely that everyone should understand our meaning; as the term *Karma*[11] would be the right one to use in this case; while the reader who would feel perplexed at the use of the term "spiritual" instead of "physical" iniquity, is reminded of the fact that there can be no physical iniquity. The body is simply the irresponsible organ, the tool of the *psychic*, if not of the "Spiritual man." In the case of the Atlanteans, it was precisely the Spiritual being which sinned, the Spirit element being still the "Master" principle in man. Thus it is in those days that the heaviest Karma of the Fifth Race was generated by our Monads.

Questions with regard to *Karma* and *Re-births* are constantly offered, and a great confusion seems to exist upon this subject. Those who are born and bred in the Christian faith, and have been trained in the idea that a new soul is created by God for every newly-born infant, are among the most perplexed. They ask whether in such case the number of incarnating Monads on earth is limited; to which they are answered in the affirmative. For, however countless, in our conceptions, the number of the incarnating Monads—even if we take into account the fact that ever since the Second Race, when their respective seven Groups were furnished with bodies, several

[11] Karma is a word of many meanings, and has a special term for almost every one of its aspects. It means, as a synonym of sin, the performance of some action for the attainment of an object of *worldly*, hence *selfish*, desire, which cannot fail to be hurtful to somebody else. Karma is action, the Cause; and Karma again is "the law of ethical causation"; the *Effect* of an act produced egotistically, when the great Law of Harmony depends on altruism.

births and deaths may be allowed for every second of time in the aeons already passed—still, there must be a limit. It was stated that Karma-Nemesis, whose bond-maid is Nature, adjusted everything in the most harmonious manner; and that, therefore, the fresh pouring-in, or arrival of new Monads, had ceased as soon as Humanity had reached its full physical development. No fresh Monads have in-carnated since the middle-point of the Atlanteans. Hence, remember-ing that, save in the case of young children, and of individuals whose lives were violently cut off by some accident, no Spiritual Entity can re-incarnate before a period of many centuries has elapsed, such gaps alone must show that the number of Monads is necessarily finite and limited. Moreover, a reasonable time must be given to other animals for their evolutionary progress.

Hence the assertion that many of us are now working off the effects of the evil Karmic causes produced by us in Atlantean bodies. The Law of KARMA is inextricably interwoven with that of Re-incarnation.

It is only the knowledge of the constant re-births of one and the same individuality throughout the life-cycle; the assurance that the same MONADS—among whom are many Dhyan-Chohans, or the "Gods" themselves—have to pass through the "Circle of Necessity," rewarded or punished by such rebirth for the suffering endured or crimes committed in the former life; that those very Monads, which entered the empty, senseless shells, or astral figures of the First Race emanated by the Pitris, are the same who are now amongst us—nay, ourselves, perchance; it is only this doctrine, we say, that can explain to us the mysterious problem of Good and Evil, and reconcile man to the terrible and *apparent* injustice of life. Nothing but such certainty can quiet our revolted sense of justice. For, when one unacquainted with the noble doctrine looks around him, and ob-serves the inequalities of birth and fortune, of intellect and capaci-ties; when one sees honour paid fools and profligates, on whom fortune has heaped her favours by mere privilege of birth, and their nearest neighbour, with all his intellect and noble virtues—far more deserving in every way—perishing of want and for lack of sympathy; when one sees all this and has to turn away, helpless to relieve the undeserved suffering, one's ears ringing and heart aching with the cries of pain around him—that blessed knowledge of Karma alone prevents him from cursing life and men, as well as their supposed Creator.

This Law—whether Conscious or Unconscious—predestines nothing and no one. It exists from and in Eternity, truly, for it is ETERNITY itself; and as such, since no act can be co-equal with

Eternity, it cannot be said to act, for it is ACTION itself. It is not the wave which drowns a man, but the *personal* action of the wretch, who deliberately places himself under the *impersonal* action of the laws that govern the ocean's motion. Karma creates nothing, nor does it design. It is man who plans and creates causes, and Karmic law adjusts the effects; which adjustment is not an act, but universal harmony, tending ever to resume its original position, like a bough, which, bent down too forcibly, rebounds with corresponding vigour. If it happen to dislocate the arm that tried to bend it out of its natural position, shall we say that it is the bough which broke our arm, or that our own folly has brought us to grief? Karma has never sought to destroy intellectual and individual liberty. On the contrary, he who unveils through study and meditation its intricate paths, and throws light on those dark ways, in the windings of which so many men perish owing to their ignorance of the labyrinth of life, is working for the good of his fellow-men. KARMA is an Absolute and Eternal law in the World of manifestation; and as there can only be one Absolute, as One eternal ever-present Cause, believers in Karma cannot be regarded as Atheists or materialists—still less as fatalists: for Karma is one with the Unknowable, of which it is an aspect in its effects in the phenomenal world.

Intimately, or rather indissolubly, connected with Karma, then, is the law of Re-birth, or of the re-incarnation of the same spiritual individuality in a long, almost interminable, series of personalities. The latter are like the various costumes and characters played by the same actor, with each of which that actor identifies himself and is identified by the public, for the space of a few hours. The *inner*, or real Man, who personates those characters, knows the whole time that he is Hamlet for the brief space of a few acts, which represent, however, on the plane of human illusion, the whole life of Hamlet. And he knows that he was, the night before, King Lear, the transformation in his turn of the Othello of a still earlier preceding night; but the outer, visible character is supposed to be ignorant of the fact. In actual life that ignorance is, unfortunately, but too real. Nevertheless, the *permanent* Individuality is fully aware of the fact, though, through the atrophy of the "spiritual" eye in the physical body, that knowledge is unable to impress itself on the consciousness of the false personality.

THE CIVILIZATION AND DESTRUCTION OF THE THIRD AND FOURTH RACES

43. THEY (*the Lemurians*) BUILT HUGE CITIES. OF RARE EARTHS AND METALS THEY BUILT. OUT OF THE FIRES (*lava*) VOMITED. OUT OF THE WHITE STONE OF THE MOUNTAINS (*marble*) AND THE BLACK STONE (*of the subterranean fires*) THEY CUT THEIR OWN IMAGES, IN THEIR SIZE AND LIKENESS, AND WORSHIPPED THEM.

As the history of the first two *human* races—the last of the Lemurians and the first of the future Atlanteans—proceeds, we have at this point to blend the two, and speak of them collectively.

Here reference is also made to the *divine* Dynasties, such as were claimed by the Egyptians, Chaldeans, Greeks, etc., to have preceded their *human* kings. Our modern geologists are now being driven into admitting the evident existence of submerged continents. But to confess their presence is not to accept that there were men on them during the early geological periods;—ay, men and civilized nations, not Palaeolithic savages only; who, under the guidance of their *divine* Rulers, built large cities, cultivated arts and sciences, and knew astronomy, architecture and mathematics to perfection. This primeval civilization did not, as one may think, immediately follow their physiological transformation. Between the final evolution and the first city built, many hundred thousands of years had passed. Yet, we find the Lemurians in their sixth sub-race building their first rock-cities out of stone and lava.[1] One of such great cities of primitive

[1] Our best modern novelists, who are neither Theosophists nor Spiritualists, begin to have, nevertheless, very psychological and suggestively Occult dreams: witness Mr. Louis Stephenson and his Dr. Jekyll and Mr. Hyde, than which no grander psychological essay on Occult lines exists. Has the rising novelist, Mr. Rider Haggard, also had a prophetic or rather a retrospective clairvoyant dream before he wrote *She*? His imperial Kor, the great city of the dead, whose surviving living men sailed northwards after the plague had killed almost a whole nation, seems to step out in its general outlines from the imperishable pages of the old archaic records. Ayesha suggests "that those men who sailed north may have been the fathers of the first Egyptians"; and then seems to attempt a synopsis of certain letters of a MASTER quoted in "Esoteric Buddhism." For, she says, "Time after time have nations, ay, and rich and strong nations, learned in the arts, been, and passed away, and been forgotten, so that no memory of them remains. This (the nation of Kor) is but one of several; for time eats up the work of man unless, indeed, he digs in caves like the people of Kor, and *then mayhap the sea swallows them, or the*

structure was built entirely of lava, some thirty miles west from where Easter Island now stretches its narrow piece of sterile ground, and was entirely destroyed by a series of volcanic eruptions. The oldest remains of Cyclopean buildings were all the handiwork of the Lemurians of the last sub-races; and an occultist shows, therefore, no wonder on learning that the stone relics found on the small piece of land called Easter Island by Captain Cook, are "very much like the walls of the Temple of Pachacamac or the Ruins of Tia-Huanuco in Peru," (*The Countries of the World*, by Robert Brown, Vol. 4, p. 43); and that they are in the CYCLOPEAN STYLE. The first large cities, however, appeared on that region of the continent which is now known as the island of Madagascar. There were civilized people and savages in those days as there are now. Evolution achieved its work of perfection with the former and Karma—its work of destruction on the latter. The Australians and their like are the descendants of those, who, instead of vivifying the spark dropped into them by the "Flames," extinguished it by long generations of bestiality.[2] The Aryan nations could trace their descent through the Atlanteans from the more spiritual races of the Lemurians, in whom the "Sons of Wisdom" had personally incarnated.

It is with the advent of the divine Dynasties that the first civilizations were started. And while, in some regions of the Earth, a portion of mankind preferred leading a nomadic and patriarchal life, and in others savage man was hardly learning to build a fire and to protect himself against the Elements, his brothers—more favoured than he by their *Karma*, and helped by the divine intelligence which informed them—built cities, and cultivated arts and sciences.

Gradually, mankind went down in stature, for, even before the real advent of the Fourth or Atlantean Race, the majority of mankind had fallen into iniquity and sin, save the Hierarchy of the "Elect," the followers and disciples of the "Sons of Will and Yoga"—called later the "Sons of the Fire Mist."

earthquake shakes them in. . . . Yet were not these people utterly destroyed, as I think. Some few remained in the other cities, for their cities were many. But the barbarians . . . came down upon them, and took their women to wife, and the race of the Amahagger that is now is a bastard brood of the mighty sons of Kor, and behold it dwelleth in the tombs with its fathers' bones. . . " (pp. 180, 181.)

[2] See Stanza 2, *ante.* This would account for the great difference and variation between the intellectual capacities of races, nations, and individual men. While incarnating, and in other cases only informing the human vehicles evolved by the first brainless (*manasless*) race, the incarnating Powers and Principles had to make their choice between, and take into account, the past Karmas of the *Monads*, between which and their bodies they had to become the connecting link. Besides which, as correctly stated in *Esoteric Buddhism*, "the fifth principle, or human (intellectual) soul, in the majority of mankind is not even yet fully developed."

Then came the Atlanteans; the giants whose physical beauty and strength reached their climax, in accordance with evolutionary law, toward the middle period of their fourth sub-race. But, as said in the Commentary:—

The last survivors of the fair child of the White Island (the primitive Sveta-dvipa) *had perished ages before. Their* (Lemuria's) *elect, had taken shelter on the Sacred Island* (now the "fabled" Shamballah, in the Gobi Desert), *while some of their accursed races, separating from the main stock, now lived in the jungles and underground* ("cave-men"), *when the golden yellow race* (the Fourth) *became in its turn "black with sin." From pole to pole the Earth had changed her face for the third time. . . . The demi-gods of the Third had made room for the semi-demons of the Fourth Race.*

The earliest pioneers of the Fourth Race were not Atlanteans, nor yet the human *Asuras* and the *Rakshasas* which they became later. In those days large portions of the future continent of Atlantis were yet part and parcel of the ocean floors. Lemuria, as we have called the continent of the Third Race, was then a gigantic land.[3] It covered the whole area of space from the foot of the Himalayas, which separated it from the inland sea rolling its waves over what is now Tibet, Mongolia, and the great desert of Shamo (Gobi); from Chittagong, westward to Hardwar, and eastward to Assam. Thence, it stretched South across what is known to us as Southern India, Ceylon, and Sumatra; then embracing on its way, as we go South, Madagascar on its right hand and Australia and Tasmania on its left, ran down to within a few degrees of the Antarctic Circle; when, from Australia, an inland region on the Mother Continent in those ages, it extended far into the Pacific Ocean, not only beyond Rapa-nui (Teapy, or Easter Island) which now lies in latitude 26 S., and longitude 110 W. This statement seems corroborated by science, even if only partially; as, when discussing continental trends, and showing the infra-Arctic masses trending generally with the Meridian, several ancient continents are generally mentioned, though inferentially. Among such the "Mascarene continent,'' which included Madagascar, stretching north and south, is spoken of, and the existence of another *ancient* continent running "from Spitzbergen to the Straits of Dover, while most of the other parts of

[3] Neither the name of Lemuria nor even Atlantis are the real *archaic* names of the lost continents, but have been adopted by us for the sake of clearness. Atlantis was the name given to those portions of the submerged Fourth-Race continent which were "beyond the pillars of Hercules," and which happened to keep above water after the general cataclysm. The last remnant of these—Plato's *Atlantis,* or the "Poseidon" (another *substitute* or rather a translation of the real name)—was the last of it some 11,000 years ago.

Europe were sea bottom," is taught. The latter corroborates, then, the Occult teaching which shows the (now) polar regions as the earliest of the seven cradles of Humanity, and as the tomb of the bulk of the mankind of that region during the Third Race, when the gigantic continent of Lemuria began separating into smaller continents. This is due, according to the explanation in the Commentary, to a decrease of velocity in the earth's rotation:—

"*When the Wheel runs at the usual rate, its extremities* (the poles) *agree with its middle circle* (equator); *when it runs slower and tilts in every direction, there is a great disturbance on the face of the Earth. The waters flow toward the two ends, and new lands arise in the middle belt* (equatorial lands), *while those at the ends are subject to pralayas by submersion. . . . "*

And again:—

. . . "*Thus the wheel* (the Earth) *is subject to, and regulated by, the Spirit of the Moon, for the breath of its waters* (tides). *Toward the close of the age* (Kalpa) *of a great* (Root) *Race, the Regents of the Moon* (the Pitar fathers, or Pitris) *begin drawing harder, and thus flatten the wheel about its belt, when it goes down in some places and swells in others, and the swelling running toward the extremities* (poles) *new lands will arise and old ones be sucked in.*"

In the Puranas every reference to the North of Meru is connected with that primeval Eldorado, now the North Polar region, which, when the magnolia blossomed there where now we see an unexplored endless desert of ice, was then a continent again. Science speaks of an ancient continent which stretched from Spitzbergen down to the Straits of Dover. The Secret Doctrine teaches that, in the earliest geological periods, these regions formed a horse-shoe-like continent, whose one end, the Eastern, far more northward than North Cornwall, included Greenland, and the other contained Behring Straits as an inland piece of ground, and descended southward in its natural trend down to the British Isles, which in those days must have been right under the lower curve of the semi-circle. This continent was raised simultaneously with the submersion of the equatorial portions of Lemuria. Ages later, some of the Lemurian remains re-appeared again on the face of the oceans. Therefore, though it can be said without departing from truth that Atlantis is included in the seven great insular continents, since the Fourth Race Atlanteans got some of the Lemurian relics, and, settling on the islands, included them among *their* lands and continents, yet a difference should be made and an explanation given, once that a fuller and more accurate account is attempted, as in the present work. Easter Island was also taken possession of in this manner by some Atlanteans; who, having escaped from the cataclysm which befell their own land, settled on that remnant of Lemuria, only to perish thereon, when destroyed in one day by its volcanic fires and lava.

Science refuses to sanction the *wild* hypothesis that there was a time when the Indian peninsula at one end of the line, and South America at the other, were connected by a belt of islands and continents. The India of the pre-historic ages . . . was doubly connected with the two Americas. The lands of the ancestors of those whom Ammianus Marcellinus calls the 'Brahmans of Upper India' stretched from Kashmir far into the (now) deserts of Schamo. A pedestrian from the north might have reached—hardly wetting his feet—the Alaskan peninsula, through Manchuria, across the *future* Gulf of Tartary, the Kurile and Aleutian islands; while another traveller, furnished with a canoe, and starting from the South, could have walked over from Siam, crossed the Polynesian Islands and trudged into any part of the continent of South America.

In the epoch we are treating of, the Continent of Lemuria had already broken asunder in many places, and formed new separate continents. There was, nevertheless, neither Africa nor the Americas, still less Europe in those days, all these slumbering yet on the ocean floors. Nor was there much of present Asia; for the cis-Himalayan regions were covered with seas, and beyond this stretched the "lotus leaves" of *Sveta-dwipa*, the countries now called Greenland, Eastern and Western Siberia, etc., etc. The immense Continent, which had once reigned supreme over the Indian, Atlantic, and Pacific Oceans, now consisted of huge islands which were gradually disappearing one after the other, until the final convulsion engulfed the last remains of it. Easter Isle, for instance, belongs to the earliest civilization of the Third Race. Submerged with the rest, a volcanic and sudden uplifting of the ocean floor raised the small relic of the Archaic ages untouched, with its volcano and statues, during the Champlain epoch of northern polar submersion, as a standing witness to the existence of Lemuria. It is said that some of the Australian tribes are the last remnants of the last descendants of the Third Race.

It is to this period that we have to look for the first appearance of the Ancestors of those who are termed by us the most ancient peoples of the world—now called respectively the Aryan Hindus, the Egyptians, and the oldest Persians, on the one hand, and the Chaldees and Phoenicians on the other. These were governed by the DIVINE DYNASTIES, *i.e.*, Kings and Rulers who had of mortal man only his physical appearance *as it was then*, but who were Beings from spheres higher and more celestial than our own sphere will be, long Manvantaras hence.

If we regard the second portion of the Third Race as the first representatives of the *really human race* with solid bones, then Haeckel's surmise that "the evolution of the primitive men took place ... in *either* Southern Asia or ... Lemuria"—Africa, whether Eastern or Western being out of the question—is correct enough, if not entirely so. To be accurate, however, in the same way that the evolution of the First Race (from the bodies of the *Pitars*) took place on seven distinctly separated regions of the (then) only Earth at the Arctic Pole —so did the ultimate transformation of the Third occur. It began in those northern regions, which have just been described as including Behring's Straits, and what there then was of dry land in Central Asia, when the climate was semi-tropical even in the Arctic regions and most adapted to the primitive wants of nascent physical man. That region, however, has been more than once frigid and tropical in turn since the appearance of man. The Commentary tells us that the Third Race was only about the middle point of its development when:—

"*The axle of the Wheel tilted. The Sun and Moon shone no longer over the heads of that portion of the* SWEAT BORN; *people knew snow, ice, and frost, and men, plants, and animals were dwarfed in their growth. Those that did not perish* REMAINED AS HALF-GROWN BABES[4] IN SIZE AND INTELLECT. *This was the third Pralaya of the Races.*[5]

Which means again, that our Globe is subject to seven periodical *entire* changes which go *pari passu* with the Races. For the Secret Doctrine teaches that, during this Round, there must be seven terrestrial *Pralayas*, three occasioned by the change in the inclination of the earth's axis. It is a *law* which acts at its appointed time, and not at all blindly, as science may think, but in strict accordance and harmony with *Karmic* law. In Occultism this inexorable Law is referred to as "the great ADJUSTER."

Thus, since Vaivasvata Manu's Humanity appeared on this Earth, there have already been four such axial disturbances; when the old continents—save the first one—were sucked in by the oceans, other lands appeared, and huge mountain chains arose where there had been none before. The face of the Globe was completely changed

[4] "Half-grown babes" in comparison with their giant Brethren on other zones.
[5] Relates to Lemuria.

each time; the *survival of the fittest* nations and races was secured through timely help; and the unfit ones—the failures—were disposed of by being swept off the earth.

The *Sub*-races are subject to the same cleansing process, as also the side-branchlets (the family-races). Let one well acquainted with astronomy and mathematics take notes of what he knows of the history of peoples and nations, and collate their respective rises and falls with what is known of astronomical cycles—especially with the *Sidereal Year*, equal to 25,868 of our solar years. If the observer is gifted with the faintest intuition, then will he find how the weal and woe of nations is intimately connected with the beginning and close of this Sidereal Cycle. Every Sidereal Year the tropics recede from the pole *four degrees* in each revolution from the equinoctial points, as the equator rounds through the Zodiacal constellations. Now, as every astronomer knows, at present the tropic is only twenty-three degrees and a fraction less than half a degree from the equator. Hence it has still 2½ degrees to run before the end of the Sidereal Year; which gives humanity in general, and our civilized races in *particular*, a reprieve of about 16,000 years.

After the Great Flood of the Third Race (the Lemurians)—

"*Men decreased considerably in stature, and the duration of their lives was diminished. Having fallen down in godliness they mixed with animal races, and intermarried among giants and pigmies* (the dwarfed races of the Poles) ... *Many acquired* DIVINE, *more*—UNLAWFUL *knowledge, and followed willingly the* LEFT PATH."

Thus were the Atlanteans approaching destruction in their turn. How many geological periods it took to accomplish this *fourth* destruction who can tell? But we are told that—

44. THEY (*the Atlanteans*) BUILT GREAT IMAGES, NINE YATIS HIGH (27 *feet*)—THE SIZE OF THEIR BODIES (*a*). INNER [? LUNAR] FIRES HAD DESTROYED THE LAND OF THEIR FATHERS (*the Lemurians*). WATER THREATENED THE FOURTH (*Race*) (*b*).

(*a*) It is well worth noticing that most of the gigantic statues discovered on Easter Island, a portion of an undeniably submerged continent—as also those found on the outskirts of Gobi, a region which had been submerged for untold ages—are all between 20 and 30 feet high. The statues found by Cook on Easter Island measured almost all *twenty-seven* feet in height, and eight feet across the shoulders.

We are told that it is after the destruction of Lemuria by subterranean fires that men went on steadily decreasing in stature—a process already commenced after their *physical* FALL—and that finally, some millions of years after, they reached between six and seven feet, and are now dwindling down (as the older Asiatic races) to nearer five than six feet. As Pickering shows, there is in the Malay race (a sub-race of the Fourth Root Race) a singular diversity of stature; the members of the Polynesian family (Tahitians, Samoans, and Tonga islanders) are of a *higher stature than the rest of mankind;* but the Indian tribes and the inhabitants of the Indo-Chinese countries are decidedly below the general average. This is easily explained. The Polynesians belong to the very earliest of the surviving sub-races, the others to the very last and transitory stock. As the Tasmanians are now completely extinct, and the Australians rapidly dying out, so will the other old races soon follow.

(*b*) The sinking and transformation of Lemuria beginning nearly at the Arctic Circle (Norway), the Third Race ended its career in Lanka, or rather on that which became Lanka with the Atlanteans. The small remnant now known as Ceylon is the Northern highland of ancient Lanka, while the enormous island of that name was, in the Lemurian period, the gigantic continent described a few pages back. As a MASTER says (See *Esoteric Buddhism*, p. 65):—"Why should not your geologists bear in mind that under the continents explored and fathomed by them . . . there may be hidden, deep in the fathomless, or rather unfathomed ocean beds, other and far older continents whose strata have never been geologically explored; and that they may some day upset entirely their present theories? Why not admit that our present continents have, like Lemuria and Atlantis, been several times already submerged, and had the time to re-appear again and bear their new groups of mankind and civiliza- tions; and that at the first great geological upheaval at the next cataclysm, in the series of periodical cataclysms that occur from the beginning to the end of every Round, our already autopsized con- tinents will go down and the Lemurias and Atlantises come up again?"

Not the *same* identical continents, of course.

But here an explanation is needed. No confusion need arise as regards the postulation of a Northern Lemuria. The prolongation of that great continent into the North Atlantic Ocean is in no way subversive of the opinions so widely held as to the site of the lost Atlantis, and one corroborates the other. It must be noted that Lemuria, which served as the cradle of the Third Root-Race, not only embraced a vast area in the Pacific and Indian Oceans, but extended in the shape of a horse-shoe past Madagascar, round "South Africa" (then a mere fragment in process of formation), through the Atlantic up to Norway. The great *English fresh-water deposit called the Wealden—which every geologist regards as the mouth of a former great river—is the bed of the main stream which drained Northern Lemuria in the Secondary Age*. The former reality of this river is a fact of science. Professor Berthold Seeman not only accepted the reality of such a mighty continent, but regarded *Australia and Europe as formerly portions of one continent*—thus corroborating the whole "horse-shoe" doctrine already enunciated. No more striking confirmation of our position could be given than the fact that the ELEVATED RIDGE in the Atlantic basin, 9,000 feet in height, which runs for some two or three thousand miles southwards from a point near the British Islands, first slopes towards South America, then *shifts almost at right angles* to proceed in a SOUTH-EASTERLY *line toward the African coast*, whence it runs on southward to Tristan da Cunha. This ridge is a remnant of an Atlantic continent, and, could it be traced further, would establish the reality of a submarine horse-shoe junction with a former continent in the Indian Ocean. (*Cf.* chart adapted from the *Challenger* and *Dolphin* soundings in Mr. Donnelly's *Atlantis, the Antediluvian World*, p. 47.)

The *Atlantic portion of Lemuria* was the geological basis of what is generally known as Atlantis. The latter, indeed, must be regarded rather as a development of the Atlantic prolongation of Lemuria, than as an entirely new mass of land upheaved to meet the special requirements of the Fourth Root-Race. Just as in the case of Race-evolution, so in that of the shifting and re-shifting of continental masses, no hard and fast line can be drawn where a new order ends and another begins. Continuity in natural processes is never broken. Thus the Fourth Race Atlanteans were developed from a nucleus of Northern Lemurian Third Race Men, centred, roughly speaking, toward a point of land in what is now the mid-Atlantic Ocean. Their continent was formed by the coalescence of many islands and peninsulas which were upheaved in the ordinary course of time *and became ultimately the true home of the great Race known as the Atlanteans*. After this consummation was once attained it follows that "Lemuria should no more be confounded with the Atlantis Continent, than Europe with America." (*Esoteric Buddhism*, p. 58.)

Of still standing witnesses to the submerged continents, and the colossal men that inhabited them, there are still a few. Besides the Easter Island statues mentioned already, to what epoch do the colossal statues, still erect and intact near Bamian, belong? Archaeology assigns them to the first centuries of Christianity, and errs in this as it does in many other speculations.

All those numberless gigantic ruins discovered one after the other in our day, all those immense avenues of colossal ruins that cross North America along and beyond the Rocky Mountains, are the work of the Cyclopes, the true and actual Giants of old.

Central Asian traditions say the same of the Bamian statues. What are they, and what is the place where they have stood for countless ages, defying the cataclysms around them, and even the hand of man? Bamian is a small, miserable, half-ruined town in Central Asia, half-way between Kabul and Balkh, at the foot of Kobhibaba, a huge mountain of the Hindu-Kush chain, some 8,500 feet above the level of the sea. In days of old, Bamian was a portion of the ancient city of Djooljool, ruined and destroyed to the last stone by Genghis Khan in the XIIIth century. The whole valley is hemmed in by colossal rocks, which are full of partially natural and partially artificial caves and grottoes, once the dwellings of Buddhist monks who had established in them their *viharas*. It is at the entrance of some of these that five enormous statues, of what is regarded as Buddha, have been discovered or rather *rediscovered* in our century, as the famous Chinese traveller, Hiouen-Thsang, speaks of, and saw them, when he visited Bamian in the VIIth century.

The Buddhist Arhats and ascetics found the five statues, and many more now crumbled down to dust, and as the three were found by them in colossal niches at the entrance of their future abode, they covered the figures with plaster, and, over the old, modelled new statues made to represent Lord Tathagata. But the five statues belong to the handiwork of the Initiates of the Fourth Race, who sought refuge, after the submersion of their continent, in the fastnesses and on the summits of the Central Asian mountain chains. Moreover, the five statues are an imperishable record of the Esoteric Teaching about the gradual evolution of the Races.

The largest is made to represent the First Race of mankind, its ethereal body being commemorated in hard, everlasting stone for the instruction of future generations, as its remembrance would otherwise never have survived the Atlantean Deluge. The second—120 feet high—represents the Sweat-born; and the third—measuring 60 feet—immortalizes the Race that fell, and thereby inaugurated the first *physical* race, born of father and mother, the last descendants of which are represented in the statues found on Easter Isle; but they were only from 20 to 25 feet in stature at the epoch when Lemuria was submerged, after it had been nearly destroyed by volcanic fires. The Fourth Race was still smaller, though gigantic in comparison with our present Fifth Race, and the series culminated finally in the latter.

45. THE FIRST GREAT WATERS CAME. THEY SWALLOWED THE SEVEN GREAT ISLANDS (*a*).

46. ALL HOLY SAVED, THE UNHOLY DESTROYED. WITH THEM MOST OF THE HUGE ANIMALS PRODUCED FROM THE SWEAT OF THE EARTH (*b*).

(*a*) As this subject—the fourth great Deluge on our Globe in this Round—is fully treated in the chapters that follow the last Stanza, to say anything more at present would be mere repetition. The seven great Islands (Dwipas) belonged to the continent of Atlantis. The Secret Teachings show that the "Deluge" overtook the Fourth, giant Race, not on account of their depravity, or because they had become "black with sin," but simply because such is the fate of every continent, which—like everything else under our Sun—is born, lives, becomes decrepit, and dies. This was when the Fifth Race was in its infancy.

(*b*) Thus the Giants perished, but "all holy saved," and alone the "unholy were destroyed." This was due, however, as much to the *prevision* of the "holy" ones, who had not lost the use of their "Third Eye," as to Karma and natural law. Speaking of the subsequent race (our Fifth Humanity), the Commentary says:—

"*Alone the handful of those Elect, whose divine Instructors had gone to inhabit that Sacred Island—'from whence the last Saviour will come'—now kept mankind from becoming one-half the exterminator of the other* [as mankind does now—H. P. B.]. *It* (mankind) *became divided. Two-thirds of it were ruled by Dynasties of lower, material Spirits of the earth, who took possession of the easily accessible bodies; one-third remained faithful, and joined with the nascent Fifth Race—the Divine Incarnates. When the Poles moved* (for the fourth time) *this did not affect those who were protected, and who had separated from the Fourth Race. Like the Lemurians—alone the ungodly Atlanteans perished, and 'were seen no more.' . . .*"

STANZA 12

THE FIFTH RACE AND ITS DIVINE INSTRUCTORS

47. Few (*men*) REMAINED. SOME YELLOW, SOME BROWN AND BLACK, AND SOME RED, REMAINED. THE MOON-COLOURED (*of the primitive Divine Stock*) WERE GONE FOR EVER (*a*) . . .

48. THE FIFTH RACE PRODUCED FROM THE HOLY STOCK (*remained*). IT WAS RULED BY HER FIRST DIVINE KINGS.

49. THE "SERPENTS" WHO RE-DESCENDED, WHO MADE PEACE WITH THE FIFTH (*Race*), WHO TAUGHT AND INSTRUCTED IT (*b*) . . .

(*a*) This Sloka (47) relates to the Fifth Race. History does not begin with it, but living and ever-recurring tradition does. History—or what is called history—does not go further back than the fantastic origins of our fifth sub-race, a "few thousands" of years. It is the sub-divisions of this first sub-race of the Fifth Root-Race which are referred to in the sentence, "Some yellow, some brown and black, and some red, remained." The "moon coloured" (*i.e.*, the First and the Second Races) were gone for ever—without leaving any traces whatever; and that, so far back as the third "Deluge" of the Third Lemurian Race, that "Great Dragon," whose tail sweeps whole nations out of existence in the twinkling of an eye. And this is the true meaning of the verse in the COMMENTARY which says:

"*The* GREAT DRAGON *has respect but for the* 'SERPENTS' *of* WISDOM, *the Serpents whose holes are now under the triangular stones,*" *i.e.*, "the Pyramids, at the four corners of the world."

(*b*) This tells us clearly that which is mentioned more than once elsewhere in the Commentaries; namely, that the Adepts or "Wise" men of the three Races (the Third, Fourth and the Fifth) dwelt in subterranean habitats, generally under some kind of pyramidal structure, if not actually under a pyramid. For such "pyramids" existed in the four corners of the world and were never the monopoly of the land of the Pharaohs, though until found scattered all over the two Americas, under and over ground, beneath and amidst virgin forests, as in plain and vale, they were supposed to be the exclusive property of Egypt. If the true geometrically correct pyramids are no longer found in European regions, many of the supposed early *neolithic* caves, of the colossal triangular, pyramidal and conical *menhirs* in the Morbihan, and Brittany generally; many of the Danish tumuli and even of the "giant tombs" of Sardinia with their inseparable companions, the *nuraghi*, are so many more or less clumsy copies of the pyramids. Most of these are the works of the first settlers on the newly-born continent and isles of Europe, the—"some yellow, some brown and black, and some red"—races that remained after the submersion of the last Atlantean continents and islands (850,000 years ago), with the exception of Plato's Atlantean island, and before the arrival of the great Aryan races; while others were built by the earliest immigrants from the East.

There were *several* Deluges mixed up in the memories and traditions of the sub-races of the Fifth Race. The first great "Flood" was astronomical and cosmical, while several others were *terrestrial*. The Pyramids are closely connected with the ideas of both the Great Dragon (the constellation), the "Dragons of Wisdom," or the great Initiates of the Third and Fourth Races, and the Floods of the Nile, regarded as a divine reminder of the great Atlantic Flood. The astronomical records of Universal History, however, are said to have had their beginnings with the Third Sub-race of the Fourth Root-race or the Atlanteans. When was it? Occult data show that even since the time of the regular establishment of the Zodiacal calculations in Egypt, *the poles have been thrice inverted.*

WESTERN SPECULATIONS, FOUNDED ON THE GREEK AND PURANIC TRADITIONS

We believe in the seven "continents," four of which have already lived their day; the fifth still exists, and two are to appear in the future. We believe that each of these is not strictly a continent in the modern sense of the word, but that each name, from Jambu down to Pushkara[1] refers to the geographical names given (i) to the dry lands covering the face of the whole earth during the period of a Root-Race, in general; and (ii) to what remained of these after a geological (Race) *Pralaya*—as Jambu, for instance: and (iii) to those localities which will enter, after the future cataclysms, into the formation of new *universal* continents, peninsulas, or dwipas[2]—each continent being, in one sense, a greater or smaller region of dry land surrounded with water.

[1] Jambu, Plaksha, Salmali, Kusa, Krauncha, Saka, and Pushkara.
[2] Such as Saka and Pushkara, for instance, which do not yet exist, but into which will enter such lands as some portions of America, of Africa, and Central Asia, with the Gobi region. Let us bear in mind that *Upadwipas* means "*root*" islands, or the dry land in general.

Thus, we believe *we know* that, though two of the Puranic "islands"—the *sixth and seventh* "continents"—are yet to come, nevertheless there *were*, or there *are*, lands which will enter into the composition of the future dry lands of new earths whose geographical faces will be entirely changed, as were those of the past. Therefore we find in the Puranas that Saka-dwipa is (or will be) a continent, and that Sankha-dwipa, as shown in the Vayu Purana, is only "a minor island," one of the nine divisions (to which Vayu adds six more) of Bharata Varsha.

There was a time when the whole of the Sahara desert was a sea, then a continent as fertile as the Delta, and then, only after another temporary submersion, it became a desert similar to that other wilderness, the desert of Shamo or Gobi.

That not only the last island of Atlantis, spoken of by Plato, but a large continent, first divided, and then broken later on into seven peninsulas and islands (called *dwipas*), preceded Europe, is sure. It covered the whole of the North and South Atlantic regions, as well as portions of the North and South Pacific, and had islands even in the Indian Ocean (relics of Lemuria).

Surely, if the Hindu Puranas give a description of wars on continents and islands situated beyond Western Africa in the Atlantic Ocean; if their writers speak of *Barbaras* and other people such as Arabs—they who were known to navigate, or cross the *Kala pani* (the black waters of the Ocean) in the days of Phoenician navigation—then their Puranas must be older than those Phoenicians (placed at from 2,000 to 3,000 years B.C.). At any rate those traditions must have been older; as—

"In the above accounts," writes an Adept, "the Hindus speak of this island as *existing* and in great power; it must, therefore, have been more than *eleven thousand years ago*."

But another calculation and proof may be adduced of the great antiquity of these Hindu Aryans who knew of (because they had once dwelt in it) and described the last surviving island of Atlantis—or rather of that remnant of the Eastern portion of that continent which had perished soon after the upheaval of the two Americas[3]—the two Varshas of Pushkara. Recalling what the Orientalist had brought forward concerning the Mount Ashburj "at the foot of which the sun sets," where was the war between the Devatas and the Daityas,[4] he says:—

[3] America, the "new" world—is thus, though not *much*, older; still it *is* older than Europe, the "old world."
[4] If Div or Dev-Sefid's (the Taradaitya's) abode was on the *seventh stage*, it is because he came from Pushkara, the *Patala* (antipodes) of India, or from America.

"We will consider, then, the latitude and longitude of the lost island, and of the remaining Mount Ashburj. It was on the seventh stage of the world, *i.e.*, in the seventh climate (which is between the latitude of 24 degrees and latitude 28 degrees north) . . . This island, the daughter of the Ocean, is frequently described as lying in the West; and the sun is represented as setting at the foot of its mountain (Ashburj, Atlas, Teneriffe or Nila, no matter the name), and fighting the White Devil of the 'White Island.' "

Since, in the Puranic accounts, the island is *still existing*, then those accounts must be older than the 11,000 years elapsed since Sancha dwipa, or the Poseidonis of Atlantis, disappeared. Is it not barely possible that Hindus should have known the island still earlier? Let us turn again to astronomical demonstrations, which make this quite plain if one assumes, according to the said Adept, that "at the time when the summer tropical 'colure' passed through the *Pleiades*, when *Cor-Leonis* would be upon the equator; and when Leo *was vertical* to Ceylon at sunset, then would *Taurus* be vertical to the island of *Atlantis at noon*."

This explains, perhaps, why the Sinhalese, the heirs of the Rakshasas and Giants of Lanka, and the direct descendants of *Sinha*, or *Leo*, became connected with Sancha dwipa or Poseidonis (Plato's Atlantis). Only, as shown by Mackey's "*Sphinxiad*," this must have occurred about 23,000 years ago, *astronomically;* at which time the obliquity of the ecliptic must have been rather more than 27 degrees, and consequently Taurus must have passed over "Atlantis" or "Sancha dwipa." And that it was so is clearly demonstrated.

"*The sacred bull Nandi was brought from Bharata to Sancha to meet Rishabha* (Taurus) *every Kalpa. But when those of the White Island* (who descended originally from Sveta dwipa),[5] *who had mixed with the Daityas* (giants) *of the land of iniquity, had become black with sin, then Nandi remained for ever in the "White Island"* (or Sveta dwipa.) "*Those of the Fourth World* (race) *lost AUM*"—say the *Commentaries*.

The latter touched the walls, so to say, of Atlantis, before the latter sank finally. The word *Patala*, meaning both the antipodal countries and infernal regions, thus became synonymous in ideas and attributes as well as in name.

[5] Neither Atlantis, nor yet Sancha dwipa, was ever called "White Island." When tradition says that "the White Island became black on account of the sins of people" it only means the denizens of the "White Island," or Siddhapura, or Sveta dwipa, who descended to the Atlantis of the Third and Fourth races, to "inform the latter; and who, having incarnated, became black with sin"—a figure of speech. All the Avatars of Vishnu are said to come originally from the White Island. According to Tibetan tradition the White Island is the only locality which escapes the general fate of other dwipas and can be destroyed by neither fire nor water, for—it is the "eternal land."

Asburj (or Azburj), whether the peak of Teneriffe or not, was a volcano, when the sinking of the "western Atala" (or hell) began, and those who were saved told the tale to their children. Plato's Atlantis perished between water below and fire above; the great mountain vomiting flames all the while. "The 'fire-vomiting Monster' survived alone out of the ruins of the unfortunate island."

ADDITIONAL FRAGMENTS FROM A COMMENTARY ON THE VERSES OF STANZA 12

THE MS. from which these additional explanations are taken belongs to the group called "*Tongshaktchi Sangye Songa,*" or the Records of the "Thirty-five Buddhas of Confession," as they are *exoterically* called. These personages, however, though called in the Northern Buddhist religion "Buddhas," may just as well be called Rishis, or Avatars, etc., as they are "Buddhas who have preceded Sakyamuni" only for the Northern followers of the ethics preached by Gautama. These great Mahatmas, or Buddhas, are a universal and common property; they are *historical* Sages—at any rate, for all the Occultists who believe in such a hierarchy of Sages, the existence of which has been proved to them by the learned ones of the Fraternity. They are chosen from among some ninety-seven Buddhas in one group, and fifty-three in another,[1] mostly imaginary personages, who are really the personifications of the powers of the first-named.[2] These "baskets" of the oldest writings on "palm leaves" are kept very secret. Each MS. has appended to it a short synopsis of the history of that sub-race to which the particular "Buddha-Lha" belonged. The one special MS. from which the fragments which follow are extracted, and then rendered into a more comprehensible language, is said to have been copied from stone tablets which belonged to a Buddha of the earliest day of the Fifth Race, who had witnessed the Deluge and the submersion of the chief continents of the Atlantean race. The day when much, if not all, of that which is given here from the archaic records, will be found correct, is not far distant. Then the modern symbologists will acquire the certitude

[1] Gautama Buddha, named Shakya Thüb-pa, is the *twenty-seventh* of the last group, as most of these Buddhas belong to the *Divine Dynasties* which instructed mankind.

[2] Of these "Buddhas," or the "Enlightened," the far distant predecessors of Gautama the Buddha, who represent, we are taught, once living men, great Adepts and Saints, in whom the "Sons of Wisdom" had incarnated, and who were, therefore, so to speak, minor Avatars of the Celestial Beings—eleven only belong to the Atlantean race, and 24 to the Fifth Race, from its beginnings. They are identical with the Tirtankaras of the Jainas.

that even Odin, or the god Woden, the highest god in the German and Scandinavian mythology, is one of these thirty-five Buddhas; one of the earliest, indeed, for the continent to which he and his race belonged is also one of the earliest. So early, in truth, that in the days when tropical nature was to be found, where now lie eternal un-thawing snows, one could cross almost by dry land from Norway *via* Iceland and Greenland, to the lands that at present surround Hudson's Bay. Just, as in the palmy days of the Atlantean giants, the sons of the "Giants from the East," a pilgrim could perform a journey from what in our days is termed the Sahara desert to the lands which now rest in dreamless sleep at the bottom of the waters of the Gulf of Mexico and the Caribbean Sea. Events which were never written outside the human memory, but which were religiously transmitted from one generation to another, and from race to race, may have been preserved by constant transmission "within the book and volume of the brain," and through countless aeons, with more truth and accuracy than inside any written document or record. "That which is part of our souls is eternal," says Thackeray; and what can be nearer to our souls than that which happens at the dawns of our lives? Those lives are countless, but the soul or spirit that animates us throughout these myriads of existences is the same; and though "the book and volume" of the *physical* brain may forget events within the scope of one terrestrial life, the bulk of collective recollections can never desert the Divine Soul within us. Its whispers may be too soft, the sound of its words too far off the plane perceived by our physical senses; yet the shadow of events *that were*, just as much as the shadow of the events *that are to come*, is within its perceptive powers, and is ever present before its mind's eye.

This is what is written in one passage:—

"THE KINGS OF LIGHT HAVE DEPARTED IN WRATH. THE SINS OF MEN HAVE BECOME SO BLACK THAT EARTH QUIVERS IN HER GREAT AGONY. . . . THE AZURE SEATS REMAIN EMPTY. WHO OF THE BROWN, WHO OF THE RED, OR YET AMONG THE BLACK (*races*), CAN SIT IN THE SEATS OF THE BLESSED, THE SEATS OF KNOWLEDGE AND MERCY! WHO CAN ASSUME THE FLOWER OF POWER, THE PLANT OF THE GOLDEN STEM AND THE AZURE BLOSSOM?"

The "Kings of Light" is the name given in all old records to the Sovereigns of the Divine Dynasties. The "azure seats" are translated "celestial thrones" in certain documents. The "flower of power" is now the Lotus; what it may have been at that period, who can tell.

They had become bereft of their "azure" (celestial) Kings, and "they of the *Deva* hue," the moon-like complexion, and "they of the refulgent (golden) face" have gone "to the Land of Bliss, the land of metal and fire"; or—agreeably with the rules of symbolism—to the lands lying North and East, from whence "the great waters have been swept away, sucked in by the earth and dissipated in the air." The wise races had perceived "the black storm-dragons, called down by the Dragons of Wisdom"—and "had fled, led on by the shining Protectors of the most Excellent Land"—the great ancient Adepts, presumably; those the Hindus refer to as their Manus and Rishis. One of them was Vaivasvata Manu.

They "of the yellow hue" are the forefathers of those whom Ethnology now classes as the Turanians, the Mongols, Chinese and other ancient nations; and the land they fled to was no other than Central Asia. There entire new races were born; there they lived and died until the separation of the nations. Nearly two-thirds of one million years have elapsed since that period. The yellow-faced giants of the post-Atlantean day had ample time, throughout this forced confinement to one part of the world, and with the same racial blood and without any fresh infusion or admixture in it, to branch off during a period of nearly 700,000 years into the most heterogeneous and diversified types. The same is shown in Africa; nowhere does a more extraordinary variability of types exist, from black to almost white, from gigantic men to dwarfish races; and this only because of their forced isolation. The Africans had never left their continent for several hundred thousands of years. If to-morrow the continent of Europe were to disappear and other lands to re-emerge instead; and if the African tribes were to separate and scatter on the face of the earth, it is they who, in about a hundred thousand years hence, would form the bulk of the civilized nations. And it is the descendants of those of our highly cultured nations, who might have survived on some one island, without any means of crossing the new seas, that would fall back into a state of relative savagery. Thus the reason given for dividing humanity into *superior* and *inferior* races falls to the ground and becomes a fallacy.

Such are the statements made and facts given in the archaic records. Collating and comparing them with some modern theories of Evolution, *minus natural selection*, these statements appear quite reasonable and logical. Thus, while the Aryans are the descendants of the *yellow* Adam, the gigantic and highly civilized Atlanto-Aryan race, the Semites—and the Jews along with them—are those of the red Adam; and thus both de Quatrefages and the writers of the Mosaic *Genesis* are right. For, could chapter v. of the First Book of Moses be compared with the genealogies found in our Archaic Bible, the period from Adam unto Noah would be found noticed therein, of course under different names, the respective years of the Patriarchs being turned into periods, the whole being shown symbolical and allegorical. In the MS. under consideration many and frequent are the references to the great knowledge and civilization of the Atlantean nations, showing the polity of several of them and the nature of their arts and sciences. If the Third Root-Race, the Lemuro-Atlanteans, are already spoken of as having been drowned "with their high civilizations and gods" (*Esoteric Buddhism*, p. 65), how much more may the same be said of the Atlanteans!

It is from the Fourth Race that the early Aryans got their knowledge of "the bundle of wonderful things," the *Sabha* and *Mayasabha*, mentioned in the Mahabharata, the gift of Mayasur to the Pandavas. It is from them that they learnt aeronautics, *Vimana Vidya* (the "knowledge of flying in air-vehicles"), and, therefore, their great arts of meteorography and meteorology. It is from them, again, that the Aryans inherited their most valuable science of the hidden virtues of precious and other stones, of chemistry, or rather alchemy, of mineralogy, geology, physics and astronomy.

Several times the writer has put to herself the question: "Is the story of Exodus—in its details at least—as narrated in the Old Testament, original? Or is it, like the story of Moses himself and many others, simply another version of the legends told of the Atlanteans?" For who, upon hearing the story told of the latter, will fail to perceive the great similarity of the fundamental features? The anger of "God" at the obduracy of Pharaoh, his command to the "chosen" ones to spoil the Egyptians, before departing, of their "jewels of silver and jewels of gold" (Exod. xi.); and finally the Egyptians and their Pharaoh drowned in the Red Sea (xiv.). For here is a fragment of the earlier story from the Commentary:—

. . . "*And the 'great King of the dazzling Face,' the chief of all the Yellow-faced, was sad, seeing the sins of the Black-faced.*

"*He sent his air-vehicles* (Vimana) *to all his brother-chiefs* (chiefs of other nations and tribes) *with pious men within, saying: 'Prepare. Arise ye men of the good law, and cross the land while* (yet) *dry.'*

'*The Lords of the storm are approaching. Their chariots are nearing the land. One night and two days only shall the Lords of the Dark Face* (the Sorcerers) *live on this patient land. She is doomed, and they have to descend with her. The nether Lords of the Fires* (the Gnomes and fire Elementals) *are preparing their magic Agnyastra* (fire-weapons worked by magic). *But the Lords of the Dark Eye* ("Evil Eye") *are stronger than they* (the Elementals) *and they are the slaves of the mighty ones. They are versed in Ashtar* (Vidya, the highest magical knowledge). *Come and use yours* (i.e., your magic powers, in order to counteract those of the Sorcerers). *Let every lord of the Dazzling Face* (an Adept of the White Magic) *cause the Vimana of every Lord of the Dark Face to come into his hands* (or possession), *lest any* (of the Sorcerers) *should by its means escape from the waters, avoid the rod of the Four* (Karmic Deities) *and save his wicked'* (followers, or people).

'*May every Yellow face send sleep from himself* (mesmerize?) *to every Black face. May even they* (the Sorcerers) *avoid pain and suffering. May every man true to the Solar Gods bind* (paralyze) *every man under the Lunar Gods, lest he should suffer or escape his destiny.*

'*And may every Yellow face offer of his life-water* (blood) *to the speaking animal of a Black face, lest he awaken his master.*[3]

'*The hour has struck, the black night is ready, etc., etc.*

.   .   .   .

'*Let their destiny be accomplished. We are the servants of the Great Four.*[4] *May the Kings of Light return.'* "

"*The great King fell upon his dazzling Face and wept. . . .*

"*When the Kings assembled the waters had already moved. . . .*

"(But) *the nations had now crossed the dry lands. They were beyond the water mark. Their Kings reached them in their Vimanas, and led them on to the lands of Fire and Metal* (East and North)."

.   .   .   .

Still, in another passage, it is said:—

" *. . . Stars* (meteors) *showered on the lands of the Black Faces; but they slept.*

"*The speaking beasts* (the magic watchers) *kept quiet.*

"*The nether Lords waited for orders, but they came not, for their masters slept.*

"*The waters arose, and covered the valleys from one end of the Earth to the other. High lands remained, the bottom of the Earth* (the lands of the antipodes) *remained dry. There dwelt those who escaped; the men of the Yellow-faces and of the straight eye* (the frank and sincere people).

"*When the Lords of the Dark Faces awoke and bethought themselves of their Vimanas in order to escape from the rising waters, they found them gone.*"

Then a passage shows some of the more powerful magicians of the

---

[3] Some wonderful, artificially-made beast, similar in some way to Frankenstein's creation, which spoke and warned his master of every approaching danger. The master was a "Black Magician," the mechanical animal was informed by a *djin*, an Elemental, according to the accounts. The blood of a pure man alone could destroy him.

[4] The four Karmic Gods, called the Four Maharajahs in the Stanzas.

"Dark Face"—who awoke earlier than the others—pursuing those who had "spoilt them" and who were in the rear-guard, for—"*the nations that were led away were as thick as the stars of the milky way*," says a more modern Commentary, written in Sanskrit only.

"Like as a dragon-snake uncoils slowly its body, so the Sons of men, led on by the Sons of Wisdom, opened their folds, and spreading out, expanded like a running stream of sweet waters . . . many of the faint-hearted among them perished on their way. But most were saved."

Yet the pursuers, "whose heads and chests soared high above the water," chased them "for three lunar terms" until, finally reached by the rising waves, they perished to the last man, the soil sinking under their feet and the earth engulfing those who had desecrated her.

This sounds a good deal like the original material upon which the similar story in *Exodus* was built many hundred thousands of years later. The biography of Moses, the story of his birth, childhood and rescue from the Nile by Pharaoh's daughter, is now shown to have been adapted from the Chaldean narrative about Sargon. And if so, the Assyrian tile in the British Museum being a good proof of it, why not that of the Jews robbing the Egyptians of their jewels, the death of Pharaoh and his army, and so on? The gigantic magicians of Ruta and Daitya, the "lords of the Dark Face," may have become in the later narrative the Egyptian Magi, and the yellow-faced nations of the Fifth Race the virtuous sons of Jacob, the "chosen people." . . . One more statement has to be made: There have been several Divine Dynasties—a series for every Root Race beginning with the Third, each series according and adapted to its Humanity. The last Seven Dynasties referred to in the Egyptian and Chaldean records belong to the Fifth Race, which, though generally called Aryan, was not entirely so, as it was ever largely mixed up with races to which ethnology gives other names. It would be impossible, in view of the limited space at our disposal, to go any further into the description of the Atlanteans, in whom the whole East believes as much as we believe in the ancient Egyptians. The civilization of the Atlanteans was greater even than that of the Egyptians. It is their degenerate descendants, the nation of Plato's Atlantis, who built the first Pyramids in the country, and that certainly before the advent of the "Eastern Æthiopians," as Herodotus calls the Egyptians. This may be well inferred from the statement made by Ammianus Marcellinus, who says of the Pyramids that "there are also subterranean passages and winding retreats, which, it is said, men skilful in the ancient mysteries, by means of which they divined the coming of a flood, constructed in different places lest the memory of all their sacred ceremonies should be lost."

These men who "divined the coming of floods" were not Egyptians, who never had any, except the periodical rising of the Nile. Who were they? The last remnants of the Atlanteans, we maintain.

Broadly calculated, it is believed by the Egyptologists that the great Pyramid was built 3,350 B.C., and that Menes and his Dynasty existed 750 years before the Fourth Dynasty (supposed to have built the Pyramids) had appeared. Thus 4,100 years B.C. is the age assigned to Menes. Now Sir J. Gardner Wilkinson's declaration that *"all the facts lead to the conclusion* that the Egyptians had already made very great progress in the arts of civilization *before the age of Menes, and perhaps before they immigrated into the valley of the Nile"* (*Rawlinson's* "*Herodotus*," *vol. ii. p.* 345) is very suggestive, as destroying this hypothesis. It points to great civilization in *prehistoric* times, and a still greater antiquity. The *Schesoo-Hor* ("the servants of Horus") were the people who had settled in Egypt; and, as M. G. Maspero affirms, it is to this *prehistoric* race that "belongs the honour ... of having founded the principal cities of Egypt, and established the most important sanctuaries." This was *before* the great Pyramid epoch, and when Egypt had hardly arisen from the waters. Yet "they possessed the hieroglyphic form of writing special to the Egyptians, and must have been already considerably advanced in civilization." It was, says Lenormant, "the country of the great prehistoric sanctuaries, seats of the sacerdotal dominion, which played the most important part in the origin of civilization." What is the date assigned to this people? We hear of 4,000, at the utmost of 5,000 years B.C., (Maspero). Now it is claimed that it is by means of the cycle of 25,868 years (the Sidereal year) that the approximate year of the erection of the Great Pyramid can be ascertained. "Assuming that the long narrow downward passage was directed towards the pole star of the pyramid builders, astronomers have shown that ... Alpha Draconis, the then pole-star, was in the required position about 3,350 B.C., as well as in 2,170 B.C. (Proctor, quoted by Staniland Wake). But we are also told that "this relative position of Alpha Draconis and Alcyone being an extraordinary one ... it could not occur again for a whole sidereal year" (*ibid*). This demonstrates that, since the Dendera Zodiac shows the passage of three sidereal years, the great Pyramid must have been built 78,000 years ago, or in any case that this possibility deserves to be accepted at least as readily as the later date of 3,350 B.C.

Now on the Zodiac of a certain temple in far Northern India, as on the Dendera Zodiac, the same characteristics of the signs are found.

Those who know well the Hindu symbols and constellations will be able to find out, by the description of the Egyptian, whether the indications of the chronological time are correct or not.

The last three family races of the fourth Sub-race of the Fifth Root-race must each have lived approximately from 25 to 30,000 years. The first of these (the "Aryan-Asiatics") witnessed the doom of the last of the populations of the "giant Atlanteans" who perished some 850,000 years ago (the Ruta and Daitya Island-Continents) toward the close of the Miocene Age. The fourth sub-race witnessed the destruction of the last remnant of the Atlanteans—the Aryo-Atlanteans in the last island of Atlantis, namely, some 11,000 years ago. In order to understand this the reader is asked to glance at the diagram of the genealogical tree of the Fifth Root-Race—generally, though hardly correctly, called the Aryan race, and the explanations appended to it.

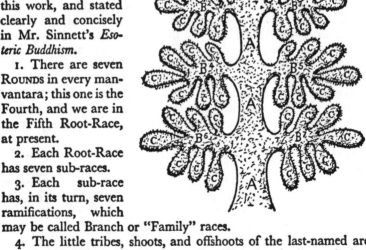

Let the reader remember well that which is said of the divisions of Root Races and the evolution of Humanity in this work, and stated clearly and concisely in Mr. Sinnett's *Esoteric Buddhism.*

1. There are seven ROUNDS in every manvantara; this one is the Fourth, and we are in the Fifth Root-Race, at present.

2. Each Root-Race has seven sub-races.

3. Each sub-race has, in its turn, seven ramifications, which may be called Branch or "Family" races.

4. The little tribes, shoots, and offshoots of the last-named are countless and depend on Karmic action. Examine the "genealogical tree" hereto appended, and you will understand. The illustration is purely diagrammatic, and is only intended to assist the reader in obtaining a slight grasp of the subject, amidst the confusion which exists between the terms which have been used at different times for

the divisions of Humanity. It is also here attempted to express in figures—but only within approximate limits, for the sake of comparison—the duration of time through which it is possible to definitely distinguish one division from another. It would only lead to hopeless confusion if any attempt were made to give accurate dates to a few; for the Races, Sub-Races, etc., down to their smallest ramifications, overlap and are entangled with each other until it is nearly impossible to separate them.

The human Race has been compared to a tree, and this serves admirably as an illustration.

The main stem of a tree may be compared to the ROOT-RACE (A).

Its larger limbs to the various SUB-RACES; seven in number (B¹, B²).

On each of these limbs are seven BRANCHES, OR FAMILY-RACES (C).

After this the cactus-plant is a better illustration, for its fleshy "leaves" are covered with sharp spines, each of which may be compared to a nation or tribe of human beings.

Now our Fifth Root-Race has already been in existence—as a race *sui generis* and quite free from its parent stem—about 1,000,000 years; therefore it must be inferred that each of the four preceding Sub-Races has lived approximately 210,000 years; thus each Family-Race has an average existence of about 30,000 years. Thus the European "Family Race" has still a good many thousand years to run, although the nations or the innumerable spines upon it vary with each succeeding "season" of three or four thousand years. It is somewhat curious to mark the comparative approximation of duration between the lives of a "Family-Race" and a "Sidereal Year."

The knowledge of the foregoing, and the accurately correct division, formed part and parcel of the Mysteries, where these Sciences were taught to the disciples, and where they were transmitted by one Hierophant to another.

CONCLUSION

The duration of the periods that separate, in space and time, the Fourth from the Fifth Race—in the historical[1] or even the legendary beginnings of the latter—is too tremendous for us to offer, even to a Theosophist, any more detailed accounts of them. During the course of the post-diluvian ages—marked at certain periodical epochs by

[1] The word "historical" is used, because, although historians have dwarfed almost absurdly the dates that separate certain events from our modern day, nevertheless, once that they are known and accepted, they belong to history. Thus the Trojan War *is* an historical event; and though even less than 1,000 years B.C. is the date assigned to it, yet in truth it is nearer 6,000 than 5,000 years B.C.

the most terrible cataclysms—too many races and nations were born, and have disappeared almost without leaving a trace, for any one to offer any description of the slightest value concerning them. Whether the Masters of Wisdom have a consecutive and full history of our race from its incipient stage down to the present times; whether they possess the uninterrupted record of man since he became the complete physical being, and became thereby the king of the animals and master on this earth—is not for the writer to say. Most probably they have, and such is our own personal conviction. But if so, this knowledge is only for the *highest* Initiates, who do not take their students into their confidence. The writer can, therefore, give but what she has herself been taught, and no more.

But even this will appear to the profane reader rather as a weird, fantastic dream, than as a possible reality.

If Troy was denied, and regarded as a myth; the existence of Herculaneum and Pompeii declared a fiction; the travels of Marco Polo laughed at and called as absurd a fable as one of Baron Münchausen's tales, why should the writer of *Isis Unveiled* and of *The Secret Doctrine* be any better treated? When Leverrier and Adams predicted a planet by calculation, it was gravely asserted in some quarters that the planet which had been calculated was not *the* planet but another which had clandestinely and improperly got into the neighbourhood of the true body. *The disposition to suspect hoax is stronger than the disposition to hoax.*

Thus let it be. No disbeliever who takes the "Secret Doctrine" for a "hoax" is forced or even asked to credit our statements. Nor is it, after all, necessary that any one should believe in the Occult Sciences and the old teachings, before one knows anything or even believes in his own soul. No great truth was ever accepted *a priori*, and generally a century or two passed before it began to glimmer in the human consciousness as a possible verity, except in such cases as the positive discovery of the thing claimed as a fact. The truths of to-day are the falsehoods and errors of yesterday, and *vice versa*. It is only in the XXth century that portions, if not the whole, of the present work will be vindicated.

Enough was said to show that evolution in general, events, mankind, and everything else in Nature proceed in cycles. We have spoken of seven Races, five of which have nearly completed their earthly career, and have claimed that every Root-Race, with its subraces and innumerable family divisions and tribes, was entirely distinct from its preceding and succeeding race.

Nevertheless our general proposition will not be accepted. It will be said that whatever forms man has passed through in the long pre-

historic Past there are no more changes for him (save certain variations, as at present) in the future. Hence that our Sixth and Seventh
Root Races are fictions.

To this it is again answered: How *do you* know? Your experience
is limited to a few thousand years, to less than a day in the whole age
of Humanity and to the present types of the actual continents and
isles of our Fifth Race. How can you tell what will or will not be?
Meanwhile, such is the prophecy of the Secret Books and their no
uncertain statements.

Since the beginning of the Atlantean Race many million years
have passed, yet we find the last of the Atlanteans, still mixed up
with the Aryan element, 11,000 years ago. This shows the enormous
overlapping of one race over the race which succeeds it, though in
characters and external type the elder loses its characteristics, and
assumes the new features of the younger race. This is proved in all
the formations of mixed human races. Now, Occult philosophy
teaches that even now, under our very eyes, the new Race and Races
are preparing to be formed, and that it is in America that the transformation will take place, and has already silently commenced.

Pure Anglo-Saxons hardly three hundred years ago, the Americans of the United States have already become a nation apart, and,
owing to a strong admixture of various nationalities and inter-
marriage, almost a race *sui generis*, not only mentally, but also
physically.

Thus the Americans have become in only three centuries a
"primary race," *pro tem.*, before becoming a race apart, and strongly
separated from all other now existing races. They are, in short, the
germs of the *sixth* sub-race, and in some few hundred years more
will become the pioneers of that race which must succeed to the
present European or fifth sub-race, in all its new characteristics.
After this, in about 25,000 years, they will launch into preparations
for the seventh sub-race; until, in consequence of cataclysms—the
first series of those which must one day destroy Europe, and still
later the whole Aryan race (and thus affect both Americas), as also
most of the lands directly connected with the confines of our continent and isles—the Sixth Root-Race will have appeared on the
stage of our Round. When shall this be? Who knows save the great
Masters of Wisdom, perchance, and they are as silent upon the
subject as the snow-capped peaks that tower above them. All we
know is, that it will silently come into existence; so silently, indeed,
that for long millenniums shall its pioneers—the peculiar children
who will grow into peculiar men and women—be regarded as abnormal oddities physically and mentally. Then, as they increase, and

their numbers become with every age greater, one day they will awake to find themselves in a majority. It is the present men who will then begin to be regarded as exceptional mongrels, until these die out in their turn in civilized lands; surviving only in small groups on islands—the mountain peaks of to-day—where they will vegetate, degenerate, and finally die out, perhaps millions of years hence, as the Aztecs have, as the Nyam-Nyam and the dwarfish Moola Koorumba of the Nilghiri Hills are dying. All these are the remnants of once mighty races, the recollection of whose existence has entirely died out of the remembrance of the modern generations, just as we shall vanish from the memory of the Sixth Race Humanity. The Fifth will overlap the Sixth Race for many hundreds of millenniums, changing with it slower than its new successor, still changing in stature, general physique, and mentality, just as the Fourth overlapped our Aryan race, and the Third had overlapped the Atlanteans.

This process of preparation for the Sixth great Race must last throughout the whole sixth and seventh sub-races (*vide supra*, the diagram of the Genealogical Tree of the Fifth Race). But the *last* remnants of the Fifth Continent will not disappear until some time after the birth of the *new* Race; when another and *new* dwelling, the Sixth Continent, will have appeared above the *new* waters on the face of the globe, so as to receive the new stranger. To it also will emigrate and settle all those who shall be fortunate enough to escape the general disaster. When this shall be—as just said—it is not for the writer to know. Only, as nature no more proceeds by sudden jumps and starts, than man changes suddenly from a child into a mature man, the final cataclysm will be preceded by many smaller submersions and destructions both by wave and volcanic fires. The exultant pulse will beat high in the heart of the race now in the American zone, but there will be no more Americans when the Sixth Race commences; no more, in fact, than Europeans; for they will have now become a *new race, and many new nations*. Yet the Fifth will not die, but survive for a while: overlapping the new Race for many hundred thousands of years to come, it will become transformed with it—slower than its new successor—still getting entirely altered in mentality, general physique, and stature. Mankind will not grow again into giant bodies as in the case of the Lemurians and the Atlanteans; because while the evolution of the Fourth Race led the latter down to the very bottom of materiality in its physical development, the present Race is on its ascending arc; and the Sixth will be rapidly growing out of its bonds of matter, and even of flesh.

Thus it is the mankind of the New World—one by far the senior of our Old one, a fact men had also forgotten—of *Patala* (the Antipodes), whose mission and Karma it is to sow the seeds for a forthcoming grander, and far more glorious Race than any of those we know of at present. The Cycles of Matter will be succeeded by Cycles of Spirituality and a fully developed mind. On the law of parallel history and races, the majority of the future mankind will be composed of glorious Adepts. Humanity is the child of cyclic Destiny, and not one of its Units can escape its unconscious mission, or get rid of the burden of its co-operative work with nature. Thus will mankind, race after race, perform its appointed cycle-pilgrimage. Climates will, and have already begun, to change, each tropical year after the other dropping one sub-race, but only to beget another higher race on the ascending cycle; while a series of other less favoured groups—the failures of nature—will, like some individual men, vanish from the human family without even leaving a trace behind.

Such is the course of Nature under the sway of KARMIC LAW, of the ever present and the ever-becoming Nature. For, in the words of a Sage, known only to a few Occultists:—"THE PRESENT IS THE CHILD OF THE PAST; THE FUTURE, THE BEGOTTEN OF THE PRESENT. AND YET, O PRESENT MOMENT! KNOWEST THOU NOT THAT THOU HAST NO PARENT, NOR CANST THOU HAVE A CHILD; THAT THOU ART EVER BEGETTING BUT THYSELF? BEFORE THOU HAST EVEN BEGUN TO SAY 'I AM THE PROGENY OF THE DEPARTED MOMENT, THE CHILD OF THE PAST,' THOU HAST BECOME THAT PAST ITSELF. BEFORE THOU UTTEREST THE LAST SYLLABLE, BEHOLD! THOU ART NO MORE THE PRESENT BUT VERILY THAT FUTURE. THUS ARE THE PAST, THE PRESENT, AND THE FUTURE, THE EVER-LIVING TRINITY IN ONE—THE MAHAMAYA OF THE ABSOLUTE IS."

A SELECT BIBLIOGRAPHY OF WORKS

ON H. P. BLAVATSKY AND *THE SECRET DOCTRINE*

Incidents in the Life of Madame Blavatsky. A. P. SINNETT. (The First Edition) 1886.

H.P.B. In Memory of Helena Petrovna Blavatsky. By some of her Pupils. 1891.

Reminiscences of H. P. Blavatsky and "The Secret Doctrine". COUNTESS CONSTANCE WACHTMEISTER. 1893.

Helena Petrovna Blavatsky. KATHERINE TINGLEY. 1921.

*H. P. Blavatsky as I knew her. 1923.

*H. P. Blavatsky. Her Life and Work for Humanity. 1922.

*H. P. Blavatsky. A Great Betrayal. 1922.

The Real H. P. Blavatsky. WILLIAM KINGSLAND. 1928.

The Personality of H. P. Blavatsky. C. JINARAJADASA. 1930.

Reminiscences of H.P.B. BERTRAM KEIGHTLEY. 1931.

My Guest. H. P. Blavatsky. FRANCESCA ARUNDALE. 1932.

Personal Memoirs of H. P. Blavatsky. Compiled by MARY NEFF. 1937.

H. P. Blavatsky and the Theosophical Movement. C. J. RYAN. 1937.

Studies in "The Secret Doctrine". Book I and Book II. B. P. WADIA. 1961.

Obituary. The "Hodgson Report" on Madame Blavatsky. 1885-1960 ADLAI E. WATERMAN. 1963.

* Separately, or in one volume. 1924. ALICE LEIGHTON CLEATHER.

INDEX

INDEX

255